Magic
In the New Testament

For Morton Smith

Magic
In the New Testament

A Survey and Appraisal of the Evidence

Robert Conner

Published by
Mandrake of Oxford
PO Box 250
OXFORD
OX1 1AP (UK)

A CIP catalogue record for this book is available from the British Library and the US Library of Congress.

Cover art by Christopher Cochran

978-1-906958-27-5

Preface

Of all the sagas of dead men, none has exhibited more potential for imaginative reiteration than the story of Jesus of Nazareth. It is a powerful narrative which has been retold, recast, and embellished for nearly two thousand years to form a myth that resonates in every corner of the Western world.

To call Jesus a *sorcerer* contradicts nearly two millennia of Christian teaching and iconography. Indeed, any claim that goes so firmly against the grain of this founding cultural myth might seem on first sight preposterous, even to the non-believer. However, Jesus was regarded as a magician in antiquity by Jews and Gentiles alike, and Christian apologists were forced to defend him from such charges for centuries after his death.

Closer to the present, a re-evaluation of Jesus' career began as part of the search for the elusive historical Jesus. As a result of that effort, scholars steadily accumulated evidence for magical practices in the New Testament throughout much of the 20th century —in the 1920s occasional articles on the subject began to appear in specialty journals, and by the 1970s books setting out the evidence for magic in primitive Christianity were published. In the final decades of the past century academic interest in magic in the Greco-Roman world increased dramatically, with the result that further connections between Christian and pagan magic were documented.[1] It is that continuously expanding body of knowledge and commentary that has made this survey of the evidence possible.

---

[1] Notably with Campbell Bonner (1927) and P. Samain (1932). Samain's article stands as one of the most completely documented and tightly reasoned early summaries in the literature. Among the early book length treatments are John Hull's *Hellenistic Magic and the Synoptic Tradition* (1974) and Morton Smith's *Jesus the Magician* (1978). More recent works include Clinton Arnold's *Ephesians: Power and Magic* (1989), Hans-Josef Klauck's *Magic and Paganism in Early Christianity*, first published in German in 1996, Naomi Janowitz' *Magic in the Roman World: Pagans, Jews and Christians* (2001), Rick Strelan's *Strange Acts* (2004), and David Aune's *Apocalypticism, Prophecy, and Magic in Early Christianity* (2009), a collection of previously published essays.

1

Progress in this area has been impeded, however, by the double barrier of theology on one hand and Enlightenment rationalism on the other. As Rick Strelan has pointed out, the subject of magic has been placed off limits to New Testament scholars in particular "by a scientific method that ruled out the supernatural *a priori*" and to publish on any aspect of the supernatural "put their credibility and academic acceptability on the line..."[2]

Until quite recently, magic was dismissed as beneath the dignity of academic discourse, if not, in fact, beneath contempt. As Peter Brown noted in his epic study, until very recently most scholars considered "the study of exorcism, the most highly rated activity of the early Christian church, a historiographical 'no-go' area."[3] Horsley has characterized "modern western interpreters" as "skittish about demon possession and exorcism"[4] because these phenomena, which were central to primitive Christian experience, cannot be squared with modern scientific rationalism.

However, it is not rationalism but advocacy scholarship that has been and remains the single greatest barrier to understanding the founding documents of Christianity.[5] Regarding the editor and contributors to the *Theologisches Wörterbuch zum Neuen Testament*, the German corpus translated into English as the *Theological Dictionary of the New Testament*, a work much admired by some scholars, David Aune remarks, "[they] write as if they were involved in a conspiracy to ignore or minimize the role of magic in the New Testament and early Christian literature."[6] In fact, they were involved in somewhat more than that. Kittel and a number of his contributors were Nazi collaborators who were attempting to systematically write the Jewish background out of the life of Jesus, to make Jesus of Nazareth *judenfrei* the better to adapt German Christianity to a virulently racist ideology.[7]

---

[2] *Strange Acts*, 9.
[3] *The Cult of the Saints*, 108.
[4] *Experientia*, Volume I, 41.
[5] Such as *Deliver Us from Evil: Interpreting the Redemption from the Power of Satan in New Testament Theology*, to cite a recent example. The book concedes "there may be some similarities" between Jesus and pagan magicians, but claims "there is really no basic similarity when one views the context of these miracles." The author, Richard Bell, finds it "highly problematic that some have understood Jesus' 'career' as that of a magician." (185-186)
[6] *Aufstieg und Niedergang der Römischen Welt*, II.23.2: 1508.
[7] See Ericksen, *Theologians Under Hitler: Gerhard Kittel, Paul Althaus, and Emanuel Hirsch*.

Samson Eitrem, a very thorough scholar, drew multiple detailed parallels between the miracles of Jesus and the spells of the magical papyri only to conclude, "It is, indeed, very difficult to detect any *magical method* in the cures of Jesus...He was no thaumaturge trained in magical technique: this, at least, we know from our sources."[8] In fact, what we know from ancient sources is that magic was practiced in Palestine from the beginning of recorded history, that magic was practiced in Palestine in the time of Jesus, and that early Christians were accused of practicing magic by their pagan opponents, by their Jewish contemporaries, *and by other Christians*. The notion that Jesus somehow transcended his own time, place and culture, while simultaneously using its language and frame of reference, is based on the theological position that Jesus was "the Son of God" and therefore could not have engaged in activity tainted by magic.

Apologetic study of ancient texts is hardly limited to Christianity, however. Following the discovery of the trove of manuscripts in the Cairo *genizah*, the two Jewish scholars who most thoroughly examined the material "had to sift through the thousands of magical texts strewn there," eventually producing thorough coverage of the material "with the glaring exception of its numerous fragments which deal with magic, divination, and the occult sciences, fragments which both scholars simply treated as if they did not exist."[9]

These are merely a few examples of distortion which could be cited in the long history of scholarly accomodationism. If the gospels are to be allowed as evidence, it would appear that the origins of Christianity itself began to be falsified soon after Jesus' death. This book explores how Jesus' apocalyptic message, which was central to his preaching, came to be explained away and then quietly abandoned. It also examines how magical details of Jesus' performance of miracles were excised from the gospels and how spirit possession, once central to what became normative Christianity, was allowed to wither. It is a pivotal argument of this book that faith-based scholarship is frequently dishonest scholarship which does violence to the evidence.

It is no difficult matter to find recently published discussions of exorcism and spirit possession in early Christianity that use exquisitely technical arguments and subtle distinctions aimed at exonerating Jesus

---

[8] *Some Notes on the Demonology in the New Testament*, 40.
[9] *Ancient Jewish Magic. A History*, 8.

of all charges of performing magic. The gist of these arguments can be simply stated: (1) Christian magical technique does not always dupli- cate the praxis of non-Christian magic in each and every detail and (2) the vocabulary of the gospels sometimes substitutes Christian terms for the terms most often found in pagan texts. From these superficial differences it therefore follows that Jesus and early Christians were not practicing magic. Unlike modern apologists with sectarian motives, ancient critics who actually witnessed the Christians in action were not so easily fooled.

The present essay will not attempt a detailed reconstruction of the brief career of the prophet from Galilee. Instead, this work examines the following topics which I believe to be of particular importance to a modern nonsectarian understanding of Christian origins:

- The nature of the earliest Christian documents, the de- fects of their transmission, and the evidence for the sup- pression of descriptions of magical acts.
- The closely related problem of the New Testament ac- counts as historical sources.
- The radically apocalyptic nature of Jesus' message and its connection with magical performance.
- The failure of the apocalypse to occur and the theological reaction to that failure.
- The role of magic and mystery cult in early Christianity.

The evidence for magical practice by Jesus and the early church is so variable and extensive that the presentation given herein may be re- garded as at best a summation of the arguments for the case. In fact, such a volume of material exists that it is often difficult to know how to accommodate all of it.[10] There are many non-biblical documents that are potentially relevant to an understanding of early Christian magic, not the least of which are the Greek magical papyri and the spells of such Hebrew works as the *Sepher Ha-Razim* which illustrate numerous similarities between ancient magicians and Jesus of Naz- areth. The pre-Nicene church fathers, Clement of Alexandria, Origen, and Justin Martyr above all, as well as the apocryphal Acts, are other important sources of information about early Christian magic. Even

---

[10] See Becker, *A Kind of Magic*, 87-88, for a longer list of recent works.

though I've drawn on those sources, I have focused primarily on the text of the New Testament.

The facticity of Jesus' miracles are not the concern of this book. I have taken the miracles at face value, neither tentatively accepting them as merely psychosomatic manifestations, nor flatly denying them as quaint relics of an ignorant age. In any case, the fact remains that *there is no Jesus apart from miracles*; they are by far the most extensively attested feature of his life —not even his opponents tried to deny their reality. Jürgen Becker says of Jesus,

> "To no miracle worker of Antiquity were as many miracles attributed as there were to Jesus. All four gospels, including their sources (the synoptic sayings source and the Johannine signs source), without exception bear witness to Jesus as a powerful miracle worker..."[11]

I am in agreement with Hull on the subject: "The crucial point of inquiry into the miracles of Jesus, as of those of the early church, was not whether they had in fact happened but the nature and origin of the power used to perform them. By means of such as these 'the apostles gave witness with great power', i.e., not simply with great impact but the aid of a mighty force (Acts 4.33)."[12] A Jesus with no wonders to perform is a historical perversion, as much a reflection of the materialist philosophy of our culture as of the superstition of his. Had Jesus no fame for performing wonders, it is doubtful whether there would be any such religion as Christianity or that the world would even recall his existence.[13] I leave it to readers to make of Jesus' miracles what they will.

This is as good a place as any to briefly address the proposed differences between *religion* and *magic*, a distinction designed to raise the petticoats of faith above the gutter of superstition. I will spare the reader a lengthy rehearsal of the contorted logic behind that exercise. Suffice to say that scores of scholars have written many hundreds of pages in an attempt to establish some difference, an observation which suggests ipso facto that there is no clear distinction to be made.

---

[11] *Jesus of Nazareth*, 170.
[12] John Hull, *Hellenistic Magic and the Synoptic Tradition*, 108.
[13] A point emphasized by Ramsay MacMullen, *Christianizing the Roman Empire*, 22.

In the early 20th century, it was proposed that religion *honors* spiritual forces, and *pleads* with them for whatever favors they may be disposed to grant, whereas magic *manipulates* and *threatens* them. Such a distinction seems to work best in the context of a 19th century Eurocentric culture that regards magic as part of an evolutionary continuum culminating in high church theology, but it quickly falls apart outside that context. Accordingly, it has been generally abandoned as useless for the study of religion in the ancient Near East. "The notion of magic as distinct from religion seems to be alien to the Hebrew Bible."[14]

It was next proposed that religion could be distinguished from magic on the basis of *ritual*. In this case, it was alleged that magic uses ritual in a *manipulative* way to achieve specific ends. What specific ends Christians are thought to achieve by rituals that involve bowing, kneeling, prostrating, clapping, raising their hands in the air or laying them on one another, dunking, marking themselves with ashes, chanting, hymning, making the sign of the cross, sprinkling holy water, swinging censers, lighting candles, walking in processions, making pilgrimages, swallowing wafers, speaking in tongues, displaying imagery such as the crucifix and the 'Jesus fish,' or by fasting, hooding and flogging, abstinence from sex, meat, coffee, tea, and alcohol, or the collection and veneration of relics, and whether such ritualistic behavior should ever be considered magical, is once again left to the reader to decide. However, attempts to distinguish religion from magic in the New Testament and primitive Christianity will not repay the effort, a claim this work intends to verify in extenso. As Reimer observes, "The death blow for absolute definitions for miracle and magic is simply the ambiguous nature of the ancient evidence itself."[15] I believe the same death blow may be aimed at the supposed distinction between magic and religion.

Therefore for the purposes of this book we will define *religion* as *magic for the masses* and *magic* as *religion for the individual.* Religion typically deals with the future after death, and magic with more immediate concerns, but when the immediate concern *is* death, religion more or less openly displays its magical face in various rituals of last rites. To see the fluid boundary between magic and religion in our sources, we need look no further than the stories of the Old Testament where the magical ser-

---

[14] Peter Schäfer, *Envisioning Magic*, 33.
[15] *Miracle and Magic*, 7.

pent staff fashioned to relieve victims of snakebite,[16] later becomes a named object of religious veneration and is for that reason destroyed.[17]

Several additional points remain to be made. This work assumes that Jesus was a real person and that the gospels contain at least some historical material. Although it has been argued for several hundred years that Jesus of Nazareth never existed and that the gospels are a complete fabrication, a recent summary of the evidence for such claims concludes, "The theory of Jesus' non-existence is now effectively dead as a scholarly question."[18] Jesus was scarcely mentioned outside the New Testament for a century or more because he was not regarded as important, not because he was fictional. However, it should be clearly stated at the very beginning that the existence of a 'historical Jesus' has not and cannot be conclusively proven on the evidence.[19]

The discussion which follows entirely dispenses with the pleasant pretext that the life of Jesus was truly relevant to much of anything in the era in which he actually lived. Christianity began as an obscure apocalyptic sect of Palestinian Judaism. Its 'founder' thought the world would end in his lifetime. It is certainly fair to say that Jesus was personally unknown to the majority of Christians —"a tiny, peculiar, antisocial, irreligious sect"[20] from a Roman perspective— who could have been his contemporaries. In fact, it appears that he was personally unknown even to Saul of Tarsus who, writing as the apostle Paul, became orthodox Christianity's chief spokesman. In any case, the Lord Jesus Christ of Paul's religion is first and foremost a construct of faith, not of history. If his epistles are any indication, it appears that Paul knew little and cared less about the historical Jesus.

The emergence and survival of Christianity is an example of the confluence of apparently trivial coincidences on which human history so often seems to turn. That said, it is irrelevant whether the following arguments apply to a historical Jesus or to a Jesus who exists primarily in myth. In either case, they still apply. Like most mainstream students of the New Testament, I believe that the story of Jesus represented therein is a combination of history and myth, but the question we

---

[16] Numbers 21:6-9.
[17] 2 Kings 18:4.
[18] *Jesus Outside the New Testament*, 14.
[19] See particularly Avalos' *The End of Biblical Studies*, a work which should be required reading for anyone contemplating a career in any aspect of religious studies.
[20] *The Christians as the Romans Saw Them*, xv.

should be asking is not whether Jesus is historical or mythological, and to what degree. The question we should be asking is if the message preached by Jesus is in any way relevant to humanity's present situation. Consistent with that goal, the text which follows rejects the fanciful, the apologetic, the incoherent, the misinformed and allegorical, together with interpretation clouded by personal drama and sectarian commitment.

Obviously this book makes no attempt to disabuse literalist Christian believers. Literalists are in a paradoxical situation: many feel commited by faith to the belief that the Bible has all the answers that matter, but pick and choose among those answers, ignoring whatever makes them uncomfortable. Although most fundamentalists profess to want a church that operates 'by the book,' they dispute endlessly over what their book means and disregard the clear implications of its text whenever it suits them. Many argue that behavior —particularly sexual behavior— they find objectionable is contrary to nature, but in the next breath claim that nature is 'fallen.' When it comes to issues of religion or science, most appear unable to discern the difference between explaining and explaining away, or between ideas and ideologies. That said, it is hypocritical to claim the Bible must be taken seriously but to ignore or offer facile explanations for the parts believers find inconvenient.

I certainly make no claim to have written a book that will sway the opinion of that large and vociferous group of people who claim that what 'scripture' says counts for everything. This work is a secular book about Christianity, and like most pagans[21] I regard any and all scripture with suspicion. Unlike some authors, I do not advocate a *rapprochement* between pagans and Christians.[22] Graham Harvey mentions several radical differences between pagan and Christian spirituality and notes, correctly in my opinion, "in dialogue with Christians, however 'liberal,' it is usually clear that bridges are illusory." Salvation, as the author points out, is simply not an issue in most religions, least of all paganism.[23] In point of fact, pagan critics of antiquity noted some of the

---

[21] "Pagan" in that it rejects sweeping, universal truth claims based on special revelation, proselytizing and coercion of belief.
[22] Gus diZerega's *Pagans and Christians: The Personal Spiritual Experience*, for example. Although his book is an excellent presentation of modern pagan spirituality, this work will argue that Christianity apocalyptic, dualistic, and totalitarian. I cannot imagine what modern pagans hope to gain by a dialogue with believers in such a system.
[23] *Contemporary Paganism*, 223.

many logical inconsistencies posed by Christian preaching and even pointed to discrepancies between the various gospel accounts.[24]

Strictly speaking, the New Testament consists of 27 documents written in Greek. No informed person disputes that translation from a source language into a target language is an interpretive, even creative, act which involves decisions not only about vocabulary and tone, but also inevitably reflects what the translator thinks the source document as a whole means. While enabling a measure of comprehension by rendering texts into a familiar language, translation inevitably loses most of the rich field of association that every word has in its own language, era and culture.

In many cases the identity of the authors of the New Testament books is unknown, and both the process by which their texts were composed as well as the intentions of their texts are matters of dispute. New Testament writers sometimes coin words, or use established vocabulary in idiosyncratic ways. A number of famous passages exist for which no satisfactory explanation has ever emerged. But even if the language is clear and the translator can tell the reader word for word what the author *said*, that still doesn't necessarily clarify what the author *meant*. Jesus' saying about men who castrate themselves for the sake of the kingdom[25] is a case in point. Scholars are often divided about which words Jesus actually said, if said, in what context, and differ in their opinion about what is meant by them assuming they are authentic. The mere fact that a clear dictionary definition exists for each word does not necessarily clarify the intended meaning of a text.

Although the failings of translators are widely acknowledged, it is less often conceded that translators more often overachieve. Translators paper over grammatical inconcinnities and non sequiturs, glide over missing sections of texts, assign definitions to unknown words,[26] and make sense of statements that are incomprehensible in the original. A rigorously honest translation of most ancient texts would bracket many words and expressions as untranslatable, but this rarely occurs, particularly in bibles. In actual practice, most translations are also *emen-*

---

[24] See Hoffman's *Celsus On the True Doctrine* and *Julian's Against the Galileans.*
[25] Matthew 19:12.
[26] An easy example from the New Testament is the term δευτεροπρωτος (deuteroprōtos), "second-first," of Luke 6:1. Comparing various English translations will reveal that no one actually knows what it means.

dations. In this manner also, translation misrepresents by creating the false impression of a smooth, uncomplicated text the meaning of which seems readily apparent. Which word (if any) in English appropriately translates a word in Hebrew or Greek is often a matter of conjecture, particularly it seems at those points where the text is of greatest interest to us.

Within the discussion that follows there will be occasions to point to manipulation of language, as well as to comment on occasional words which may have functioned as a form of early Christian jargon. Since the documents were preserved in Greek, to discuss what the New Testament says about nearly anything can involve some discussion about what words mean in Greek. The notion that the meaning of the New Testament can be determined with certainty from arguments based on translations, my own included, is not entertained in this work. To partially address the lost-in-translation issue, I have reproduced the details of numerous passages in Greek and have attached comments on the vocabulary. Even though the body of the text can be easily read with no knowledge of Greek, familiarity with the language confers some advantage.

It is my expectation that those for whom this book has been written will easily rise above disputes about personalities and credentialism, and judge the arguments made herein on their factual merits. Few of the broad conclusions of mainstream New Testament scholarship will be rehashed here. Those who are interested in the details of these larger questions should find them adequately covered in standard references.

A penultimate observation should be made regarding citations from the magical papyri. The two collections most often referenced, the *Papyri Graecae Magicae* and the *Supplementum Magicum*, are cited somewhat differently. In the case of the *Papyri Graecae Magicae*, the individual papyri are cited by number and by line of text. Therefore *PGM* IV, 24 would refer to papyrus document number 4, line 24. The papyri included in the *Supplementum Magicum*, issued in two volumes, are numbered by document, but are accompanied by additional pages of commentary. The documents in this collection are referenced in the footnotes by number, the commentary on those documents by volume and page. *Supplementum Magicum* 24 therefore refers to document 24, whereas *Supplementum Magicum* II, 329 refers to commentary in Volume 2, page 329.

Unless otherwise noted, all translations from Greek sources are my own.

Chapter 1: The Question of Sources

For all practical purposes the reconstruction of Jesus' life and teaching is based entirely on the documents of the New Testament. By some estimates over thirty gospels were produced in the first two centuries following Jesus' death,[27] but most of those gospels have disappeared and the few outside the New Testament that survive are fragmentary, distorted by fabulist tendencies, and contain little to nothing of biographical interest.

Physical evidence exists for as many as four non-canonical gospels which possibly date from the 1st century. A passion story, possibly part of a longer Greek gospel called the *Gospel of Peter*, was recovered from a grave in Akhmim, Egypt in 1886. The *Egerton Gospel*, also written in Greek, was purchased from an antiquities dealer in Egypt in 1934. Its provenance is unknown. Two other extremely fragmentary papyri exist, both recovered from Oxyrhynchus, *POxy 840* and *POxy 1224*. It is speculated that the latter may once have belonged to a copy of the *Gospel of Peter*, but the amount of preserved text is too small to make a firm determination. Other apocryphal gospels, several of which are Coptic translations of Greek originals, appear to contain primitive tradition, but the fragments that remain indicate that the text of these books was subject to revision, hence unstable.

Pagan accounts mention Christians in passing, but not until about seventy years after the death of Jesus when the Romans realized that the Christians were not simply another Jewish sect. Surviving Jewish sources are even more reticent on the subject of Jesus and the primitive church for reasons which should require no explanation. We are therefore unable to compare the gospel accounts with those of contemporaries outside the earliest Christian communities. In addition to the lack of verification outside the circle of believers, we are con-

---

[27] Some 21 gospels in various states of preservation are known, as well as the names of 13 others that have not survived. *Journal of Early Christian Studies* 11:139.

The content of papyrus fragments believed to carry primitive text has been compiled by Andrew Bernhard, *Other Early Christian Gospels: A Critical Edition of the Surviving Greek Manuscripts*.

fronted with the problem that the gospels often contradict each other on details both large and small.

For reasons I will begin to discuss in a subsequent chapter, it is unlikely that Jesus' followers even considered a written record of his teachings to be of much importance until long after his death. Whatever the case, the fact remains that if it were not for the gospels of the New Testament, Jesus would have long since disappeared into the black hole of the undocumented, so it is with a brief examination of the gospels and their formation that we must begin.

...the oral tradition

In daily conversation Jesus and his disciples spoke a dialect of Palestinian Aramaic, a Semitic language closely related to Hebrew. In a few places the writer of the gospel of Mark records Aramaic words or phrases and provides a Greek translation, particularly when the words in question are 'words of power' that accompany the performance of healings and exorcisms.[28] In the technical literature, a 'power word' is often called a *vox magica* (plural: *voces magicae*).

> Foreign words are a very familiar feature of magic spells and the papyri are full of examples...In the Coptic magical papyri Greek appears as the strange and forbiddingly authentic sound, while in the Greek magical world Jewish names and words had special prestige...The foreign expressions are sometimes translated into Greek for the professional use of healers and exorcists...The continued use of Ephphatha in the baptismal ritual of the church (which was also exorcism) can hardly be accounted for except by the supposition that the word was believed in itself to possess remarkable power.[29]

Two clear examples are ταλιθα κουμ (talitha koum), "get up, little girl,"[30] and εφφαθα (ephphatha), "be opened."[31] Commenting on the words of power used in Mark 5:41, Morton Smith noted of the formula used by Peter to raise a dead woman —Ταβιθα αναστηθι:

---

[29] Hull, *Hellenistic Magic and the Synoptic Tradition*, 85-86.
[30] Mark 5:41.
[31] Mark 7:34.

"Tabitha, rise!"[32]— "*Tabitha* is a mispronunciation of *talitha*, which the storyteller mistook for a proper name."[33] Magical invocations tend to gain in length and complexity with the passage of time and in some later manuscripts, Peter's "Tabitha rise!" has accordingly expanded to include "in the name of our Lord Jesus Christ."

The magical words of Mark 5:41 are missing in the parallel texts of Matthew 9:22 and Luke 8:54. Matthew and Luke appear to have carefully edited material that might implicate Jesus in the practice of magic, and the power words of Mark 7:34 are omitted in the parallel text of Matthew 15:29-31.

David Aune addresses the motive for the retention of such words in the oldest gospel:

> Why then are these Aramaic healing formulas preserved in the tradition used by Mark? In view of the importance attributed to preserving adjurations and incantations in their original languages, these formulas were probably preserved for the purpose of guiding Christian thaumaturges in exorcistic and healing activities. In early Christianity, therefore, these Aramaic phrases may have functioned as magic formulas.[34]

Of course the official language of Rome and the Italian peninsula was Latin, but in most of the eastern Roman territories of Jesus' time the language most commonly used from day to day was not Latin, but Greek. Much elevated discourse, writing on philosophy and theology in particular, was carried forward in Greek. The New Testament is also written in Greek, but not in the polished language of the rhetoricians of classical literature:

> As we study the New Testament…the first great impression we receive is that the language to which we are accustomed in the New Testament is on the whole just the kind of Greek that simple, unlearned folk of the Roman Imperial period were in the habit of using.[35]

---

[32] Acts 9:40.
[33] *Jesus the Magician*, 95.
[34] *Aufstieg und Niedergang der Römischen Welt*, II.23.2:1535.
Aune's extensively referenced essay, "Magic in Early Christianity," reproduced in *Apocalypticism, Prophecy, and Magic in Early Christianity*, is an invaluable resource.
[35] *Light from the Ancient East*, 62.

Whether Jesus spoke any language other than Aramaic or was even able to read has been the subject of some debate. Modern societies expend enormous resources to educate their populations, but pre-industrial societies had neither the resources nor the motivation to teach many people to read and write. Reading was simply not necessary for the types of work that the majority of people performed. It has been estimated that about 90% of the population in the 1st century was completely illiterate and the New Testament specifically states of Peter and John that they were αγραμματος (agrammatos), "without letters," unable to read or write.[36] Peter betrays himself by his rustic Galilean Aramaic.[37] Since Jesus' closest disciples were predominantly men who worked with their hands, an inability to read or write would have been completely in keeping with their era and station in life.

Early Christian converts were most frequently women, slaves, servants, and laborers, i.e., members of groups with very low rates of literacy. Making a virtue of necessity, Paul openly acknowledged Christianity's appeal to the humble and disenfranchised: "not many wise by human standards, not many powerful, nor many well-born..."[38] "Not many" in this case evidently meant "precious few." Paul's first letter to the Corinthians begins by making the case for more or less pure fideism, dumbing down the gospel historically, and early pagan critics such as Celsus clearly considered gullibility and ignorance to be notable Christian attributes, "to believe without reason."[39] In his biography of the colorful religious huckster Peregrinus, the Roman satirist Lucian described the Christians as "ill-informed men,"[40] gullible rubes eager to believe and therefore easily misled.

The low social status of the early Christians and of Jesus himself reflects a bitter reality of the ancient world generally. Lane Fox: "By itself, a specialized ability in a craft was not a source of upward mobility. Its adepts were often slaves themselves, and even if they were not,

---

[36] Acts 4:13.
[37] See Watt, *Diglossia and Other Topics in New Testament Linguistics*, 107-120.
[38] 1 Corinthians 1:26.
[39] *Contra Celsum*, I, 9.
[40] ιδιωταις ανθρωποις: "**ill-informed** men," from ιδιωτης (idiōtēs), *ignorant, unskilled*, from whence the English *idiot*.
Περι της Περεγρινου Τελευτης (On the Death of Peregrinus) 13, in Macleod, *Lucian: A Selection*, 154.

they were competing with slave labour, which kept the price of their own labour low."[41]

All the gospels agree that Jesus taught in synagogues. On one such occasion the gospel of Luke has Jesus being handed a scroll from which he reads a passage from Isaiah,[42] but the accuracy of this account, like the rest of Luke's history, is highly questionable. Regarding the reaction to Jesus' teaching, John says, "Consequently the Jews were amazed, saying, 'How does this man know letters when he has not been taught?'" The clear implication is that Jesus himself was "without letters,"[43] or at the very least exhibited some evident deficiency. Joseph Hoffman: "...even the members of the synagogue in Nazareth, not the most cultivated of towns (see John 1:46), were offended at the sight of someone with this background teaching in public."[44]

Jesus is sometimes referred to as "rabbi," which means *teacher* or *master*. However, just what the speakers meant by this title is unclear. In Mark 9:5, for instance, Jesus is so addressed after Peter, James, and John witness the transfiguration. In John 3:2, Nicodemus also calls Jesus "rabbi," but appears to do so in recognition of his miraculous signs. In other words, it is not Jesus' remarkable erudition that calls forth this title of respect, but rather the visions and miracles associated with him. In a subsequent chapter, I will briefly make the case that Jesus' 'teaching' had nothing to do with reading and everything to do with the performance of miracles. Whether anything like the office of rabbi as currently understood even existed in the 1st century is doubtful, but in any case several recent assessments of Jesus conclude that he did not conform to "the rabbinic model," but instead "fits well with the general image of a traveling exorcist and miracle-worker."[45]

The villagers of Nazareth ask concerning Jesus, "Isn't this the laborer, the son of Mary and the brother of James and Joses and Judas and

---

[41] *Pagans and Christians*, 59.

[42] Luke 4:16-20.

"The spirit of the Lord is upon me" (4:18) is cited as an apologetic 'proof text' from Isaiah 61:1 and likely reflects theological conviction more than historical fact.

[43] John 7:15. "Letters," γραμματα (grammata), i.e., *reading and writing*. The villagers of Nazareth raise the same question according to Matthew 13:34-38.

Γραμμα (gramma), a *character* or *letter*, from which *grammar*, the rules for combining letters, from which *grimoire*, a DIY book for combining magical symbols.

[44] *Jesus Outside the Gospels*, 29.

[45] *Judaism from Cyrus to Hadrian*, II, 521.

Simon, and aren't his sisters here among us?"⁴⁶ In this passage, the word τεκτων (tektōn), *laborer*, refers to a person who works with wood or stone, a person who in Jesus' times would hardly have been expected to be literate. Matthew, on the other hand, rephrases the question to avoid making Jesus out to be a mere laborer: ουκ ουτος εστιν ο του τεκτονος υιος: "Isn't this the son **of the laborer**…?"⁴⁷ Luke and John simply omit any reference to Jesus' day job. Modern historians tend to place 1ˢᵗ century artisans such as carpenters below agricultural workers in the social hierarchy.⁴⁸

Might Jesus have spoken Greek or at least understood it to some degree? The idea derives some support from the fact that a Hellenistic enclave, Sepphoris, lay a mere four miles from Jesus' boyhood home of Nazareth. It has been claimed by some that Jesus might have spent part of his youth working in Sepphoris as a carpenter and may have thus acquired some familiarity with Greek language and culture. However, there is no evidence in the gospels that Jesus spent any time in any pro-Roman city of his day. In fact, Sepphoris is not mentioned in the New Testament and it is doubtful that a very large Greek-speaking population existed in the Galilee of Jesus' day. Much of the reconstruction of Galilee in Jesus' time is based on remains dating from centuries after his death.⁴⁹ The complexity of the question of who spoke what in 1ˢᵗ century Palestine has been recently addressed by Stanley Porter.⁵⁰

Contrary to seeking out non-Jews, Jesus appears to have actively avoided any contact with major towns and cities, and his disciples were specifically instructed not to enter Gentile or Samaritan cities.⁵¹ "When Jesus engages in his ministry, according to our Gospels, he *avoids* all major cities but spends his time in small villages and remote rural areas, until his final trek to Jerusalem to celebrate Passover."⁵² Of an apparently long-standing antipathy Crossan notes: "Peasant hatred for administrative centers such as Sepphoris and Tiberias…points toward social revolution or…at least toward social insurrection. The Galilean peasants might not have been able to imagine a new social order, but

---

⁴⁶ Mark 6:3.
⁴⁷ Matthew 13:55.
⁴⁸ *The Historical Jesus*, 46.
⁴⁹ *Biblical Archaeology Review* 33/4: 43-50.
⁵⁰ *Diglossia and Other Topics in New Testament Linguistics*, 53-75.
⁵¹ Matthew 10:5.
⁵² *The New Testament: A Historical Introduction to the Early Christian Writings*, 254.

they could well imagine a world with certain administrative centers razed to the ground."[53] Freyne notes that in antiquity the elites "lived for each other to the exclusion of the vast majority of the population" and from that observation it follows that even Hellenistic enclaves with substantial Jewish populations "were alien centres as far as peasant Jews were concerned."[54]

Despite occasional encounters with Gentiles, Jesus' general attitude toward them appears to have been openly antagonistic. Jesus refers to Gentiles as "dogs" as at Mark 7:27 where he tells the Gentile woman whose daughter he eventually heals, "It is not right to take the children's bread and throw it to the curs." The fact that Jesus uses κυναριον (kunarion), the diminutive of κυων (kuōn), *dog*, has been interpreted by some as ironic, but as corrected by Grant, "the diminutive form rather expresses contempt and distaste."[55] Jesus intends to draw the strongest possible distinction between the Jews, to whom alone he has been sent[56] and the Gentiles, which he generally avoids.[57]

Absent any other evidence, the proximity of Hellenistic colonies is not proof that Jesus had enough dealings with speakers of Greek to have acquired proficiency in their language. It is also to be expected that Greek language skills dropped off dramatically as one moved from city to village, and from all indications Jesus taught primarily in villages and rural settings. Indeed, Greek in 1st century Palestine may have functioned as French once did in colonial Algeria, a means of social empowerment for some, as a symbol of external control for others. Under such circumstances, the emerging elite embrace the language, while others actively resist assimilation. From the details revealed by the gospels, there is good reason to think that Jesus was not numbered among the assimilated.

There is no evidence that Jesus wrote down any of his teachings. Based on careful study of the surviving gospels, it is certain that Jesus' sayings circulated for several decades in oral form —almost certainly in Aramaic— before any were written down. But if any of the earliest Christian documents were written in Aramaic, no trace of them re-

---

[53] *The Historical Jesus*, 193.
[54] Freyne, *Galilee, Jesus and the Gospels*, 173.
[55] *Jesus*, 122.
[56] Matthew 15:24.
[57] Matthew 10:5.

mains. All of the earliest surviving Christian writings are in Greek. As Deissmann observed, "The Christian missionaries with an Aramaic book of gospels in their hands would have been powerless to make propaganda in what was in fact a Greek or rather Hellenized world. An Aramaic gospel-book would have condemned Christianity to remain a Palestinian sect."[58]

At some point, likely decades after Jesus' death, the teachings that had been passed on orally were committed to writing. Some scholars envision this process to have involved compilations of lists of sayings and lists of miracles which were only later put into the context of a narrative: "...the first of his signs...the second sign...many other signs not written in this book..." may be part of the surviving framework of just such a list.[59] On the basis of textual analysis, it has been proposed that a more primitive source, designated the *Gospel of Signs*, stands somewhere behind the present-day gospel of John.[60]

There exists a collection of dicta called the *Gospel of Thomas*, a Coptic translation of a Greek original, which consists of nothing but isolated sayings unconnected by any narrative.[61] It is not hard to imagine various sayings uttered at different points of Jesus' career being collected into 'sermons,' and it would appear obvious that the context of much of what Jesus said was rephrased or simply lost in the decades between the earliest oral tradition and the beginning of the writing of the first documents. The New Testament itself suggests as much.[62]

...the autographs

Before the invention of the press, every document was handwritten and every copy made by hand. In the event an original wore out from use or was lost or destroyed, subsequent readers would have to rely on copies or even copies of copies. The process of reproduction by hand was laborious, time-consuming, and expensive, and abundant mistakes crept into handwritten copies. Besides unwitting errors, it is clear that

---

[58] *Light from the Ancient East*, 65.
[59] John 2:11, 4:54, 20:30.
[60] *The Complete Gospels*, 180-193. This is an accessible source for all surviving gospels.
[61] "The Gospel of Thomas has no christological titles, no narrative material, and no reference within its sayings to any action of Jesus or any event in his life." *Jesus Outside the New Testament*, 189.
[62] John 21:25.

passages were often deliberately changed to reflect the theology of the copyists, or as Ehrman has so aptly expressed it, "make them *say* what they were already known to *mean*."[63]

In other cases it appears the text was merely paraphrased. The earliest copies of New Testament manuscripts often exhibit the handwriting of unprofessional scribes, and the text reproduced by some of them is charitably described as "free." Of one such early copyist it has been observed that "he worked at reproducing what he imagined to be the thought of each phrase...he transposed and omitted many words and deleted several phrases."[64] In fact, apart from a minute fragment of the gospel of John, there is no secure manuscript evidence for any canonical gospel during the first hundred years following their composition, and as noted by Helmut Koester, "Textual critics of classical texts know that the first century of their transmission is the period in which the most serious corruptions occur. Textual critics of the New Testament writings have been surprisingly naïve in this respect."[65]

When textual scholars speak of an *autograph*, they are referring to the original document as it came fresh from the pen of the author. It is universally conceded that none of the autographs of the New Testament books survive. All the documentary evidence known to exist consists of copies of copies of copies of the autographs.

There is abundant evidence that the books of our present-day New Testament were not the only documents, nor were they necessarily the first. Papyrus *Egerton 2*, for example, dated from the early 2nd century, consists of four fragmentary pages of a passion story with similarities to parts of Mark and John. The text, first published in 1935, is widely believed to represent an early lost gospel.[66] In addition to those gospels for which we have some fragmentary evidence, other lost gospels such as *The Gospel of the Twelve Apostles*, a *Gospel of the Egyptians*, the *Gospel of Basilides*, the *Gospel According to the Hebrews*, and a *Gospel of Matthias* are mentioned by early Christian writers. There were also numerous forged epistles, acts, and apocalypses. The *Second Epistle of Clement*, composed around CE 150, is the only letter of the Apostolic Fathers which appears to contain verbatim quotations of Jesus. Of this epistle,

---

[63] *The Orthodox Corruption of Scripture*, xii.
[64] *The Text of the Earliest New Testament Manuscripts*, 161.
[65] *Gospel Traditions in the Second Century*, 19.
[66] *Ancient Christian Gospels*, 205-216.

Koester observes, "Nowhere does one find allusions to narrative materials from any written gospel known to us."[67] In other words, the gospel(s) from which the author quoted does not appear to have included those currently in the New Testament.

The majority of scholars accept that the writers of the gospels of Matthew and Luke used the gospel of Mark and an additional early gospel, called *Q* (from the German *Quelle, source*), as their primary sources of information. Both Matthew and Luke also incorporated material peculiar to each of them from other sources. The gospels of Matthew and Luke therefore contain material from *at least* four different sources: quotations from Mark, quotations from Q, material peculiar to Matthew (i.e., not from Mark, Q, or Luke), and material peculiar to Luke (i.e., not from Mark, Q, or Matthew). In New Testament studies this is known as the *four source hypothesis*. According to this interpretation of the evidence, the New Testament contains four presumably complete gospels, Matthew, Mark, Luke and John, remnants of a fifth, *Q*, which survives in part in the form of quotations in Matthew and Luke, and probable traces of yet another, the *Gospel of Signs*, some part of which is thought to live on in the text of John.

The abrupt ending of the gospel of Mark, the earliest of our surviving gospels, has led to persistent speculation that some amount of text has been lost, but the evidence is inconclusive. Moreover, it has been convincingly argued that the text of Mark as it appears in today's bible is not the edition copied by Matthew and Luke. "With respect to Mark, one can be fairly certain that only its revised text has achieved canonical status, while the original text (attested only by Matthew and Luke) has not survived."[68]

The extensive borrowing from these primary sources explains why we often see near verbatim agreement among the gospels Matthew, Mark, and Luke. The first three gospels, because of their close similarities of viewpoint, are known as the *synoptic* ("seen together") gospels. The gospel *Q*, which obviously antedated Matthew and Luke since they quote from it, is now lost to us although textual scholarship has managed to reconstruct it at least in part based on comparisons between the texts of Matthew and Luke.

---

[67] *Gospel Traditions in the Second Century*, 27.
[68] Ibid, 37.

That the gospel of John does not share the viewpoint of the synoptic gospels is obvious even to the casual reader. Nevertheless, that there is a close relationship between the gospel of Mark and the gospel of John is also evident to most scholars. Regarding the *Semeia Source*, the list of miracle stories[69] probably used by the author of John, Koester says: "The stories of the Markan cycles describe Jesus as a man with extraordinary powers who is not above using magical techniques; he employs magical words, uses magical manipulations, and holds a long discourse with a demon."[70] The presentation of wonder-working in the gospel of John, however, differs significantly from that of Mark while still retaining evidence of magical technique. By the time the fourth gospel was written, Jesus was slipping the surly bonds of history and becoming the face of God.

The most important point to emerge is that *the writers of the gospels were not eyewitnesses of the events they describe.* If they had been eyewitnesses, there would be little reason for them to have relied so extensively on previously written accounts. The complex question of unnamed sources is summarized by Van Voort, who says regarding them, "No manuscript evidence has survived, and no ancient Christian author mentions them...the communities that used and copied them also disappeared, most likely into the churches that used the fuller Gospels."[71]

Even the question of an autograph itself is not as straightforward as we might at first suppose. If a writer produced more than one edition of his text, as is suspected to be the case with the gospel of Mark and the book of Acts, which should be considered the real autograph, the first document or a subsequent variation, both presumably by the same hand? If a scribe produced ten copies of a letter written for wide distribution, all containing slight variations in the wording, which copy would be considered the inspired original? A textual critic, Johann Hug, writing nearly two centuries ago, posed the problem in this way:

Let us now suppose, as it is very natural to do, that the same [copyist] who was employed to make this copy, made copies likewise for opulent individuals and other churches—and there

---

[69] Jerome Neyrey points out that the miracles mentioned in Matthew 11:5 and Luke 7:22 "is a list which was narrated in great detail much later by the evangelists." *The Resurrection Stories*, 15.

[70] *Ancient Christian Gospels*, 204.

[71] *Jesus Outside the New Testament*, 176.

was no original at all, or there were perhaps ten or more [origi-
nals] of which none could claim superiority.[72]

The process of recovering the original text of any New Testament
book is complicated and the results uncertain. Noted textual critic Eldon Epp has proposed no less than four classifications of texts: (1) an
"autographic text-form," i.e., the text as originally written, (2) a
"predecessor text-form," one (or more) forms of the text discernible
behind the form we now possess, (3) a "canonical text-form," the
form of the text at the time it was declared authoritative by the church,
and (4) an "interpretive text-form," the form the text acquired during
"any and each interpretive iteration…as it was used in the life, worship, and teaching of the church."[73] The New Testament books as they
now exist are variable combinations of Epp's four text-forms.

Additionally, it is now widely recognized that the names attached to
the gospels and most of the other New Testament books are not the
names of the actual authors. Among the letters attributed to Paul, only
Romans, the letters to the Corinthians, Galatians, Philippians, 1 Thessalonians and Philemon are considered with any degree of certainty to
be authentic. Attribution of the gospel which bears Matthew's name
does not occur until the 2nd century, and even then it is not clear that
the reference is to the canonical gospel of Matthew.

Ancient writers often attributed their writings to more famous persons. These documents, produced under false names, are called *pseude-
pigrapha*, an elegant term borrowed from Greek which means *forgeries*.
There is virtually no doubt that the majority of New Testament books,
including the gospels, the pastoral epistles (1 and 2 Timothy and Titus), and Revelation, are pseudonymous. Lane Fox: "By withholding
his name, the writer lent authority to texts which had none…However
we try to justify the authors' practice, at bottom they used the same
device: falsehood."[74] Ironically, the second letter to the Thessalonians,
widely regarded to be a forgery, warns its readers about "letters as if
from us," i.e., forgeries.[75]

---

[72] Quoted from Epp, *Harvard Theological Review* 92:246.
[73] Ibid, 276-277.
 Epp's article is indispensible reading for anyone interested in the question of the
original text of the New Testament books.
[74] *Pagans and Christians*, 340.
[75] 2 Thessalonians 2:2.

Of the many gospels rejected by the early church, Eusebius remarked, "they obviously turn out to be inventions of heretical men."[76] In point of fact, the victors of the various early doctrinal wars declared their gospels to be orthodox, and labeled the numerous gospels and Acts used by the losers heretical.

...transmission of the text

The study of texts which have come down to us in multiple handwritten copies is quite complex and the details of such study are well beyond the scope of this book. Nevertheless, the principle obstacles to the reconstruction of a lost original from imperfect copies are easy enough to understand.

1. If the original of a document is lost and only imperfect copies survive, the reading of any given portion of the text of the original can still be established *assuming that at least one of the imperfect copies preserves the correct reading of that particular portion of the original.*[77]
2. If the original text contained a reading that seemed inadequate to the copyist and the copyist 'improved' it, and all surviving copies contain that 'improvement,' then the original reading is lost.
3. If a copy of the original text contained a corrupted reading, and all surviving copies are descended from that corrupted copy, then the original reading is lost —textual critics call this "primitive error."
4. If, on comparison, copies judged to be of equally probable authority are found to preserve conflicting readings, and one of those readings is assumed to be the original, then in principle it is still not possible to establish the original text with certainty.

Knowing that there are well over 5000 manuscripts of the Greek New Testament which have been compared one to another, and that *they*

---

[76] *Ecclesiastical History*, III, 25, 7.

[77] The assumption that the original text of each portion of each New Testament document is to be found in at least one surviving manuscript is accepted as a mostly unspoken article of faith by many textual critics. If this assumption is not correct, then recovery of the original text can never be assured and the project of classical textual criticism —establishing the exact text of the original documents— ultimately fails.

contain over 300,000 variant readings,[78] the perceptive reader will immediately get some sense of the enormity of the problem of establishing the original wording of the New Testament. The wording of the text is different in each New Testament manuscript.

Given the humble origins of the earliest Christians, it is unlikely that professional scribes were regularly employed to copy their texts until around the middle of the 4th century. On the contrary, based on study of the handwriting of the earliest copies of the New Testament books, it seems clear that most copies were produced ad hoc by literate amateurs, with the result that the surviving copies are known to contain "far more variants than there are words in the New Testament."[79] Elsewhere Ehrman notes, "...the earliest copyists appear to have been untrained and relatively unsuited to the tasks..."[80]

Like Christianity today, early Christianity encompassed a very diverse set of interpretations of the gospels and epistles. After the Roman emperor Constantine declared Christianity to be the official religion of the Empire in the 4th century, the question of whose interpretation of Jesus' teachings represented Christian truth suddenly assumed greater importance. Under pressure from the Roman state and motivated by personal antagonism, bishops in the major cities met to formulate an official —"orthodox"— Christian theology and began to actively suppress the many unofficial interpretations which were declared to be heresy. Constantine's policy of toleration toward Christianity, aimed at unity within the Roman Empire, may paradoxically have escalated the competition among Christian sects "by declaring tax exemptions for Christian clergy and offering churches immense patronage."[81]

For a long time it was assumed by scholars that only the 'heretical' sects sought to change the text of the New Testament. However, recent attention to the evidence has demolished that comfortable position. There are abundant indications that the suppression of the many early forms of Christianity that diverged from the orthodox position

---

[78] There are 138,000 words more or less in the New Testament.

Many of the variant readings are variations in spelling which probably reflected regional differences in pronunciation which existed in Greek as in every other language.

[79] Bart Ehrman in a lecture, "The Neglect of the Firstborn in New Testament Studies," 2.

[80] *Lost Christianities,* 49.

[81] *The Closing of the Western Mind,* xviii, 178.

also entailed making 'refinements' of the New Testament text.[82] Even after several centuries of exacting study of thousands of manuscripts, the text of the New Testament remains to some extent unsure, a situation which has led one textual critic to ask, "Why is almost no one... willing to claim, at least with any substantial degree of confidence, that with our current critical texts we have recovered the N[ew] T[estament] in the original Greek?"[83]

The 4th century church historian Eusebius made this revealing complaint about the copying and alteration of gospels up to his time, alterations which may have involved a primitive form of textual criticism:

> For this reason [i.e., confidence in "the techniques of unbelievers," *my note*] they fearlessly put their hands on the divine scriptures, purporting to have corrected them, and that I utter no false allegation against them anyone who wishes can learn, for if any man so desire, collect the copies to closely compare each with the other. He would find many discrepancies and variances between those of Asklepiades and Theodotus, and it is possible to acquire an abundance of them since their disciples have copied them diligently, "set aright" as they call it, but in fact corrupted.
>
> Again, the copies of Hermophilus do not agree with these, nor do those of Apollonides even agree with one another, for the copies they produced first can be compared to those which later on they even further corrupted, and they will be discovered to differ greatly.[84]

---

[82] Ehrman's *The Orthodox Corruption of Scripture*, which concentrates on the effects of the emerging christological controversies on the New Testament text, is the most comprehensive examination of the evidence for doctrinally motivated textual tampering. The corrupted form of the text is essentially that of the *King James Version*, the so-called "majority text."

For a thorough discussion of the majority text and its ever thinning ranks of defenders, Daniel Wallace's essay in *The Text of the New Testament in Contemporary Research* is recommended.

[83] Holmes, *Text of the New Testament*, 348-350.

A *critical text* is a master text thought to preserve the most accurate wording of the New Testament based on close comparison of the most generally reliable existing manuscripts. The critical text used for this work is the 27th edition of the Nestle-Aland *Novum Testamentum Graece*.

[84] *Ecclesiastical History*, V.28.17-18.

In short, for at least the first two centuries of Christianity there was no sacred canon, no agreed upon body of authoritative scripture, no New Testament as we now know it. Primitive Christianity encompassed wildly divergent beliefs and practices —Epiphanius of Salamis "was able to list no less than eighty heresies…and Augustine in his old age came up with eighty-three."[85] Some divergent forms of Christianity were supported by quasi-historical concoctions called "gospels." All existing lines of evidence point to a laissez-faire attitude toward the text of gospels, with creations and alterations being made as exigency demanded. The net result is gospel texts of questionable historicity.

…conclusions

Because modern Bibles are printed, it is natural to assume that the books therein follow the rules of other printed books with which we are familiar. Unfortunately, the text of each New Testament gospel is known to have a complex, multilayered —*to say nothing of an additional unknown and unverifiable*— history that requires a level of sophistication unnecessary for the reading of any modern book. The text of the gospels is in a very real sense a trap for the unwary and uninformed. In fairness it must be pointed out that New Testament scholars have written extensively in an attempt to disseminate their understanding of these complexities, yet the majority of Christians appear blissfully unaware of controversies that are common knowledge in the field of New Testament studies.

As Hector Avalos has pointed out, the search for an autograph —even if it were to ultimately succeed— which stands behind the surviving texts would still not return us to the authentic sayings of Jesus. A "Greek translation, by definition, cannot be the 'original' text of anything Jesus said in Aramaic."[86]

That the quest for the 'authentic' Greek text of the New Testament is a fool's errand is now more commonly acknowledged by central figures in biblical studies: "A text, not protected by canonical status, but used in liturgy, apologetics, polemics, homiletics, and instruction of catechumens is most likely to be copied frequently and is thus subject

---

[85] *The Closing of the Western Mind*, 308.
[86] *The End of Biblical Studies*, 71.

to frequent modifications and alterations."[87] Seen from the vantage point of textual criticism or source criticism, it is somewhat ironic that "gospel" is a vernacular synonym for "truth."

In subsequent chapters I will examine various examples of textual alteration, particularly in the ways in which Matthew and Luke treated potentially embarrassing material in the gospel of Mark. Although it is customary for scholars to refer to such manipulation as 'editing,' it is in fact an early example of spin, of tweaking the text, recasting it to make it say something rather different, or more commonly, evading problematic topics by saying nothing at all. Much of the 'editing' of the New Testament was effectively censoring. Nevertheless, a subject raised by one author that is met with deafening silence by a subsequent editor is often just as revealing as what is openly acknowledged.

Minus the original gospels, the only thing that can be known a priori on the basis of the surviving copies is that all the copies are different and all the copies contain errors. The extensive use of sources reveals that the gospels were not written by eyewitnesses —it is inconceivable that an eyewitness would not have used his own recollections. According to Christian apologists, Jesus' life was the most important life ever lived, and yet amazingly none of our surviving documents appear to contain the direct personal account of anyone who actually saw it. The best evidence indicates that oral traditions were considered more authoritative than written texts until well into the 2nd century,[88] so it is quite possible that no direct eyewitness account of Jesus' life was ever produced.

It was long the assumption of New Testament criticism that as layers of theology were stripped away from the texts of the gospels the 'historical' Jesus would emerge into the light, a hope now recognized as too optimistic by half. It is assumed in this book that earlier traditions with multiple attestation have a higher probability of being authentically historical, but it must be acknowledged that that is an assumption and nothing more. There is no *non-theological* Jesus —or for the purposes of this book, no *non-magical* Jesus— which is exactly why there is any record of Jesus at all.

---

[87] *Gospel Traditions in the Second Century*, 20.
[88] *The Closing of the Western Mind*, 137.

Chapter 2: The Holy Family

To the modern reader, a history is by definition a dispassionate examination of the facts, and many Christians past and present have read the gospels as if they were histories in this sense: simple, unbiased accounts of facts. From the representations of the New Testament writers themselves, the reader might easily assume that a history in the modern sense is being proposed:

> Inasmuch as many have set their hand to organize a coherent narrative concerning the events which have been fulfilled in our midst, even as those who from the beginning became eyewitnesses and attendants of the word handed down to us, I too resolved to carefully trace the course of events from the beginning and to write them down in a logical sequence for you, most excellent Theophilus,[89] so that you might know with certainty the matters about which you have been instructed.[90]

A close reading of the introduction reveals that the writer was not himself an eyewitness, but is drawing on accounts which were "handed down to us," the "us" in question being Christians of Luke's generation who had not personally witnessed the events of Jesus' life. Moreover, the stated goal of Luke's narrative is *correct religious instruction*, not mere acquaintance with the facts of Jesus' career. The gospels are not simple reportage. The purpose of the gospels is to convince.[91]

---

[89] **Κρατιστε Θεοφιλε**: "**most excellent** Theophilus." *Most excellent* –κρατιστος (kratistos)– is used elsewhere in the New Testament only by Luke and only in addressing the Roman officials Felix (Acts 23:26, 24:3) and Festus (Acts 26:25). Lane Fox concludes that Theophilus ("beloved of God") "is the cover name for a highly placed figure in Roman circles...Acts and the third Gospel are the first, and greatest, of Christian apologies to be addressed to highly placed pagans." *Pagans and Christians*, 430.

[90] Luke 1:1-4.

[91] Regarding the "Barabbas episode," Carmichael notes that the account "has an artificial, histrionic, and tendentious effect," but is "flagrantly contrary to all probability" meaning "historical probability or fact, a notion alien to the writers and editors of the Gospels, who were interested solely in discovering occasions for edification." *The Un-riddling of Christian Origins*, 90.

It is estimated that at least 30 years passed between the events of Jesus' life and the writing of the gospels. To appreciate the implications of the time lapse between the end of Jesus' life and the writing of the gospels, try to imagine the eyewitness accounts of the assassination of John F. Kennedy, which occurred in 1963, being passed from person to person in oral form until about the year 2000, at which point someone finally commits an *edited* version of *some* of the oral accounts to written form. Our confidence in the reliability of such reports would likely be quite low.

The gospels are religious propaganda, missionary literature with a double agenda: the conversion of unbelievers and the defense of Christianity before a skeptical pagan audience. The gospels also make absolute religious assertions, a point not missed by astute critics of early Christianity such as Porphyry who questioned how a cult confined to a remote corner of Syria could possibly claim universal application.

The declaration of Christianity in this regard is clear:

> "I am the way and the truth and the life. No one comes to the Father except through me."[92]

> "And there is no salvation in anyone else, for there is no other name under heaven given among men by which we must be saved."[93]

Whether or not Jesus himself ever spoke the words attributed to him, they nevertheless categorically exclude believers in other religions as well as the billions who never heard of Jesus from any approach to God. Every invitation to belief should be an occasion for scrutiny, and a claim as sweeping as this invites the most rigorous form of examination.

To the modern mind, the gospels contain a host of glaring omissions. There is no physical description whatever of Jesus or of any of his disciples. "Nobody remembered what Jesus looked like...by c. 200, he was being shown on early Christian sarcophagi in a stereotyped pagan image, as a philosopher teaching among his pupils or as a shepherd

---

[92] John 14:6.
[93] Acts 4:12.

bearing sheep from his flock."[94] The very earliest representation of Jesus appears to be the Roman *Alexamenos grafitto*, which depicts Jesus as a crucified man with a donkey's head. Interestingly, the Egyptian Seth, a god particularly associated with magic, is often pictured with a donkey-like head.[95]

The familiar Jesus of the rather elongated, bearded face comes to us from the 6th century when such a likeness is said to have been miraculously imprinted on a facecloth or *mandylion*, becoming the ancestor of the Greek (and later Russian) Orthodox icon. Such a miraculous image is known as an *acheiropoietos*, 'made without hands.'

Only Jesus' mother, brothers, and sisters are referred to in Mark,[96] — Joseph is never mentioned in Mark— and none of the gospels has anything to say about his father once Jesus' career begins. Of Jesus' own marital status, nothing is said and it is difficult to know just what to make of the gospels' silence on this subject. A strand of the early tradition claimed that Jesus had a twin brother, Judas Thomas —*Thomas* is derived from the Aramaic word for *twin*— also known as *Didymus* from the Greek word for *twin*. He may be the same as the famous Doubting Thomas of the gospel of John,[97] and is the subject of the apocryphal *Acts of Thomas*. However, the New Testament is opaque about the "factual origins of Jesus" and a case has even been made on the basis of ancient sources that Jesus was conceived as a result of Mary having been raped by a Roman soldier named Pantera.[98]

Even more to the point, apart from the mention that he was at one time a disciple of John the Baptist, the gospels provide no information on the source of Jesus' ideas. According to the most primitive tradition, Jesus does not become a person of interest until after he receives the spirit. In other words, John the Baptist and Jesus simply pop up in the narrative like cardboard figures: "John the Baptizer *appeared* in the wilderness."[99] Similarly, Jesus simply "comes from Nazareth of Gali-

---

[94] *Pagans and Christians*, 392.
[95] *Supplementum Magicum*, 69.
[96] Mark 3:31.
    Jesus' brothers are also mentioned at John 7:3, 1 Corinthians 9:5, and Galatians 1:19. According to Paul, Jesus' brothers and the other apostles were married.
[97] John 20:27-28.
[98] *Palestine in the Time of Jesus*, 57-58.
[99] Mark 1:4.

lee."[100] This may be compared with the more elaborate account of the gospel of John[101] which is ultimately no more revealing.[102]

Despite all attempts by historians to determine them, the exact dates of Jesus' birth and death remain a matter of conjecture. The length of Jesus' career is also uncertain; the chronology of the gospel of John suggests a career of about three years, but the earlier account of Mark is consistent with a much shorter period, perhaps less than a year in length.

The later synoptic gospels, Matthew and Luke, both polish Mark's prose and ease into Jesus' story by including infancy narratives which are clearly fictitious. Matthew and Luke also omit many of the more radical details and sayings found in Mark, features with which they were apparently uncomfortable. There were unquestionably two phases to Jesus' career: a longer one in Galilee and a much shorter one in Judea, but beyond this generalization it is risky to proceed. Grant: "...the Gospels, vague about dates and times, and differing sharply, moreover, one from another, fail to provide the materials for any safe chronological framework. It is therefore not possible to offer even a likely or approximate order of events."[103]

...Infancy Narratives

Of the city of Bethlehem the prophet Micah wrote:

> But you, O Bethlehem Ephrathah, who are little to be among the clans of Judah, from you shall come forth for me one who is to be ruler in Israel, whose origin is from of old, from ancient days.[104]

---

[100] Mark 1:9.

[101] John 1:19-34.

[102] This is a remarkable contrast with the documentation of a later religious career: "[Mother] Teresa's supporters have worked endlessly to compile a complete volume of records documenting her case. More than 100 witnesses answered a 263-question survey, and a 35,000-page, 80-volume report was assembled, according to the promoter of her cause, the Rev. Brian Kolodiejchuk." *Austin American-Statesman*, October 17, 2003.

[103] *Jesus*, 10.

[104] Micah 5:2, (RSV)

The first Christians were eager to apply this prediction to Jesus, but to do so they had to get Jesus born in Bethlehem. There was, unfortunately, a problem: Jesus and his family were from Nazareth, a village so insignificant that it is never even mentioned in the Old Testament. "There seems no good reason why anyone should have invented a connection with a place otherwise so little known."[105] Mark, the writer of the earliest gospel,[106] simply ignored the issue, but Matthew and Luke, who had an excellent motive for making a connection between Jesus and Bethlehem, elected to take it up. John knew of the controversy,[107] but did not invent an infancy fable.

It is well known that people of Jesus' time often concocted fantastic stories about the birth and childhood of famous figures. In the centuries after Jesus' death, apocryphal tales about him and his mother were collected in the form of books, two of which, the *Infancy Gospel of Thomas*[108] and the *Gospel of James*, still survive. Matthew and Luke needed to get Jesus born in Bethlehem, in David's city,[109] so that David, the past king of Israel, could function as a prophetic prototype of Jesus, the future King of Kings. Toward this goal they created our earliest recorded fables about Jesus' childhood, but their fictional solutions created many more difficulties than they resolved.

Matthew places Jesus in the family line of Abraham and David, two pivotal characters in Jewish salvation history, and even enumerates a span of 42 generations between Abraham, David, and Jesus. Strangely enough, Matthew includes several women of ill repute in Jesus' family tree: Tamar,[110] who, posing as a prostitute has sex with her father-in-law,[111] Rahab,[112] a prostitute by profession,[113] and Bathsheba, the wife of Uriah,[114] an adulteress.[115] Assuming that Matthew could just have easily omitted these women, one can only wonder why he chose to

---

[105] Wilcox, *Aufstieg und Niedergang der Römischen Welt*, II.25.1: 143.
[106] That Mark was written before the other gospels is agreed upon by the majority of New Testament scholars. A summary of the evidence for Markan priority has been written by Daniel Wallace: "The Synoptic Problem," *www.bible.org.*
[107] John 7:41-42.
[108] Not to be confused with the Coptic *Gospel of Thomas.*
[109] David's father, Jesse, was a native of Bethlehem (1 Samuel 16:1).
[110] Matthew 1:3
[111] Genesis 38:13-26.
[112] Matthew 1:5.
[113] Joshual 2:1.
[114] Matthew 1:6.
[115] 2 Samuel 11:2-5.

include them. It is not impossible that they are meant to be read as a subtext to the story of Jesus' own parentage.

Matthew wishes to complete Jesus' connection to David by having him born in Bethlehem,[116] after which time magi from the east appear at the court of the Judean king, Herod the Great:

> In the days of Herod the king, after Jesus was born in Bethlehem of Judea, magi came from the east to Jerusalem, saying, "Where is he who has been born King of the Jews? For we saw his star ascend,[117] and we came to render homage to him." But after hearing this, King Herod became troubled and all Jerusalem with him, and he assembled all the chief priests and scribes of the people and inquired of them where the Christ was to be born.[118]

Herod then sends the magi on to Bethlehem with orders to report back.

A μαγος (magos) is usually understood to have been a Persian court official, an expert in astrology, dream interpretation, and the occult arts generally.[119] However, in the Greek speaking world the practice of magic was often attributed to foreigners, particularly Persians and Egyptians, simply as a matter of custom. An intriguing parallel in the Greek translation of the Old Testament recounts how Nebuchadnezzar, disturbed by a prophetic dream, summons the "enchanters," — επαοιδος (epaoidos), enchanter— the "magi," —μαγος (magos), magician— and the "sorcerers," —φαρμακος (pharmakos), sorcerer— to interpret his dream.[120] Georg Luck: "The history of the terms magos, mageia, suggests and old misunderstanding. What, for the Persians, was their national religion, was, in the eyes of the Greeks, ritual magic."[121] Morton Smith believed that the story was meant to mark Jesus out as "the supreme magus and master of the art," worthy of the submission of other magi.[122] Jesse Rainbow has made a case that the gold, fran-

---

[116] Matthew 1:1, 17, 2:1.
[117] If the star was a comet or some other spectacular celestial event, why had Herod and his court not seen it? Matthew probably had in mind Isaiah 60:3 (*RSV*): "And nations shall come to your light and kings to the brightness of your rising."
[118] Matthew 2:1-4.
[119] See especially Becker, *A Kind of Magic*, 87-106.
[120] Daniel 2:2.
[121] *Witchcraft and Magic in Europe: Ancient Greece and Rome*, 95.
[122] *Jesus the Magician*, 96.

kincense and myrrh brought to Jesus by the magi[123] were gifts fit for an accomplished magus.[124]

According to Matthew,[125] the star goes ahead of the magi and stops over the house —*not*, it should be noted, *a manger*— where the infant Jesus lives — εως ελθων εσταθη επανω ου ην το παιδιον: "until [the star] stopped over the place where the child was." The sign of the star given to the magi finds a nearly exact parallel in the magical papyri where a "sign"[126] given to a magician is a star that "after descending will stop over the middle of the house" —κατ' ελθων στησεται εις μεσον του δωματος.[127] So similar is the language of the gospel that it is tempting to think Matthew might have copied his story from some magical text.

The magi are warned in a dream not to return to Herod, and an angel appears to Joseph in a dream and warns him to flee with his family to Egypt. Herod, seeing that the magi have not returned as promised, kills all the children in Bethlehem who are under two years of age. When Herod dies, an angel again appears in a dream to Joseph and orders him to return from Egypt to Judea, but on returning, Joseph discovers that Archelaus, Herod's son, is ruler of Judea (and Bethlehem) and warned yet again in a dream, resettles his family in Nazareth of Galilee. "The most important of all the modes of divination which link the Hebrews with other nations is that by dreams."[128]

These events —the flight to Egypt, the slaughter of the children, and the move to Nazareth— supposedly fulfill Old Testament predictions.[129]

Concerning dreams the papyri recommend the magician call "the heavenly gods and chthonic demons[130]...and whenever [Apollo] comes in, ask him what you wish for, about prophecies, about divina-

---

[123] Matthew 3:11.

[124] *Harvard Theological Review* 100: 263.

[125] Matthew 2:9, 11.

[126] σημειον: a "sign." This is the usual term for working wonders in the gospel of John.

[127] *Papyri Graecae Magicae* I, 75.

[128] *Magic, Divination, and Demonology among the Hebrews and their Neighbors*, 77.

[129] Matthew 2:8-23.

[130] καλων τους ουρανιους θεους και χθονιους δαιμονας: "calling the heavenly gods and chthonic demons..."

tion by means of Homeric verses,[131] about sending dreams, revelations in dreams, interpretation of dreams,[132] sending diseases, about everything included in the craft of magic..."[133]

There are many problems with Matthew's story, beginning with the magi, who, if represented to be Persian officials, could be presumed to have some slight knowledge of royal courts and how they worked. They appeared before Herod the Great —who no doubt regarded *himself* as King of the Jews— inquiring about "he who has been born King of the Jews." Although his reputation for rapacious cruelty was not out of keeping with the standards of his times, this is the same Herod widely known to have murdered two of his ten wives, three sons, a brother-in-law, and a wife's grandfather.[134] How did the magi think that Herod would react to the news of the birth of a rival king?

Herod dispatches the magi to Bethlehem on the promise that they will return and report the child's location to him, but according to the story, they evade Herod, returning to their country by a different route. But if Herod was so disturbed by the news of the kingly birth, "and all Jerusalem with him," why didn't he simply have the magi followed? Why, for that matter, didn't Herod just kill all the children in Bethlehem at once and call it done, having learned about Bethlehem from the prophecy of Micah, not the magi?[135]

---

[131] A reference to *bibliomancy* or *stichomancy*, an ancient form of divination using first the epics of Homer (*sortes Homerica*) and later the gospels (*sortes sanctorum*). A passage, selected at random, was interpreted prophetically. Homeric verses are used in magical spells in the Greco-Egyptian papyri; New Testament passages were used similarly in later Christian magic. Randomly heard voices were also thought to carry indications of the divine will, as in the famous case of "tolle, lege" which resulted in the conversion of Augustine (*Confessions* XIII, 28-29).

[132] Dreams were considered of enormous importance in antiquity and Greek has an impressive number of terms for dream work, only a fraction of which occur here: ονειροπομπεια (oneiropompeia), *dream-sending*, ονειραιτησια (oneiraitēsia), *dream revelation*, and ονειροκρισια (oneirokrisia), *dream interpretation*.

[133] εν τη μαγικη εμπειρια: "in the **craft** of magic..." *Papyri Graecae Magicae* I, 266, 327-331.

Εμπειρια (empeiria), *experience*, from εμπειραω, to *try, attempt*, hence εμπειρος, *practiced, experienced*, from whence *empiric*. Magical spells, like recipes, were evidently based upon trial and error. Experience was therefore more valuable than theory.

[134] Metzger, *The New Testament: Its Background, Growth and Content*, 24.

[135] As pointed out by Becker, the Old Testament prophets, not the stars, are the only true guide to the identity of the Messiah (*A Kind of Magic*, 104), but that still fails to solve the problem of Matthew's illogical narrative.

When the magi set out from Herod's palace on their mission to find Jesus, the star again appears and stops over the house where Jesus and his parents live. But if the star led them to Jesus, why didn't it just take them there in the first place? Why did it lead them first to Herod and why would they need to inquire of Herod's scribes and priests where the Christ would be born if the star stopped over the very house where Jesus lived? Obviously the story as we have it traces a ridiculously convoluted path to Bethlehem. However, there was a possible theological motive for the story of the slaughter of the children by Herod: it might have served to create a parallel between Jesus and Moses by recalling Pharaoh's murder of Israelite boys.[136]

Joseph Hoffman has suggested a strong secondary motive for Matthew's elaborations, namely a "Christian counter-polemic" made necessary by the charge in the Talmud "that Jesus had learned magic and sorcery in Egypt...The Talmud knows Egypt as the center of the magical arts: 'Ten measures of sorcery descended in the world: Egypt received nine, the rest of the world one.' (Talmud b. Qidd. 49). Thus, to say that Jesus learned magic in Egypt is to say that he is more powerful as a worker of signs than the local variety of wonder-workers (see Matt. 9:33)."[137]

To posit a connection between Jesus of Nazareth and the magicians of Egypt and their techniques might seem at first to be the pursuit of an exegetical phantom, but it is the New Testament itself that connects Jesus both with *magicians* and with *Egypt*.[138] Of particular interest is Koester's observation that the concept of virgin birth, which is foreign to Judaism, "is Hellenistic and, ultimately, Egyptian. No other religious or political tradition of antiquity can be identified as its generator."[139]

According to this reading, Matthew's infancy story reflects accusations of magical practice leveled against Jesus and seeks to disarm them by explaining Jesus' association with Egypt and its magic as strictly circumstantial and not as the true source of his amazing powers. Nevertheless, Christian apologists found themselves defending Jesus against charges of practicing sorcery for several centuries after his death, including allegations that he had returned from Egypt with spells tat-

---

[136] Exodus 2:15-16.
[137] *Jesus Outside the Gospels*, 40, 45.
[138] Matthew 2:1-2, 13, 19.
[139] *Ancient Christian Gospels*, 306.

tooed on his body:[140] "But did not Ben Stada [Jesus, *my note*] bring forth witchcraft from Egypt by means of scratches/tattoos upon his flesh?"[141] The Jews, like many ancients, regarded Egypt as the cradle of magic; of the world's magic, Egypt possessed nine parts, the rest of the world only one.[142] Clement of Alexandria famously referred to Egypt as "the mother of magicians" and even Pythagoras was rumored to have traveled to Egypt. The pagan polemicist Celsus, writing about 180 CE, also knew of such charges leveled against Jesus, likely from Jewish informants.[143] Fritz Graf: "...those who accused Jesus of being a magician (they were not few among the pagans) argued that he, after all, had spent part of his youth in the homeland of magic, after the escape from Palestine..."[144]

If Matthew's infancy story is to be judged improbable, Luke's is even worse. The birth narrative of Luke starts, not with Jesus, but with his predecessor, John the Baptist. According to this version of events, a priest named Zechariah was married to a barren woman named Elizabeth. While Zechariah fulfilled his priestly duties in the temple, the angel Gabriel appeared to him and announced that Elizabeth would bear a son who would be called John. When Zechariah objected that both he and his wife were too old to have children, Gabriel struck him mute.[145] The impregnation of barren women was practically a cottage industry in the Old Testament —Sarah, the wife of Abraham and mother of Isaac, was barren[146] as was Hannah, the mother of Samuel.

In the sixth month of Elizabeth's pregnancy, Gabriel appeared to Mary, a virgin girl living in Nazareth of Galilee.

> In the sixth month, the angel Gabriel was sent forth from God to a city of Galilee called Nazareth to a virgin, the finacée of a man named Joseph of David's house. The virgin's name was Mary.
>
> When [Gabriel] came in, he said, "Greetings, favored one, the Lord is with you." But she became very troubled by this an-

---

140 *Magic in Ancient Egypt*, 47.
141 *Jesus in the Talmud*, 16.
142 Talmud *Kiddushin* 49b.
143 *Contra Celsum*, I, 28.
144 *Envisioning Magic. A Princeton Seminar and Symposium*, 94-95.
145 Luke 1:5-20.
146 Genesis 17:17-19.

nouncement and began to wonder what kind of greeting this might be.

And the angel said to her, "Do not fear, Mary, for you found favor before God, and behold, you will conceive in your womb and give birth to a son and you will call his name Jesus. This one will be great and will be called Son of the Most High, and the Lord God will give him the throne of David his father, and he will rule over the house of Jacob for all ages and of his kingdom there will be no end."

Mary said to the angel, "How will this happen, since I have no husband?"[147] And the angel said to her in answer, "The holy spirit will come upon you,[148] and power of the Most High will overshadow you,[149] and therefore what is begotten will be called God's son."[150]

Mark has little to say about Jesus' childhood and nothing to say about Jesus' virgin birth. John appears not to have heard of the virgin birth; the disciple Philip identifies Jesus simply as "Jesus the son of Joseph from Nazareth"[151] and the Jews also identify Jesus as "the son of Joseph."[152] Mark describes Jesus as "the son of Mary,"[153] which, given the custom of patrilineal genealogy (as at Matthew 1:1-17, for example), implies that the identity of Jesus' father was a matter of dispute. On the subject of fatherhood, his opponents chide him, "we were not born from fornication,"[154] a taunt which would be pointless unless Jesus' legitimacy was already in question. Luke says of Jesus ων υιος **ως ενομιζετο Ιωσηφ**: "being a son —**so it was thought**— of Joseph" (Luke 3:23). It is interesting to compare this remark with the explanation of Jesus' parentage at Matthew 1:18-20.

---

[147] επει ανδρα ου γινωσκω: (literally) "since I know not a man…"

[148] πνευμα αγιον **επελευσεται** επι σε: "the holy spirit **will come upon** you…" The same expression occurs in Acts 1:8: λημψεσθε δυναμιν **επελθοντος** του αγιου πνευματος εφ υμας: "you will receive power when the holy spirit **comes upon** you…" The barely concealed violence of the idiom is considered in another chapter.

[149] Moses cannot enter the tabernacle because the cloud representing Yahweh's presence "overshadows" it, Exodus 40:34-35. Compare the "cloud" at Matthew 17:5.

[150] Luke 1:26-35.

[151] John 1:45.

[152] John 6:42.

[153] Mark 6:3.

[154] John 8:41.

The Greek word παρθενος (parthenos), *virgin*, used of Mary in Matthew 1:23 and echoed in Luke 1:27, is a quotation of Isaiah 7:14 in the *Septuagint*,[155] the Greek translation of the Old Testament favored by early Christians. The translators of the *Septuagint* used παρθενος to translate the Hebrew word עלמה (almah), *young woman*, in Isaiah 7:14. The word *almah*, the feminine form of עלם (elem), *young man*, primarily indicates the *age* of a woman and only by implication her virginity — reflecting the culturally based assumption that any young woman not married would necessarily be a virgin or a slut. However, Hebrew has a different word, בתולה (bethulah), which nearly always means *virgin*.

The story of the virgin birth is a clumsy attempt to make Jesus fulfill the prophecy of Isaiah 7:14, based, *not on a reading of the Hebrew text —* which few early Christians could have read anyway— *or its context*, but on a Greek translation used by the early church. Indeed, the context of Isaiah 7:14 indicates that a particular woman, at whom the prophet might very well have pointed while uttering his prediction, would bear a son and that "before the child knows how to refuse the evil and choose the good, the land before whose two kings you are in dread will be deserted."[156] In other words, Isaiah specifically states that the birth of the male child was a short-term prediction given as a sign to king Ahaz, not to people born centuries later. The interpretation of Isaiah 7:14 offered by Matthew and Luke is one of the more blatant examples of how the gospel writers misappropriated anything in the Old Testament that could be construed —by however great a stretch of the imagination— as applying to Jesus of Nazareth.

Having established the connection between Jesus and his forefather David through Gabriel's announcement, Luke must now somehow get Mary to David's home town of Bethlehem where she will deliver the promised child. It is here that Luke makes an egregious misstep, for according to him[157] the Roman Caesar Octavian (titled *Augustus*) issued a decree that "all the world" must go to the town of their forefathers to be registered. Luke says this occurred while Quirinius was governor

---

[155] The text of the *Septuagint* reads: δωσει κυριος αυτος υμιν σημειον ιδου η **παρθενος** εν γαστρι εξει και τεξεται υιον και καλεσεις το ονομα αυτου Εμμανουηλ:"the Lord himself will give you a sign, behold, **the virgin** will conceive and bear a son and will call his name Emmanuel." The latter part of verse is quoted verbatim by Matthew.
[156] Isaiah 7:16, *RSV*.
[157] Luke 2:1-4.

of Syria, an event which, according to Luke 1:5, was contemporaneous with the rule of Herod the Great.

There are two fatal problems with this part of Luke's story: Quirinius was, in fact, a governor in Syria, but not until ten years *after* Herod's death. And of the worldwide census supposedly ordered by Augustus, there is no record, nor indeed could there have been. How could people all over the empire have possibly known where their ancestors had lived *a thousand years previously* and gone there to be registered as Luke claims Joseph did? Ancient sources are understandably silent about this fictitious registration as noted by Ehrman who asks, "…are we to imagine that this massive migration of millions of people, all over the empire, took place without any other author from the period so much as *mentioning* it?"[158]

There are other problems in harmonizing the infancy narratives of Matthew and Luke. In Luke, we are informed that following Mary's ritual purification according to Jewish law, she and her husband "returned to Galilee, *to their town Nazareth,*" where the child grew up and that *every year thereafter* his parents went down to Jerusalem for the Passover festival.[159] Where, then, does the family's flight to Egypt and their return to Palestine fit in? In Luke's account of Jesus' childhood, there is never any sense that Jesus is in danger. To the contrary, following the saccharine tale of Jesus being left behind in the temple, Luke assures us that the young Jesus increased in favor with both God and men,[160] a fairly unlikely observation to record if Herod had really attempted to murder him, slaying other children in the process.

Luke's reconstruction of events forges yet another, less obvious, link between Jesus and his forefather David: even as the prophet Samuel, conceived by a barren woman, anointed David, John, also conceived by a barren woman, baptizes Jesus. The correspondence between the two stories is far too extensive to be coincidental. Indeed, it appears that Luke has taken what he regarded as the essential elements of one story and used them as a framework for the construction of his own account. Luke was particularly adept at raiding the text of the Old Testament for material with which to construct Luke-Acts. For ease of

---

[158] *Jesus: Apocalyptic Prophet of the New Millennium,* 38-39.
[159] Luke 2:39-41. The ritual period of purification, in the case of a male child, lasted 33 days according to Leviticus 12:4.
[160] Luke 2:42-52.

comparison, I have listed the similarities between the two stories below:

1. Elizabeth is barren. Hannah is barren.
2. Elizabeth miraculously conceives John. Hannah miraculously conceives Samuel.
3. Zechariah sings a psalm of praise. Hannah signs a psalm of praise.
4. Israel will be saved from its enemies. Israel's enemies will be shattered.
5. Jesus grows in favor with God and the people. Samuel grows in favor with God and the people.
6. John baptizes Jesus. Samuel anoints David.[161]

The parallelism between the stories of Samuel the Anointer and John the Baptizer suggests that Luke deliberately used the Old Testament as a model for his story, seeking to show another, deeper, correspondence between David, the king of Judah, and Jesus, to whom God will give "the throne of David his father." Despite the piling up of historical references at Luke 2:1-2, the author of the gospel was not writing history as we know it, but rather locating Jesus and his predecessor John in the stream of salvation history. Thus Samuel becomes a prototype of John even as David becomes a prototype of Jesus —what the first of each pair did, the second will do in an even larger way. In Acts 3:24, Luke even has Peter say that the prophet *Samuel* predicted the coming of Jesus.

...Jesus and the family

The foregoing discussion illustrates some of the ways in which the text of the gospels was composed to score theological points. It is probable that we catch a brief glimmer of the real Jesus and the controversy surrounding him in the references to magi and Egypt, but it is clear that these stories do not approximate any modern definition of history.

The gospel of Mark contains this revealing snatch of dialogue:

Peter began to say to him, "Look, we have given up everything and followed you."
Jesus replied, "Truly I say to you, there is no one who has left house or brothers or sisters or mother or father or children or

---

[161] Luke, chapters 1-3. 1 Samuel, chapters 1-16.

fields on my account and on account of the good news who will not receive a hundred times as much now in this present time, houses and brothers and sisters and mothers and children and fields —with persecutions— and in the age to come, eternal life."[162]

It appears that Jesus' closest disciples abandoned their homes, families —*including wives and children*— and means of living to follow him. This naturally raises the question of what happened to those families his disciples left behind —*wives and children* are never mentioned as a part of Jesus' entourage. "Jesus appears to have challenged some to a lifestyle which left local family responsibilities behind. He, himself, appears to have lived such a lifestyle."[163] Jesus' admonition to his followers to make eunuchs of themselves is "yet another extravagant gesture of renunciation" that included abandonment of family, wealth, and concern for daily cares.[164] How Jesus and his band of disciples managed to support themselves is also unclear, but the accounts imply that while on the road they lived from the charity of those receptive to Jesus' message.[165]

Luke 18:29 specifically includes *wives* along with brothers, parents, and *children* among those renounced.[166] While various writers have speculated that Jesus married, none to my knowledge have read Jesus' statements as evidence that he abandoned his family. Could Jesus have led by example, leaving behind a wife and children and insisting his followers do likewise? Thirty years old when he appeared for baptism,[167] he was old enough to have been married and to have had children. Did Jesus hate his own wife and children? Did he leave them behind?

Several passages indicate that Jesus was alienated from his immediate family:

---

[162] Mark 10:28-30.
[163] *Sexuality and the Jesus Tradition*, 134.
[164] *The Manly Eunuch*, 259.
[165] Women are mentioned who provided for Jesus (Luke 8:1-4), and John notes that the disciples kept a purse (John 12:6, 13:29).
[166] Aune's comments on this passage are particularly cogent. *Apocalypticism, Prophecy, and Magic in Early Christianity*, 68-70.
[167] Luke 3:23.

And his mother and brothers came, and standing outside, they sent for him, calling him. A crowd sat around him, and they said to him, "Look, your mother and brothers and sisters are outside asking for you."

He answered, "Who are my mother and brothers?" And looking at those who were sitting around him, he said, "Behold my mother and my brothers! For whoever does the will of God, this is my brother and sister and mother."[168]

This episode is also reported by Matthew and Luke.[169]

Myers is certainly correct when he when he states, "kinship is the backbone of the very social order Jesus is struggling to overturn," and notes that "community of discipleship"[170] is the basis for a new apocalyptic society.

The brief exchange between Jesus and his mother at the wedding in Cana contains this startling comment:

And when they ran out of wine, Jesus' mother said to him, "They don't have any wine."

Jesus said to her, "What have I to do with you, woman? My time is not yet here."

His mother said to the servants, "Do whatever he tells you."[171]

I have translated the idiom τι εμοι και σοι —literally "what to me and to you"— as "What have I to do with you?" It is a carryover of a Semitic expression into Greek that means something like "What do you have against me?" or "What have I done to you that you should attack me?" It is, in fact, the identical idiom used by the demons when addressing Jesus: "What have we to do with you, Jesus the Nazarene? Have you come to destroy us?"[172] The expression, fairly common in the Greek translation of the Hebrew Old Testament, is often linked by

---

[168] Mark 3:31-35.
[169] Matthew 12:46-50, Luke 8:19-21. Jesus' saying that his disciples must hate their families as well as their own lives (Luke 14:26) may reflect an element of his own psychology as suggested by Smith. *Jesus the Magician*, 24-28.
[170] Myers, *Binding the Strong Man*, 168.
[171] John 2:3-5.
[172] Mark 1:24: τι ημιν και σοι Ιησου Ναζαρενε: **"What have we to do with you, Jesus the Nazarene?"**

the context to violent intentions.[173] The hostility implicit in this idiom has been papered over by any number of apologists of the Mary-Mother-of-God persuasion, whose diligent misreading of the passage has successfully generated an enduring fog of misimpression. Jesus' disciples must hate their parents, siblings, wives, and children according to the form of the saying in Luke 14:26.

Jesus' prickly family relationship appears repeatedly in the gospels in connection with his mission. As noted by Barton, Capernaum and the inner circle of the twelve "replaces Nazareth and the community of Jesus' own family," and concludes that the ominous "those outside" for whom everything is obfuscation includes Jesus' own relatives[174] — Jesus' own brothers did not believe in him.[175] Those looking for support for conventional 'family values' may take cold comfort from the words of Jesus of Nazareth. As Andrew Jacobs notes, the language of the gospels is the language of "domestic demolition."[176]

> ...Jesus hated families...By "family values" conservative politicians mean "hierarchical values," imposed not only on children but on lots of adults, often punitively. "Family values" forcibly infantilize most of the population. Jesus rejects families in part because he insists upon a different hierarchy: God is the father, which means that all humans are children, which means that all humans are equal in relation to one another...That slaves were attracted to Christianity is not surprising.[177]

Jesus' family tensions were hardly the end of his troubled relationships, however. After two thousand pigs rush headlong into the sea and drown, the people of the region beg Jesus to leave[178] —likely to prevent any further decimation of their economy— and after the cities where he healed numbers of people failed to repent, Jesus denounced them.[179] The members of the synagogue in his home territory recognize his humble origins and take offense, and he can perform few

---

[173] As at Judges 11:12, 1 Kings 17:18, 2 Chronicles 35:21, for example, where in each case one party contemplates the death of the other.
[174] *Discipleship and Family Ties in Mark and Matthew*, 68, 72.
[175] John 7:5.
[176] *Journal of Early Christian Studies* 7: 107.
[177] Gary Taylor, *Castration: An Abbreviated History of Western Manhood*, 199-200.
[178] Mark 5:16-17.
[179] Matthew 11:20.

powerful works there.[180] Many of his first disciples are offended by his teaching and desert him.[181] Most commentators on the New Testament regard these reports as fundamentally reliable. It could hardly have served the interest of the early church to retain them, but they had likely become too firmly embedded in the oral tradition to merely ignore.

...Jesus the bachelor

We have touched on the subject of Jesus' marital status. Few scholars competent in the field of New Testament studies seem to question the conclusion that Jesus was a confirmed bachelor. Now and then a conspiracy theorist wades into the murky texts of later apocryphal books, or discerns a previously unnoticed 'code' in paintings created more than a millennium after Jesus' death. Such excursions into the world of fantasy sometimes make for best-selling books and blockbuster movies, as well as provoking a state of near hysteria among the pious. However, this level of naïveté in regard to either religion or art is barely worthy of serious address.

As to Jesus' sex life, the relevant facts are these: at thirty years of age, Jesus was a single man, a feature of his life that would have been remarked upon in his time and culture: "Singleness—an unmarried lifestyle—was exceptional, even suspicious among the Jews, because it was seen as an offense to the divine obligation to procreate (Gen. 1:28). Jesus, however, was apparently single."[182] If a childless woman was considered a scandal worthy of intervention from On High, we can barely imagine the amount of malicious whispering a wifeless man must have produced among the village busybodies. "Celibacy is prohibited in Jewish law. The rabbis consider procreation the first command recorded in the Bible...Marriage and study of Torah are put ahead of all other religious obligations."[183]

It is not that celibacy was unknown in 1st century Judaism. The Essenes practiced celibacy as a part of their apocalyptic and isolationist religious movement, or possibly because of "the embattled character of

---

[180] Mark 6:3-5.
[181] John 6:60.
[182] *Homoeroticism in the Biblical World*, 119.
[183] *Sex Laws and Customs in Judaism*, 141.

the Community as a whole,"[184] but there is no evidence that Jesus was isolationist to the same extent, so one might fairly ask why he remained unmarried. Dale Martin, who discusses various forms of asceticism practiced in Jesus' day, notes that sexual abstinence usually accompanied other forms of abstinence or avoidance (wine, food, social relations, contact with the dead) and concludes, "...though we can now admit that sexual abstinence was indeed practiced by Jews of Jesus' day, what we know about Jesus does not fit any of the forms of ascetic Judaism we know about. If Jesus was a sexual ascetic, he was a queer one."[185]

Of course, various motives for celibacy may have overlapped: Jesus' intensely apocalyptic fixation (discussed in a subsequent chapter) may have been expressed as avoidance of sex, as well as a concern for purity, defined both in Jesus' cultural milieu and in the magical papyri as "abstention from sexual activity," which in certain extreme cases extended to not speaking to women and avoiding food served by them.[186]

Sexual abstinence was also commonly connected to magic. A book of magical spells, the *Sepher Ha-Razim*, repeatedly admonishes the magician, "Perform the entire rite in purity, and you will succeed."[187] Morton Smith pointed to Paul's "recommendation of celibacy on the ground that it would free the Christian from distractions and make him *euparedron* for the Lord...the lack of normal sexual satisfaction is likely to lead to compensatory connections with spirits, hence the requirement of celibacy by many shamanistic and priestly groups has probably some functional justification."[188] Temporary sexual abstinence was a condition of purity for Egyptian priests[189] —who practiced magic as part of their duties— and sexual abstinence played a significant role in Greco-Egyptian magic which in the 1st century included the characteristically Jewish element of exorcism: "virginity...

---

[184] *The Body and Society: Men, Women and Sexual Renunciation in Early Christianity*, 38.
[185] *Sex and the Single Savior*, 97.
[186] Rebecca Lesses, *Harvard Theological Review* 89:57.
[187] *Sepher Ha-Razim*, 31, 42, etc.
"You must lie down on green reeds, being pure from a woman, your head being turned toward the south," etc. *The Leyden Papyrus: An Egyptian Magical Book*, 51.
[188] *Harvard Theological Review* 73: 244.
Paul's term ευπαρεδρος (euparedros) receives further comment in a subsequent chapter.
[189] *Ancient Egyptian Magic*, 38.

gave efficacy to the exorcist's words."[190] The *Leyden Papyrus*, an Egyptian magical text, is another witness to the importance of purity, defined by the formula "a boy, pure, before he has gone with a woman."[191]

...the saying about eunuchs

Jesus himself may have offered an oblique answer to the question of his sexuality in his saying regarding the self-made eunuch: "some made eunuchs of themselves for the sake of the kingdom of heaven."[192] The implication is that Jesus himself was indisposed to marriage, either physically, emotionally, or due to prophetic calling. Nevertheless, this is a curious saying given that castrated or emasculated men were specifically excluded by Jewish law from cultic participation.[193] "The law prohibits castration either of man or beast or fowl...the castrated person was despised in biblical times, for he was not accepted in marriage in Jewish families, as the castrated animal was not acceptable as an offering upon the altar."[194]

Hester notes that the saying about eunuchs rejects the notion of "divinely sanctified sexed morphologies whose complementarity is demonstrated by the procreative fitness of anatomical design" —crudely known as 'the plug and socket theory'— and asks,

> Where does the eunuch fit in such a sexed ideology? Outside of it altogether. The eunuch is a figure that not only violates the heterosexual binary dualism, but cannot participate in it at all...in the saying of Mt. 19.12 there is absolutely no suggestion that to be a eunuch is to be someone who is in any way in need of 'fixing', 'healing' or 'reintegrating' into society...there is no implication whatsoever of 'illness' or social 'deformity' in need of restoration. Instead, the eunuch is held up as a model to follow...the rhetorical direction is away from reinforcement of the binary sex para-

---

[190] Brenk, *Aufstieg und Niedergang der Römischen Welt*, II, 16.3, 2112.

[191] *Leyden Papyrus*, III, 11; XXV, 20; XXVII, 15.

[192] Matthew 19:12.

[193] Deuteronomy 23:1.

As noted elsewhere, a number of early Christians took Jesus' words literally and castrated themselves.

[194] *Sex Laws and Customs in Judaism*, 138-139.

digm and its function to establish and naturalize heterosexual marriage and procreativity.[195]

Meier notes of the saying about eunuchs,

> ...this violent imagery could possibly derive from the fact that the logion echoes slurs and jibes aimed at the celibate Jesus —or possibly some of his disciples— as he hobnobbed with the religious low life of Palestine and traveled around the countryside with a strangely mixed entourage of men and women "on leave" from their spouses.[196]

Loader also regards the saying about eunuchs as "perhaps even formulated in response to personal ridicule."[197]

Although the saying about eunuchs has been the subject of extensive comment, Jesus also said that childless women would be better off,[198] and warned pregnant women and mothers of the hardships of the coming apocalypse.[199]

Nevertheless, while the points made above about sexual purity and its role in magic are possibly germane, they do not entirely address the issue as it existed in the world of Jesus' day. "Intercourse with castrated children was often spoken of as being especially arousing, castrated boys were favorite 'voluptates' in imperial Rome, and infants were castrated 'in the cradle' to be used in brothels by men who liked buggering young castrated boys."[200]

Contrary to modern expectations, castrating children for purposes of sexual pleasure was not confined to some shadowy criminal class of child rapists. The custom, which may have originally gained traction among the Medes and Persians,[201] was known at all levels of Roman society. According to the historian Dio Cassius, the emperor Titus

---

[195] *Journal for the Study of the New Testament* 28: 38.
   Self-castration is the renunciation of a body part, hardly different from tearing out an eye or cutting off a hand (Matthew 5:9-10).
[196] *A Marginal Jew*, I, 344.
[197] *Sexuality and the Jesus Tradition*, 133.
[198] Luke 23:28,29.
[199] Mark 13:17.
[200] *The History of Childhood*, 46.
[201] *Sexual Life in Ancient Greece*, 497, 510-511.

"had shown a great attraction to eunuchs" and his successor, Domitian, who subsequently passed a law forbidding castration, "was himself passionate for a certain eunuch named Earinus."[202]

Domitian's law against castration was celebrated by Martial, who wrote,

> The boy, mutilated by the grasping slave-dealer's art, does not lament the loss of his ravished manhood, nor does a needy mother giver her prostituted infant the pittance which the haughty pander is to count out...bodies immature suffered unutterable outrage. The Father of Italy could not endure such enormities, even he who of late succoured tender youths, that cruel lust might not make barren men.[203]

It would seem, prima facie, that the existence of such a brutal and repulsive practice, hated among Jews and many pagans alike, was known at least by reputation in every nook and corner of the empire. If authentic, the tradition that Jesus called a child forward, and having stood him in the midst of the disciples, said, "See that you do not treat one of these little ones with contempt, for I tell you that their angels in heaven always look upon the face of my Father in heaven"[204] may reflect an awareness of the depraved uses to which children were put. Given this cultural background, it is even more surprising that Jesus chose to characterize himself as a eunuch, albeit a eunuch with 'children.'[205]

Regarding the saint's (in)famous self-castration, Brown points out that Origen appears to have regarded sexuality as "a mere passing phase," as "a dispensable adjunct of the personality" which would vanish soon enough along with the earthly body.[206] Such an attitude toward sexuality generally may also reflect the attitude of Jesus, who said of those resurrected that "they neither marry, nor are they given in marriage, but are like angels in heaven."[207] Taylor notes that Christian eunuchs would have served in the kingdom of God in much the same way that

---

[202] *Roman History*, LXVII, 2, 3.
[203] *The Epigrams of Martial*, IX, 6, 8.
[204] Matthew 18:1-2, 10.
  See particularly William Loader, *Sexuality and the Jesus Tradition*, 60.
[205] John 1:12.
[206] *The Body and Society: Men, Women and Sexual Renunciation in Early Christianity*, 168.
[207] Matthew 22:28.

eunuchs served in royal courts in keeping with a tradition of sacred slavery in which slaves were marked for life. By breaking the cycle of birth, the eunuch "ends a world," and if the gospels are clear on any point they are clear on Jesus' belief that the world was about to die.[208]

...Jesus, disciples, and questions of sex

It is remarkable how closely Jesus' words to his disciples match those of an αγωγη (agōgē), a sexual attraction spell:

> If anyone comes to me and does not hate his father and mother and wife and children and brothers and sisters and his own soul as well, he cannot be my disciple.[209]

> Make her leave father, mother, brothers, sisters, until she comes to me...with an endless divine passion and frenzied devotion.[210]

> Frenzied,[211] let [Name] throw herself at my doors, forgetting children, and life with her parents, detesting the race of men and women, let her hold me and me alone..."[212]

> ...may you forget your parents, children, friends![213]

Faraone, who has analysed the Greek love spells, points out that erōs-type spells, which urge the victim to abandon family relationships, is typically employed by "men, courtesans, or whores."[214]

It may be simple coincidence that the language of religious devotion tends to mimic the language of sexual infatuation, but Jesus is quoted as using metaphors of virgins[215] and brides[216] in connection with his

---

[208] Taylor, *Castration*, 201-203.
   "...the Christian bishops themselves held power as feminine consorts of an even more powerful ruler. They were brides of Christ. Bishops used the image of the bride of Christ as a central feature of their authority, despite its unmanly connotations." *The Manly Eunuch*, 137.
[209] Luke 14:26.
[210] *Supplementum Magicum*, I, 45, quoted by Martinez, *Ancient Magic and Ritual Power*, 358.
[211] μαινομενη: "frenzied..."
[212] *Papyri Graecae Magicae* IV, 2756-2761.
[213] *Papyri Graecae Magicae* XV, 4.
[214] *The World of Ancient Magic*, 279.
[215] Matthew 25:1-13.
[216] Mark 2:19-20, John 3:29.

followers, and the trope is carried over into the letters of Paul.[217] It is well known from modern examples that a certain erotic glamour is sometimes associated with the most unlikely religious figures, at least in the minds of their followers, and such appears to have been the case with Paul. In the *Acts of Paul and Thecla*, a leering novella about virginity retained, Thecla, a maiden betrothed, sits "like a spider at the window ...bound by [Paul's] words" in a "a fearful passion."[218]

The effect of Paul's enchantment is sexual renunciation, leading the people of the city to shout, "Away with the sorcerer!"[219] Brown notes of *Paul and Thecla*, "The ancient scenario of supernatural violence exercised through love-spells was a device exploited with gusto by all writers in the second century."[220] However, the acrobatics in Thecla's case are revealed to be more psycho than sexual, as perfect an example as could be hoped for that abstinence is merely one of the many uses to which the sexual impulse may be put. The pure Christian 'nottie' as 'hottie' has an ancient pedigree.

Jesus relationship to his body of disciples is frequently likened to marriage, particularly in the apocalyptic passages of the New Testament.[221] The 144,000 who are the collective "bride" of the Lamb are virgin males: "these are the ones who were not defiled with women, for they are virgins. These are the ones who follow the Lamb wherever he goes ..."[222] It may be difficult for the post-modern reader to avoid seeing a camp *bouleversement* in this image, a twee Sunday school Jesus accompanied by a fey army of professional virgins, and it would come as little surprise if some early Christian sects interpreted the union as more than merely spiritual.

Indeed, the language of the gospels frequently contains overtly sexual connotations, a fact obscured by the usual selection of English equivalents for Greek words. Jesus is the οικοδεσποτης (oikodespotēs), the *master of the house*, or if a more literal but still accurate rendering is preferred, the *house despot*, a term "redolent with hegemonic

---

[217] 2 Corinthians 11:2.
[218] Henneke, *Acts of Paul*, 9.
[219] Ibid, 15.
[220] *The Body and Society: Men, Women and Sexual Renunciation in Early Christianity*, 157.
  Thecla is the first of the holy women to dress as a man, a so-called 'transvestite saint.' See *The Manly Eunuch*, 223.
[221] As at Matthew 9:15, 25:1-10, Mark 2:19-20, Revelation 18:23, 21:2, for instance.
[222] Revelation 14:4.

assumptions about masculine destiny."[223] The lord and master of the house 'can do as he pleases with what belongs to him.'[224] In several parables, the master of the house commands slaves[225] —a further evocation of a patriarchal household— and "the kingdom of the heavens may be compared to a man who sowed good seed in his field."[226] The good seed —καλον σπερμα (kalon sperma)— is a clear sexual metaphor and the sowing is promiscuous: on the path, the rocks, among the thorns, and on good soil.[227] The metaphor is carried over into the epistle of John: "Every man who has been begotten from God cannot commit a sin because his seed remains in him,[228] and he is not able to sin because he has been begotten."[229]

In the culture of the day, an allusion to 'seed sowing' carried an undeniable masculine swagger, much like the expression "sowing wild oats."

Jesus' most thoroughly attested emotional attachment was to another man, and a young man —νεανισκος (neaniskos)— at that.[230] Close male relationships were probably not unusual in Jesus' day, particularly since the society in which he lived was sexually segregated and casual contact between the sexes was considered suspect. The gospel of John contains this bit of dialogue: "His disciples came along and they were astonished that he was speaking with a woman. However no one said, 'What are you after?' Or, 'Why are you talking to her?'"[231] Strictly historical nor not, the passage reveals what must have been a common attitude toward casual interaction between the sexes.

---

[223] *New Testament Masculinities*, 79, 102. The term occurs in Matthew 13:52, 20:1, 21:33, Mark 14:14, Luke 12:39, 13:25, 14:21, 22:11, for example.

[224] Matthew 20:15.

[225] Matthew 13:27, for instance: οι δουλοι του οικοδεσποτου: "the housemaster's slaves" which often rendered by innocuous translation, "the householder's servants."

[226] Matthew 13:24.

[227] Mark 4:1-9.

[228] οτι σπερμα αυτου εν αυτω μενει: "because his **seed** remains in him..." 1 John 3:9.

[229] 1 John 3:9.

The erotic subtext of Christian discourse is discussed at length in Benko, *Pagan Rome and the Early Christians*, 79-102.

[230] Of νεανισκος (neaniskos), "a young man in his prime as a sexual object...A word with strong connotations of erotic desire." *Same Sex Unions in Premodern Europe*, 143-146. See Mark 14:51, 16:5; John 13:23.

In our own culture, the announcement that someone is "seeing a young man" implies that sensations other than sight are in play.

[231] John 4:27.

There were women in Jesus' retinue, but speculation to the contrary, it is a man, not a woman, who is repeatedly designated by the gospel of John as the disciple particularly loved by Jesus, the disciple who lay against Jesus' breast.[232]

Working within the framework of conventional scholarship, Nissinen concludes, "The custom of a student resting against his teacher's chest manifests cultural conventions rather than homoeroticism; in this sense the relationship between Jesus and his favorite disciple evinces homosociability that tolerates also physical expressions of mutual attachment...Finally, there is the basic question of the historical authenticity of the Gospel of John. Even if this Gospel allows for some homosocial interpretations, this would not necessarily reveal anything about Jesus' actual life."[233] Obviously, if the gospels do not "necessarily reveal anything about Jesus' actual life," then for all practical purposes they can be regarded as on par with fairy tales and historical inquiry be abandoned as foolish. Marvin Meyer eludes the (homo?) sexual question by proposing that the beloved disciple is "the paradigmatic disciple" or "prototype disciple"[234] although there is nothing in the text of the gospels that encourages this interpretation. Given the delicacy with which the topic of Jesus' sexuality is approached by commentators, it is easy to suspect the existence of some unrelieved anxiety about the subject.

Mark notes of the young man who met Jesus on the road that Jesus "gazed upon him and loved him,"[235] a passage that could also be translated, "gazed upon him and caressed him." There are six references to the beloved disciple, all occurring late in the gospel of John, where he is "the one he loved."[236]

A consensus of Sunday school scholarship has long held that the noun αγαπη (agapē) and the corresponding verb, αγαπαω (agapaō), the words most frequently used by New Testament writers for love and loving, refer to a pure and ethereal *love-of-God-for-man*, a platitude that has been repeated for so long and so often that it has become an *idée*

---

[232] John 13:23; 21:20.

[233] *Homoeroticism in the Biblical World*, 122.

[234] *Secret Gospels*, 128.

[235] ο δε Ιησους εμβλεψας αυτον και ηγαπησεν αυτον: "but Jesus gazed at him and **loved** him..." Mark 10:21.

[236] John 13:23, 19:26, 21:7, 20 where he is ον ηγαπα: "the one **he loved**," and 20:2 where he is referred to as ον εφιλει: "the one **he loved**."

fixe which fairly begs to be demolished —a closely related word, αγα-πημα, means *darling*. John Boswell's trenchant observation on the vocabulary of love may well apply here: "Only a naïve and ill-informed optimism assumes that any word or expression in one language can be accurately rendered in another…"[237] The New Testament writers consistently shun the *other* Greek word pair for love: ερoω (eroō) and ερως (erōs) —from whence *erotic*— both of which generally denote sexual activity. Do the New Testament writers protest too much?

Another word pair, φιλια (philia) and φιλεω (phileō), are widely held to refer to fraternal affection —as in *Philadelphia*, still called "the City of Brotherly Love" despite its burgeoning reputation for homicide— but φιλος (philos), the word used to describe Lazarus,[238] for example, can carry a connotation that exceeds the meaning of *friend*. The related verb can mean *to kiss*, as in "whoever I kiss, that's him,"[239] and the cognate noun, φιλημα (philēma), means *kiss*, as in "Greet one another with a holy kiss."[240] And of course there is φιλτρον (philtron), *love potion*. It is clear that the meaning of φιλεω can include carnality: it is the term used in the *Septuagint* of the love of the demon Asmodeus for Sarah — οτι δαιμονιον **φιλει** αυτην: "because the demon **loves** her…"[241]

Several other observations merit inclusion.

When asked by the disciples where he wanted to eat the Passover, Jesus told them to go into the city where they will be met by a man carrying a jar of water.[242] It was the duty of women to draw water and the prerogative of men to demand a drink as illustrated by Jesus' conversation with the Samaritan woman at the well.[243] As Morton Smith pointed out:

> When he sent a couple of disciples to make preparations for the Passover meal, he did not tell them the address, but told them to look for a man carrying a pitcher of water. (Carrying water was

---

[237] *Same Sex Unions in Premodern Europe*, 3.
[238] Λαζαρος ο φιλος ημων: "Lazarus our friend…" John 11:11.
[239] ον αν **φιλησω** αυτος εστιν: "whoever **I kiss**, that's him…" Mark 14:44.
[240] Romans 16:16.
[241] Tobit 6:14.
[242] Mark 14:13, Luke 22:10.
[243] John 4:7.
Compare 1 Kings 17:10 where a woman fetches water for God's prophet.

woman's work, so this was like saying, "Look for a man wearing lipstick.")[244]

The disciples were to follow this man into the house he entered and speak to the owner, who would provide a room for the Passover celebration.

Like many cultures in modern times, the culture in which Jesus lived traditionally divided labor according to sex, making particular tasks marks of gender. Distinguishing gender extended to a religious prohibition against men and women wearing each other's clothing.[245] Among the curses David pronounced against Joab and his descendents, "one who holds a spindle," —presumably an effeminate man— was included along with venereal disease, leprosy, violent death, and hunger.[246] Given such cultural animosity toward those who bent gender, one might fairly ask how Jesus knew a man who carried water, and why he directed his disciples to prepare Passover in his home.

A second point, raised by Theodore Jennings, concerns the ritual of foot washing.[247] John relates the story of Jesus washing the feet of his disciples, the point of which is that the servant is not above his master.[248] In the Greco-Roman world, the washing of feet as a gesture of hospitality was the work of slaves, and lacking slaves, quite naturally the work of women.[249] In cases where men invite other men to stay for supper, the guests wash their own feet, otherwise it is the job of women and never men.[250] In the New Testament it is the women who wash feet, and rather dramatically at that, drying them with their hair.[251] Although normally the work of slaves —and Jesus says as much— Jesus was certainly too poor to own slaves himself and none of his circle are mentioned as owning slaves.[252] Therefore, when Peter

---

[244] *Secret Gospel*, 80.

[245] Deuteronomy 22:5.

[246] 2 Samuel 3:29.

[247] *The Man Jesus Loved*, 163-165.

[248] John 13:1-16.

[249] In their article, "La lavanda dei piedi di Giovanni 13,1-20," Pesce and Destro argue that the washing of the disciples' feet, which takes place *during*, not before the meal, has ritual, even initiatory, significance, but slight the biblical evidence on foot washing, particularly its connection to women. *Biblica* 80: 240-249.

[250] Genesis 18:4, 19:2, 24:32, 43:24, Judges 19:21, 2 Samuel 11:8, Song of Solomon 5:3, 1 Samuel 25:41, 1 Timothy 5:10.

[251] Luke 7:38, John 12:3.

[252] John 13:6.

tells Jesus, "You will never wash my feet!" is he objecting to Jesus performing the work of a slave, the work of a woman, or both?[253]

It is in connection with the sort of devotion, "the likes of which not even a slave would do," that David Martinez notes "the close parallel between magical ερως θειος and the exclusive devotion demanded by Jesus in Lk 14:26" where the oft-repeated demand to hate one's family members is stipulated as a requirement for discipleship.[254] The phenomenon of ερως θειος (erōs theios), *the love due a god*, or φιλια μανικη (philia manikē), *maniacal devotion*, is a feature of the eroto-magical spells in the papyri as previously noted. The connection between nocturnal mystery rites and sexual acts, a point further explored in a subsequent chapter, is also well attested.[255] It seems unlikely that the nearly identical language of the gospels and the language of magical love spells is merely coincidental.

Samuel Angus:

> Another conception of communion with the deity in the Mysteries was a religious marriage—a conception the roots of which can be traced back to the Egyptian and Asiatic belief and practice of copulation with deity...Such *synousia* had a double underlying idea: first, an erotic-anthropomorphic, in which *synousia* has the character of an offering or sacrifice (of purity); secondly, the magical, whereby the worshippers participated in the god's *Mana* and secured life and salvation.[256]

A few commentators, most famously Morton Smith, have suggested that primitive Christian ritual may have included an overtly sexual element, a claim which is not particularly controversial if read against the background of possession cults generally: "ecstatic possession seizures are sometimes explicitly interpreted as acts of mystical sexual inter-

---

[253] John 13:8.

[254] *Ancient Magic and Ritual Power*, 357, 358.
Compare Matthew 10:37, 19:29, Mark 10:29-30, Luke 14:26, 18:29.

[255] "The modern use of the word 'orgies,' from *orgia*, reflects the puritan's worst suspicions about secret nocturnal rites. There is no doubt that sexuality was prominent in mysteries." *Ancient Mystery Cults*, 104.
The term οργια (orgia) referred to *worship* generally, rites and sacrifices, but when applied to the mystery cults, it meant the *secret rite* practiced by an initiate.

[256] *The Mystery Religions*, 222-223.
Συνουσια (sunousia), *communion, social intercourse*, or even *unio mystica, mystical union*.

course between the subject and his or her possessing spirit...all over the world we find this conception of a spiritual union, paralleling human marriage, used to image the relationship between a spirit and its regular devotee."[257]

Androgyny also played a part in ecstatic religion: "Many ancient observers noted that women (and effeminate men) were especially prone to orgiastic religious seizure, and such moods were of particular value for prophecy and for the production of important results in nature by means of sympathetic magic."[258]

That sex magic played a central role in some early 'gnostic' sects was claimed by their opponents. The Basilidians were alleged to "employ magic and images, incantations, invocations and all the rest of the arsenal of magic" and gnostic rites were said to include the use of sexual secretions:

> Man and woman take the male sperm in their hands, step forward, look up to the sky, and with the defilement still on their hands, evidently pray..."We present unto you this gift, the Body of Christ." So they eat it while participating in their infamies...They behave in a similar way with what comes from the woman when she menstruates: the monthly blood of impurity from her is collected by them; they take it, eat it in common and say: "This is the blood of Christ."...They prohibit the generation of children during intercourse...they smear their hands with the ignominy of their seminal ejaculation, and rise and pray with polluted hands, completely naked...The power which is contained in the blood of menstruation and the reproductive organs, however, is the Psyche, which we collect and eat.[259]

Whatever the claims made about Christian 'gnostics,' there is no doubt that sex magic figured in the wider culture:

> Over [seminal] emission, a good [spell]. After intercourse say: "I have poured out the blood of Abrathiaou into the vagina[260] of

---

[257] *Ecstatic Religion*, 58-59.
[258] *The Cults of the Greek States*, III, 111.
[259] *Gnosis: Character and Testimony*, 43, 71-73.
  The specific references to sylexis are from Epiphanius' *Panarion*.
[260] εις την φυσιν: literally "into the nature..." In keeping with the broad definition of φυσις (phusis), *nature*, the principle "which causes growth and preservation in

woman [Name]. Give your pleasure to [Name]. I have given you part of my pleasure, O [Name], I poured the blood of Babraōth in your womb."[261]

Φυσικλειδιον[262]

The spell to say:
"I say to you, uterus of [Name], open and receive the sperm of [Name], the incontinent sperm of Iarphe Arphe (write it!). Make her, [Name], love me for all her time as Isis loved Osiris..."[263]

Some spells name frankly sinister ingredients:

...the fat of a spotted goat and blood and pollution,[264] the fetus of a dog, and watery discharge[265] from a maiden untimely dead and the heart of a young boy...[266]

Is it possible that similar sexual elements appeared among some early Christian sects as charged by their opponents? Such accusations have typically been dismissed by modern scholars as over-heated rhetoric similar to accusation spells (διαβολαι), but given the admittedly lim-

---

plants and animals" (Liddell & Scott, *Greek-English Lexicon*, 1965), and by extension, the sex organs.

[261] *Supplementum Magicum*, 79.

Semen is often referred to in the magical papyri as the water or blood of various gods. "The general notion can be explained in the light of the fact that blood and semen (also saliva, milk, urine, wine, water, honey, etc) were thought to emanate from or to share something with an eternal flow of divine light, which was also viewed as a liquid." (Ibid, II, 158).

[262] φυσικλειδιον (phusikleidion), derived from the words for "vagina" and "key," a 'key-to-the-vagina' spell to gain entrance to that enchanted passage.

For further informative commentary on sex magic in the papyri, see particularly Gregory Smith's "The Myth of the Vaginal Soul," *Greek, Roman and Byzantine Studies* 44: 199-225.

[263] *Papyri Graecae Magicae*, XXXVI, 286-288.

[264] μυσαγμα: "pollution..."

Given the context, some bodily fluid, probably semen, is meant.

[265] ιχωρα παρενου αωρου: "**watery discharge** from a maiden untimely dead..."

The same as the ιχωρ (ichōr), *ichor* or *juice*, that flowed in the place of blood in the veins of the gods. Otherwise, serous or purulent discharge, in this case from a corpse.

[266] *Papyri Graecae Magicae* IV, 2644-2648. It should be noted that the text is part of a διαβολη, a spell that accuses the intended victim of violating the sanctity of a ritual, arousing the wrath of the offended deity. In short, the text is an *accusation*, almost certainly not literally true.

ited evidence from the magical papyri they cannot be discounted absolutely. In any case, the New Testament contains language that could be interpreted sexually: "a man will leave his father and mother behind and stick closely to his wife and the two will be one flesh. This is a great mystery —I am speaking of Christ and the church."[267]

The erotic undercurrents of the New Testament are of interest in the context of magic, however, not because they are so frequently appropriated in the discourse of modern socio-religious debate. Speculation about Jesus' possible sexual orientation is certainly no more pointless than conjecture about any other of his personal quirks, beliefs, or behavior, but any attempt to assign Jesus of Nazareth to either of our culture's principle sexual categories —straight or gay— is liable to criticism on several counts. It is first of all an anachronistic enterprise, inevitably based on guesswork, and is fatally liable to a predisposition to read the evidence in a way that supports the belief of the investigator. Moreover, a propensity to regard such an inquiry as meaningful almost certainly reflects present sexual anxieties or is part of an effort to enlist Jesus in support of a socio-religious agenda.

Lest I be misunderstood, let me make clear that I regard homosexual orientation as a normal variant of human behavior and discrimination against homosexuals as repulsive. But as far as Jesus and sexuality is concerned, his ethical teachings as represented by the gospels rise at best to the level of common decency and common sense even as pointed out by ancient critics.[268] Jesus has precious little to teach us either by precept or example, so his desires, whatever they may have been, are irrelevant. Jesus the apocalyptic prophet has little of substance to say to us about family or about sexual orientation. Commenting on 'recontextualizing' the Bible, Avalos remarks, "the Bible is so foreign to modern life that it can only survive if people pretend that it is something other than it is. The fact that people reappropriate scripture is not an argument that they should do so."[269]

---

[267] Ephesians 5:31-32.
[268] *Contra Celsum*, 1, 9.
[269] *The End of Biblical Studies*, 270.

Above: The Alexamenos graffito.
Below: Image of Egyptian Seth

Chapter 3: The Looming Apocalypse

All four gospels agree that Jesus came from Nazareth to John the Baptist and was baptized by him in the Jordan River. The descent of the spirit following his baptism constitutes Jesus' anointing and it is from this point onward that we first hear of his teachings and miracles.

"...into the wilderness"

That wonder-working Judean prophets or a receptive public were rarely in short supply is confirmed by the Jewish historian Flavius Josephus who wrote in the 1st century.[270] Among them were Theudas, who Josephus calls both a γοης (goēs), which may mean either *sorcerer* or *impostor*, and a προφητης (profētēs), *prophet*. Just what sort of prophet Theudas was is answered by the report that at his command the river Jordan was expected to part so the mob that followed him into the desert could cross over it on dry land.[271] In short, Theudas promised to perform a miracle. Anitra Bingham Kolenkow: "In the Jewish world, the major motif is proof of prophecy by miracle-sign."[272]

Theudas' actions constituted insurrection; he was killed and his head brought back to Jerusalem, likely to be put on display as a warning to other would-be magician-prophets.

Notwithstanding Theudas' sticky end, Josephus soon tells us of "those deceived by a certain man, a magician, who proclaimed salvation and an end to their troubles" if they chose to follow him "into the wilderness."[273] This man and his followers were also promptly killed. In the

---

[270] Koskenniemi: "Many sources, especially the NT and Josephus, recount Jewish and Samaritan miracle workers at the time of Jesus. It is not even difficult to name more than ten of them." *Journal of Biblical Literature* 117: 465.

[271] *Jewish Antiquites*, 20, 97.
  Theudas and his fate are noted at Acts 5:36.

[272] *Aufstieg und Niedergang der Römischen Welt* II.23.2: 1471.

[273] τους απατηθεντας υπο τινος **ανθρωπου γοητος** σωτηριαν επαγγελλου-μενου: "those deceived by a certain **man, a magician**, who proclaimed salvation..." *Jewish Antiquites*, XX, 188.

light of these reports, the beheading of the apocalyptic prophet known to us as John the Baptist should come as little surprise.

Josephus also tells us about an Egyptian false prophet: "A man came into the countryside, a magician, who established a reputation as a prophet..."[274] This man led 30,000 into the desert, up to the Mount of Olives, and attacked Jerusalem, but was repulsed and escaped.

The attraction of the Jordan River and the adjoining wilderness for prophets and miracle workers was no doubt based on the exploits of Elijah and Elisha, the legendary holy men of Hebrew scripture. Elijah parted the waters of the river by striking them with his cloak, a wonder which Elisha duplicated, and Elijah ascended heavenward in a chariot of fire from the bank of the river.[275] The waters of the Jordan cured Naaman's leprosy, and at the Jordan Elisha performed magic by causing an iron ax head to float.[276]

Michael Grant has suggested that John the Baptist chose a particular area of the Jordan in which to baptize because it was reputed to be the place where Elijah had ascended and where his successor, Elisha, had commanded the leper Naaman to wash and be cured.[277] After carefully tracing the way in which his message was adapted to meet Christian needs, Crossan notes "that John's message was an announcement of imminent apocalyptic intervention by God and not at all about Jesus" and of John's execution observes, "No matter what John's intentions may have been, Antipas had more than enough materials on which to act. Desert and Jordan, prophet and crowds, were always a volatile mix calling for immediate preventive strikes."[278] In other words, apocalyptic prophets were *political* figures, preaching what we today might call "dominion theology." As pointed out by Horsley: "these prophets and their followers thought they were about to participate in the divine

---

As pointed out by David Aune, apocalypticism and magic were "nearly an international phenomenon in the ancient world..." *Apocalypticism, Prophecy, and Magic in Early Christianity*, 348.

[274] παραγενομενος γαρ εις την χωραν ανθρωπος γοης και προφητου πιστιν επιθεις: "A man came into the countryside, **a magician**, who established a reputation as a prophet..." *Jewish War*, II, 259.

According to Acts 21:38, Paul was mistaken for this man.

[275] 2 Kings 2:6-14.

[276] 2 Kings 5:14, 6:5-6.

[277] Matthew 3:13, Mark 1:9, Luke 3:21, John 1:32.

Jesus, 79.

[278] *The Historical Jesus*, 235.

transformation of a world gone awry into a society of justice, willed and ruled by God...”[279]

The suppression of ecstatic religious movements was not isolated to Palestine. The celebration of the Bacchanalia was savagely crushed when the Roman senate became suspicious that a play for political power lay behind it: “vast numbers of adherents of the cult —men and women, noble and plebian— were executed or imprisoned.”[280] By the time Jesus appeared, the Roman state had made it clear that it would brook no opposition from apocalyptic or ecstatic religious cults.

About John himself the gospels have little to report. Herod Antipas, one of the sons of Herod the Great, had John executed after he rashly criticized Antipas’ marriage to Herodias, the wife of his brother Philip.[281] Aside from John’s critique of Herod’s irregular family life, the gospels have this to say about his message:

> So he said to the crowds that were coming out to be baptized by him, “Nest of vipers! Who showed you how to flee from the coming wrath?”
>
> “Therefore produce fruits worthy of repentance and do not start to say among yourselves, ‘We have Abraham for a father,’ for I tell you that God can raise up children for Abraham from the stones. The ax is already laid at the root of the tree! Every tree not producing good fruit will be cut down and thrown into the fire!”
>
> “The winnowing fork is in his hand, ready to clean out the threshing floor and gather the wheat into his barn, but the husks he will burn with fire that cannot be put out!”[282]

John proclaims a message of rapidly impending judgment that no Jew can escape by pleading special status as a son of Abraham. The separation of righteous from the unrighteous is imminent: the ax is already laid at the root of the tree. We are never informed about what circumstances prompted John’s denunciations, but the fact that Jesus came to him and was baptized indicates that he agreed with John’s message and became his disciple.

---

[279] *Bandits, Prophets and Messiahs: Popular Movements in the Time of Jesus*, 161.
[280] *Europe’s Inner Demons*, 12.
[281] Mark 6:17-18.
[282] Luke 3:7-9, 17.

Whether John performed powerful works as part of his prophetic repertoire, we do not know. In Luke it is promised that John "will go before him in the spirit and power of Elijah,"[283] an apparently clear prediction that John would perform miracles. The gospel of John denies that he did,[284] likely out of deference to the wonder-working of Jesus, but we are also informed that John's opponents said, "He has a demon," the very charge Jesus' opponents level against him for performing exorcisms.[285] Jesus himself observes that John "is more than a prophet," but just how much more we are not told.[286] In any case, prophets were expected to perform miracles and John enjoyed quite a reputation in that regard.

After Jesus feeds the multitude, John tells us, "When the men saw the sign he performed, they said, 'Surely this is the prophet, the one coming into the world!'"[287] and after Jesus brings a young man back from the dead, the crowd, seized with fear, exclaims, "A great prophet has arisen among us!"[288] However, being identified as a prophet did not mean that momentous events had to be predicted, or great wonders performed: when Jesus tells the woman at the well that she has had four husbands and that the man she currently lives with is not legally her husband, she also replies, "I see that you are a prophet."[289]

"...by no means will this generation disappear"

According to Mark, Jesus' career begins even as John's is about to end, and Jesus adopted John's apocalyptic message:

It happened in those days that Jesus came from Nazareth of Galilee and was baptized in the Jordan by John. And at once, while he was coming up out of the water, he saw the heavens

---

[283] Luke 1:17.

[284] John 10:41.

[285] δαιμονιον εχει: "He has a demon." (Matthew 11:18; Luke 7:33).

The meaning of this charge made against Jesus (Mark 3:22; John 7:20) is discussed at length in a later chapter.

Samson Eitrem noted, "...it marks the proper distance between John the Baptist and Jesus when John is said to 'have a demon' (Matt. xi.18) but Jesus to 'have Beelzebub' (Mark iii.22)." *Some Notes on the Demonology in the New Testament*, 4.

[286] Luke 7:26.

[287] John 6:14.

[288] Luke 7:16.

[289] John 4:19.

being ripped open[290] and the spirit descending on him like a dove.[291] And a voice came out of the heavens, "You are my son, the beloved. In you was I pleased."

At once the spirit drove him out into the wilderness, and he was in the wilderness for forty days being tempted by Satan and he was with the wild animals and the angels served him.

But after John had been arrested, Jesus came into Galilee proclaiming the good news of God, and saying, "The time allotted has run out and the kingdom of God has arrived! Repent and believe in the good news!"[292]

Like John the Baptist, Jesus proclaimed a message of impending judgment and called for repentance. The kingdom of God was coming quickly. But just how quickly? What sort of judgment did Jesus visualize? And what sort of kingdom? Despite later editing, the gospels provide coherent answers to these questions.

That Jesus imagined the kingdom to be coming soon —*very soon*— is made abundantly clear by Mark:

He said to them, "Truly I say to you, there are some standing here who will by no means taste death until they see the kingdom of God already arrived in power."[293]

---

[290] The curtain which closes off the Holy of Holies where God is symbolically present is similarly ripped from top to bottom following Jesus' death.

Though separated by nearly the entire text of the gospel, the "ripping" pericopes are a clear case of chiasmus: the heavens are sundered (σχιζω) and Jesus receives the spirit (πνευμα) in Mark 1:10. Jesus gives up the spirit (εκπνεω) and the curtain that conceals the Holy of Holies is torn in two (σχιζω) at Mark 15:38. Each member of the "frame" is meant to be understood in terms of the other. It is also significant that Mark limited the use of σχιζω to these two verses in his gospel, thereby calling attention to their complementarity.

[291] το πνευμα ως περιστεραν καταβαινον εις αυτον: "the spirit descending on him like a dove." Regarding the preposition Ehrman observes, "The prepositon εις commonly means "into," so that the text as Mark originally wrote it is especially vulnerable to the Gnostic claim that at Jesus' baptism a divine being entered into him. Whether Mark himself understood the event in this way is not the question I'm concerned to address here. It is worth noting, however, that both Matthew and Luke changed the preposition to επι ('upon')." *The Orthodox Corruption of Scripture*, 141.

[292] Mark 1:9-15.

[293] Mark 9:1.

The "some of those standing here" likely included a reference to Jesus' opponents who are being warned of impending judgment.

According to Matthew's version, the disciples will not die before seeing the Son of Man "coming in his kingdom" (16:28). The note of immediacy is also present in Luke (4:22).

> "Truly I tell you, by no means will this generation disappear until all these things happen."[294]

> The High Priest was standing in their midst, and he asked Jesus, "Have you nothing to say in response? What are these men testifying against you?"
> But he kept silent and did not reply to anything. Again the High Priest asked him, "Are you the Christ, the son of the Blessed One?"
> Jesus said, "Am I?[295] You will see the Son of Man seated at the right hand of power and coming with the clouds of heaven!"[296]

According to Jesus, the High Priest himself will witness the coming of the heavenly Son of Man. Jesus own generation —"*this* generation"— will not disappear before "*all* these things" happen, nor will most of his followers die before personally seeing the kingdom of God arrive "in power."

When Jesus sends his disciples out on a round of healing and kingdom preaching, he tells them,

> "But whenever they run you out of one town, flee to another, for truly I tell you, by no means will you finish going through all the towns of Israel before the Son of Man arrives."[297]

The immediate arrival of the kingdom of God is also assumed in Jesus' saying, "…by no means will I drink the fruit of the vine until that day when I drink it anew in the kingdom of God."[298] Such vows of absten-

---

[294] Mark 13:30.

[295] Greek does not use inverted word order to indicate a question, so Jesus' reply, εγω ειμι (*I am*), could also be translated, "Am I?" As pointed out by Borg and Crossan, the ambiguous answers recalled by the gospels of Matthew (26:64) and Luke (22:70) seem to favor rendering Jesus' response as neither confirming or denying the charges. *The Last Week*, 24.

[296] Mark 14:60-62.

[297] Matthew 10:23.

[298] Mark 14:25. Compare Luke 22:16, 18.

tion are examples of אסר (issar),[299] a binding oath to abstain (usually from eating or drinking) until a goal is accomplished. A similar New Testament usage occurs in Acts 23:12: "The Jews bound themselves with a curse,[300] saying they would neither eat nor drink until they killed Paul." Similar binding vows of abstinence are well known elements of the erotic spells of the Greek magical papyri, formulae which, as previously noted, find very close parallels in Jesus' repeated demands for exclusive devotion.[301] Uttering a vow not to eat or drink until an oath is fulfilled clearly does not presume that the consummation is centuries away.

It is probable that Jesus thought his confrontation with the Jewish leaders would somehow trigger the entry of the New Age, an interpretation nearly demanded by the phraseology of the so-called "eucharistic words":

"Truly I tell you that I will never by any means drink of the fruit of the vine until that day when I drink it anew in the kingdom of God."[302]

"Truly I tell you that I will by no means eat [the Passover] until it is consummated in the kingdom of God...I tell you that from now on I will by no means drink from the fruit of the vine until the kingdom of God arrives."[303]

As noted by David Martinez, such a self-binding vow of abstinence is employed "to activate the realm in which divine power operates." By vowing abstinence from the Passover meal, the supreme cultic celebration of Judaism,

---

[299] The root meaning of אסר (issar) denotes *binding* or *bond* and is similar in meaning to the Greek καταδεσμος (katadesmos) or *magical bond*. The concept of magical binding and releasing is discussed at length in a subsequent chapter.

[300] ανεθεματισαν εαυτους: **bound** themselves **with a curse**, or made themselves αναθεμα (anathema), *accursed*, until their goal was achieved.

[301] As, for example, at Matthew 10:37 and Luke 14:26.

[302] Mark 14:25.

[303] Luke 22:16, 18.

"by no means": the formula ου μη + the aorist subjunctive used in these passages constitutes the most negative statement possible in Greek, denying not only the fact, but even the possibility that an event might take place.

Jesus consecrates himself to the necessary action, making himself the instrument through which God will establish the new order... He seals his absolute commitment to the apocalyptic age with the vow that he will not partake of the sacred bread and wine until that age is ushered in.[304]

Regarding the connection between prophecy and magic, Crossan notes that "among colonized people there appear not only thaumaturgical or magical but also millennial or revolutionary prophets, or, more simply, magicians and prophets."[305]

...the comparative study of millennial movements has shown that magic functions in such a way that the leaders of such movements are supernaturally legitimated, so the thaumaturgical activities of Jesus appear to have functioned as a form of supernatural legitimation supporting his role as messianic prophet.[306]

Jesus is quite explicit about what the coming of the Son of Man will mean for both the righteous and the wicked:

"But in those days, after that affliction, the sun will be darkened and the moon will not give its light and the stars will fall out of the sky and the powers in the heavens will be shaken. And they will see the Son of Man coming in the clouds with great power and glory. Next he will send forth his angels and gather his chosen ones from the four winds, from the ends of the earth to the ends of the sky."

"Learn this comparison from the fig tree: whenever you see its branch sprout and put forth leaves, you know that summer is almost here. In the same way, whenever you see these things happening, you know that he is at your door. Truly I tell you, under no circumstances will this generation disappear until all these things happen."[307]

"Just the way it happened in the days of Noah, that is the way it will be in the days of the Son of Man. They were eating and drinking, marrying and giving brides away right up to the day

---

[304] David Martinez, *Ancient Magic and Ritual Power*, 346, 350-351.
[305] *The Historical Jesus*, 137.
[306] Aune, *Aufstieg und Niedergang der Römischen Welt*, II.23.2: 1527.
[307] Mark 13:24-30.

Noah went into the ark, and the Deluge came and destroyed everyone."

"It happened the very same way in the days of Lot. They were eating, drinking, buying and selling, planting and building, but the day Lot left Sodom, fire and sulfur rained from heaven and destroyed everyone. It will be like that the day the Son of Man is revealed."[308]

The verb translated "to reveal" in Luke 17:30 is αποκαλυπτω (apokaluptō), and the corresponding noun, αποκαλυψις (apokalupsis), is the source of our word *apocalypse*. *Apocalypticism* is the ideological substrate of the most primitive Christian theology, the sudden revelation of God's judgment with all that that implies. In this passage Jesus describes how in the remote past the mundane façade of everyday life was suddenly ripped away by revelations of divine judgment. In the case of Sodom[309] and the near extinction of the human race during the Deluge,[310] the overthrow of the wicked was sudden, violent, and complete. The reversal of fortune for people then living was also total: the complacent wicked were utterly annihilated, the watchful righteous exalted.

The notion of apocalyptic confrontation seized the imagination of Jesus just as it apparently seized the imagination of some of his contemporaries. Of the monastic community at Qumran, Michael Grant says, "…they were glad to pronounce the revelation of a blood-thirsty holocaust at the end of the world when the Kingdom of God would come …the Qumran devotees expected this final event in the extremely near future. Indeed, they believed that the great battles destined to herald it would be fought in their own lifetimes and that they themselves, as recipients of a New Covenant replacing the Covenant bestowed upon Moses, had been chosen to play a vital part in the world-shattering events of those days."[311]

Did Jesus mean to identify himself with the apocalyptic Son of Man whose coming he foretold? The evidence is ambiguous, and like many other issues dealing with the correct interpretation of Jesus' words, the controversy has raged back and forth only to end in stalemate. In the

---

[308] Luke 17:26-30.
[309] Genesis 19:24-27.
[310] Genesis 7:1-5.
[311] *Jesus*, 18.

passages concerning world judgment such as the ones quoted above, Jesus speaks of the Son of Man in the third person. A reader unacquainted with Christian belief might easily assume that Jesus was speaking of someone else and not himself.

What is clear is that Jesus' earliest followers came to identify him as the Son of Man, probably due to the influence of an apocalyptic passage from Daniel.[312] Mark has Jesus refer to himself as the Son of Man in connection with his betrayal, death, and resurrection,[313] and Matthew relates the term to Jesus' authority to forgive sins, heal on the Sabbath, and with his identification as the Messiah.[314] It has been argued that in these passages the church was simply reading its subsequent understanding of Jesus' mission back into the institutional memory of his life.

> As far as we can determine, this was not a message about himself, but a message about the coming day of judgment on which the Son of Man...would be licensed by God to take direct control of a new kingdom (c.f. Mark 14:62). *The failure of these signs to materialize led to the curious result that Jesus was retroactively declared 'Son of Man'...by his followers after his death...*"[315]

It is notable that apart from the gospels, the disciple Stephen is the only other person to identify Jesus as the Son of Man,[316] and oddly enough, Paul, for whom the resurrection *cum* glorification of Jesus is the theological event of all time, never speaks of Jesus as the Son of Man, nor do the early church fathers seem at all interested in the term.

Desperate times, it has been said, call for desperate measures. If Jesus really believed in the impending end of the political and religious order, we would logically expect to hear it reflected in his ethical advice, and we do. The disciples are not to imagine that Jesus came to bring peace on earth. Indeed, family members will turn on one another, be-

---

[312] Daniel 7:13-14.
[313] Mark 8:31, 9:31, 10:33-34.
[314] Matthew 9:5-6, 12:8, 16:13-17.
[315] *Jesus Outside the Gospels*, 11-12.
  Neither Hebrew nor 1st century Greek employed lower case letters, so the mere convention of capitalizing "Son of Man" in English makes it into a title, implying that the ancients so regarded it. That, of course, is not necessarily the case.
[316] Acts 7:56.

coming bitter enemies[317] and those who expect to follow Jesus into the coming kingdom should do so now, not even stopping to say goodbye to those left behind.[318] A man on his roof must not linger to gather his possessions, and a man in the field must not stop even to pick up his cloak.[319] The urgency of the times abrogates even the most basic filial responsibilities:

> Another of his disciples said to him, "Lord, first permit me to go and bury my father." But Jesus said to him, "Follow me and let the dead bury their dead."[320]

For those who expect to inherit the coming kingdom, the costs will be steep. No one can become a disciple without hating his own father, mother, brothers and sisters, or even his wife and children, as well as relinquishing all possessions. The would-be disciple must therefore count the cost. Little wonder that the rich heard Jesus' words with regret.[321] Of Jesus' anti-family stance, Pitre says,

> However, one set of similar texts [the beatitudes, *my note*] has repeatedly failed to draw the detailed attention of the Jesus questers: the beatitudes for childless and barren women (Lk. 23.29; *Gos. Thom.* 79b) and the warnings to pregnant women and mothers (Mk 13.17-19; Lk. 23.28, 30-31)…when the beatitudes and woes to women are understood in the context of Jewish apocalyptic eschatology, they function together as an injunction against procreation…[Jesus'] message of renouncing reproduction in light of imminent tribulation stands firmly in the tradition of an ancient prophetic predecessor (Jer. 16:1-9)…Jesus' words of renunciation are congruent with his negative response to an unnamed woman who blesses 'the womb that bore' him and 'the breasts that nursed' him (Lk. 11.27-28; *Gos. Thom.* 79a)…His retort, 'Blessed rather are those who hear the word of God and

---

317 Matthew 10:34-37, Luke 12:49-53.
318 Luke 9:61-62.
319 Matthew 24:17-18.
320 Matthew 8:21-22.
321 Luke 14:26-28, 33, 18:23-25.
    Compare "For the days will come when you will say, Blessed is the womb which has not conceived and the paps which have not given suck!" *Gospel of Thomas*, 79, quoted from *Gnosis: Character and Testimony*, 271.

obey it!' makes a good deal of sense if, as we have seen, part of his message was to warn women against bearing children.[322]

In short, nothing should distract from the nearness of the end: neither self-regard,[323] nor standing within the community — "I swear to you that the tax farmers and the whores are going ahead of you into the kingdom of God!"[324] The flight to safety should not be delayed for any reason. The nearness of the end has rendered the distinctions of daily life irrelevant: "the abandonment of worldly hostilities was not motivated by gentleness, or compassion, or pacifism, but by his concentration on the Kingdom and the all-important task of securing admission to it..."[325]

Even Jesus' exorcisms are evidence of the coming kingdom:

> "For if I cast out the demons by means of Beezeboul, by whom do your sons cast them out? That is why they will become your judges. But if I cast them out the demons by the finger of God, then the kingdom of God has already overtaken you."[326]

The "finger of God" had previously established magical connotations,[327] so Matthew changed it to "spirit of God." John Hull: "Matthew's reticence about technique is seen in 12:28 (= Luke 11:20) where the change from 'finger' to 'spirit' is to be explained in terms of the association with magical technique which the finger of God had. They only place in the gospel where Jesus seems to be on the point of disclosing his method is thus spiritualized."[328] Regarding the significance of the expression "finger of God" Twelftree says,

> This is evidence that [Jesus] understood that he was not operating unaided but was using a power-authority—the Spirit or finger of God. Also, in the previous verse ('If I cast out daimons by Beel-

---

[322] *Journal for the Study of the New Testament* 81: 60, 78.
[323] Matthew 18:3,4.
[324] Matthew 21:31.
[325] Grant, *Jesus*, 30.
[326] Luke 11:19-20.
[327] Exodus 8:19.
  A brief but informative discussion of the 'finger-hand-arm' metaphor and its use in magical texts can be found in Eitrem's *Some Notes on the Demonology in the New Testament*, 42-44.
[328] *Hellenistic Magic and the Synoptic Tradition*, 129.

zebul, by whom do your sons cast them out?'), Jesus places himself on a level with other healers and takes up the assumption that he is using a power-authority for his exorcisms...it is plain that he shared the same view of exorcism as some of those involved in ancient magic: using a power-authority to perform an exorcism.[329]

Works of wonder have a meaning which extends beyond them. Jesus' exorcisms are harbingers of the coming kingdom. The raising of the dead foreshadows the raising of all the dead at the final judgment, the healing of the sick foretells the elimination of all disease, and casting out demons anticipates the final expulsion of the Prince of Demons. So sure is Jesus of this that he describes it proleptically, as if already done:

> And the seventy-two returned with rejoicing, saying, "Lord, even the demons are subject to us in your name!" And he said to them, "I saw Satan thrown down from heaven like lightening!"[330]

If Satan is overthrown, then his followers must also fall. The metaphor of opposing kingdoms of light and darkness is a powerful element in the apocalyptic view. "The figure of Satan becomes, among other things, a way of characterizing one's actual enemies as the embodiment of transcendent forces. For many readers of the gospels ever since the first century, the thematic opposition between God's spirit and Satan has vindicated Jesus' followers and demonized their enemies."[331]

It is, in fact, quite possible to see most of the events of Jesus' career as parables-in-action. The confrontation with the temple authorities is a preview of God's impending judgment of the temple and his rejection of its leadership. Jeremiah is understood —probably by Jesus himself— as a prototype or forerunner. Jesus takes up both the Old Testament prophet's mantle of office and his words. All the judgments of the past, the Deluge, the end of Sodom, and the destruction of Solo-

---

[329] *A Kind of Magic*, 81-82.

[330] Luke 10:17-18.

"This passage, in which Jesus remarks that he saw Satan 'fall like lightening from the sky,' depicts an unabashedly apocalyptic scene in the midst of a document not usually considered to be 'apocalyptic.'" *The Demise of the Devil*, 46.

The arrest of Jesus therefore became a temporary triumph of "the power of darkness" (Luke 22:53). The meaning is clear: the Jewish leaders are the minions of Satan, doing his bidding.

[331] *The Origin of Satan*, 13.

mon's temple, foretell the judgment Jesus speaks against his own generation, "this generation" that will not pass away until all Jesus' words are fulfilled upon it. In addition to Jesus' openly apocalyptic statements, there are other indications of his intense animosity toward the temple and its leaders: the cursing of the fig tree, which withers "to the roots," is a sign given to the disciples,[332] a sign rapidly followed by the parable of the vineyard: "What will the master of the vineyard do? He will come and he will destroy the cultivators and give the vineyard to others."[333]

Jesus' disciples envisioned a physical kingdom that would replace the kingdoms soon to be swept away. And how could they have thought otherwise? Jesus had promised them that he would drink wine with them in the kingdom, where they would enjoy families, houses, and fields, and sit on thrones, judging the twelve tribes of Israel. Even the mother of two of the disciples asks Jesus to seat her sons at his right and left hand in his coming kingdom.[334] Paul predicted that the Christian saints would sit in judgment of the world and the angels.[335]

According to Luke, as Jesus approached Jerusalem for his final Passover celebration, the disciples supposed that the kingdom was about to appear, and after Jesus' resurrection they again asked if he was about to restore the kingdom to Israel.[336] In the earliest phase of Christianity, expectations of Jesus' triumphant return ran so high that those with property sold off what they had and Jesus' followers lived communally.[337]

Writing to the newly converted, Paul advised slaves to remain slaves, and virgins and the unmarried to remain in their present state. Married men were to behave as if they had no wife, which probably meant that married couples acted as if celibate, for "the time allotted has become short."[338] The ascetic tendencies provoked by the looming parousia

---

[332] Mark 11:12-25.
[333] Mark 12:9.
[334] Mark 10:30, 14:25, Matthew 19:28, 20:20-21.
[335] 1 Corinthians 6:2-3. Paul almost certainly had in mind the fallen angels he believed were the real rulers of the world (2 Corinthians 4:3-4).
[336] Luke 19:11, Acts 1:6.
[337] Acts 4:34-35.
[338] 1 Corinthians 7:21-31.

result in "a household of brothers and sisters rather than husbands and wives, fathers and mothers."[339]

So pervasive was the sense of impending doom that the early Christians resorted to the most extreme behavior: Origen, a church father of the 2nd century went so far as to castrate himself, using Matthew 19:12 as justification, and Justin Martyr, another early church father, praised a young Alexandrian convert who petitioned the Roman governor to give a surgeon permission to castrate him. Like many apocalyptic movements since, early Christianity was characterized by sexual psychopathology and extremism.

Convinced that Jesus had risen and would soon return, the believers waited expectantly. But nothing happened. Albert Schweitzer, in what is perhaps the most important New Testament studies text of the 20th century, wrote:

> There is silence all around. The Baptist appears, and cries "Repent, for the kingdom of God is at hand." Soon after that comes Jesus, and in the knowledge that He is the coming Son of Man lays hold of the wheel of the world to set it moving on that last revolution which is to bring all ordinary history to a close. It refuses to turn, and He throws Himself upon it. Then it does turn; and crushes Him. Instead of bringing in the eschatological conditions, He has destroyed them. The wheel roles onward, and the mangled body of the one immeasurably great Man, who was strong enough to think of Himself as the spiritual ruler of mankind and to bend history of His purpose, is hanging upon it still. That is His victory and His reign.[340]

It is hardly surprising that Christian believers are unhappy with this evaluation of the evidence of the gospels and that they have concocted a theology which ignores the spectacular failure of Jesus' predictions. In a recent survey of the New Testament evidence regarding the end-of-the-world beliefs of Jesus and the primitive church and the modern theological response, Dale Allison concludes, "I myself do not know what to make of the eschatological Jesus. I am, for theological reasons, unedified by the thought that, in a matter so seemingly crucial, a lie has

---

[339] *Sex and the Single Savior*, 108.
[340] *The Quest of the Historical Jesus*, 370-371.

been walking around for two thousand years while the truth has only recently put on its shoes. But there it is."[341]

Generations of people come and go, and as one year passed into the next, the people of Jesus' generation began to die. There was no Apocalypse, no host of angels, no Judgment Day for the wicked, no glorious return of the Son of Man, and no Kingdom of Heaven to re-place the kingdoms of this world. In 70 C.E., only a few years after the finishing touches were put on it, Herod's temple was destroyed, not by the wrath of God, but by wrathful Roman soldiers who burned the magnificent structure to the ground. Some stones were left standing upon stones; the massive blocks of the Western Wall —the present-day Wailing Wall— which in Jesus' day towered as much as 100 feet above the surrounding terrain, survived the Roman siege engines.

...Paul and his parousia

The letter of Paul to the church in Thessalonika is thought to be the oldest surviving Christian document. Its principle subject is the dead, specifically those of the first generation of Christians who died await-ing Jesus' return. What, the faithful wondered, would become of those who had already died? What hope could Paul hold out for them?

Here are the parts of Paul's letter that specifically touch on those con-cerns:

> ...And to wait for his Son from the heavens, who he raised from the dead, Jesus, the one who delivers us from the coming wrath
> ...For what is our hope, or joy, or crown of exaltation? Is it not you in the presence[342] of our Lord Jesus Christ at his coming?
> ...In order to strengthen your hearts, blameless in holiness, be-fore our God and Father at the coming of our Lord Jesus with all his holy ones...For we do not wish you to be ignorant, brothers,

---

[341] *Journal of Biblical Literature* 113: 668.

[342] The παρουσια (parousia), or *presence*. It is the opposite of απουσια (apousia), *absence*. In Paul's time the word appears to have had two main uses: it was used in the pagan cultus for the revelation of divine beings, and for the arrival of persons of exalted rank who had come to visit a province. The phrase seems to have already become a Christian cultic formula which Paul uses repeatedly: εμπροσθεν του κυριου ημων Ιησου εν τη αυτου παρουσια: "before our Lord Jesus in his presence."

concerning those who are sleeping, so that you do not grieve like the others, those who have no hope. For if we believe that Jesus died and rose again, in the same way, through Jesus, God will bring those who have fallen asleep with him. For this we tell you by the word of the Lord, that we the living who are left remaining until the coming of the Lord will by no means get ahead of those who sleep [in death]. Because the Lord himself will descend from heaven with the commanding voice of an archangel and with the sound of God's trumpet, and the dead in Christ will be raised first. Then we the living who are left remaining will be snatched away in the clouds together with them to meet the Lord in the air, and so we will always be with the Lord...But concerning the times and the seasons, brothers, you have no need to have any-thing written to you. For you yourselves know exactly that the day of the Lord is coming like a thief in the night. Whenever they are saying, "Peace and security," then suddenly destruction will overtake them like the labor pains that come upon a pregnant woman, and they will by no means escape.

But you, brothers, are not in darkness so that the day might catch you like a thief, for you are all sons of light and sons of day. We are not of the night or of the darkness. Therefore let us not sleep like the others do, but let us keep watch and stay sober. For those who sleep, sleep at night, and those who get drunk, drink at night, but we who belong to the day should be sober, having on the breastplate of faith and the hope of salvation as a helmet.

For God has not consigned us to wrath, but to the gaining of salvation through our Lord Jesus Christ, who died for us so that whether we stay awake or fall asleep, we might live together with him. Therefore comfort one another and edify one another just as you are doing.

...May the God of peace sanctify you completely and may your spirit, soul, and body be preserved blameless at the coming of our Lord Jesus Christ. He who calls you is faithful and he will do this.[343]

Paul escapes the dilemma of the delayed parousia —for the moment, at least— by making the resurrection of dead believers a part of the coming of the Lord. The dead will be raised and swept up, as if snatched away by the wind, to meet those still alive in the clouds. But the astute reader will have already detected the slippage: gone are the

---

[343] 1 Thessalonians 1:10, 2:19, 3:13, 4:13-17, 5:1-11, 23-24.

houses, relatives, and fields to be replaced a hundred-fold in the age to come as described by the gospels. The coming of the Lord has already shifted from a glorious promise made to a generation still living to words of comfort and edification made to a generation already dying.

The letter to the Thessalonians reveals the intensely apocalyptic orientation of the early church. That focus on their expectations for the near future —"we the living who are left remaining until the coming of the Lord"— very naturally shifted their attention away from the historical Jesus and onto the exalted Lord Jesus Christ who might at any moment arrive in glory to collect his saints. Schweitzer described the result in *The Quest of the Historical Jesus*:

> Paul shows us with what complete indifference the earthly life of Jesus was regarded by primitive Christianity. The discourses in Acts show an equal indifference, since in them also Jesus first becomes the Messiah by virtue of his exaltation…The fact is, if one reads through the early literature one becomes aware that so long as theology had an eschatological orientation and was dominated by the expectation of the parousia, the question of how Jesus of Nazareth 'had been' the Messiah not only did not exist, but was impossible. Primitive theology is simply a theology of the future, with no interest in history.[344]

Paul himself informs his converts that in the (unlikely) event that they had known Jesus "according to the flesh" they know him so no more.[345] That they would not know him so from Paul is clear: regarding the "transformation of the historical Jesus into the cultic Christ," Hoffmann remarks on the "comparative disinterest in the facts of his life and the substance of his teaching. Paul's preaching clearly reflects this lack of interest," and adds that the writing of the gospels took place "*under the influence of specific doctrines about Jesus as the Christ*, and not out of any purely historical interest in preserving the facts of his existence."[346]

By Paul's time, the Galilean carpenter-turned-prophet has completely disappeared behind the dazzling glory of the exalted Christ. We strain to catch some glimpse of him in Paul's writings, but are blinded by the

---

[344] *The Quest of the Historical Jesus*, 344-345
[345] 2 Corinthians 5:16.
[346] *Jesus Outside the Gospels*, 34.

light. But as Jesus' contemporaries continued to die off and hope in the parousia began inevitably to wane, the attention of the church shifted backward, to the historical figure of Jesus, and finally, even further back, to the Word who coexisted with God from deep time, before the beginning of the world. That shift in theological focus is not the subject of this book, but the point to be made is this: by the time the attention of the church moved back to the historical figure of Jesus, most of the eyewitnesses to his life were likely dead. The writers of the gospels were forced to fall back on oral and fragmentary written traditions to construct an official biography, traditions which had already been in circulation for decades. It is at this point that the early church began in earnest to ransack the texts of the Old Testament in search of 'prophecy' that Jesus might 'fulfill.'

As time passed and the doubts about its reality increased, Christian teaching about the Second Coming became more complex and the language used to describe it ever more shrill.

First know this, that in the last days will come ridiculers with their derision, living in accord with their own lusts, and saying, "Whatever happened to the promise of his coming? Ever since our fathers fell asleep [in death], everything goes on just like it has from the beginning of creation!"

By maintaining this opinion it escapes their notice that there were heavens long ago and an earth that emerged from the water and through water by the word of God, and that afterward the world was destroyed by being flooded with water. By the same word, the heavens and earth that are now have been stored up for fire. They are being reserved until the day of judgment and the destruction of the ungodly men.

But do not let this one point escape your notice, beloved ones, that for the Lord a day is like a thousand years and a thousand years like a day. But the Lord of the promise does not delay as some define slowness, for he is patient with you, not desiring that anyone be destroyed, but that everyone attain repentance.

But the day of the Lord will come like a thief in which the heavens will come to an end with a roar and the elements will be destroyed by fire and the earth and all that is done on it will be uncovered. If all these things are to be destroyed in this way, what kind of people should you be in holy conduct and godliness, awaiting and hastening the coming of the day of God by which the heavens will be destroyed by fire and the elements will melt? For we await a new heavens and a new earth according to his promise in which righteousness will dwell.[347]

It is clear from the language of this passage that the tone has changed from one of questioning to one of frank skepticism. All the previous generation has apparently died by now —"our fathers fell asleep in death"— and the promise made to the fathers has yet to be fulfilled.[348] A minor adjustment —"the dead in Christ will be raised first"— will no longer suffice. Instead, the writer conjures up vast vistas of time: lest we forget, a day to the Lord is like a thousand years!

As pointed out by Norman Cohn, the earliest Christians were convinced that the world "was about to go under in a sea of fire," and therefore interested "only in the speedy end of the world, they took no part in the daily life of the city and refused to make even token gestures of loyalty to the emperor, or of reverence to the gods of Rome."[349] This was hardly an attitude which would allow Christianity to become the official religion of the Empire, and by the end of the 2nd century fascination with the apocalypse had been abandoned, never to be taken up again by any orthodox sect.

By the time the last books of the New Testament were composed, Christianity had already followed the apocalyptic road to a dead end, and the explanations for its non-occurrence had become as preposterous as the language used to describe it. The parousia is first delayed, then indefinitely postponed, then finally —and *thankfully* most would agree— forgotten by all but a fringe element. Concerning the theological demise of the parousia in one of its final expressions, the book of Revelation, Lane Fox says,

> ...Dionysus [the bishop of Alexandria, Egypt, *my note*] explained away the plain words of Revelation as an allegory, and when Irenaeus' tract against heresy was translated into Latin in the early

---

[347] 2 Peter 3:3-15.

[348] There is a near consensus among New Testament scholars that neither letter attributed to Peter was written by the apostle, and that 2 Peter was written by a different author than 1 Peter. In fact, the epistle of Jude is so similar to 2 Peter that one is almost certainly a copy of the other. Peter the apostle was martyred in Rome about the year 64, but both epistles that bear his name appear to have been written near or after the end of the 1st century. Some put the terminus a quo for 2 Peter as late as 110 CE.

[349] *Europe's Inner Demons*, 13-14.

fifth century, the translator omitted the millennium from its text. To many thinking Christians it had become an embarrassment.[350]

...coming to terms

As we move away from the relative simplicity of the gospels' vision of the coming of the heavenly Son of Man, we find ourselves ever more entangled in the thickets of theological jargon. It seems to be a recurring fantasy among fundamentalist Christians that the Greek of the New Testament is a species of *über*-language, a divine speech of infinite precision, logic, and clarity. No human language fits such a description, of course, and the conviction that the New Testament was written in such a tongue could only be voiced from the depths of the most profound naïveté. In point of fact, nearly all words are polysemous; they carry multiple meanings and shades of meaning, and words used to describe spiritual experience are among the most slippery of all —even the early Christians acknowledged that Paul's letters contained language that was hard to understand.[351]

The New Testament is without a doubt the world's most intensively scrutinized set of documents, and its interpreters have spotted some highly significant meaning lurking in the tense of every verb and in every preposition. Indeed, so much emphasis has been placed on the supposed subtlety of the Greek text that the modern reader could be forgiven for thinking that the authors of the New Testament were the world's most polished grammarians instead of moderately literate members of society. Yet oddly enough, despite centuries of relentless study and an outpouring of commentary that continues unabated, there appears to be doubt and disagreement about the meaning of nearly everything the New Testament says. As one scholar wryly notes, "The Bible may, in fact, be the only feature of the Christian religion that all Christians have in common."[352]

---

[350] *Pagans and Christians*, 266.

[351] 2 Peter 3:16.

Wenham, in his classic introductory grammar, observes, "It needs to be stressed that words in one language seldom have a precise equivalent in another language. Any word has a range of meanings and the nearest equivalent word in another language will have a range of meanings which overlaps but does not exactly coincide with it." *The Elements of New Testament Greek*, 192.

[352] Burton Mack, *Who Wrote the New Testament*, 276.

That Jesus preached an apocalyptic message of imminent judgment is as sure as any feature of his teaching. Indeed, the preaching of Jesus forms a seamless continuum of apocalyptic thought that begins with his predecessor, John the Baptist, and extends to the early churches founded in his name. This observation, which is crucial for locating Jesus and his first followers in the stream of religious ideas, has been emphasized recently by Bart Ehrman:

> This means that Jesus' ministry began with his association with John the Baptist, an apocalyptic prophet, and ended with the establishment of the Christian church, a community of apocalyptic Jews who believed in him. The only connection between the apocalyptic John and the apocalyptic Christian church was Jesus himself. How could both the beginning and the end be apocalyptic, if the middle was not as well? My conclusion is that Jesus himself must have been a Jewish apocalypticist.[353]

Both the historian who has spent his life studying Jesus and the theologian who believes that Jesus is the Christ, the Son of God, purely as a matter of faith, work from the assumption that Jesus is relevant in some way to the modern world. Both understandably want Jesus to speak to each and every generation, including ours. They want a Jesus who *matters*. But a Jesus who foretells an end of the world that never happens, a Son of Man whose kingdom never arrives, is an embarrassment, or worse, a complete failure. Albert Schweitzer, the author of one of the first and finest modern analyses of the historical Jesus, came to this rather grim conclusion: "The historical Jesus will be to our time a stranger and an enigma."[354] Michael Grant made this stark comparison:

> The historian has to assume that [Jesus] meant what he said, and its consequence, that he turned out to be wrong. His wrongness did not deter the Adventists of the early nineteenth century from once again deciding in their turn that the world was about to come to an end. William Miller, who founded their movement, forecast that this would happen in 1843 or 1844. He proved to be wrong. Jesus, too, had been wrong. His ministry was based on an error.[355]

---

[353] *Jesus: Apocalyptic Prophet of the New Millennium*, 139.
[354] *The Quest of the Historical Jesus*, 400.
[355] *Jesus*, 20.

The early church found itself stuck with a terrible problem: its theology had been built on the coming of the glorified Lord, and initially the message of his coming must have been a most effective inducement to discipleship. Yet with every year that passed and every believer that died, the parousia became a more hollow promise. What was the church to do?

To the pagan world, *deification* would have recommended itself as an obvious first step. Why not simply declare Jesus to be a god and have done with it? And as Christianity gradually changed from a Jewish splinter sect to become an increasingly cosmopolitan cult, that is, in effect, what happened.[356] I do not mean to leave the impression that the Christians cleanly extricated themselves from the impasse of the deferred parousia, deifying Jesus in a series of neat, logical steps. Their progress was tentative and centuries in the making, and there were divergent solutions along the way, most of which the church subsequently declared to be heretical.[357] But as the church moved ever closer to its deified Lord, it pushed his Second Coming ever further away. As reported by Eusebius, by at least the 3rd century the doctors of the church had begun to characterize belief in the earthly rule of Christ as "trivial and befitting mortals and too like the present,"[358] and by the time of Augustine, *chiliasm*,[359] the belief in a 1000-year reign on earth entertained by many early churches, had been relegated to the uttermost fringes of Christian belief though never formally declared heretical.

---

[356] That some measure of deification has already occurred in the later documents of the New Testament is beyond question (John 1:1, 18, 20:28, Hebrews 1:8, for example), but the exact doctrinal significance of these passages has been debated ad nauseam up to the present day.

[357] See particularly Richard Rubenstein's *When Jesus Became God: The Epic Fight Over Christ's Divinity in the Last Days of Rome.*

Joseph Hoffman, who appears to be more agnostic than I am about rescuing much of historical value from the gospels, gives a lucid presentation of the problem of the delayed parousia in *Jesus Outside the Gospels*, 9-34.

[358] *Ecclesiastical History*, VII, 24.4-5. The receiving of houses and land as well as the restoration of the kingdom of Israel presupposes and earthly kingdom (Mark 10:29-30, Acts 1:6) and many of the first Christians so believed.

[359] From χιλια (chilia), *one thousand* (Revelation 20:4-5). Most of the early Christians who accepted the book of Revelation apparently believed the number to be literal.

Chapter 4: The Final Confrontation

The gospels pass over the life of Jesus quite rapidly, concentrating most of their attention on his trial and execution. Indeed, it was the death and resurrection of Jesus that became essential both to early Christian theology and Christian miracle, and an enormous amount of firepower is expended on this subject, particularly by Jesus' chief advocate, the apostle Paul. The first letter to the Thessalonians, widely believed to be the oldest surviving Christian document, defines the centrality of Jesus' death and resurrection, a theme which is sounded again in the letter to the Corinthians:

> Concerning us, they report what sort of welcome we had from you, and how you turned away from idols to serve a living and true God, and to wait for his Son to come from the heavens, who he raised from the dead, Jesus, who delivers us from the coming wrath.[360]

> Because in the wisdom of God the world did not know God through its wisdom, God resolved through the foolishness of what is proclaimed to save those believing. Because Jews ask for signs and Greeks demand wisdom, but we proclaim Christ crucified, for the Jews a cause of revulsion, to the Gentiles foolishness, but to those who are called, both Jews and Greeks, Christ the power of God and the wisdom of God. So that the foolish thing of God is wiser than the wisdom of men, and the weakness of God is stronger than the strength of men.
>   And coming to you, brothers, I did not come with superior speech or wisdom proclaiming the mystery of God to you. No, for I decided not to know anything among you except Jesus Christ and him crucified.[361]

These passages are the verbal equivalent of a crucifix Paul thrusts forth before his readers. Given that the death and resurrection of Jesus is the bedrock on which both Paul's apocalyptic theology and wonder-

---

[360] 1 Thessalonians 1:9-10.
[361] 1 Corinthians 1:21-25, 2:1-2.

working rests —he rarely specifically quotes Jesus' teachings and shows almost no interest in his biography[362] —it is important to examine the accounts of those key events.

...confrontation at the temple

Six days before the feast of Passover, Jesus and his disciples arrived at Bethany, a small town within walking distance of Jerusalem.[363] Jesus sent two of the disciples into the village where they found a donkey. The disciples threw their cloaks over the animal, Jesus mounted it, and rode into Jerusalem much as described in the prophecy of Zechariah:

Rejoice greatly, O daughter of Zion! Shout aloud, O daughter of Jerusalem! Lo, your king comes to you; triumphant and victorious is he, humble and riding on an ass, on a colt, the foal of an ass.[364]

The gospel of Matthew reconstructs this prophetic scene as follows:

This happened to fulfill what was spoken through the prophet, saying, "Tell the daughter of Zion, Behold, your king is coming to you, humble, and mounted on a donkey and on a colt, the foal of a donkey."

And the disciples went and did just as Jesus directed them. They brought the donkey and the colt, and laid their outer garments over them, and he sat upon them. And a very large crowd spread their outer garments in the road, and others cut branches from the trees and were spreading them in the road. And the crowds that preceded him and those following him shouted, saying, "Hosanna to the son of David. Blessed is the one coming in the name of the Lord! Hosanna in the highest heavens!"

And coming into Jerusalem, the whole city was in commotion, saying, "Who is this?" And the crowd said, "This is the prophet Jesus from Nazareth in Galilee."[365]

The writer of the gospel was obviously not an eyewitness of the events he describes. He misunderstands the parallelism of the Old Testament

[362] Michael Grant: "...Paul was amazingly ignorant of Jesus' teaching." *Jesus*, 89.
[363] Mark 11:1, John 12.1.
[364] Zechariah 9:9, *RSV*.
[365] Matthew 12:4-11.

passage, misreading the text of Zechariah to refer to *two* animals —
Mark, Luke, and John[366] all have one donkey— and presents the
reader with the absurd image of Jesus astraddle two animals, an adult
and its colt. The gospel of John nearly concedes that the connection
between Jesus' trip into Jerusalem on a donkey and the prophecy of
Zechariah is a later invention:

> His disciples did not realize these things about him at first, but
> after he had been glorified, then they recalled that these things
> had been written about him and they had done these things to
> him.[367]

On the day of his arrival, possibly the first day of the six days mentioned in John,[368] Jesus went to Jerusalem, entered the temple for a
look around, and then left, "as it was already late," and went back to
Bethany to spend the night.[369] On the following day —day two
according to Mark— he returned from Bethany with a group of disciples and created a disturbance in the temple, overturning the tables of
the moneychangers and generally obstructing business, but was not
arrested by the temple police at that point. This so-called "cleansing of
the temple"[370] was, as noted by Crossan, "not at all a purification of
the Temple but rather a symbolic destruction."[371]

Jesus and his followers left the city that evening and returned on the
following day, the third day of Jesus' temple activities according to
Mark's account. At this point the temple authorities confronted him,
but were unable to arrest him in public for fear of the crowds that Jesus attracted —the gospels are unanimous on this point.[372] The Temple authorities *feared* Jesus.

---

[366] Mark 11:2, Luke 19:30, John 12:14. In John's account, Jesus finds the donkey on
his own.

[367] John 12:16.

[368] John 12:1.

[369] John 12:1, Mark 11:11.

It seems likely that Mark and John drew the account of the Jerusalem phase of Jesus'
career, including the story of Lazarus, from a common source.

[370] Mark 11:12.

[371] *The Historical Jesus*, 357.

Regarding the aggressive and violent imagery in the gospels, Stroumsa notes that the
"deep-seated ambiguity is directly related to the radical nature of earliest Christianity, a
movement born within the chiliastic context of Jewish apocalypticism." *Barbarian
Philosophy*, 10.

[372] Matthew 21:26, Mark 11:32, Luke 20:19, John 12.19.

Sean Freyne observes that "reports of [Jesus'] mighty deeds brought the crowds flocking to him," a situation bound to be regarded as subversive of the religious and political order. As Freyne notes, "the miracle stories [were] propagandist within early Christianity," as well as a focus of suspicious popular enthusiasm during Jesus' lifetime.[373]

The confrontations the gospels describe between Jesus and the temple authorities were an ugly business. Jesus denounced them in offensive terms, quoting from the prophet Jeremiah:

And he was teaching them, saying, "Has it not been written, my house will be called a house of prayer for all the nations? But you have made it a hideout of robbers!" And the chief priests and the scribes heard about this and they began to seek how they might kill him, for they feared him because the whole crowd was overwhelmed by his teaching.[374]

"Woe to you, scribes and Pharisees! Hypocrites! You build the tombs of the prophets and you adorn the graves of the righteous, and you say, 'If we lived in the days of our forefathers, we would not have been their partners in shedding the blood of the prophets.' So you testify against yourselves that you are sons of those who killed the prophets!"

"Fill up the measure of your fathers, you! Snakes! Offspring of vipers! How are you to flee from the judgment of Gehenna?"

"Why for this reason I am sending forth prophets and wise men and scribes to you. You will kill and crucify some of them and some of them you will whip in your synagogues and pursue from city to city, so that there may come upon you all the righteous blood spilled on earth from the blood of innocent Abel down to the blood of Zechariah the son of Barachiah who you murdered between the sanctuary and the altar."

"Yes, indeed, I say to you, all this will come upon this generation!"

"Jerusalem, Jerusalem, she who kills the prophets and stones those sent forth to her! How many times I wanted to gather your children to me the way a hen gathers her chicks under her wings, but you did not want it. Now look! Your house is left desolate!

---

[373] *Galilee, Jesus and the Gospels*, 228.
[374] Mark 11:17-18.

For I say to you, from now on you will by no means see me until you say, 'Blessed is he who comes in the name of the Lord!'"[375]

As extreme as these words are, the modern reader can scarcely appreciate the offense they must have caused the temple authorities. The Gehenna to which Jesus refers is the valley of Hinnom,[376] a steep narrow ravine outside the southern wall of Jerusalem. In Jesus' day the valley was the receptacle into which the city's sewage drained and rubbish was thrown to be burned. Gehenna was a combination of cesspool and garbage dump. As Grant observed, Jesus' denunciation "is the language not only of invective but of white-hot anger...What Jesus felt and displayed was violent rage."[377] Lacey Baldwin Smith: "Jesus did everything possible to goad the authorities into action. In effect, he got himself executed."[378]

The valley's unsavory associations dated from the remote past; the area is the likely site where the apostate king Solomon built an altar to Moloch, a 'Canaanite' deity associated with child sacrifice by burning.[379] Long after the reign of Solomon, the Judean king Josiah led a violent religious reformation movement during which the altars and furnishings of the temples of 'foreign' gods were destroyed, their priests killed, and the grounds of their holy sites desecrated by the burning of human bones.[380]

In this scathing denunciation, Matthew even has Jesus include converts to Judaism, calling them "sons of Gehenna."[381] In short, the context of this bitter denunciation repeatedly associates the temple offi-

---

[375] Matthew 23:29-39.

[376] Greek γεεννα (Gehenna), a transliteration of the Aramaic for "valley of Hinnom."

[377] *Jesus*, 77.

[378] *Fools, Martyrs, Traitors: The Story of Martyrdom in the Western World*, 81.

[379] 1 Kings 11:4-8, 2 Kings 16:2-4, 2 Chronicles 28:1-4.

As pointed out by Schmidt, "Isa[iah] 30:33 clearly connects Yahweh and Tophet, and if no such connection was intended in this allusion to Assyria's destruction, then one would have expected some disclaimer to that effect. In any case, the sacrifice of the first born to Yahweh and the Molek sacrifice were possibly related, if not one and the same cult." It is possible "that Molek was Yahweh's chthonic aspect or an independent netherworld deity of the Yahwistic cult." *Magic and Ritual in the Ancient World*, 248-249.

[380] 2 Kings 22:1 – 23:25.

[381] Matthew 23:15.

cials not only with filth, but with apostasy. Do these exchanges reflect the words of the historical Jesus?[382]

It is nearly certain that they do. The woes pronounced against the temple leadership culminate in the prediction that the temple itself will be destroyed.

> As he left the temple, one of his disciples said to him, "Teacher, look what large stones and amazing buildings!" And Jesus said to him, "Do you see these great buildings? By no means will a stone be left upon a stone here and not be demolished!"[383]

Jesus' curse upon the temple is reported by all four gospels, repeated by his accusers at his hearing before the temple authorities, and is thrown back in his face as a taunt during his crucifixion. It appears in the Coptic *Gospel of Thomas*, and in Acts the witnesses against Stephen accuse him of repeating Jesus' prediction that the temple will be destroyed.[384] Jesus' curse on the temple finds an eerie echo in the magical spells of the *Sepher Ha-Razim*: "Smite it to dust and let it be overturned like the ruins of Sodom and Gemorah, and let no man place stone upon stone on the place..."[385]

There is certainly no reason to doubt Jesus' animosity toward the temple authorities and their fear of him is well documented. They believed the crowd would riot if they arrested him publicly.[386] Sean Freyne describes how the tension between Jesus and the religious authorities builds to a crescendo in the gospel of John:

> John's Pharisees...send emissaries to investigate the identity of John (1:19,24) and they are obviously concerned about the success of new religious movements (4:1); they send servants to arrest Jesus (7:32,ff.); they cross-examine the parents of the man

---

[382] Some of the details of these diatribes are certainly anachronistic: none of Jesus' followers were being pursued or flogged in synagogues at this stage, and the Pharisees were never in charge of the temple cult. As the only religious sect to survive the Roman invasion following the Jewish revolt in 68 CE, they became the source of modern rabbinic Judaism.

[383] Mark 13:1-2.

[384] Matthew 24:1-2, Luke 21:5-6, John 2:19-21, Mark 14:58, 15:29-30, Gospel of Thomas, 71 ("I shall destroy this house and no one will be able to build it."), Acts 6:13-14.

[385] *Sepher Ha-Razim*, 28.

[386] Mark 14.2.

born blind and it is they who will be responsible for expulsion from the synagogue (9:13,ff.); they are deeply involved in the decision to have Jesus removed, actually summoning a meeting of the council (11:46f.).[387]

Needing a pretext to cover Jesus' arrest, the authorities approached him with a trick question: should Jews pay Roman taxes, taxes that helped support the Roman occupation of Judaism's holy city?[388] A flat refusal would both implicate Jesus openly in the advocacy of insurrection, agreement would alienate those in the crowd who were unenthusiastic about paying for their own subjugation.

Two types of coinage were used in Jerusalem. Jewish coins had no human or animal images in keeping with the prohibition against such imagery. Roman coins, on the other hand, typically had images of Caesar. By calling attention to the fact that the Jewish authorities used such Roman coins,[389] Jesus pointed to their collaboration. Jesus responded, in effect, "It's Caesar's coin —give it back to him."[390]

The apocalyptic content of Jesus' preaching has been previously touched upon. Jesus came proclaiming the imminent arrival of the kingdom of God and the overthrow of the old order, including, as we have seen, the destruction of Herod's temple. As pointed out by Horsley in a discussion of the social context of Jesus' exorcisms, Moses' miracles done 'by the finger of God' preceded the deliverance from Egypt. "Such an understanding suggests that Jesus's exorcisms as manifestations of the kingdom of God entail the end of Roman rule."[391] It is impossible to imagine that any prophet foretelling the overthrow of kings and kingdoms in the midst of the vast Passover throngs —caught up during the festival on the high tide of nationalistic religious fervor— would be tolerated. It is also impossible that Jesus did not realize this.

Preventing disturbances during Passover was the job of the Jewish temple police operating under the authority of the High Priest, Joseph Caiaphas. For the sake of all involved, it was acknowledged that the

---

[387] *Galilee, Jesus and the Gospels*, 125-126.
[388] Mark 12:14.
[389] Mark 12:13-17.
[390] *The Last Week*, 64.
[391] *Experientia*, I, 55.
  Compare Luke 11:20 and Exodus 8:19.

administration of Jewish affairs was best left in the hands of the Jewish authorities whenever possible. The provocation of pagan soldiers entering the sacred temple grounds during this most holy of festivals would be a recipe for disaster, so Roman intervention within the temple precinct would have been used only as a last resort. An inscription putting Gentiles on notice not to enter the sacred precinct read as follows: "Let no foreigner enter within the screen and enclosure surrounding the sanctuary. Whosoever is taken so doing will be the cause that death overtaketh him."[392]

Given the potential for rioting among the Passover crowds, the Roman prefect —Pontius Pilate at the time of Jesus' arrest— traveled to Jerusalem from his usual residence in the sea coast city of Caesarea accompanied by a contingent of 3000 troops. A permanent Roman garrison in the fortress of Antonia, adjacent to the temple precinct, warily surveyed the Jewish pilgrims from the ramparts of the heavily fortified walls and towers, alert for any signs of disturbance. In the event of problems during Passover, the entire political leadership, Jewish and Roman, would present a united front, quickly and efficiently dealing with troublemakers.

Pontius Pilate, *praefectus* of Judea from CE 26-36, possessed *imperium*, supreme administrative power, which entitled him to deal with virtually any situation as he saw fit, the customary practice when the indigenous people of a province presented special problems of governance. Palestine was part of the imperial province of Syria which, unlike senatorial provinces, was ruled by a military governor. The districts of the province were controlled by *prefects* or *procurators*. Pilate was such a prefect.

The festivals were perfect opportunities for cut-throats. Josephus mentions how the *sicarii*, or *daggermen*, Jewish 'terrorists' who targeted Jewish collaborators, mingled with the crowds the better to conceal themselves after committing murders. One of their victims in the years following Jesus' death was Jonathan, the high priest, an assassination which was one of the causes of the First Jewish War.[393]

---

[392] *Light from the Ancient East*, 80.
[393] *Jewish War*, II, 256.
  The First Jewish War, 66-73 CE, during which the temple built by Herod was destroyed (70), was followed by a second war, the Kitos War, 115-117 CE, and a third, the Bar Kokhba Revolt, 132-135 CE.

Joseph Caiaphas' responsibilities to his people during the festival were particularly extreme: if a mob should slip from the control of the Jewish temple police, the Roman prefect would be forced to intervene, a provocation that would incite the restive population to open rebellion. Should that occur, Pilate would next petition for legions of troops from the neighboring Syrian legate. All of Judea could erupt into war with incalculable loss of life, a disaster for Caiaphas and a tragedy for the Jewish nation.

> Therefore the chief priests and the Pharisees assembled the High Council and they said, "What will we do? This man is performing many signs! If we tolerate him like this, everyone will believe in him and the Romans will come and take over both our place and people!"
>
> But one of them, Caiaphas, being the High Priest that year, said to them, "You don't understand anything! You don't even take into account that it is more advantageous for you that one man die for the people than to have the whole nation destroyed." He did not say that of his own accord, but being High Priest that year he prophesied that Jesus was about to die for the nation, and not only for the nation, but to gather together God's dispersed children into one.
>
> So from that day forward they planned how they might kill him.[394]

The betrayal, arrest, and trial of Jesus are deeply overlaid with Christian iconography and facts are hard to separate from fable. Luke reports that the temple police used spies to follow Jesus[395] in preparation for his delivery to the authorities, so it makes little sense to suppose that they would pay Judas to betray Jesus' location. It has been suggested that Judas betrayed the content of Jesus' secret teaching, an idea supported by the charge that Jesus considered himself the future "King of the Jews."[396] But as Geza Vermes observes, "That Jesus never asserted directly or spontaneously that he was the Messiah is admitted by every serious expert...The firmness of early Christian emphasis on Jesus' Messianic status is matched by the reluctance of Syn-

---

Elsewhere Josephus documents other disturbances that occurred during Passover. *Jewish Antiquities*, XX, 106, ff.

[394] John 11:47-53.

[395] Luke 20:20.

[396] *Jesus, Apocalyptic Prophet*, 216-219. During his ministry, Jesus never calls himself "King of the Jews" (Mark 15:12).

optic tradition to ascribe to him any unambiguous public, or even private, declaration in this domain."[397]

Joel Carmichael points out that the gospel accounts of Jesus' arrest and trial are told "in contradictory and ambiguous ways; both the procedure and the content of the trial are deeply confused."[398] Mark has Judas indicate which man is Jesus by approaching him and kissing him. In John's gospel, on the other hand, Jesus steps forward, asks the temple police who they are seeking, and identifies himself not once but three times while Judas simply stands by. At the time of his arrest, the disciples initially offer armed resistance, and then flee.[399]

Significantly, Jesus asks if the temple police have come to arrest him as if he were a λησϛης (lēstēs). The word is multivalent: it can mean *highwayman, robber,* or *insurrectionist, guerrilla,* i.e., any person who incited rebellion against Roman authority.[400] Based on material from the gospels, Carmichael has made a case that Jesus attempted an insurrection, concluding:

> Since the Romans could scarcely have bothered giving actual trials to the multitude of Kingdom of God activists they crucified, it is clear that "trying" Jesus—if they did—and identifying him as "King of Jews" was a natural way of explaining the point of Jesus' execution; it represented the crushing of a national rebellion.[401]

While sympathetic to this line of argument and in no way able to disprove it, I should note that there does not seem to be any line of evidence *outside* the gospels which indicates that Jesus led "a national rebellion." That said, it must also be acknowledged that insurrection was very much in the eye of the beholder, and that during Passover, with its huge emotional crowds, crossing the line into rebellion likely required the expenditure of very little effort. Additionally, there is no reason to think that each and every violent suppression of excited religious crowds would have been recorded, so I regard it as possible, based on the internal evidence of the gospels, that Carmichael is right.

---

[397] *Jesus the Jew,* 140, 152.
[398] *The Unriddling of Christian Origins,* 83. The author's "The Trial of Jesus, Dissected," is an excellent summary of the multiple mutually contradictory elements of the gospel accounts.
[399] Mark 14:43-45, John 18:3-10, Matthew 26:56, Mark 14:50.
[400] Mark 14:48.
[401] *The Unriddling of Christian Origins,* 136.

It is, of course, quite probable that insurrection in Jesus' day was funded by theft in much the same way that unconventional warfare of today is funded by illegal activity, so the two categories no doubt overlapped. Given that the gospel was written during the last years of the Jewish revolt, certainly after the destruction of Herod's temple, it raises the possibility that Jesus advocated subversion. The term is also used of the two men crucified along with Jesus.[402] "Social banditry and millennial prophecy may, indeed, go hand in hand...Messianic claimants invoke human violence but with divine violence undergirding it."[403] Religiously motivated violence in Palestine is a phenomenon with a distinguished pedigree.

If the disciples abandoned Jesus in disarray and followed the subsequent progression of events from a safe distance,[404] then it was, of course, impossible for them to overhear Jesus' exchanges with his accusers. It is already established by the gospels themselves that the Jewish authorities arrested Jesus by night, hastily interviewed him, pronounced his guilt, and hustled him away to Pilate for speedy execution because they were in fear of the reaction of the crowd of Jesus' supporters. To have Pilate stand Jesus before the crowd and argue repeatedly for his acquittal is a patently absurd apologetic ploy when examined against the rest of the evidence.

The recasting of events that tends to exonerate Pilate is completely contradicted by what is known of his rule. "These elements of the story of Jesus' last hours derive from the desire of the Christians to get along with Rome and to depict the Jews as their real opponents."[405] The cruelty and arbitrary violence of Pilate's administration is well-attested by his contemporaries, and he was eventually recalled from Palestine on that account.

In summary, the chain of events leading up to Jesus' execution seems to have run roughly like this: Jesus and his disciples left the temple area and crossed the Kidron valley to a garden where Jesus was arrested by the temple police.[406] He was taken before Annas, the father-in-law of Caiaphas, and other members of the High Council, where he

---

[402] Luke 23:40.
[403] *The Historical Jesus*, 163, 168.
[404] Matthew 26:56, Mark 14:50.
[405] *The Historical Figure of Jesus*, 273.
[406] John 18:1-3.

was questioned by some number of Jewish rulers, including the High Priest.[407] The Jewish authorities, satisfied that Jesus was recalcitrant, then sent Jesus posthaste to Pilate with the recommendation that he be executed. Pilate briefly interrogated him and sent him away to die.[408]

Even the accounts of the crucifixion present difficulties. Mark informs us that certain women among Jesus' followers watched his crucifixion from a distance, an observation probably in keeping with historical possibility.[409] *Women* viewing the execution *from a distance* would not likely have aroused the suspicions of the Romans. John, on the other hand, has female members of Jesus' family, along with at least one male disciple, standing at the foot of the cross engaging the dying Jesus in conversation.[410] This admittedly adds a nice dramatic touch, often portrayed in religious art, but seems historically improbable. Crucifixion was a grisly punishment designed to instill terror.

Luke exonerates the Romans by shifting the blame for Jesus' death to the chief priests and the scribes,[411] omits the presence of Romans at the moment of Jesus' arrest[412] —in contrast with John[413]— and deletes the reference to Gentile "sinners" found in Matthew and Mark.[414] Luke has Herod Antipas' officers abuse Jesus,[415] not the Romans who perform this task in Matthew and Mark.[416] Nevertheless, that Pilate murdered Jews is conceded, perhaps inadvertently, by Luke.[417] Even the interrogation of Jesus is problematic. If Pilate spoke Latin and Greek, and Jesus spoke Aramaic, then the prolonged philosophical discussions reported in the gospels, particularly the gospel of John, could only have transpired through an interpreter and it is extremely doubtful that Jesus received that much of a hearing from Pilate, a man who apparently despised the Jews and their religion.

---

[407] John 18:12-14, 19-24. This proceeding was a close to a formal trial as Jesus was to get.
[408] John 18:28, 19:1-16.
[409] Mark 15:40.
[410] John 19:25-27.
[411] Luke 22:2.
[412] Luke 22:52.
[413] John 18:12.
[414] Matthew 26:45, Mark 14:41.
[415] Luke 23:11.
[416] Matthew 27:27-31, Mark 15:16-20.
[417] Luke 13:1.

...the accusation of sorcery

One further detail, the most relevant to this investigation, must be addressed. It would appear that the Jewish leaders accused Jesus of sorcery. As Eitrem noted, "common Jewish people considered Jesus a μαγος [magician, *my note*]..."[418]

The gospel evidence for such an accusation, considered apart from other information, is not entirely conclusive, but given the editing to which the gospel accounts have been subjected, one could hardly expect the situation to be otherwise. Whatever the case, an accusation of sorcery was not trivial: "There was thus no period in the history of the empire in which the magician was not considered an enemy of society, subject at the least to exile, more often to death in its least pleasant forms."[419]

The imputations of practicing sorcery are based on two passages, one of which is found in John. Asked by Pilate what charges they are bringing against Jesus, the Jewish leaders reply:

> "If this man were not an evildoer, we would not have handed him over to you."[420]

It is apparent from the context that whatever evil Jesus was accused of doing, it was a capital offense, but the charges are vague. Eric Plumer notes, "In the Johannine trial of Jesus the material evidence for the prosecution has conveniently gone missing!" Plumer concludes that the "material evidence" in question was the Beelzeboul controversy, i.e., the accusation that Jesus practiced sorcery.[421] In any case, it is clear from the gospels that the Jewish authorities considered Jesus to be in control of evil spirits. In addition to *evildoer*, the term κακοποιος (kakopoios) could also mean *sorcerer*, and under Roman law many forms of sorcery, in particular the attempt to predict the death of Caesar by any form of divination, was considered lèse majesté and was punish-

---

[418] *Some Notes on the Demonology in the New Testament*, 41.
[419] MacMullen, *Enemies of the Roman Order*, 125-126.
[420] John 18:30.
  Ει μη ην ουτος **κακον ποιων** ουκ αν σοι παρεδοκαμεν αυτον: "If this man were not an **evildoer**, we would not have handed him over to you."
[421] *Biblica* 78: 359-361.

able by death.[422] The performance of exorcisms, to say nothing of resurrecting Lazarus, whose appearance in Jerusalem advertized Jesus' power and drew a substantial crowd of supporters,[423] "blatantly and publicly defied the emergent Jewish standards of ritual boundaries."[424]

The custom of calling sorcerers *evildoers* was apparently very old even in Jesus' day. François Lenormant:

> As a rule the sorcerer was called "the evildoer, and the malevolent man" in the old Accadian conjurations…his rites and formulae for enchantment subjected the demons to his orders… He could even take away life with his spells and imprecations…"[425]

Although not typically cited as evidence favoring an accusation of magic, Luke specifies that the charge made against Jesus was "**perverting** our people"[426] —διαστρεφοντα το εθνος ημων— which is perhaps *not* coincidentally the very same term he has Paul use against the *magician* Bar-Jesus: ου παυση **διαστρεφων** τας οδους του κυριου: "will you not stop **making crooked** the paths of the Lord?"[427]

The second passage cited in support of a charge of sorcery comes from Matthew, and is again voiced by the Jewish authorities to Pilate:

> "My Lord, we remember that that magician said while still alive, 'After three days I will raise myself.'"[428]

If construed as the middle voice, εγειρομαι would mean *I will raise myself*. Most translators, accepting the claim that God raised Jesus from the dead, translate the passage as *I will be raised*, reading the verb as passive. However, in defense of this rendering it must be pointed out that Jesus clearly foretold that he would raise *himself* from the dead:

---

[422] On the use of κακοποιος in magical texts, see Kotansky, *Greek Magical Amulets*, 102.
[423] John 12:9-11.
[424] *Medicine, Miracle and Magic in New Testament Times*, 74.
[425] *Chaldean Magic*, 60-61.
[426] Luke 23:2.
[427] Acts 13:10.
[428] Matthew 27:63.

εκεινος ο **πλανος** ειπεν ετι ζων μετα τρεις ημερας εγειρομαι: "that **magician** said while still alive, 'After three days I will raise myself.'"

In response the Jews said to him, "What sign are you showing us that you are doing these things?"

In reply Jesus said to them, "Destroy this temple and in three days I will raise it."[429]

Then the Jews said, "This temple was built in forty-six years and in three days you will raise it?" But he said that about the temple of his body.[430]

"Instead of displaying another sign on the spot, Jesus promises one—it will be his greatest and will give the best apology imaginable for his death. That he is to accomplish his own resurrection is virtually unique in the N[ew]T[estament]. If there was any doubt that he had been alluding to his own death (and resurrection), it is dispelled by the formula, *in three days*."[431]

The gospel of John is quite explicit on this point:

This is why the Father loves me, because I lay aside my life in order that I might take it up again. No one takes it from me, but I lay it aside of my own volition. I have the authority to lay it down and I have authority to take it up again.[432] This is the order I received from my Father.[433]

It is after this surprising announcement that the Jews respond, "He has a demon and he's raving!"[434] —a charge (as will be shown) that Jesus was a magician. The contrast is clear: Jesus claims to have *authority*, his opponents claim he has a *demon*. Both are claims that Jesus can per-form amazing works of power, so the question, as the context reveals,[435] concerns the source of Jesus' power. Jesus' *authority* is consistently linked to the working of magic.

The gospel of Mark contains very similar wording regarding the death and resurrection of the Son of Man: "after three days he will raise

---

[429] και εν τρισιν ημεραις **εγερω** αυτον: "and in three days **I will raise** it."
[430] John 2:18-21.
[431] *The Complete Gospels*, 187 (footnote on John 2:19).
[432] **εξουσιαν** εχω θειναι αυτην και **εξουσιαν** εχω παλιν λαβειν αυτην: "I have the **authority** to lay it down, and I have the **authority** to take it up again."
[433] John 10:17-18.
[434] δαιμονιον εχει και μαινεται: "He has a demon and he's raving!"
[435] John 10:19-21.

himself."[436] The tense of the verb is the future middle indicative, a 'reflexive' formation which indicates what the subject will do *to or for himself*. The identical formula is found in another prediction regarding the death of the Son of Man: "and after three days he will raise himself."[437] After the first such prediction Mark notes that the disciples did not understand what Jesus was talking about and were afraid to ask.[438] But if Jesus 'merely' predicted that a divine agent would raise the Son of Man from the dead as the Old Testament prophets had raised people from the dead and as Jesus himself raised people from the dead, what was there to misunderstand? To the best of my knowledge there is no text within normative Judaism that speaks of a person raising *himself* from the dead.

The remarkable notion that Jesus could raise himself from the dead receives passing mention in a letter of Ignatius, an early martyr, composed around the beginning of the 2nd century. Writing against the Docetist heresy, which claimed that Jesus was a spirit that only appeared to suffer in the flesh, Ignatius says, "He suffered all these things on our account that we might be saved, and he truly suffered as also he truly raised himself…"[439]

The remarkable forecast that Jesus would raise himself from the dead was evidently known to Christianity's early opponents. Origen felt obligated to address it in his defense against Celsus, but ascribed it to "false witnesses" who testified at Jesus' trial:

At last, two came forward and stated, "This man said, 'I can tear down the temple of God and in three days build it up.'"[440]

The term πλανος (planos), which I have translated *magician*, can also mean *deceiver* or *sorcerer* and as an adjective is used elsewhere in the New

---

[436] Mark 9:31. μετα τρεις ημερας **αναστησεται**: "after three days **he will raise himself**."

[437] **και** μετα τρεις ημερας **αναστησεται**: "and after three days **he will raise himself**."

[438] Mark 9:32.

[439] ως και αληθως **ανεστησεν εαυτου**: "as also he truly **raised himself**…" *Ad Smyrnaeos*, II.

[440] δυναμαι καταλυσαι τον ναον του θεου και δια τριων ημερων οικοδομησαι: "I can tear down the temple of God and in three days build it up." *Contra Celsum, Præfatio* I.

Testament in relation to spiritism.[441] After a lengthy analysis of the passage in question, Samain concluded:

> ...by the epithet πλανος, Matthew refers to a man who has won over the crowd not only by his doctrines and his words, but also by his activities and his wonders, that is to say, a magician.[442]

In a seminal essay, David Aune has characterized Samain's evidence as "an ironclad case for understanding the charge of imposture as an accusation that Jesus performed miracles by trickery or magical techniques."[443] Stanton concludes,

> The allegations that Jesus was a magician and that he was a false prophet were known at the time the evangelists wrote. Matthew knew the double form of the accusation. John (certainly) and Luke (probably) were aware that Jewish opponents of Christian claims allege that Jesus was a false prophet who led God's people astray.[444]

The apologist Justin Martyr (c. 100-165 CE), born in Palestine, knew of Jewish charges that Jesus practiced sorcery —he quotes Jews who called Jesus a μαγος, a *magician*, and a λαοπλανος, a *deceiver of the people*.[445] Origen reports that Celsus described Jesus as "a worthless sorcerer, hated by God."[446] Such charges were widely known even in Jesus' day and must be taken seriously. In the *Acts of Thomas* the terms μαγος (magos), *magician*, and πλανος (planos), *sorcerer or fraud*, are applied to the apostle Thomas and the terms are clearly equated: ηκουσα γαρ οτι ο μαγος εκεινος και πλανος τουτο διδασκει: "for I heard that **magician** and **sorcerer** teaches this..."[447]

---

[441] As at 1 Timothy 4:1: προσεχοντες πνευμασιν **πλανοις** και διδασκαλιαις δαιμονιων: "turning to **deceptive** spirits and teachings of demons..."

[442] My translation of: "pour...l'épithète de πλανος Matthieu désigne un homme qui a séduit la foule, non seulement par sa doctrine et ses paroles, mais aussi par ses gestes prodiges: c'est à dire un magicien." *Ephemerides Theologicae Lovanienses* 15:458-459.

[443] *Aufstieg und Niedergang der Römischen Welt* II, 23.2, 1540.

[444] *Gospel Truth? New Light on Jesus and the Gospels*, 160.

[445] *Dialogue with Trypho*, LXIX.6.

[446] θεομισους ην τινος και μοχθηρου **γοητος**: "a worthless **sorcerer**, hated by God." *Contra Celsum*, I, 71.

[447] *Acts of Thomas*, 96.

"To begin with the terminology used in speaking of itinerant magicians: in Greek they continue to be classified as *agyrtai* or begging holy men, although sometimes they are also called *ageirontes*, a participle from the same root as *agyrtes* that means 'those taking up a collection,' and sometimes yet again as *planetai*, 'wanderers or vagabonds,' or *planoi* [plural of πλανος, *my note*], the deeply ambiguous term that means primarily 'one who creates delusions in the minds of other men,' then 'sorcerer,' but that may also have connotations of vagabond or wandering beggar; the term *laoplanos*, 'one who deludes the masses,' is also found."[448]

That πλανος can also refer to apocalyptic prophets is clear from Josephus who describes "magicians and deceivers" who led crazed multitudes into the wilderness promising that God would give them "signs of deliverance."[449] Significantly, the same authorities who accuse Jesus of controlling demons also say "he **deceives** the crowd" — πλανα τον οχλον.[450] That magical works of power and apocalyptic predictions inflicted damage on Jesus' reputation long after his death is certain. The gospel of John refers to Jesus' miracles as "signs" (σημειον, *sign*) as opposed to "works of power" (δυναμις, *powerful work*), likely because of the association of the latter term with magic,[451] and it is relevant to note as well that the apocalyptic content of Jesus' preaching has nearly disappeared from the fourth gospel.

That Paul and his companions were regarded ως πλανοι: "as **impostors**"[452] in certain circles may acknowledge that they were charged with practicing magic —Paul's relation to Jewish and pagan magicians and the charge that he was a magician himself are the subjects of subsequent chapters.

The Jewish historian Josephus, in a passage which is likely authentic, refers to Jesus as "a performer of amazing works," which as Van Voort notes "can be read to mean simply that Jesus had a reputation as a wonder-worker,"[453] but would also be consistent with a charge of

---

[448] *Magic and Magicians in the Greco-Roman World*, 224-225.
[449] *Jewish Wars* II. 229. πλανοι γαρ ανθρωποι και απατεωνες: "men, magicians and deceivers..." σημεια ελευθεριας: "**signs** of deliverance..."
[450] John 7: 12, 20.
[451] "The Absence of Exorcisms in the Fourth Gospel," *Biblica* 78: 350-368.
[452] 2 Corinthians 6:8.
[453] παραδοξων εργων ποιητης: "a performer **of amazing works**..." *Jesus Outside the New Testament*, 89.

performing feats of magic. Raising oneself from the dead would seem to qualify.

The Babylonian Talmud contains similar accusations:

> The master said, "Jesus the Nazarene practiced magic and deceived and led Israel astray."
> "And a herald went forth before him 40 days: Jesus the Nazarene is going forth to be stoned because he practiced sorcery and instigated and seduced Israel (to idolatry)."[454]

Denunciation of Christians for practicing magic continued for over two centuries following Jesus' death. Morton Smith's observations in this regard merit an extended quote:

> ...These persecutions require explanation both because of their frequency and because of the general tolerance throughout the Roman empire for cults of oriental gods and deified men. Occasional exceptions to this tolerance might be explained by peculiar local circumstances; but the consistent opposition to Christianity evidently resulted from something characteristic of the new religion. What was it? The common answer is, the Christians' refusal to worship other gods. But other worshippers of Yahweh —the Jews and the Samaritans—also refused to worship other gods, and they were not generally persecuted. Consequently, the Christians had to explain the persecutions as inspired either by the demons or by the Jews who, they said, denounced them to the authorities...But for what could the Jews denounce them? Certainly not for refusing to worship other gods —that was the hallmark of the Jewish faith generally...What they were accused of was the practice of magic and other crimes associated with magic: human sacrifice, cannibalism, and incest...Magic figures conspicuously in charges against Christians from the second century on...Moreover, as the passages from Eusebius show— and they could be paralleled by many more from Irenaeus, Hippolytus, and Epiphanius—the Christians made considerable use of this charge against one another. Presumably they knew what they were talking about.[455]

---

[454] *Jesus in the Talmud*, 35, 64.
[455] *Clement of Alexandria*, 234.

...some additional conclusions

The gospels are simultaneously missionary literature, apologies, and polemics, written to defend a Jewish sect emerging from obscurity before the greater Greco-Roman world while at the same time quashing unwanted theological speculation within Christian ranks by defending correct teaching. The gospels are back formations, responses to unexpected historical developments which put the most primitive theological tradition in serious doubt.[456]

As to whether Jesus practiced sorcery, we have thus far the allusions to Egypt in Matthew's infancy narrative and the direct accusations made by the Jewish leaders when they turned him over to Pilate. Taken alone, this evidence is perhaps not completely conclusive, but the aim of the gospel writers was to *exonerate* Jesus before the world, not convict him of charges of practicing magic. Christian belief is on trial in the gospels and at no point would we expect full disclosure.

Jesus' confrontation with the temple authorities appears on the best evidence to have been a premeditated act of self-immolation.[457] "His actions were deliberate decisions to initiate a course of events which the evangelists, because of hindsight, and Jesus, because of foresight, knew must end in death."[458] Given recent history, the following description of Jesus' action, written in 1977, assumes a chilling currency:

> In a country seething with frustration and discontent, martyrdom increasingly seemed to Palestinians a glorious fate.[459]

---

[456] On the apologetic function of the gospel of Mark, see Davies, *Jesus the Healer*, 96-97.

[457] Compare Matthew 16:21-23; Luke 13:31-33.

[458] *Fools, Martyrs, Traitors*, 80.

[459] *Jesus*, 140.

Lilith

Chapter 5: Resurrection or Ghost Story?

If what happened when the Jewish leaders turned Jesus over to the Roman authority was predictable, what happened after the Roman authority turned Jesus over to history was nothing short of amazing.

Like other New Testament stories, the accounts of the resurrection are riddled with contradictions large and small. Although it is claimed that Jesus' disciples removed his body and buried it,[460] in a passage from Acts the apostle Paul —who appears to have known little about the historical Jesus— clearly states that "those living in Jerusalem and their rulers...asked Pilate to put him to death, even as they fulfilled all the things written about him, and taking him down from the gibbet, they laid him in a tomb."[461] Paul, in his previous incarnation as Saul, was an avid persecutor of the early church[462] and so may have known for a fact that the authorities who had Jesus executed were the ones who then removed the body from the cross and disposed of it. Reimer suggests Paul may have had some relationship with the temple police in his role of "enforcing Jewish religious law...in a punitive fashion, initiating policy, enforcing it with considerable zeal, and casting judgment against those caught."[463]

Peter Kirby lists four plausible scenarios other than an empty tomb: "Jesus was left hanging on the cross for the birds," the Romans dumped the body in a mass grave, the body was buried by the Jews, or the body was buried by his disciples and remained in a tomb.[464]

Jesus' post mortem appearances fall generally into three categories: visions, epiphanies, and apparitions, but the distinctions are not always maintained, nor are the details wholly consistent. For example, the

---

[460] John 19:38.

[461] Acts 13:27-29.

[462] Acts 7:58-8:3; 22:6-11; Galatians 1:13-14.

[463] *Miracle and Magic*, 65-66.

[464] *The Empty Tomb*, 233.

Kirby's essay, "The Case Against the Empty Tomb," from which the quotation above is extracted, presents a thorough discussion of the difficulties in the gospel narratives.

account of Jesus' appearance to Saul on the road to Damascus, reported in three places in the book of Acts,[465] differs in detail with each retelling. According to the first report, the men with Paul hear a voice but see no one,[466] and in the second the men see a light but do not hear a voice.[467] In the first account, Paul alone falls to the ground,[468] but in the third retelling, all the men fall to the ground.[469]

Soon after his conversion, Saul (aka Paul) again sees Jesus, but under different circumstances:

> It happened that after returning to Jerusalem, while I was praying in the temple, I came to be in a state of ecstasy, and I saw him saying to me, "Hurry and leave Jerusalem at once because they will not accept your testimony about me."[470]

Jesus' appearance to Paul in the temple is an ecstatic vision,[471] whereas his manifestation on the road to Damascus has characteristics of post-resurrection epiphanies: light, voices, glowing raiment,[472] supernatural entities, and natural upheavals.[473] Visions during prayer are well documented,[474] and as Strelan observes,

> That [Paul's] prayer included an ecstatic vision is not at all unusual...It is quite likely that Temple prayer had rhythm and a repetitive element. In addition, it is possible that the body moved in harmony with the rhythm of the prayer. Such a method of praying is often mantra-like and can induce a hypnotic, ecstatic state.[475]

---

[465] Acts 9:1-19, 22:6-16, 26:12-18.
[466] Acts 9:7.
[467] Acts 22:9.
[468] Acts 9:4.
[469] Acts 26:14.
[470] Acts 22:17-18.
[471] The term εκστασις (ekstasis), which literally means "to be outside oneself," is the obvious source of *ecstasy*. An altered state of consciousness is apparently in view, and the word is often translated *trance*. Peter also sees a vision while in a state of ecstasy (Acts 10:10-11).
[472] As at Matthew 28:3, Luke 24:8.
[473] Matthew 28:2, 5.
[474] Daniel 9:20, for example.
[475] *Strange Acts*, 180.

Throughout the Mediterranean world the dead were expected to be up and around by early morning, a belief that persists even today in the form of Easter 'sunrise services.' "The funeral was finished and the slow process of death completed when the soul finally departed at the coming of dawn…"[476] "The 'Spell for Coming Forth by Day'…draws the parallel between the sun's passage from night to day, and the deceased's emergence from the tomb to the daylight."[477]

A text often cited as the first report of Jesus' post-resurrection appearances comes to us from a letter written by Paul:

> For I passed on to you as of first importance what I also received, that Christ died for our sins according to the scriptures, and that he was buried, and that he was raised on the third day according to the scriptures, and that he appeared to Cephas,[478] then to the twelve, then he appeared to more than five hundred brothers at one time, the greater number of whom remain until now, but some have fallen asleep [in death].
> Then he appeared to James, then to all the apostles. Last of all, he appeared even to me, as to one born before his time.[479]

However, the claim that Jesus appeared to 500 witnesses at one time is the sort of exaggeration one would expect from a later apocryphal account and the fact that none of the gospels, although written later than 1 Corinthians, report this remarkable confirmation of the resurrection almost certainly marks the passage as having been inserted into the text after Paul's death.[480] Riley concludes, "A simple comparison of the Gospels and 1 Corinthians 15 shows that the two traditions cannot be reconciled."[481]

Robert Price has proposed that the chain of connectives —"*that* Christ died…*that* he was buried…*that* he was raised…*that* he appeared"— is

---

[476] *Aspects of Death in Early Greek Art and Poetry*, 21.

[477] *Religion and Magic in Ancient Egypt*, 84.

[478] The usual words meaning to "see" are βλεπω (blepō) and θεωρεω (theōreō), but here Paul repeatedly uses forms of οραω (horaō), a verb often employed in the New Testament for preternatural visions and similar experiences. The related noun, οραμα (horama), usually denotes *vision* in the sense of "supernatural experience."

[479] 1 Corinthians 15:3-8.

[480] Price: "If the claim of 500 witnesses were early tradition, can anyone explain its total absence from the gospel tradition?" *The Empty Tomb*, 80.

[481] *Resurrection Reconsidered*, 89.

the relic of an interpolated liturgical confession,[482] i.e., not written by Paul,[483] which if true, would make the gospel of Mark the oldest report of the resurrection:

> When the Sabbath had passed, Mary the Magdalene and Mary the mother of James and Salome bought spices so that they might go and anoint him, and very early in the morning[484] on the first day of the week, the sun having risen, they went to the tomb. They were saying to one another, "Who will roll the stone away from the door of the tomb for us?"
>
> Looking up, they saw that the stone —which was extremely large— had been rolled away. And entering the tomb, they saw a young man clothed in a white robe, sitting off to the right, and they were alarmed. But he said to them, "Do not be alarmed. You are seeking Jesus of Nazareth who was crucified. He is not here. He has been raised. Look at the place where they laid him! But go tell his disciples and Peter that he goes ahead of you into Galilee. You will see him there just as he told you."[485]
>
> And after they left, they fled from the tomb, for trembling and panic[486] seized them. And they said nothing to anyone because they were afraid.[487]

The account contradicts our expectations for several reasons, most clearly because the women do not actually see Jesus, but a young man usually assumed to be an angel.[488] Moreover, there is no sense of reassurance —the women flee the tomb in panic, too frightened to speak of their experience. Later manuscripts of the gospel of Mark append spurious endings designed to improve on the original conclusion, a conclusion some readers obviously found to be theologically deficient.

The writers of Matthew and Luke were also dissatisfied with Mark's ending and set about repairing it, introducing a number of new diffi-

---

[482] This seems to be the consensus. See Neyrey, *The Resurrection Stories*, 14, for example.
[483] *Journal of Higher Criticism* 2/2: 69-99.
[484] Three days in the tomb reflects the Jewish belief that the soul remained in the vicinity of the tomb for three days following burial. *Ancient Christian Gospels*, 235.
[485] Contradicting Acts 1:4 where the disciples are ordered to stay in Jerusalem.
[486] Another occurrence of εκστασις (ekstasis), which I have rendered *panic*. The Greeks believed the sight of the nature divinity Pan induced irrational fear, hence our word.
[487] Mark 16:1-8.
[488] In a subsequent chapter I will make the case the *young man* is the resurrected Lazarus, the beloved disciple, whose resurrection prefigures that of Jesus.

culties in the process. Matthew appropriates the youth's words from Mark,[489] but in his retelling the women are not struck silent from fear but run joyfully to inform the apostles that Jesus has risen, being met by Jesus on the way.[490] Matthew's expansion has the eleven remaining apostles go to Galilee where they receive the commission to make disciples of all nations, but, we are told, "*some doubted.*"[491]

The doubt of some of the apostles clearly troubled the early church — the resurrection and glorification of Jesus was already the keystone in the arch of Christian belief as Paul explains to the Corinthians:

> If Christ has not been raised, your faith is useless. You are still in your sins and those who have fallen asleep in Christ are truly dead. If in this life only we have hoped in Christ, we alone among all men are the most pathetic.
> But now Christ has been raised from the dead, the beginning of the harvest of those who have fallen asleep in death.[492]

When Luke set about removing the last element of doubt about the reality of Jesus' resurrection, he created a startling narrative shift: the appearances of the risen Christ begin to take on the characteristics of ghost stories. Deborah Thompson Prince, who has published a thorough comparison of the features of Luke's account with classical ghost stories, finds that the stories in Luke incorporate a mixture of classical features and concludes, "the method at work in Luke 24 is an attempt to disorient the reader in order to reconfigure the traditions known to the author and reader in light of the disciples' extraordinary experience of the resurrected Jesus."[493] This conclusion appears to assume both that ancient readers shared our sense of confusion when confronted with apparently contradictory traits —apparitions that are physical and yet not physical— and that the disciples' "experience of the resurrected Jesus" was extraordinary by ancient standards. Neither assumption is unquestionably true. In fact, Prince cites a number of examples of ghosts who were corporeal yet changed appearance at will, and engaged in various physical activities including sexual intercourse.[494]

---

489 Matthew 28:5-7.
490 Matthew 28:9-10.
491 Matthew 28:17.
492 1 Corinthians 15:17-20.
493 *Journal for the Study of the New Testament* 29: 297.
494 ibid, 294.

Few ancient people appear to have believed that the physical body would persist after death or could be restored in any form. Yet the disembodied dead could talk, walk, eat and drink with the living and food offerings and libations were brought to tombs even in cases where the body had been cremated.[495] It appears the dead could exist in various modes or states, to use modern terminology, and could evidently change modes at will. The phantom or ειδωλον (eidōlon) — from ειδος (eidos), *that which is seen*, a *form* or *shape*— is a *reflected image* of an eternal entity, the ψυχη (psuchē), or *soul*. But the phantom, which represents a *deathless* entity, could be considered more 'real' than the corruptible body.[496]

What the earliest Christians believed about the matter is not entirely clear. A text adduced as prophetic[497] is quoted in Acts: "my flesh will dwell[498] in hope…because you will not abandon my soul in Hades, nor allow your Holy One to see corruption."[499] Paul taught that there are "**heavenly** bodies" —σωματα επουρανια— which seems to be the same as a σωμα πνευματικον a "**spiritual** body."[500] What characteristics such bodies were thought to possess in actual practice is not specified.

The longest of Luke's stories concerns the stranger that two disciples meet on the road to Emmaus. As they walk with him, they repeat the details of the story of the women at the tomb and the vision of angels. Jesus, who they have been prevented from recognizing, then explains all the prophecies relating to himself in the Old Testament. Finally, as they eat the evening meal together, Jesus blesses the bread, breaks it, and hands it to them.[501] The account of the appearance comes to this jarring conclusion, a conclusion which is particularly unsettling be-

---

[495] Following his self-immolation the religious figure Peregrinus was reported to be seen walking about dressed in white. *On The Death of Peregrinus*, 173.

[496] See Riley, *Resurrection Reconsidered*, 49.

[497] Psalm 16:9-10.

[498] A curious verb, κατασκηναω, based on σκηνη (skēnē), *tent*, meaning to *encamp*, but also used of birds alighting to roost in trees. Generally speaking, the *body* was thought of as the tent in which a deathless soul temporarily 'encamped.' The gist of the passage seems to be that the body, or some form of the body, will be preserved.

[499] Acts 2:27.

[500] 1 Corinthians 15:40, 44.

[501] Neyrey points to the "remarkable parallelism" of the breaking of bread during the Emmaus meal and the Last Supper. *The Resurrection Stories*, 41. By implication, one story could have served as a template for the other.

cause of the association between invisibility, transformation, and magic:

> Their eyes were opened and they recognized him and he became invisible to them.[502]

This is the only specific mention of disappearance in connection with the resurrection —καὶ αυτος **αφαντος εγενετο** απ᾽ αυτων: "and he **became invisible** to them"— and the only occurrance of αφαντος (aphantos) in the New Testament. The preposition απο (apo) in the construction απ᾽ αυτων is often used with verbs of concealment and separation, and could be taken to imply that Jesus' manifestation became invisible to them *as he left*, i.e., dematerialized in some way.

The spells of the papyri demonstrate a strong connection between magic and invisibility:

> But if you wish to become invisible, rub just your face with some of the mixture, and you will be invisible[503] for as long as you want.[504]

> And say, "Depart as you please, lord, blessed god, where you [live] forever," and the god is invisible.[505]

> "Arise, demon from the realm below...whatever I may command of you, I, [Name],[506] in that way obey me...if you wish to become invisible, just smear your forehead with the mixture and you will be invisible for however long you want."[507]

The wording of the spells, αφαντος γενεσθαι, "to become invisible," duplicates the phraseology of Luke's story.

---

[502] Luke 24:31.

[503] καὶ **αφαντος** εση: "and you will be **invisible**..."

[504] *Papyri Graecae Magicae* I, 256-257.

[505] καὶ **αφανης** εστιν ο θεος: "and the god is **invisible**." *Papyri Graecae Magicae* I, 94-95.

[506] The Greek ο δεινα (ho deina), which I translate [*Name*], means *a certain one*, indicating that the name of the magician or the subject of the incantation is to be supplied as the occasion requires. The term is very common in the spell books.

[507] *Papyri Graecae Magicae*, I, 14.

One of the more grisly ghost stories of antiquity concerns Polykritos, a man who died only days after the consummation of his marriage. In time his widow delivered a hermaphroditic child. This event was considered to be an ominous omen, and as the citizens were deliberating what course of action to take, the ghost of Polykritos appeared and asked that the child be handed over to him. When the people hesitated to comply, the ghost seized the child, tore it limb from limb, consumed all but the head, and "suddenly disappeared."[508] The phrase — αυτικα αφανης εγενετο, literally, "at once **became invisible**"— exactly duplicates the language of Luke.[509]

Surely Luke was not unaware of the ghostly nature of his resurrection story. Indeed, the next account he relates appears designed to prove that the stranger on the road to Emmaus was not a ghost:

> But while they were talking about these things, he stood in their midst and said to them, "Peace be with you!" But they were alarmed and became afraid, thinking they were seeing a spirit. And he said to them, "Why are you terrified, and why do doubts arise in your hearts? Touch me and see,[510] because a spirit does not have flesh and bones as you see I have." And saying this, he showed them his hands and feet.
>
> But even in their joy they did not believe him, and while they were wondering, he said to them, "Do you have anything here to eat?" And they gave him a piece of fish. And he took it and ate it in front of them.[511]

In this passage Jesus proves his corporeal nature to his disciples by having them touch him and by eating food in their presence. In fact, eating is taken as proof of return from the dead in Mark.[512] But the disciples wonder —as well they might— how a body of flesh and bones has suddenly appeared from nowhere. A rather similar case is encountered in Apuleius' story of the miller slain by a crone who turns

---

[508] Keller, *Rerum Naturalium Scriptores Graeci Minores*, I, 65.

For an English translation of this and other *paradoxa*, see Hansen, *Phlegon of Tralles' Book of Marvels*.

[509] The term αφανης is also used by Lucian to describe the disappearance of the magician Pancrates (*The Lover of Lies*, 36).

Compare the passage about Philip and the eunuch in Acts 8:39-40.

[510] ψηλαφησατε με και ιδετε: "touch me and see.."

[511] Luke 24:36-43.

[512] Mark 5:43. Compare Acts 1:3; 10:41.

out to be a ghost.[513] Of this story Ogden observes, "The fact that the ghost could touch the miller's arm suggests that it had a solid form, but the fact that it could then disappear from a locked room suggests, perplexingly, that by contrast it was ethereal."[514]

The 4th century church historian Eusebius quotes an ancient variant of the Emmaus story: εφη αυτοις λαβετε ψηλαφησατε με και ιδετε οτι ουκ ειμι **δαιμονιον ασωματον**: "He said, take, touch me and see that I am not **a bodiless demon**…"[515] "Demon" in this context might reflect a Christian belief that ghosts were evil spirits pretending to be dead people, or may simply mean "ghost."

That this textual variant is of great antiquity is supported by its quotation in an epistle of Ignatius, written at the beginning of the 2nd century:

> For I know and I believe him to have been in the flesh after the resurrection, when he came to those with Peter and said to them, "Take, touch me and see that I am not a bodiless demon,"[516] and immediately they touched him and believed…but after the resurrection he ate and drank with them as made of flesh,[517] although spiritually united[518] with the Father.[519]

The reference to a disembodied demon "is clearly a free saying with a long history" known to Ignatius, Jerome, who believed that it came from the now lost *Gospel According to the Hebrews*, and Origen, who cites the Latin version, "*Non sum daimonium incorporeum.*" Riley concludes, "Both Luke and Ignatius have drawn on a common source. That source sought to demonstrate a material resurrection body by means of physical proofs."[520]

---

[513] Apuleius, *Metamorphosis* IX, 29-31.

[514] *Night's Black Agents: Witches, Wizards and the Dead in the Ancient World*, 70.

[515] *Ecclesiastical History*, 3, 36.11.

[516] Λαβετε ψηλαφησατε με και ιδετε οτι ουκ ειμι δαιμονιον ασωματον: "take, touch me and see that I am not a bodiless demon…"

[517] ως σαρκικος: "as made of flesh…"

[518] καιπερ πνευμαικως ηνωμενος τω πατρι: "although spiritually united with the Father."

[519] *Ad Smyrnaeos*, III.

According to the *Acts of John* (93), Jesus' body during life was sometimes solid and at other times immaterial. This presentation probably reflects a later docetic understanding of Jesus' nature.

[520] *Resurrection Reconsidered*, 95-96.

Interestingly, Jesus' appearances tend to occur at night or in the intervals between day and night, i.e., 'between times' typically associated with works of sorcery.[521] It is plain from the frequent mention of lamps in the papyri that most magical ritual took place at night. On this feature of the magician's work, the late Samson Eitrem noted,

> Lamp or lantern magic (Lampenzauber) plays a major role here as generally in Egyptian magic —for light, the nocturnal sun, was something to be exploited. The night with its horde of dead spirits and eerie ways —the night through which the sun god navigated in his vessel to reach the east through the dark kingdom of the underworld while the moon shone or the heavens were starry —offered the magician the best opportunity for exercising his art or arts.[522]

Nicodemus also came to Jesus by night and the subject of his inquiry was also how one entered the kingdom of God.[523]

The nocturnal workings of the magician are, in part, a simple reflection of human physiology: "In general the association between sleep, death, dreams, and night was tight."[524] —the author of Matthew's gospel clearly considered dreams to be supernatural in origin.[525] The world of the New Testament, the world before artificial light, was literally a darker place, a place where night and the dreams that haunt it held a larger place in life. Nighttime was particularly associated with works of sorcery, and Greek preserves several relevant terms such as νυκτι-πλανος (nuktiplanos), *roaming by night*, and νυκτοπεριπλανητος (nuktoperiplanētos), *wandering around by night*, that refer to such activities.

"Alongside public Dionysiac festivals there emerge private Dionysos mysteries. These are esoteric, they take place at night; access is through an individual initiation, *telete*."[526] Georg Luck: "It seems that the magos had a little bit of everything —the bacchantic (i.e. ecstatic) element, the initiation rites, the migratory life, the nocturnal activities."[527] "In mod-

---

[521] Matthew 28:1; Mark 16:2; Luke 24:29; John 21:4.
[522] *Magika Hiera*, 176.
[523] John 3:1-5.
[524] *Greek and Roman Necromancy*, 77.
[525] Matthew 2:12, 19, etc.
[526] *Greek Religion*, 291.
[527] *Witchcraft and Magic in Europe: Ancient Greece and Rome*, 104.

ern languages the word *mystery* is mainly used in the sense of 'secret,' a usage that goes back to the New Testament. In fact, secrecy was a necessary attribute of ancient mysteries…Secrecy and in most cases a nocturnal setting are concomitants of this exclusiveness."[528]

Jesus' appearances in the gospel of John convey a spectral quality. Twice Jesus appears in the disciples' midst even though the doors are locked:

> So being the evening of that day, the first of the week, and the doors having been locked[529] where the disciples were for fear of the Jews, Jesus came and stood in their midst and said to them, "Peace to you!" and having said this, showed his hands and side to them. Consequently the disciples rejoiced at seeing the Lord.
> …
> And after eight days his disciples were again indoors and Thomas was with them. Jesus came, the doors having been locked, and stood in their midst and said, "Peace to you!"
> Then he said to Thomas, "Put your finger here, and look at my hands, and reach out your hand and stick it into my side, and be not unbelieving, but believing."
> Thomas exclaimed, "My Lord and my God!"
> Jesus said to him, "You have seen me and believed. Happy are those who not having seen yet believe."[530]

John does not disclose how Jesus left following these appearances, but it is probably safe to assume that he did not simply walk out the door.

In these various manifestations Jesus exhibits traits of a *revenant*, an embodied ghost that appears once or for a brief period of time following the death of the subject[531] and performs bodily functions such as speaking and eating, displays premortem wounds, is associated with an empty tomb, and vanishes suddenly without leaving any physical trace, all of which are characteristics noted by Debbie Felton, a scholar who has produced a productive analysis of the ancient Greco-Roman

---

[528] *Ancient Mystery Cults*, 7-8.
[529] The verb κλειω (kleiō) means *to lock, to shut with a key* –κλεις (kleis), *key*. Translations that render the verb as simply *to shut* fail to fully convey the idea that the doors were locked, not merely closed, and that in spite of that fact, Jesus "came and stood in their midst."
[530] John 20:19-20, 26-29.
[531] Evans, *Field Guide to Ghosts*, 19.

ghost story.[532] As noted by Finucane, "…late classical tradition attributed various activities to ghosts, such as informing, consoling, admonishing, and pursuing, the living."[533] Vermeule's observation regarding ghosts is pertinent to Jesus' appearances: "wounding the flesh means wounds in the shade below…"[534]

It is well known that people of antiquity thought certain classes of the dead especially likely to become ghosts: the αωρος (aōros), the *prematurely dead*, the αγαμος (agamos), the *unmarried*, the αταφος (ataphos), the *unburied*, and the βιαιοθανατος (biaiothanatos), the *dead by violence*. It is clear that Jesus could be numbered among at least three of these groups, all of whom share a commonality: "Those who died before completing life were understood to linger between categories, unable to pass into death because they were not really finished with life."[535]

It is possibly significant that the Greek of Luke's gospel reveals a higher social register than that of Matthew or Mark —the historiographic preface to Luke's gospel, in keeping with official histories of the era, "indicates that the author has done extensive research."[536] If that is the case, it is not unlikely that the writer was also familiar with accounts of ghosts included in secular histories and the popular *paradoxa*, collections of uncanny and bizarre events which quite naturally included ghost stories. Phlegon of Tralles' story of the newly dead Philinnion who returns by night to have sex with her family's guest and vanishes each morning can be cited as a particularly famous example. A fragment of an ancient novel, included among the Greek magical papyri, alludes to a "handsome phantom"[537] which appears to a woman, apparently one of many who have "fallen in love with fantastic bodies" —"fantastic" because they are the bodies of ghosts.[538]

The disappearance, return, and redisappearance of the famous dead is not limited to the story of Jesus. Here, according to Plutarch, is how the career of Romulus is reported to have come to its end:

---

[532] *Haunted Greece and Rome*, 7, 14, 17, 23-26, 28.
[533] *Ghosts*, 25
[534] *Aspects of Death in Early Greek Art and Poetry*, 49.
[535] Johnston, *Restless Dead*, 149.
   Such a person was considered ατελεστος (atelestos), *unfulfilled*.
[536] Ehrman, *The New Testament*, 115.
[537] καλον ειδωλον: "handsome **phantom**…"
[538] *Papyri Graecae Magicae* XXXIV, 20-21.

...Romulus was perceived to transform suddenly, and no part of his body or shred of clothing was seen. Some speculated that the senators, gathered in the temple of Hephaistos, rose up against him and killed him, and distributed pieces of his body to each to carry away hidden in the folds of his clothing. Others believe it was neither in the temple of Hephaistos, nor when the senators alone were present that he disappeared, but when he held an assembly around the so-called Marsh of the Goat. Suddenly wonders strange to describe occurred in the air, incredible changes, the light of the sun faded, and night fell, not gently or quietly, but with terrible thunder and gusts of wind driving rain from every direction, during which the great crowd scattered in flight, but the influential men huddled together with one another. When the tempest had passed and the sun broke out and the mass reassembled there was an anxious search for the king, but the men in power neither inquired into the matter nor investigated it, but loudly exhorted all of them to honor and worship Romulus as a man imbued with divinity, a god favorably disposed to them rather than a worthy king. The mass of people, believing these things, left rejoicing with high hopes to worship him. However, some bitterly contested the matter in a hostile way, and accused the patricians of foisting a stupid story on the people, being themselves the perpetrators of murder.

At this point, a man from among the patricians, high born, reliable and most esteemed, a trusted intimate of Romulus himself, a colonist from Alba, Julius Proculus, went into the forum and swore by the most sacred emblems that as he traveled along the road he saw Romulus approaching him face to face, handsome and strong as ever, decked out in bright, shining armor. He himself, struck with fear at the sight, said, "O king, what were you thinking, subjecting us to unjust and evil accusations, the whole city an orphan in tears, weeping for having been abandoned?" Romulus answered, "It pleased the gods, Proculus, that I be with men for just so long a time, and having founded a city of superlative glory, dwell again in heaven. Farewell, and proclaim to the Romans that if they practice self-control with manliness, they will achieve the very heights of human power. And I will be your propitious daemon, Quirinus."[539]

---

[539] ευμενης εσομαι δαιμων Κυρινος: "I will be your propitious daemon, Quirinus." Quirinus, the deified Romulus, together with Jupiter and Mars, forms the Capitoline

These things seemed believable to the Romans, based on the character of the man who related them and because of his oath, besides feeling some participation in divine destiny, equal to possession by the gods.[540] No one objected, but all set aside suspicion and opposition and prayed to Quirinus, calling upon him as a god.

...Romulus is said to have been fifty-four years old, in the thirty-eighth year of his rule when he disappeared from among men.[541]

If Luke sought, consciously or not, to imitate the genre of the classical ghost story or other fabulous 'histories' in framing his accounts of Jesus' post-resurrection appearances, his technique might at the very least have set a precedent for the author of the gospel of John. Alternatively, of course, it is possible that the accounts of Luke and John were not influenced by Greco-Roman literary conventions, in which case we are confronted with a primitive New Testament tradition that contains examples of independently drawn ghost stories.

...the polymorphic Jesus

An additional point of interest is the ancient tradition that Jesus appeared post mortem in various physical forms. In addition to his manifestation as a stranger on the road to Emmaus,[542] he appears on the shore of the Sea of Galilee, again initially unrecognized.[543] In the century that follows, the apocryphal Gospels and Acts tell of additional appearances in the form of "an old man, a youth, a boy...in the form of Paul...in the form of Andrew...To Drusiana he appears in the form of John, and of a young man...to John he appears as an old man, to James, who was with John, as a youth...and to a young married

---

Triad, the gods of the state cult. At a later date, the manly Quirinus and Mars were dropped in favor of Juno and Minerva.

[540] δαιμονιον τι συνεφαψασθαι παθος ομοιον ενθουσιασμω: "feeling some participation in divine destiny, equal to **possession by the gods.**"

[541] *Plutarch's Lives* I, 27.5 — 28.3, 29.7.

Robert Price notes that resurrection stories are "embodied in tales all over the world and throughout history" and cites Oedipus, Adonis, Tammuz, Osiris, Attis, Hercules, Romulus, Empedocles and Apollonius as examples from the ancient Mediterranean world. *The Empty Tomb*, 14.

[542] Luke 24:15-16.

[543] John 21:4.

couple on their wedding night he appears as Thomas...The world of the apocryphal acts...is, in many ways, the Hellenistic world in which magic and sorcery were quite at home."[544]

To the pagan mind, there would be little to distinguish Jesus from any other divinity, Hermes or Hekate, for instance, who manifests in various forms,[545] but perhaps that was exactly the point. Supernatural entities were commonly thought of as having many forms as well as many names.

> Klōthō and Lachesis and Atropos are you, Three-Headed, Persephonē and Megaira and Allēktō, Many Formed..."[546]

> Prayer:[547] I invoke you, double-horned Mēnē, in every shape and many-named,[548] whose form no one knows for certain except the one who made the entire world, Iaō, the one who formed [you] into the twenty-eight shapes of the world...[549]

In the apocryphal Acts, the body of the risen Jesus is both "solide et immatériel," —like a revenant's— as well as polymorphic.[550] Self-transformation, otherwise known as shape-shifting, is an expected magical ability of superhuman entities: "Another element common to Hellenistic magical beliefs was the power of a magician to turn himself...into another form, i.e., metamorphosis."[551]

In the apocryphal *Acts of Thomas*, a demon is addressed as "O Many-formed,[552] who reveals himself as he wishes, but cannot change his nature..."[553] In its next two occurrences the term πολυμορφος (polumorphos), *polymorphic*, is used of the risen Jesus (*Acts of Thomas* 48, 153). In the apocryphal *Acts of John* (91) Jesus is described as a "a unity

---

[544] *Aspects of Religious Propaganda in Judaism and Early Christianity*, 167-168.

[545] Compare Lucian's **πολυμορφον** τι θεαμα: "some **polymorphous** wonder..." in reference to Hecate. *Lover of Lies*, 14.

[546] **πολυμορφε**: "Many-Formed..." *Papyri Graecae Magicae* IV, 2796-2798.

[547] ευχη: "Prayer..." As pointed out elsewhere in this work, *prayers* and *spells* are indistinguishable in the magical books.

[548] **πανμορφον και πολυωνυμον**: "in every shape and many-named..."

[549] *Papyri Graecae Magicae* VII, 756-757.

[550] *Acta Apostolorum Apocrypha*, II, 475.

[551] Ibid, 155.

[552] ο **πολυμοφος**: "Many-formed..."

[553] *Acts of Thomas*, 44.

within many faces" —πολυπροσωπον (poluprosōpon), *many faces.*
Lalleman, who has produced a valuable discussion of Jesus' polymor-
phism in the apocryphal Acts, claims that "Polymorphy in the narrow
sense is not found in texts that are older than the [Acts of John] and
the [Acts of Peter] (second century AD),"[554] but notes a tradition of
shape-shifting in the spurious ending of Mark which says, "Afterward,
when two of them went walking into the country, he appeared in another form."[555]

...ascending from the cross

It appears, however, that not all early Christians believed in a bodily
resurrection. The fragmentary gospel of Peter, mentioned previously,
describes Jesus' death and departure rather differently from the canonical gospels:

> And the Lord cried out, "My power, O power, did you abandon
> me?"[556] And when he said this, he was taken up.[557]

This variant report suggests that, having given up his power, Jesus
somehow ascended from the cross. Of course whether this account —
or any gospel account for that matter— contains anything historical is
not the point. What they seem to demonstrate is that during the formative period, Christian sects explained the circumstances of Jesus'
death and what happened to him next in wildly divergent ways. Given
the accounts of Jesus' burial in the canonical gospels, how are we to
understand Origen's passing remark about Jesus concerning "his sudden bodily disappearance from the stake"?[558]

Although Jesus did eventually find his way from the insignificant village of Nazareth to the right hand of God, the New Testament writers
were unclear about when Jesus became the Son of God, and this un-
certainty apparently existed prior to the composition of any of the
New Testament documents.

---

[554] *The Apocryphal Acts of John,* 111.
[555] εφανερωθη εν ετερα **μορφη**: "he appeared in another **form**." (Mark 16:12).
[556] η **δυναμις** μου η **δυναμις** κατελειψας με: "my **power**, O **power**, did you
abandon me?"
[557] *Gospel of Peter* 5:5.
[558] το ευθυς απο του σκολοπος αυτον **αφανη γενεσθαι σωματικως**: "his
sudden **bodily disappearance** from the stake." *Contra Celsum* II, 69.

Paul, probably quoting from a pre-existing confession of faith, says of Jesus that he "was appointed" the Son of God "by resurrection from the dead."[559] The idea that Jesus did not become the Son of God until *after* he died may shock modern Christian sensibilities, but Paul says as much when he connects the bestowal of sonship —"You are my son, today I have begotten you"— with Jesus' resurrection —"when he raised Jesus."[560] These are hardly the only passages where such linkage occurs: Paul again says that God "appointed" Jesus to be the judge of the world and confirmed that appointment "by raising him from the dead."[561] "Paul held the belief, which to the later conventional view was startling, that it was not until after Jesus had died and supposedly risen from the dead that he became the Messiah…"[562]

A different strand of the earliest tradition has Jesus become God's son at the moment of his baptism. In Mark's gospel, a voice from heaven announces, "You are my son" as Jesus comes up out of the water,[563] and the corresponding passage in Luke, according to several of the earliest manuscripts, says, "You are my son, today I have begotten you."[564]

Christians began to fight among themselves almost from the very beginning over the question of Jesus' divinity. The proto-orthodox eventually came to believe that he had always existed with God prior to his human incarnation, and had always been God's Son, but many rejected the idea both of his pre-existence and of his virgin birth. Some —known under the blanket term *adoptionists*— taught that Jesus was a holy man who had been "adopted" by God at the time of his baptism, hence the announcement, "You are my son." Some Gnostics taught that a spirit entity, an *aeon* called "the Christ," entered Jesus at his baptism after descending in the form of a dove,[565] and abandoned his

---

[559] Romans 1:4. The grammatically ambiguous εξ αναστασεως νεκρων: "by resurrection from the dead" could also mean "starting from [his] resurrection from the dead."

[560] αναστησας Ιησουν: "when he raised Jesus" (Acts 13:33-34).

[561] Acts 17:31. Compare Acts 10:42.

[562] Grant, *Jesus*, 102.

[563] Mark 1:10-11.

[564] Luke 3:22.

Ehrman argues that the reading preserved in these ancient witnesses is the original. *Orthodox Corruption of Scripture*, 49, 62-67, 140-143.

[565] Matthew 3:16, Mark 1:10, Luke 3:22.

body prior to his death, provoking his well known cry of desperation on the cross.[566]

Jesus himself, who expected the world to end in his lifetime and apparently believed that his confrontation with the temple authorities would trigger the apocalypse —his final and greatest feat of magic[567] — made no provision for the transmission of his authority from generation to generation. After all, Jesus' generation was supposed to be the last. The sudden loss of its charismatic leader left a nearly fatal power vacuum in the emerging cult, but in the centuries after his death his followers noisily regrouped, formulated the beginnings of Christian theology, backtracked to produce quasi-historical biographies, and starting with the book of Acts, invented the "apostolic fiction" written to create the illusion of continuity between Jesus and the later community of believers. In the process the apostles became the eyewitnesses of Jesus' life, the putative authors of the New Testament books, the first missionaries, founders of the first churches, the first theologians, and the first martyrs.

> It is as important for the disciples to be apostles as it is for Jesus to be the Christ. Without the apostles, the story of Jesus would recede into the past like a tale told once upon a time without effect in shaping social history...Without the apostles the Christian church would not know how to connect its history with Jesus. The apostles are the church's guarantee that, as a social historical institution of religion, it started right and has its story straight.[568]

Apologist scholars have proposed a number of supposedly objective criteria by which the resurrection stories can be positively judged as representing real history. But as Hector Avalos has pointed out in a devastating critique of such methods, the very same criteria could be applied with positive results to full-bodied apparitions of another gospel character, the Virgin Mary.[569] Yet oddly enough, no evangelical scholars seem to take sightings of the Virgin Mary seriously, although many hundreds of witnesses over the course of centuries testify to the reality of such events.

---

[566] Matthew 27:46, Luke 23:46.
[567] *Ancient Magic and Ritual Power*, 335-359.
[568] Burton Mack, *Who Wrote the New Testament*, 225.
[569] *The End of Biblical Studies*, 191-194.

*Maenad with thursos wand, 490*BCE

Chapter 6: Magical Palestine

For many centuries Palestine has been a military and cultural cross-roads, traversed by the Egyptians as well as their rivals to the north and east. Armies of Hittites, Assyrians and Babylonians marched through the troubled land on missions of conquest, momentary events in the millennia of war and commerce that stirred the great mixing bowl of the eastern Mediterranean, blending the material and the numinous, assimilating both the military forces of earthly kingdoms and the powers of a vast spirit realm, "a pleroma of divine forces."[570]

Whether the Israelites were invaders from Egypt, as claimed by the Old Testament, or an indigenous group already present within Canaan —the land between the Mediterranean Sea and the Jordan River— cannot be determined with certainty. Sometime in the Late Bronze Age, approximately 1200 years BCE, their sacred book tells that the Hebrews embarked on a genocidal campaign against various competing tribes, a protracted conflict justified on religious grounds. The book of Joshua leaves a vivid record of this war of extermination:

> Then they utterly destroyed all in the city, both men and women, young and old, oxen, sheep, and asses, with the edge of the sword...And they burned the city with fire, and all within it; only the silver and gold, and the vessels of bronze and of iron, they put into the treasury of the house of the LORD...And all who fell that day, both men and women, were twelve thousand, all the people of Ai...And Joshua took Makkedah on that day, and smote it and its king with the edge of the sword; he utterly destroyed every person in it, he left none remaining...and the LORD gave [Libnah] also and its king into the hand of Israel; and he smote it with the edge of the sword, and every person in it...and the LORD gave Lachish into the hand of Israel, and he took it on the second day, and smote it with the edge of the sword, and every person in it...And Joshua passed on with all Israel from Lachish to Eglon...and every person in it he utterly destroyed...Then Joshua went up with all Israel from Eglon to

---

[570] Lesses, *Harvard Theological Review* 89:59.

Hebron; and they assaulted it, and took it, and smote it with the edge of the sword, and its king and its towns, and every person in it; he left none remaining...[571]

To this litany of death the account happily adds the cities of Debir, and the towns of the Negeb where Joshua "left none remaining, but utterly destroyed all that breathed as the LORD God of Israel commanded," and to those glories were soon added the cities of Gaza and Goshen,[572] followed by a long list of others. What survivors remained the Israelites put to forced labor.[573]

Aware that religions of truth are invariably supported by falsified histories, let us grant the possibility that the genocidal frenzy partially described above may have been more a priestly wish list[574] than a factual account. In any event, we are on historically solid ground when the Old Testament concedes,

...the people of Israel dwelt among the Canaanites, the Hittites, the Amorites, the Perizzites, the Hivites, and the Jebusites; and they took their daughters to themselves for wives, and their own daughters they gave to their sons; and they served their gods.[575]

And learned their magic.

It is now suspected that the abominations of the Canaanites listed in Deuteronomy,[576] including child sacrifice by burning, "were most probably originally Israelite" practices.[577] This conclusion is supported by the story of Jephthah's daughter, vowed as a burnt offering,[578] and by the story of Isaac, who was to be offered by burning.[579] The Old Testament contains abundant evidence of genocide, specifically including children, foundation sacrifices, and the offering of the first-

---

[571] Joshua 6:21, 24, 8:25, 10:28, 30-32, 34-36. All references are to the *Revised Standard Version.*

[572] Joshua 10:38, 40-43.

[573] Judges 1:28, 30, 33.

[574] Compare Psalm 137:9: "Happy shall he be who takes your little ones and dashes them against the rock!"

[575] Judges 3:5-6.

[576] Deuteronomy 18:10-14.

[577] Lange, *Legal Texts and Legal Issues*, 398.

[578] Judges 11:31-35.

[579] Genesis 22:2.

born.[580] Modern scholars are inclined to believe that the rhetoric against the 'abominations of the Canaanites' was designed to cover horrific practices among the Israelites themselves: "the Hebrew Bible hardly affords a unanimous voice on what distinguishes the domains of magic and religion, let alone how one is to recognize a Canaanite over against an Israelite."[581]

...magicians in the Old Testament

Wonder-workers are featured with some frequency in Hebrew scripture, but the exact details of their performances —which are very rarely described— is a matter of dispute. In any case, Grabbe's observations would appear to apply generally to any period in the thousand years leading up to Jesus' era:

> The esoteric arts were widely practiced...What we today would call "magic" was also a widespread feature of popular religion in antiquity...however, we have to be careful what we are talking about: in many cases it represented a perfectly respectable craft, such as healing and exorcism...Exorcism and control of the spirit world were acceptable practice in Jewish society...such skills were a common feature of the miracle worker.[582]

That magical practice formed a part of normative Yahwist religion is hardly in question. A leper can be cleansed through a complex ritual which includes, but is not limited to, placing the blood of a sacrificial lamb on the tip of the right ear, the right thumb, and right great toe of the man to be healed, followed by an application of oil which must be poured into the palm of the left hand of the priest, and sprinkled seven times with the tip of the right forefinger, after which procedure the remaining oil is to be applied to the leper's right ear, thumb and great toe, and so on.[583] A house can be cleansed of leprosy by killing one of two small birds in a clay vessel over running water, and sprinkling the walls of the house seven times with bird blood using a wand of cedar and hyssop bound together with scarlet thread. The living

---

[580] Exodus 22:29-30, Leviticus 27:28-29, Deuteronomy 2:34, Numbers 37:17-18, Joshua 6:21, 1 Kings 16:34, 2 Kings 16:3, 21:6, Psalm 106:38, Isaiah 57:5.
[581] Schmidt, *Magic and Ritual in the Ancient World*, 242. Schmidt offers a concise summary of the evidence for child sacrifice as once forming a part of cult of Yahweh.
[582] *Judaism From Cyrus to Hadrian*, II, 520.
[583] Leviticus 14: 10-20.

bird is then set loose, presumably to carry away the disease.[584] Christian scholars who regard the elaborate rites of the Egyptian magical papyri as preposterous or grotesque might gain some perspective on the matter through a careful reading of the divinely inspired grimoire called Leviticus.

According to Deuteronomy, there were not only augurs and soothsayers, diviners and sorcerers, but spell-casters, necromancers, mediums and people who sacrificed their own children in the "land of promise."[585]

The ubiquitous practice of magic in Palestine notwithstanding, an appreciation of its full extent and nature is impeded by several obstacles, the primary one being the perishable nature of most artifacts from the world before plastic. "Jews in the Talmudic period doubtless wrote amulets on papyrus, cloth, and other less durable materials, but apart from an Aramaic papyrus fragment from Oxyrhynchus these have not survived."[586] The preservation of organic material in Egypt is primarily the result of a single phenomenon: dry climate. The artifacts left to us in Palestine and adjacent areas are predominantly inorganic: stone, fired clay, metal, and leather scrolls if protected in jars and concealed in desert caves. Nevertheless, some such artifacts have survived, including two silver amulets which put the priestly blessing[587] to apotropaic use. These amulets, discovered in a tomb from the Second Temple era, are dated to the 7th or 6th century BCE.[588]

Regarding the contention that ancient Palestinian Judaism was 'contaminated' by the magical practice of neighboring peoples, Naveh and Shaked have this to say:

The *Hekhalot* literature uses the techniques of magic in order to acquire secret knowledge concerning the heavenly world...This literary tradition has its roots in Palestine. Some of its early manifestations are present in the Dead Sea Scrolls...Our present concern is however with the factual statement that magic was less prominently present in Palestine than in Babylonia, which proves

---

[584] Leviticus 14: 48-53.
[585] Deuteronomy 18: 9-14.
[586] *The History of the Jewish People in the Age of Jesus Christ*, III, Part I, 355.
[587] Numbers 6:22-27.
[588] *Ancient Jewish Magic: A History*, 30.

to be wrong...Palestine and Mesopotamia had two separate traditions, each with its own style and set of formulae. When however formulae from the two geographical areas converge, it may be invariably established the origin of the theme is Palestinian, rather than Babylonian...Jewish incantation texts very often make use of biblical verses. This phenomenon is clearly visible in all varieties of Jewish magic, in the Mesopotamian bowls, the Palestinian amulets, as well as the magic material from the Cairo Geniza, and is also widely attested in late mediaeval and modern Jewish magical practice.[589]

As a general rule, sorcery appears to have been a characteristic of the lower social strata. In the past as today, the members of the higher social orders worked their will through wealth and influence and accordingly felt less need of recourse to supernatural agencies, at least while things were going well. The members of the lower classes in antiquity were as a rule not only poor but also illiterate so their beliefs and practices were not widely celebrated in writings by their own hand, writings that might have hypothetically survived to serve as sources for our enlightenment. As a result, the magical workings of common folk were unlikely to leave a permanent residue of evidence for scholars to recover. As pointed out by Gideon Bohak, if magical ritual consisted primarily of verbal activity with some manipulation of common materials, but no writing, it would leave no trace of its existence, a situation compounded by the absence of amulets used in exorcism during this period.[590]

Additionally, the magical practices of the popular religion among the Israelites were in constant tension with the official cult, which was generally identified with the temple and its priesthood. Unapproved practices were periodically suppressed, often violently, and associated texts, implements, and sacred sites were destroyed, establishing a practice of vandalism which became Christian policy towards pagan documents and temples. The writings of the official cult, our Old Testament, tend to seriously minimize disapproved popular practices and even when they mention them provide little or no description. Nev-

---

[589] *Magic Spells and Formulae: Aramaic Incantations of Late Antiquity*, 19-22.

Regarding "the surprisingly rich vocabulary to denote different aspects of magic," Schäfer remarks that "the many warnings not to follow the abominable customs of the pagans clearly show that the Israelites precisely did what they were supposed not to do." *Envisioning Magic*, 27.

[590] *Ancient Jewish Magic. A History*, 116-118, 137-138.

ertheless, the evidence for magical practice in the Middle East is so pervasive that a recently published study of an Aramaic adjuration of Beelzebub from the Dead Sea Scrolls states,

> The era of the Second Temple was a magical time. A wealth of indirect evidence proves that, on the popular level, magic was often of greater practical significance than were many aspects of the Law of Moses...The [Dead Sea] scrolls include more magic texts than was previously realized even by the few privy to the whole collection...A rich literature of magic and incantation texts has survived from Akkadian sources, and, mutatis mutandis, its formulas and phraseology can sometimes be recognized in the magic texts produced during the long period when Aramaic dominated Mesopotamia.[591]

The activities of popular belief are nearly always under-represented in official histories. How many modern denominational histories mention that many church members regularly consult horoscopes? Certainly many Christians must, or why else would nearly every newspaper in an overwhelmingly Christian country contain a section devoted to them? How many Christians say, "Bless you!" if someone sneezes, or sit for tarot readings, or knock on wood, played with the once ubiquitous Ouija boards, cross their fingers for luck, or engage in any number of other superstitions? And where in the official histories might one find documentation of any of these very ordinary events? The *locus classicus* of necromancy in the Old Testament is related as a detail of the downfall of a king and his dynasty, not as part of a story about one of the thousands of commoners who must have made similar inquiries of spirit mediums.

Evidence for the true extent of magical practice in the remote past is therefore necessarily thin due to the ravages of time and climate, destruction due to suppression, the secrecy which often accompanied magical ritual —and may even have been understood as a condition for its success— and the fact that the sheer banality of much of what we might deem magical elicited little or no mention.

---

[591] *Journal of Biblical Literature* 113: 627-629.

Peter Schäfer, who surveyed the magical material from the Cairo geniza, was impressed by "immense quantity, tremendous both in number and variety, of fragments in the Hebrew, Aramaic, Arabic, Judeo-Arabic, Judeo-Spanish, Judeo-Persian and Syrian languages." *Journal of Jewish Studies* 41:76.

"The magician is therefore conscious of being the principle actor in a procedure that is both magical and sacred. Such a practice must be kept hidden because of the exceptional powers that it assures."[592] David Aune distinguishes magic from religion in part on the basis that magic was a private act, and that magical texts and paraphernalia were employed "in *private* (often secret) ceremonies..."[593] Against this distinction one might offer the very private entry of the High Priest into the Holy of Holies on the Day of Atonement (Leviticus 16:2; Hebrews 9:7) and the continuation of the tradition of secrecy in the Eastern Orthodox rite through the use of the iconostasis before the altar, to say nothing of the seal of the confessional.

The official proscription of magical practitioners was certainly incentive for people interested in practicing de facto magic to dress up their activities as something else —perhaps even as religion. Nevertheless, the evidence for magic, exorcism in particular, is fairly extensive. Twelftree cites the (1) Qumran scrolls, (2) writers such as Josephus and Justin Martyr, (3) rabbinical references, and (4) incantation bowls as evidence for the widespread practice of exorcism among the Jews.[594]

Official history is meant to present individuals and their cultures in the best light. Unwanted details are censored. The result is a shaping of narrative like that visible in the New Testament: the magical details of exorcisms reported by Mark are omitted in the gospel of Matthew, and accounts of exorcism itself are completely absent from the gospel of John. That a similar process occurred during the composition and transmission of the Old Testament is not unlikely.

> Magic flourished among the Jews despite strong and persistent condemnation by the religious authority...The story of how Tobias, on the advice of the angel Raphael, expelled the demon who threatened to ruin his wedding night, must surely reflect actual, contemporary magical practice (Tobit 6:3-9, 17-18; 8:1-3)... Josephus, Ant. Viii 2, 5 (46-48), gives a sharply observed account

---

[592] Scibilia, "Supernatural Assistance in the Greek Magical Papyri: The Figure of the Parhedros," in *The Metamorphosis of Magic*, 84.

[593] *Apocalypticism, Prophecy, and Magic in Early Christianity*, 349.

See also Betz, "Secrecy in the Greek Magical Papyri," in *Secrecy and Concealment*, 153-175. The secrecy involved in Jesus' magical performances is discussed in a following chapter.

[594] *A Kind of Magic*, 63-67.

of an exorcism, which he himself witnessed, performed by a Jew called Eleazar in the presence of Vespasian and his officers.[595]

Various sorts of miracle workers are mentioned in the Old Testament, but their job descriptions are never specifically detailed. Instead, we are left to feel our way along through the imperfect evidence of etymologies, words in cognate languages and the context of the Hebrew and Aramaic terms themselves. Only a few terms I have felt to be particularly relevant are explored here —happily a magisterial assessment of the evidence by Ann Jeffers is available.[596] However, as noted by Bohak, "most of these terms admit of no certain translation."[597]

...necromancy in the Old Testament

Preeminent among the Hebrew terms for necromancy is *ōb* (אוב), a word which occurs in the expression *baal ōb* (באל אוב), roughly equivalent to *ghost-master*. The etymology of the word *ōb* is murky, but a case can be made for a reference to calling up ghosts by means of a pit into which libations were poured. By metonymy the term could apply to the pit itself, the ghost that emerged from it, or the necromancer who called the spirit up.

A related term, שאל אוב (shoel ōb), is generally translated "one who consults an *ōb*." The Greek translation of the Hebrew bible, the *Septuagint*, regularly translates *ōb* as εγγαστραμυθος (engastramuthos), a word which, if defined solely by its components, means "belly speech." Some translators render it by its Latinate equivalent, "ventriloquist," in an attempt to explain the calling up of ghosts as the trick of voice projection. However, there is little evidence in the Hebrew bible or in any other source which suggests that the ancients thought mere voice projection was the explanation for necromancy.

---

[595] *The History of the Jewish People in the Age of Jesus Christ*, III, Part 1, 342.

The Essene community at Qumran used "[I]ncantations, exorcisms and apotropaic prayers...to defend the sons of light from the forces of darkness" notwithstanding the "biblical interdiction against all 'magic'...in spite of biblical prohibitions, magic was not only tolerated but actively practiced by the Qumran community." García Martínez, "Magic in the Dead Sea Scrolls," in *The Metamorphosis of Magic*, 15, 33.

[596] "Diviners, Magicians and Oracular Practitioners," in *Magic and Divination in Ancient Palestine and Syria*.

[597] *Ancient Jewish Magic. A History*, 15.

A term which often occurs with *ōb*, ידעני (yiddoni), is clearly derived from a stem meaning "to know." Davies conjectured that the word pair is a hendiadys, meaning basically "a ghost that knows."[598] Jeffers agrees, noting "the spirit so returning is knowledgeable and therefore able to answer the questions of the inquirer."[599] Schmidt also concludes that the *yiddoni* are "ghosts who have superior knowledge of the affairs of the living."[600] After a survey of the interpretive options, Tropper concluded the term *ōb* "signifies persons rather than objects," likely "deified ancestral spirits" who were conjured up in necromantic rites for interrogation about the future.[601]

Regarding the Akkadian counterpart to the ritual partially described in 1 Samuel 28, during which Saul consults the ghost of Samuel, Hoffner notes "the wholly chthonic orientation of the procedure," which included nocturnal performance, silver —the color of the moon— and the use of black sacrificial animals.[602] In the Old Testament account,[603] Saul goes by night to the woman —"a mistress of necromancy"[604]— with the request that she bring up the ghost of the prophet Samuel. Saul had previously killed such practitioners, driving them from "the land." Regarding the account of Saul and the "witch" of Endor, Lewis notes, "that necromancy was practiced within the borders of ancient Israel…the earlier statement that Saul 'expelled the necromancers and mediums *from the land*…would seem to imply that necromancy was widespread throughout Israelite society and not just in Canaanite enclaves."[605]

The Old Testament has little to say about the details of necromantic procedure, perhaps because they were already well known. However, hints appear here and there. Isaiah seems to connect the summoning of ghosts with times of national distress —just as in the case of Saul:

> And I will encamp against you round about, and will besiege you with towers and I will raise siegeworks against you. Then deep from the earth you will speak, from low in the dust your words

---

[598] *Magic, Divination and Demonology among the Hebrews and their Neighbors*, 89.
[599] *Magic and Divination in Ancient Palestine and Syria*, 172.
[600] *Israel's Beneficent Dead*, 154.
[601] *Dictionary of Deities and Demons in the Bible*, 1524-1530.
[602] *Theological Dictionary of the Old Testament*, 1, 132.
[603] 1 Samuel 28:7.
[604] Brown, Driver and Briggs, *Hebrew and English Lexicon*, 15.
[605] *Cults of the Dead in Ancient Israel and Ugarit*, 113, 126.

shall come; your voice shall come from the ground like the voice of a ghost, and your speech shall whisper out of the dust. [606]

References to the practice of consulting ghosts are sprinkled throughout the Old Testament, and the fact that there were laws against it indicates that it was both sufficiently frequent and widespread to cause concern to the gatekeepers of the official religion. And though the legal passages of the Hebrew bible rail against necromancy, the Old Testament "does not attempt to discredit the efficacy of the practice."[607]

The tombs of the holy dead are well known in the Old Testament.

At Hebron, the burial place of Sarah and Abraham,[608] the chiefs made a covenant[609] and Absalom paid his vows.[610] It was a "city of refuge"[611] and a city of the priests…[612] At Ramah, the burial place of Rachael,[613] there was a holy stone upon her grave. On the grave of Deborah below Bethel there stood a tree known as *Allôn-bakhûth*, 'the holy tree of weeping.'[614] The burial place of Miriam was *kadesh*, 'the sanctuary.'[615] Shechem, the burial-place of Joseph,[616] was the site of a holy tree called "the oak of the oracle," or "the oak of the diviners,"[617] of a holy stone,[618] of an altar,[619] and of a temple.[620] It was also a city of refuge.[621] Of similar character as sanctuaries were probably the graves of the heroes Tola, Jair, Ibzan, Elon, and Abdon.[622]

The Book of Kings records with equal care the burial places of the kings of Judah. Ezek. 43:7-9 shows clearly that in his day

---

[606] Isaiah 29:3-4.
[607] *Cults of the Dead in Ancient Israel and Ugarit*, 117.
[608] Genesis 23:19.
[609] 2 Samuel 5:3.
[610] 2 Samuel 15:7, 12.
[611] Joshua 20:7.
[612] Joshua 21:11.
[613] Genesis 35:19; 1 Samuel 10:2; Jeremiah 31:15.
[614] Genesis 35:8.
[615] Numbers 20:1.
[616] Joshua 24:32.
[617] Genesis 12:6; Deuteronomy 11:30; Judges 9:37.
[618] Joshua 24:26, f.
[619] Genesis 12:7; 22:9.
[620] Judges 9:4, 46.
[621] Joshua 20:7.
[622] Judges 10:1, f; 10:3-5; 12:8-10; 12:11, f; 12:13-15.

these were seats of worship. The words "whoredom" and "abomination" that he applies to them are the ones that are commonly used by the prophets for the cult of strange gods …This change from "holy" to "unclean" can be explained only as due to a growing consciousness that the ancient sanctity of tombs was inconsistent with the sole authority of Yahweh…That this is the correct interpretation of the taboo is shown (1) by the fact that it is called "uncleanness for a spirit" (*nephesh*),[623] which shows that the uncleanness does not come from the corpse but from the spirit associated with it; (2) by the fact that priests, who are specially connected to the worship of Yahweh, are allowed to "defile themselves for a spirit" only in a few exceptional cases,[624] and that nazirites are not allowed to defile themselves at all.[625]

Other oblique references to a cult of the dead are also found. Jeremiah refers to cutting the flesh and hair as funerary rites and connects the practice to the service of foreign gods.[626] The bones of dead holy men were credited with miraculous power —a dead man who touched Elisha's bones was instantly raised[627] — and we find a passing mention of necromantic incubation, of those "who sit in tombs, and spend the night in secret places,"[628] a probable reference to "all night vigils in tombs, presumably in order to receive an oracle from the dead."[629]

There is evidence that necromantic procedure survived over an incredible period of time, spreading from ancient Mesopotamia to Palestine and Egypt[630] where evidence of such rites persists in the magical papyri. Faraone has argued that Greek necromancy, divining with the use of skulls and corpses, "originally evolved out of a Mesopotamian and Semitic cultural milieu":

Various comments in the Mishnah show, moreover, that divination by skulls undoubtedly survived among the post-exilic Jews

[623] Leviticus 21:1, 11; 22:4; Numbers 5:2; 6:6, 11; 9:6 f, Haggai 2:13.
[624] Leviticus 21:1-4, 11.
[625] Numbers 6:6.
   Spiritism and the Cult of the Dead in Antiquity, 251-252.
[626] Jeremiah 16:6, 11-12.
[627] 2 Kings 13:20-21.
[628] Isaiah 65:4.
[629] *Cults of the Dead in Ancient Israel and Ugarit*, 175.
[630] See particularly Rittner, "Necromancy in Ancient Egypt" in *Magic and Divination in the Ancient World*, 89-96.

down into the late antique period. The Tractate Sanhedrin of the Babylonian Talmud, for example, discusses the two kinds of necromancer: "both him who conjures up the dead by soothsaying, and one who consults skulls."[631]

Although consulting the dead is mentioned in the Odyssey, it is possible that "necromancy invaded the Græco-Roman world from the Semitic Orient." Paton cited the practice of wallowing in the dust (Jeremiah 6:26; Esther 4:3, etc), sitting in the dust (Isaiah 26:19; 47:1; 52:2; Job 2:8, etc), and putting dust on the head (Joshua 7:6; 1 Samuel 4:12, etc) as a "symbolic act of communion with the dead."[632]

The discovery of "incantation bowls" dating from the early Christian era in the area of the Tigris-Euphrates has led to considerable speculation about what these vessels were thought to achieve. The spells are generally written in a descending spiral pattern from the rim to the bottom on the interior of the bowl and the vessel buried in an inverted position. Some have surmised that they are genie-in-the-bottle type 'demon traps' that captured unwary spirits lured in by the incantation. Others have proposed that they represent the evolution of skull necromancy, others that they are talismanic, meant to capture magical power and hold it in place. In any case, McCullough concluded that "the inscribed bowl was an innovation in magical technique which came into vogue only in the early Christian centuries" and further noted "its use by Christians, Jews, and Mandaeans indicates that its popularity was quite extensive."[633]

The possibility that Jesus may have engaged in some practice similar to "soothsaying" in order to "raise" John the Baptist[634] has long been suspected.

---

[631] *Mantikē: Studies in Ancient Divination*, 258, 277.

[632] *Spiritism and the Cult of the Dead in Antiquity*, 150, 250.

[633] *Jewish and Mandaean Incantation Bowls*, xii-xv.

Isbell rejected the 'demon-trap' hypothesis, but appears to favor the notion of the bowls as substitutes for skulls. *Corpus of the Aramaic Incantation Bowls*, 14.

A thorough discussion of the bowls by Michael Morony, "Magic and Society in Late Sasanian Iraq," is available as a chapter in *Prayer, Magic, and the Stars in the Ancient and Late Antique World*.

[634] Mark 6:14.

...holy men and prophets

The closest to a magical generalist in the Old Testament is the אלהימ
איש (*ish elohim*), the "man of God." The powers of the *ish elohim*, of
which Elijah and Elisha are the pre-eminent examples, are wide rang-
ing: he knows details of both the present and future,[635] he heals and
causes disease,[636] he produces food by magic,[637] raises the dead,[638] calls
down fire from heaven,[639] and spends forty days in the desert.[640] The
New Testament parallels to the career of Jesus and the apostles are so
obvious that they may be passed over for the present without further
comment.

Concerning the performance of powerful works by such "men of
God", Bohak notes that

> the range of techniques they employ to perform their feats is
> quite impressive: in some cases, a simple verbal command or a
> short prayer is all it takes; in others, they use bodily movements
> and gestures...and in many cases they use various implements,
> devices and materials, be it a garment, a staff, a plate with some
> salt, a piece of wood, a pinch of flour, or the water of the Jordan
> river...in some cases it is God Himself who instructs Moses on
> which ingredients to use to perform miracles, be it some soot
> from a furnace to get a plague going (Ex 9.8-10) or a piece of
> wood to cure a bitter water source (Ex 15.25).[641]

To the *ish elohim* may be added the תבר־חבר (*hōbēr-heber*), or "spell-
caster," who is listed in Deuteronomy along with other magical practitioners. Of this enigmatic figure, who is often associated with knot
tying as symbolic of magical binding, Jeffers says, "the [hôbêr-heber]
would be a person who binds his victims by the use of words, mutter-
ings, incantations, curses...The translation 'spell-binders,' or 'weaver
of spells' seems to me to convey best the idea of binding through oral
activity.[642]

---

[635] 2 Kings 4:14-17.
[636] 2 Kings 5:3; 8:7-13; 5:25-27.
[637] 1 Kings 17:15-16.
[638] 1 Kings 17:19-24.
[639] 1 Kings 18:38.
[640] 1 Kings 19:4-8.
[641] *Ancient Jewish Magic: A History*, 26.
[642] *Magic and Divination in Ancient Palestine and Syria*, 32, 35.

The notion of magical binding, well attested in the New Testament, is discussed in a subsequent chapter. However, the connection was noted over a century ago:

> It is not impossible that Christ's words to the disciples, "What things soever you shall *bind* on earth shall be *bound* in heaven: and what things ye shall loose on earth shall be loosed in heaven" (Matt. xviii.18), were suggested by this magical practice, known in His time and in His country as in all times and lands.[643]

The notion of binding was so fundamental to the practice of magic that representations of magical knots were included in Egyptian tombs, bound in the wrappings of mummies.[644]

The term נביא (*nabi*), "prophet," is used to designate a function of the "man of God" type. Abijah is such a prophet. He not only sees through the disguise of Jeroboam's wife, he foretells the death of her child as part of a curse against the males of Jeroboam's house.[645] A *nabi* "hears" events such as rain which is yet to fall,[646] and troops before they arrive[647] and performs healings at a distance,[648] ordering the leper Naaman to wash himself a magical seven times in the Jordan River. The *nabi* can strike a man with blindness,[649] pronounce a curse of death,[650] and his clothing possesses magical power,[651] all of which are duplicated in the works of power of Jesus and his apostles.

These terms cover only a fraction of the lexicon of magical practitioners in the Old Testament and their performances are a mere sample of the activities which carry the marks of magic. Regarding the list of evil practices of Manasseh in 2 Kings 21, an indictment that includes erecting altars to Baal, child sacrifice, divination, and consulting ghosts and familiar spirits, Grabbe remarks, "...this stereotyped list is a useful

---

[643] *Magic, Divination, and Demonology among the Hebrews and their Neighbors*, 57.
[644] *Ancient Egyptian Magic*, 88, 193-194.
[645] 1 Kings 14:6, 11-13.
[646] 1 Kings 18:41.
[647] 2 Kings 6:32.
[648] 2 Kings 5:8-14.
[649] 2 Kings 6:18.
[650] 1 Kings 1:17.
[651] 2 Kings 2:14.

source for the types of things probably fairly widely practiced in Israel at one time or another."[652]

The function of prophets in the Old Testament includes activities that millennia later are known functions of 'cunning people' in other cultures, activities as relatively mundane as finding lost objects[653] or strayed animals.[654] The fact that such activities do not receive more attention in the books of the Old Testament is no more surprising than the omission of kitchen witches from the history of the Anglican Church.

The numerous parallels between Old Testament accounts and identical reports in the New Testament strongly support the contention that a common magical culture persisted both for a considerable span of time and over a significant area and that Jesus and the primitive Christians, particularly those with Jewish roots, worked within that magical culture and employed its common techniques.

...the *Sepher Ha-Razim*

Regarding the era in which Jesus lived and in which early Christianity arose, Stone has this observation: "In general, the Hellenistic age was characterized by an interest in the occult, and magic played a great role in the world of that time. The Jews, it seems, were prominent among the magicians of this era, and there were considerable Jewish elements in Graeco-Roman magic."[655] We now have evidence that Jewish magicians of the time collected their spells in books.

The *Sepher Ha-Razim*, or *Book of Mysteries*, is a collection of Hebrew magical spells reconstructed by Mordecai Margalioth from fragmentary documents discovered in the Cairo genizah. Margalioth's original work appeared in 1966, and an English translation by Michael Morgan, the translation referenced in the present work, appeared in 1983. Naomi Janowitz points out a number of similarities between the formulae of the *Book of Mysteries* and the Greek magical books, including the organization of magical recipes, "swearing and adjuring" as magical rit-

---

[652] *Priests, Prophets, Diviners, Sages,* 124.
[653] 2 Kings 6:5-7.
[654] 1 Samuel 9:20.
[655] *Scriptures, Sects and Visions,* 82.

ual, the use of angelic helpers, recitations of hymns, and invocation of spirits of the dead which "were thought to linger near their graves."[656]

Characterized by Lapin as "a particularly baroque example of a shared cultural world,"[657] the spellbook is divided into seven sections, each corresponding to an angelic sphere of activity, each level associated with a list of angelic names the magician could invoke, 704 of them, more or less. "The simple man, driven by his impulses and instructed by his authoritative Scriptures and by the tradition that angels exist... turns to these angels and spirits for assistance. He has been reassured many times that the Lord is nigh; but angels and ministers of grace, and demons, are nigher."[658] The assistants who come to the aid of magician using the *Sepher Ha-Razim* are never characterized as anything but angels: "For him they are all not divinities but angels, in other words, ministers and emissaries of the Supreme God. The magician is very careful not to slip. Even Helios...is not the Greek sun god for the magus but only the 'angel Helios.'"[659] Of the assistants in the Greek magical papyri Ciraolo notes, "After the gods, the πάρεδροι [assistants, *my note*] are most frequently identified as ἄγγελοι [angels, *my note*] and δαίμονες [demons, *my note*] of an unspecified character."[660]

The majority of scholars date the *Sepher Ha-Razim* from the late 3rd to mid-4th century CE, but the magic it contains likely reflects much earlier ideas. That similar collections predated the spells found in the Cairo *genizah* is nearly certain:

4Q560 [part of the Dead Sea Scrolls, *my note*] is probably the remnants of a recipe book containing the texts of amulets, which a professional magician would have copied out and personified for a client's use. The client would then have worn the amulet, encased in a container, as a charm against the demons who cause the illness which it enumerates...Belief in demons was probably widespread in late Second Temple Judaism, but it should be noted that there is a particularly close affinity between the demonology of the Scrolls and the demonology of the New Testament.[661]

---

[656] *Icons of Power: Ritual Practices in Late Antiquity*, 85-95.
[657] *Religious and Ethnic Communities in Later Roman Palestine*, 14.
[658] Golden, *Aspects of Religious Propaganda in Judaism and Early Christianity*, 131.
[659] Ibid, 135.
[660] *Ancient Magic and Ritual Power*, 283.
[661] Alexander, *The Dead Sea Scrolls After Fifty Years*, II, 345, 351.

The notion of seven ascending spheres of angelic powers, based on the seven known 'planets,' was clearly a shared concept across the Middle East as this Chaldean incantation indicates:

> ...the seven gods of the vast heavens,
> the seven gods of the great earth,
> the seven gods of the igneous spheres,
> the seven gods, these are the seven gods,
> the seven malevolent gods,
> the seven malevolent phantoms,
> the seven malevolent phantoms of the flames, in the
> heavens seven, on the earth seven...[662]

As the sophistication of the *Sepher Ha-Razim* indicates, Jewish magic was not simply folk religion, but a sustained intellectual effort on the part of "learned experts who mastered a specialized body of knowledge and consulted many different sources."[663]

...the *Book of Enoch*

The clear presence of evil in a world created by a supposedly just God is the problem addressed by *theodicy*, the defense of God's benevolence in the face of overwhelming evidence to the contrary. In the apocalyptic literature of Second Temple Judaism, evil is explained by positing a rebellion of spirit entities, an explanation carried forward in some detail by a collection of writings known as *1 Enoch*.

First Enoch is a composition of five "books," each book thought by experts to have been compiled in turn from various long-lost sources. Book One, frequently called *The Book of the Watchers*, tells how fallen angels called εγρηγοροι (egrēgoroi) —source of the English *egregore*— or *Watchers*, taught heavenly secrets to mankind. *The Book of the Watchers*, likely written in the 3rd century BCE and therefore "available for reading by the time of Jesus and the early church,"[664] is a haggadic ex-

---

Some of the magical papyrus texts and amulets "can now be assigned to relatively early periods (ca. second century B.C. to early first A.D.)," Kotansky, *Greek Magical Amulets*, xvii.

[662] *Chaldean Magic: Its Origin and Development*, 17.
[663] *Ancient Jewish Magic: A History*, 36.
[664] *The Jewish Apocalyptic Heritage in Early Christianity*, 33.

pansion of the story of the antediluvian angels who succumbed to their passions for human women as recounted in Genesis.[665]

Enoch himself enjoyed an elevated reputation based on the legend that he had been "taken away" by God after living for 365 years[666] —a year for each day of the solar calendar.

The text, first known in the West only by reputation, was discovered in an Ethiopic translation by explorer James Bruce in 1773. The theory that *1 Enoch* was first composed in Aramaic is supported by the discovery of eleven Aramaic fragments of *1 Enoch* among the texts of the Dead Sea Scrolls, the oldest fragment tentatively dated from the 2nd century BCE. Additionally, five Greek exemplars as well as Latin copies are known to exist. As is the case in all ancient documents with multiple attestation, the wording varies from source to source.

First Enoch is quoted verbatim in Jude 14,[667] referenced an additional three times in an early Christian text known as the *Letter of Barnabas*, and Enoch's faith is commended in the book of Hebrews,[668] evidence that it enjoyed canonical status not only among many Jews, but in at least some sects of the early church. The mention of Jesus' descent into the underworld to preach to the "spirits in prison"[669] is also believed to reflect the influence of *1 Enoch*.[670]

For present purposes *1 Enoch*[671] is of interest owing to its description of three seemingly unrelated technologies: make up, metallurgy, and magic:

> It happened in those days that the sons of men were being multiplied and they fathered daughters, beautiful in the bloom of youth. The angels, sons of heaven, gazed upon the girls and lusted after them, and said to one another, "Come on, let's pick out women for ourselves from mankind and we will father children for ourselves."

---

[665] Genesis 6:1-4.
[666] Genesis 5:23-24.
[667] 1 Enoch 1:9.
[668] Hebrews 11:5.
[669] 1 Peter 3:19.
[670] *The Jewish Apocalyptic Heritage in Early Christianity*, 35, 62-63.
[671] My translation is based on the Greek text.

And Semaxas, who was their leader, said to them, "I fear that perhaps you will not want to perform this deed, and I alone will be the one to pay for this great sin."

They all answered him, "We will all swear an oath and bind ourselves with a curse[672] not to turn back from this intention until it be accomplished and we complete this deed." Then they swore all together and bound themselves with a curse.

In the days of Jared, two hundred of them in all descended on the peak of Mount Hermon, and they called the mountain "Hermon" because on it they swore and bound themselves with a curse.

And these are the names of their leaders: Semiaza, he was their chief...

And they began to take women for themselves, each of them, picking out women for themselves, and they cohabited with them and were defiled by them, and they taught the women potions[673] and enchantments[674] and root-cutting[675] and revealed the use of herbs to them.

And they became pregnant, and gave birth to great giants...

Azael taught the men to make short swords and long shields and round shields and breastplates, and secretly disclosed the lessons of the angels to them, the metals and how to work them, bracelets and adornment, eyeshadow and the beautifying of the eyelids, all sorts of precious stones and the dyeing of cloth. And much wantonness resulted, and they fornicated, and were beguiled and befouled in all their ways.

---

[672] αναθεματισωμεν παντες αλληλους: "we will...bind ourselves with a curse." A form of magical binding discussed at length in other chapters.
[673] εδιδαξεν αυτας φαρμακειας: "they taught the women potions..."
[674] επαοιδας: "enchantments"
[675] ριζοτομιας: "root-cutting..."

Semaxas taught enchantments and root-cutting, Armaros, the reversal of spells,[676] Rakiel, astrology, Kokiel, the meaning of signs, Sadiel, star-gazing, Seriel, drawing of the moon.

As mankind was destroyed, the cry rose to heaven.[677]

It initially seems odd that the efficacy of magic is rarely if ever denied in either the Old or New Testament. Denial of the supernatural is so ingrained in the modern mind that it is nearly instinctive, but the author and readers of *1 Enoch* knew that the working of magic, like the working of metals, had been revealed from heaven, only without divine authorization. One could no more deny the effectiveness of potions and enchantments than the superiority of swords and shields over sticks and stones, or the allure of darkened eyes, richly colored cloth, and precious stones.

A strict division of labor is also evident: cooking up potions, like cooking generally, appears to be the work of women. On the other hand metallurgy, whether the forging of weapons or the manufacture of wrist and ankle bracelets, is the work of men.

The Book of the Watchers introduces us to another trait of magical religion: deep affection for the term *mystery*.

And you see all that Azael did, who taught all wickedness on earth, and uncovered the eternal mysteries,[678] the [mysteries] in heaven which men are making it their goal to learn...

...so that all the sons of men may not die off because of the whole of the mystery[679] enjoined by the Watchers and revealed to their sons...[680]

A mystery —μυστηριον (mustērion)— is a secret doctrine, always *supernaturally revealed* as the above context shows, a divine secret that surpasses human understanding and would therefore remain forever beyond human discovery except for its revelation. The New Testa-

---

[676] επαοιδων λυτηριον: "the reversal of spells..."
[677] *1 Enoch* 6:1-7; 7:1-2; 8:1-4.
[678] **τα μυστερια** του αιωνος: "the eternal **mysteries**..."
[679] εν τω **μυστηριω** ολω: "because of the whole of **the mystery**..."
[680] *1 Enoch* 9:6; 10:7

ment puts the word into the mouth of Jesus —"to you it has been given to known the mystery of the kingdom"[681] — as well as his apostles.[682]

The Book of the Watchers is of interest on yet another count, the origin of demons. After the giant offspring of the Watchers and their concubines die in the Deluge, "wicked spirits issued from their bodies."[683] A reason for the continued hostility of such demons toward humans is also given: "They will rise up against the sons of men and women because they issued forth from them."[684] This exegetical expansion on the Genesis story reveals the origin of the demons: they are the spirits of the נפלים (nephilim),[685] invisible remnants of the offspring of angels and humans, a hybrid version of the angry ghost known in the Qumran texts as "spirits of the bastards" who, being of partly human descent, "have an affinity with humans, which allows them to penetrate the human body. Indeed, it may be implied that as disembodied spirits roaming the world like human ghosts, they particularly seek embodiment, with all its attendant problems for the one whom they possess."[686]

Annette Yoshiko Reed notes the several uses early Christians made of *1 Enoch*:

> Christian traditions about Satan's role in inspiring "heretics" are here harmonized with early Enochic traditions about the fallen angels teaching magical and divinatory arts to humankind, and it is the very assumption of an inexorable link between "heresy" and "magic"—two categories often used to denounce perceived deviance from ritual and religious norms —that makes this equation possible.

> ...Proto-orthodox Christians could critique those who adopted such practices without addressing the issue of their efficacy. If anything, the association with demonic spirits helped to explain how astrologers and diviners could predict the future, how magi-

---

[681] Matthew 13:11.
[682] 1 Corinthians 15:51, for example. The term is particularly favored by Paul and his school.
[683] 1 Enoch 15:9.
[684] 1 Enoch 15:12.
[685] Genesis 6:4.
[686] *The Dead Sea Scrolls After Fifty Years*, II, 333, 339.

cians and pagan priests could heal, and how oracles from pagan temples could prove true—even as the intrinsically demonic nature of these practices formed the basis for an argument about why they should be avoided at all costs.[687]

...magic in the era of Jesus

As noted by David Aune in a seminal essay, "The matrix of early Christianity was a Palestinian Judaism which had been permeated by Hellenistic influences to such an extent that any rigid distinction between Palestinian and Hellenistic Judaism must be regarded as untenable."[688]

The extent to which Jesus was influenced by magical practices outside the Jewish milieu is impossible to assess completely. There was a strong Hellenistic[689] presence in Galilee in Jesus' day —the Decapolis, a league of ten Greco-Roman cultural enclaves, is mentioned in the gospels[690]— but the precise antecedents of Jesus' own wonder-working powers cannot be determined. However, the gospel of Mark repeatedly mentions how quickly his fame as an exorcist spread through Galilee and beyond.[691] Herod Antipas had heard of his exploits[692] and other exorcists were quick to use his name.[693] It is clear that soon after his appearance, "Jesus" had already become a name to conjure with.

It seems incredible to think that this osmotic transfer of fame and knowledge flowed only in one direction. As pointed out by Lapin, magical techniques were a commodity characterized by "broad geographical and chronological spread" across "a shared cultural world."[694] Exorcism was a quintessentially Jewish technique[695] that

---

[687] *Fallen Angels and the History of Judaism and Christianity*, 177, 181.

[688] *Aufstieg und Niedergang der Römischen Welt*, II. 23.2: 1519.

[689] Hellenization "means only to express indigenous concepts and traditions in Greek, not to transform traditions and concepts according to a Greek mold..." Graf, *Magic in the Ancient World*, 5.

[690] At Mark 5:20, for example, where the mention is made in the context of a report of an exorcism.

[691] Mark 1:28, 45, 3:7-8, 5:20.

[692] Mark 6:14.

[693] Mark 9:38.

[694] *Religious and Ethnic Communities in Later Roman Palestine*, 14.

[695] *Aufstieg und Niedergang der Römischen Welt*, II, 16.3: 2108.

rapidly spread throughout the Roman world and the early Jewish Christians enjoyed a reputation as exorcists. The Roman Celsus said the Jews "worship angels and are devoted to sorcery, in which Moses has become their instructor."[696]

To exactly what degree Galilee had been populated by non-Jews is a subject of debate.[697] Matthew refers to "Galilee of the Gentiles,"[698] but is quoting a passage in Isaiah[699] which Jesus has supposedly fulfilled and therefore should not necessarily be taken as an accurate description of a real state of affairs. Even though peasant Jews and Gentiles in Galilee may have maintained strict segregation,[700] the purity of Galilean religious practices was evidently considered suspect, particularly in Judea, the center of the temple cult. Hence the challenge, "Are you also from Galilee? Search and see that no prophet is to arise from Galilee!"[701] Both the textual and archeological evidence for an extensive Gentile presence in Jesus' home territory are ambiguous, but it is unnecessary to posit a direct connection of any kind between Jewish and Gentile magicians since the broad outlines of magical practice were evidently quite similar all around the Mediterranean and had been so for centuries.

Regarding the magical texts recovered from the Cairo *geniza*, Gager notes that they "reveal how widespread such beliefs and practices were in the Jewish communities of the ancient world and how broadly this material circulated, crossing linguistic, chronological, cultural, and religious boundaries."[702] Confounding expectations based on the prohibitions of the Old Testament, magic was widely practiced and "in no

---

Horsley proposes that "possession by spirits is intertwined with invasion of alien forces, particularly imperial conquest and domination," and that exorcism expressed an individual and collective desire to "be independent of foreign rule, free to live directly under the rule of their God..." *Experientia*, I, 51-52.

[696] ο Μωυσης αυτοις γεγονεν εξηγητης: "in which Moses has become their instructor..." The εξηγητης (exēgētēs) —from which *exegete*— was an interpreter of omens, oracles and dreams. *Contra Celsum* I, 26.

[697] The most complete recent investigation is Chancey's *The Myth of a Gentile Galilee* to which the reader is referred.

[698] Matthew 4:15.

[699] Isaiah 9:1.

[700] Compare John 4:9, for example.

[701] John 7:41-42, 52.

[702] *Curse Tablets and Binding Spells from the Ancient World*, 107.

Jewish practice forbids the destruction of any text in which the divine name has been written. Worn out scrolls were therefore retired to a storage area called a *geniza* which was located in or next to the synagogue.

way limited to apostate Jews, or to some religiously lax strata of Jewish society."[703]

The archaeological evidence suggests that extensive cross-pollination of magical belief and practice was the rule in the Mediterranean world of Jesus' day, examples of this mindset being the magical amulets written in Aramaic which have been recovered from various sites and the frequent presence of incantation bowls in what is now Iraq. In any event, it is certain that Jesus knew of and used common magical techniques because the gospels of Mark and John record them in some detail, and the connection between Palestine and Egypt, which the ancients regarded as the cradle of magic, had been strong for over 1000 years before the birth of Jesus. As noted by Johnston, "We increasingly realize that religious practices and ideas traveled fluidly across cultural boundaries; it profits the Assyriologist to compare notes with the Hellenist, the scholar of Judaism with the Egyptologist, and so on."[704]

The similarities between Jewish and Egyptian magic are often remarkable:

> The Egyptian word *heka*, which we translate as 'magic', was one of the forces which the creator-god had used in order to bring the world into existence. Creation was a development of the spoken word, and magic was the principle through which a spoken command was turned into reality, but magic could be achieved through acts and gestures as well as speech.[705]

As will become apparent in the following chapters, Jesus used "acts and gestures as well as speech" in the performance of his powerful works and the wording of his speech often finds striking parallels in both the Greek and Hebrew magical papyri recovered from Egyptian sites.

That the magical practices mentioned in the Old Testament continued in some form into the time of Jesus may be confirmed by various allusions in the New: veneration of the dead through the decoration of

---

[703] *Ancient Jewish Magic: A History*, 11.
[704] *Religions of the Ancient World: A Guide*, 142.
[705] *Religion and Magic in Ancient Egypt*, 283-284.

tombs[706] is an example and repetition of prayer a "magical" number of times —"When you pray, do not say the same thing over and over ..."[707] — is another. That the weight of sin can be lifted by the repetition of a prescribed number of Hail Mary's and Our Father's is an atavistic survival of this frankly magical notion.

Similarities between spells recorded in magical books and spells spoken by Jesus in the gospels are anything but coincidental. Conservation of wording is —and apparently has always been— considered vital for ritual activities. One need look no further than the familiar civic religion for an abundance of examples: even a child knows that the verses of national anthems must be sung in a certain order, that a pledge of allegiance must be recited with strict attention to the wording, that oath taking involves carefully repeated gestures and the repetition of a precise phraseology, that official bodies maintain a rigid decorum when being called into session, that flags are typically handled and flown according to exacting rules, and that any deviation from the above formulas somehow vitiates the performance. In short, inexact performance or utterance breaks the spell and deliberate perversion of the rite —the burning of flags, for example— is the civic equivalent of black magic.

---

[706] Matthew 23:27, 29.
[707] Matthew 6:7.

Chapter 7: Jesus the Magician

"...Jesus' opponents accused him of black magic, an accusation which stands as one of the most firmly established facts of the Gospel Tradition."[708] We know of this accusation because it is reported —*repeatedly*— by the gospels.[709]

Over two centuries after his death, Christian apologists were still defending Jesus against the charge of sorcery and according to the apocryphal Acts, likely composed in the early 3rd century, Jesus' followers were repeatedly accused of malicious magical practice. The culture of the ancient Middle East, in which magic was pervasive, can be linked to early Christianity, in which magic was very much at home, by a wonder-working apocalypic prophet from Nazareth of Galilee.

Even though the majority of Christian scholars refuse to regard Jesus as a magician, Crossan quite cheerfully applies that label to him:

> The more ordinary term for what they describe is *magician*, and I prefer to use it despite some obvious problems. The title *magician* is not used here as a pejorative word but describes one who can make divine power present *directly through personal miracle* rather than *indirectly through communal ritual*. Despite an extremely labile continuum between the twin concepts, magic renders transcendental power present concretely, physically, sensibly, tangibly, whereas ritual renders it present abstractly, ceremonially, liturgically, symbolically...[710]

...the angels began serving him

---

[708] *Biblica* 78: 357.
[709] Mark 3:22, 6:16, John 8:48, 52, 10:20, Matthew 9:34, 10:25, 12:24, 27.
  See also Stanton, *Gospel Truth: New Light on Jesus and the Gospels*, 156-163.
[710] *The Historical Jesus: The Life of a Mediterranean Jewish Peasant*, 138.

With the exception of the signs and wonders reported by the gospel of John, Jesus' miracles are predominantly exorcisms[711] and healings, and they begin almost immediately after his return from the wilderness:

> It happened in those days that Jesus came from Nazareth of Galilee and was baptized in the Jordan by John. And at once, while he was coming up out of the water, he saw the heavens being ripped open and the spirit descending into him like a dove. And a voice came out of the heavens: "You are my son, the beloved. In you was I pleased."
>
> At once the spirit drove him out into the desert,[712] and he was in the desert for forty days, being tempted by Satan and he was with the wild animals and the angels began serving him.[713]
>
> After John had been arrested, Jesus came into Galilee proclaiming the good news of God, saying, "The allotted time has run out and the kingdom of God has arrived! Repent and believe in the good news!"
>
> They came to Capernaum and as soon as the Sabbath came, he entered the synagogue[714] and taught. They were astounded by his teaching, for he was teaching them as one having authority and not like the scribes.
>
> Now in their synagogue there was a man with an unclean spirit[715] and he shouted out, "What have we to do with you, Jesus

---

[711] However much some would like to distance themselves from the Jesus of exorcisms, there is little doubt that they derive from the earliest layer of tradition. See Bell, *Deliver Us from Evil*, 87.

[712] ευθυς το πνευμα αυτον **εκβαλλει** εις την ερημον: "at once the spirit **drove** him **out** into the desert..."

The 'holy man' of antiquity was characterized by radical *withdrawal* —αναχωρησις (anachōrēsis)— which not only included physical self isolation, often by retiring into uninhabited desert areas, but also "cultivating a fringe status" through abandonment of family and regular employment. See Reimer, *Miracle and Magic*, 39, 63-65.

[713] οι αγγελοι **διηκουν** αυτον: "the angels **began serving** him."

[714] "A common feature of the Jewish synagogues of all periods is their use as places of healing..." *Ancient Jewish Magic. A History*, 314.

[715] "Often when quoting Mark, Luke —who seems to be writing to a predominately Gentile audience— changes the term *unclean spirit* (πνευμα ακαθαρτον) to "the more familiar Hellenic term δαιμονιον [demon, *my note*]...At 4:33, he changes Mark's 'unclean spirit' to 'spirit **of an unclean demon**' (πνευμα δαιμονιου ακαθαρτου)."

As additionally noted by Paige, πνευμα (pneuma), *spirit*, used for beings of intermediate rank, is a Jewish, not pagan, usage. *Harvard Theological Review* 95: 435.

The terminology of exorcism in Mark, "demonstrates a consistent modification of the vocabulary away from πνευμα ακαθαρτον [unclean spirit, *my note*] and toward δαιμονιον [demon, *my note*]." *Jesus and the Impurity of Spirits in the Synoptic Gospels*, 88.

of Nazareth? Did you come to destroy us? I know who you are! The Holy One of God!"

Jesus rebuked it,[716] saying, "Be silenced[717] and come out of him!" The unclean spirit convulsed him and screamed with a loud voice and came out of him.

They were all amazed and they were asking one another, "What is this? A new teaching with authority![718] He commands the unclean spirits and they obey him!" Immediately the report about him spread through all the surrounding region of Galilee.[719]

Exorcism and healing were central to Jesus' career. The first powerful work that Mark, the earliest gospel, records is an exorcism. Porterfield counts seventy-two instances in the canonical gospels; forty-one refer to specific cases, and in ten cases crowds of witnesses are mentioned. "These forty-one episodes involve a variety of different literary forms, an indication of their independent origins."[720] In short, Jesus' wonder-working activity is thoroughly attested and is a basic feature of his career which cannot simply be ignored by appeal to some larger meaning in his 'ministry.'

As recorded by Mark, the spirit which has descended —literally speaking— *into* Jesus immediately drives him out into the wilderness. The verb translated "drove him out" —εκβαλλω (ekballo)— is used of driving out unclean spirits in it very next occurrence.[721] The language used of Jesus' initiatory experience is the same as that used for spirit manipulation, and it is probably for that reason that both Matthew and Luke not only changed the verb, but even recast it in the passive voice when using Mark's account: ο Ιησους ανηχθη εις την

Compare Mark 1:23-27, Luke 4:33-3y; Mark 6:7, Luke 9:1; Mark 5:1-18, Luke 8:26-38; Mark 9:17-27, Luke 9:37-42.

[716] επετιμησεν αυτω ο Ιησους: "Jesus **rebuked** it..."

[717] φιμωθητι: "**Be silenced**..." The term is usually interpreted as 'silencing' —a φιμοκατοχον is "a charm to keep men and dogs silent" (Liddel & Scott, A Greek-English Lexicon, 1943)— but generally means to *restrict any unwanted action*, not just speech. The meaning here is "stop doing what you are doing" and come out of him. The unclean spirit hardly maintains silence; the very next sentence specifies that it "screamed with a loud voice."

[718] The authority to preach is based on exorcism, not formal preparation. As we have seen in a previous chapter, Jesus is declared a prophet as a result of performing miracles.

[719] Mark 1:9-15, 21-28.

[720] *Healing in the History of Christianity*, 20.

[721] Mark 1:34.

ερημον υπο του πνευματος: "Jesus **was led up** into the desert by the spirit" (Matthew 4:1); και ηγετο εν τω πνεματι εν τω ερημω: "and he **was led** by the spirit into the desert" (Luke 4:1).

> Certainly this Pneuma of God is no innocuous spirit. According to Mark i.12, the Spirit 'drove him out' into the desert...In Matt. and Luke the miraculous experience of Jesus on this occasion is tuned down: Jesus is 'conducted by the Spirit'...[722]

However, even this change does not manage to erase the magical vocabulary. Jesus "was led" by the spirit —the verb is αγω, *lead*— even as "speechless idols" once led the Corinthians into error: ηγεσθε απαγομενοι:"**you were led**" astray.[723] An erotic *spell of attraction*, an αγωγη (agōgē), is designed to *lead* or *drive* the desired person toward the beneficiary of the spell. The term αγωγη can also mean "forcible seizure, carrying off, abduction."[724]

It is little wonder that Matthew and Luke saw fit to change the text of Mark, which has the spirit descending *into* Jesus: το πνευμα ως περιστεραν καταβαινον εις αυτον, "the spirt descending like a dove **into** him."[725] Matthew changed the preposition to επι, *upon*,[726] as did Luke.[727] Stevan Davies, who argues that Jesus' miracles were the result of possession, nevertheless appears to concede that Jesus' exact relationship to the spirit is a matter of interpretation: "The evangelists do not frequently make the forthright claim that Jesus was possessed by the spirit of God."[728]

The descent of birds as proof of connection with supernatural forces is known from the magical texts: the descent of a falcon is a "sign"[729] that the magician has been heard. In another formula, spoken to the

---

[722] Eitrem, *Some Notes on the Demonology in the New Testament*, 65.
[723] 1 Corinthians 12:2.
[724] Liddel & Scott, *A Greek English Lexicon*, 18.
[725] Mark 1:10.
[726] Matthew 3:16: το πνευμα...ερχομενον επ' αυτον: "the spirt...alighting **on** him."
[727] Luke 3:22: το πνευμα...επ' αυτον: "the spirt...**upon** him."
[728] *Jesus the Healer*, 65.
[729] σημειον: a "sign..." *Papyri Graecae Magicae* I, 65.
    This is the preferred term for wonder-working in the gospel of John.

sun, the sign that he has been heard is the descent of "a falcon onto the tree."[730]

> After saying these things three times, there will be this sign of divine communion —but you, armed by having a magical soul, do not be afraid— for a falcon from the sea swoops down and strikes your form with its wings indicating you should arise... say, "I have been united with your holy form, I have been empowered by your holy name."[731]

Semitic people of the Middle East regarded the desert and mountain peaks as the natural homes of demons.[732] "In Egypt, all things associated with the liminal world of the frontier or periphery were demonized."[733] The "howling creatures" that fill the ruins of Babylon, where shepherds refuse to graze their flocks,[734] reappear in the Qumran scrolls where "they are taken as names for some kind of demon,[735] and the לילית (lilith) that will inhabit the ruins of Edom along with wild animals[736] is widely regarded as a reference to a night demon. On Atonement Day, the High Priest will take two goats, one for sacrifice to Yahweh, and another, upon which the sins of the people are confessed, for עזאזל (azazel). The goat for Azazel is then led "into the wilderness" by a man who must subsequently bathe and wash his clothing before rejoining the people.[737] Given this Old Testament background, where better to meet the Prince of Darkness face to face than the desert wilderness where the eerie silence is broken only by the moaning of the wind and the cries of nocturnal birds and beasts?

The association of demons and wild animals is a feature of the magical texts. Regarding the multiple functions of a 'magical assistant,' the spellbook promises, "he sets [you] free from many evil demons and he stops wild beasts..."[738] Although "demons and wild animals" —δαιμονας και θηρας— are linked in the papyri, the nature of the con-

---

[730] τω ιεραξ επι το δενδρον: "the falcon onto the tree." *Papyri Graecae Magicae* III, 273.

[731] *Papyri Graecae Magicae* IV, 209-217.

[732] *Chaldean Magic: Its Origin and Development*, 31.

[733] *Magic and Ritual in the Ancient World*, 258.

[734] Isaiah 13:20-21.

[735] Alexander, *The Dead Sea Scrolls After Fifty Years*, II, 335.

[736] Isaiah 34:14.

[737] Leviticus 16:8-26.

[738] *Papyri Graecae Magicae* I, 116.

nection is not specified. It is possible that vicious wild animals were regarded as demons embodied, or that *beast* was a synonym for *demon*.[739]

The שדים (shedim), the *demons* of the Old Testament, are false gods,[740] but other entities operate in a gray zone of supernatural cause and effect. The infamous שטן (satan), *Satan*, sometimes appears to be the shadow side of Yahweh, "an objectification of the dark side of God."[741] In one place we are informed that Yahweh incited David to take a census,[742] but in another, that it was Satan,[743] and the angel sent to thwart the prophet Balaam is also a "satan" or *opposer*.[744] Ehrenreich points to an impressive series of correlations between carniverous animals and carnivore deities, citing "Jehovah's furious appetite for animal offerings and his obsessive demands for foreskins, which may have been a substitute for human sacrificial victims" as one of various examples.[745]

Modern people, conditioned by countless depictions of *putti*, the pudgy cupids which reappear in the classical revival of the Quattrocento, have lost touch with the understanding of spirit entities that existed in antiquity. Christianity corrupted the term *demon*, giving it a permanent connotation of evil, a tactically useful move since Christians could then condemn pagan oracles and healing shrines "without addressing the issue of their efficacy."[746] *Angel* —αγγελος (angelos)— has been similarly distorted from its original sense. In classical Greek, the word *angel* meant simply *messenger*, and the related αγγελια (angelia), *report* or *message*.

In Greek culture, a person's *daemon* functioned in much the same way as the modern guardian angel.[747] A δαιμων (daimōn) was basically a

---

[739] For demons as "wild animals" see Williams, *Journal of Theological Studies* 57: 42-56.

Werline: "Mark seems to suggest that Jesus has now entered into an ancient mythic struggle between God and the demonic monsters of chaos...a hostile cosmos filled with menacing forces has sprung into existence." *Experientia*, I, 62.

[740] Deuteronomy 32:17, Psalms 106:37.

[741] *The Dead Sea Scrolls After Fifty Years*, II, 342.

[742] 2 Samuel 24:1.

[743] 1 Chronicles 21:1.

[744] Numbers 22:32.

[745] *Blood Rites*, 73.

[746] *Fallen Angels and the History of Judaism and Christianity*, 181.

[747] In the context of theurgy, *demons* were creative powers which emanated from the gods. *Iamblichus. De mysteriis*, 82-83.

spirit, and the δαιμονια [demons, *my note*] were a class of "divine in-termediaries" which could be good or bad and could include ghosts.[748]

The term *angel* still has a fairly wide application even in the New Tes-tament. Paul, for example, refers to an undisclosed physical malady as "an angel of Satan,"[749] and some early Christians advocated the wor-ship of angels, in all probability in the role of intercessors, a function now fulfilled in some Christian sects by saints.[750] As "an intermediary between the worlds of gods and men," even the chthonic goddess Hecate is repeatedly called an "angel."[751] Gerhard Kittel, noting the frequent use of angel in Greek magical curse tablets, says, "There are chthonic as well as heavenly αγγελοι ["angels," *my note*]."[752] In short, there is no firm distinction between angels, spirits, and demons in the magical texts, and angel and spirit are interchangeable categories in the New Testament: "Who makes his angels spirits and his ministers flames of fire."[753]

Of the angels that appeared to Jesus in the wilderness we are told:

> Then the Devil departed and, Look! angels came and began to serve him.[754]

The angels in question first appear after Jesus has been challenged by Satan to perform magic, transforming stones into bread and flying into the air. It is only after Jesus asserts his *own* authority that the angels come and begin to serve him. To this Luke adds the specific content of the temptation, using the vocabulary of magic:

> Leading him up, the Devil showed him all the kingdoms of man-kind in a flash, and the Devil said to him, "I will give you all this

---

[748] Paige, *Harvard Theological Review* 95: 427.

[749] αγγελος σατανα: "an **angel** of Satan" (2 Corinthians 12:7).

[750] Colossians 2:18.

[751] *The Rotting Goddess*, 22.

[752] *Theological Dictionary of the New Testament*, I, 75.

[753] Hebrews 1:7.

[754] Matthew 4:11: ιδου αγγελοι προσηλθον και διηκονουν αυτω: "Look! Angels came and **began to serve** him."

Following Young, I have construed the tense as an example of the inceptive im-perfect. *Intermediate New Testament Greek*, 115.

authority[755] and all their glory because it has been handed over to me[756] and I give it to whoever I wish.[757]

The New Testament reflects an assumption that worldly wealth and power is under the control of demonic forces —the chthonic god Pluto is called πλουτοδοτης (ploutodotēs) "giver of riches"[758] because precious metals come from his subterranean realm. When a boy plagued by a demon successfully repels it by means of a magical ring, the demon cries out, "Take away the ring...and I will give you all the world's silver and gold!"[759] The notion that a man might sell his soul to the Devil in exchange for supernatural power was well known in antiquity.[760]

After the angels began to serve him, "Jesus returned to Galilee in the power of the spirit[761] and word of him spread through all the surrounding region."[762] Who these angels were can be further confirmed from the Hebrew spell book, the *Sepher Ha-Razim*. Although it was composed at least three centuries after the death of Jesus, it is likely to contain material which is similar if not identical to the spells and adjurations of Jesus' day: "The intense conservatism of magic, the theory being that formulae and rituals retain their virtue only if reproduced without deviation, is a well-documented fact...there would appear to be grounds for reading back (with due caution) the later material into the earlier period."[763]

Supernatural magical assistants are always referred to as "angels" in the magical formulas of the *Sepher Ha-Razim*; reading this text back into the context of the 1st century provides an important clue to the identity of the angels that began to serve Jesus after his test in the wilderness. Various angels are also known from the Greek magical papyri, clearly imported there from Jewish spell books since they bear Hebrew names

---

[755] την **εξουσιαν** ταυτην απασαν...: "all this **authority**..."
[756] εμοι **παραδεδοται**...: "it **has been handed over** to me..."
[757] Luke 4:5-6.
[758] Liddel & Scott, *A Greek-Enlish Lexicon*, 1423.
[759] *Testament of Solomon* I, 12.
[760] Dickie, *Byzantine Magic*, 77.
[761] εν τη **δυναμει** του **πνευματος**: "...in the power of the spirit..."
[762] Luke 4:14.
[763] *History of the Jewish People in the Age of Jesus Christ*, III, Part 1: 344, 345.

such as Michael and Gabriel.[764] A gold tablet, found in 1544 among the grave goods in a tomb, was engraved with the names of Michael, Gabriel, Raphael and Ouriel, "the standard archangelic tetrarchy... widely found in Jewish and Christian literature and in magical texts..."[765]

The only specifically magical documents roughly contemporaneous with the time of Jesus are the magical papyri, preserved in Egypt by the vicissitudes of geography and weather, and brought to light by excavations over the past century or so. The surviving specimens, handbooks of magical technique that consist of spells and instructions for casting them, are written in Greek or Coptic, or a mixture of both, and occasionally in Hebrew.[766] Against the argument that the papyri were written too late to truly reflect the time of Jesus, I would offer this observation by Joshua Trachtenberg:

> However unorthodox in principle, magic is perhaps the most tradition-bound of cultural forms...As we have had occasion to note, magic is the most conservative of disciplines —like the law it clings to archaic forms long after they have lost currency.[767]

It is now recognized that "many magical texts can now be assigned to relatively early periods (ca. second century B.C. to early first A.D.)"[768]

As previously mentioned, *angel* and *spirit* are not carefully distinguished in the New Testament. Philip, for example, hears a message "from an angel of the Lord" which is apparently the same as "the spirit."[769] In the case of Mary, *holy spirit* appears to be synonymous with *power*.[770] The Pharisees ask concerning Paul, "What if a spirit or angel spoke to him?"[771] In Acts it would appear that "the holy spirit" has become identified with "the spirit of Jesus."[772] To further the confusion, peo-

---

[764] Such as Γαβριελ πρωταγγελε: "Gabriel, first among angels" *Papyri Graecae Magicae* I, 300-305.

See also Lesses, *Harvard Theological Review* 89: 41-60.

[765] *Greek Magical Amulets*, 26.

[766] In addition to the papyri are amulets (*lamellae*) of gold and silver, gem stones, and engraved lead tablets (*tabellae defixionum*) which preserve magical images and text.

[767] *Jewish Magic and Superstition*, 75, 81.

[768] Kotansky, *Greek Magical Amulets*, xvii.

[769] Acts 8:26, 29.

[770] Luke 1:35.

[771] Acts 23:9.

[772] Acts 16:6-7.

ple are not only struck mute by demons[773] but by an angel in the case of Zechariah,[774] and stricken by a loathesome disease in the case of Herod.[775] From Herod's point of view the angel would undoubtedly have been 'demonic.'

As Georg Luck observes, "An essential part of the magician's training consisted in acquiring a *paredros* (παρεδρος, *my note*), i.e. an 'assistant' (daemon). This acquisition is a step toward complete initiation..."[776] Morton Smith: "the report that after the temptation the angels served Jesus attributes to him the success magicians strove for —to be served by supernatural beings."[777] "After the gods, the παρεδροι (plural of παρεδρος, *my note*) are most frequently identified as αγγελοι (angels, *my note*) and δαιμονες (demons, *my note*) of an unspecified character. These two types of beings occur frequently in the Greek magical papyri."[778] Παρεδρος (paredros), *associate*, is equivalent to the Latin *famulus* and the English *familiar* (spirit).

Joshua Trachtenberg:

> The peculiar rôle of the angels, heavenly counterparts of all earthly phenomena, as well as the direct servants and emissaries of God, closest to His ear, rendered powerful indeed the man who possessed the secret of bending them to his will.[779]

A curious term, ευπαρεδρος (euparedros), which is translated "undivided devotion" in the *Revised Standard Version*, is found in 1 Corinthians 7:35. Regarding the word, Morton Smith remarked,

> Such a "familiar"—to use the old English term—might play a role in the magician's life not dissimilar to that of "the spirit" in Paul's. That Paul recognized the similarity is shown by his recommendation of celibacy on the ground that it would free the

---

[773] Mark 9:17.
[774] Luke 1:20.
[775] Acts 12:23.
[776] Luck, *Witchcraft and Magic in Europe: Ancient Greece and Rome*, 108.
[777] *Jesus the Magician*, 105.
[778] Leda Jean Ciraolo, *Ancient Magic and Ritual Power*, 283. Ciraolo's "Supernatural Assistants in the Greek Magical Papyri" is an invaluable resource.
[779] *Jewish Magic and Superstition*, 25.
For further comments on angels as assistants to initiated magicians, see Graf, *Magic in the Ancient World*, 90-91, 117.

Christian from distractions and make him *euparedros* for the Lord —well suited to be joined to Jesus as a *paredros*. In modern terms, the lack of normal sexual satisfaction is likely to lead to compensatory connections with spirits, hence the requirement of celibacy by many shamanistic and priestly groups.[780]

...astounded by his teaching

The nature of Jesus' "teaching" in this case must be defined within the context of his actions: today we expect enlightenment to result from teaching, but the most frequently documented reaction of the villagers of Jesus' day was fear and amazement: και εξεπλησσοντο επι τη διδαχη αυτου: "and **they were astounded** by his teaching."[781] Davies notes the "state of near conceptual chaos regarding the message of Jesus the Teacher," noting that New Testament experts who examine the content of Jesus' message "end up with something, every time, but something different, every one."[782]

Davies regards Jesus as a healer intermittently possessed by another persona, the "spirit of God." While his book, *Jesus the Healer*, is full of interesting insights, Davies flatly denies that Jesus practiced magic: "Jesus' reported use of ad hoc placebo devices such as spitting and the application of mud is not magic."[783] I do not believe that Davies makes the case that the procedures used by Jesus were "ad hoc," or that they functioned as "placebos." There was nothing ad hoc about the use of spittle; it was universal magical praxis, and to exchange "placebo" for "magic" does no more than switch terms. To say that "placebos work" —and it is clear that they do— is no more enlightening than to say "magic works." If people were not convinced magic worked, they would not have performed it since time immemorial.

Paul, the chief spokesman for proto-orthodox Christianity, apparently cared little and knew less about Jesus' ethical teaching. Indeed, as we will see in another chapter, he built his house churches not upon the 'message' of Jesus, which he scarcely mentions, but on practices of

---

[780] *Harvard Theological Review* 73: 244.
[781] Mark 1:22, 27, 2:12, 4:41, etc.
[782] *Jesus the Healer*, 13-15.
[783] Ibid, 104.

spirit possession, specifically possession by Jesus' spirit.[784] At the level of the most primitive tradition 'teaching' and 'prophecy' are tightly linked to the performance of magic.

It is clear from the papyri that successful works of magic resulted in amazement: ην και δοκιμασας θαυμασεις το παραδοξον της οικονομιας ταυτης: "once you have tested it, **you will be amazed** by the marvel of this magical operation."[785] Once the "magical characters"[786] have been put to use the magician is assured, "you will be astounded."[787] The reaction to New Testament magic is typically amazement[788] and fear,[789] as is the case with pagan magic: "and you will be amazed."[790] As noted by Daniel and Maltomini, "stressing the astonishing efficacy of recipes is a common feature both in magical and in medical texts. θαυμαζω and its derivatives are the words usually employed..."[791] The amazing efficacy of its miracle-working was the boast of early Christianity. For the primitive church, miracle was the guarantor of truth. Beginning at the latest with the book of Acts, Christian writers brag non-stop about the power of Christian versus pagan magic.

Jesus' actions everywhere conform to those of a magician. "In Mark 1:24 the demon cries out to Christ, 'I know who you are' continuing with the holy name as proof of recognition. This is a magical formula well attested in the [magical] papyri...This is similar to the girl with the oracular spirit in Acts 16.17 who greets Paul and his friends with the warning exclamation, 'These men are servants of the most high God' just before the spirit is exorcized."[792] Naomi Janowitz: "In the first centuries in order to unmask a daimon and drive it from somebody's body the officiant himself had to have more-than-human status ...Divine names...function similarly to signatures and signature guarantees in our culture, which are understood to be legally binding

---

[784] As at Galatians 4:6-7, for example.

[785] *Papyri Graecae Magicae* IV, 233.

[786] οι χαρακτηρες (charaktēres): "the **magical characters**," in reference to a magical sigil-like symbol, χαρακτηρ (charaktēr), a *character* incised into metal or written on papyrus.

[787] εκπλαγησει: "you will be astounded..." *Papyri Graecae Magicae* VII, 921.

[788] Matthew 9:33; Luke 5:26; Acts 13:12.

[789] Mark 4:41; Acts 19:17.

[790] και θαυμασεις : "and **you will be amazed**..." *Papyri Graecae Magicae* XXX-VI, 76.

[791] *Supplementum Magicum* II, 134.

[792] Hull, *Hellenistic Magic and the Synoptic Tradition*, 67-68.

representations."[793] "…the names are the source of power by which human beings can enforce their will upon the gods or angels."[794]

The gospels are clear that Jesus' authority to preach *as a layman* is based on *exorcism and healing*, not formal preparation. As noted previously, the crowd declares Jesus to be a prophet *after* he performs signs. As Jesus himself said of his public, "Unless you see signs and wonders, you will never believe."[795]

Some have interpreted Jesus' extended time in the wilderness as having shamanistic overtones consistent with a vision quest, but due caution should be exercised in this regard; there is no evidence for an exact equivalent of shamans in the Middle East.[796] Nevertheless, as Lewis notes, shamans are 'masters of spirits'[797] and the Jesus of the gospels is nothing if not a master of spirits.

…with authority

Mark tells us that Jesus taught with "authority" and "not like the scribes." The scribes were a highly literate class charged with both copying and interpreting the laws of Moses and they worked to be self-supporting so as to impose no financial burden on the population. They were the men to whom questions of religious observance might be referred, and they were deeply respected, a fact indirectly acknowledged in Mark.[798] It is not possible that they had *no authority*.

The word Mark uses for *authority* is εξουσια (exousia); it refers particularly to "the belief that some people have supernatural powers as a gift."[799] In Jesus' case the accounts make clear that the authority in question had nothing whatever to do with interpreting the laws of Moses. Jesus had the power to command demonic spirits. Hull notes that of the ten instances of εξουσια in Mark, only one is *not* connected

---

[793] *Magic in the Roman World*, 36, 40.
[794] Lesses, *Harvard Theological Review* 89: 52.
[795] John 4:48.
[796] *Magic and Magicians in the Greco-Roman World*, 13.
[797] *Ecstatic Religion*, 56.
[798] Mark 12:38.
[799] Luck, *Witchcraft and Magic*, 99.
  Significantly, Satan offered Jesus εξουσια, "authority," which Jesus refused (Luke 4:6).

with exorcism or healing, and concludes, "The people do not admire Jesus for his learning but for his power over the demons."[800] Mark himself clearly defines what the *authority* in question meant: "He *commands* the unclean spirits and they *obey* him." François Lenormant: "the sorcerer...subjected the demons to his orders."[801]

Some of the methods by which Jesus commands obedience from unclean spirits are revealed in this account of an exorcism:

> After he got out of the boat, immediately he encountered a man controlled by an unclean spirit coming out of the tombs. He lived among the tombs since no one was able to bind him even with a chain. He had been bound with chains and shackles many times, but he snapped the chains apart and broke the shackles in pieces, and no one was strong enough to restrain him.[802]
>
> He screamed day and night in the tombs and in the hills, lacerating himself with stones.
>
> When he saw Jesus from far away, he ran and fell at his feet and screamed out in a loud voice, "What have I to do with you, Jesus, son of the Most High God? I beg you in God's name do not torture me!"
>
> Because Jesus had said to it, "Come out of the man, unclean spirit!" and asked him, "What is your name?"
>
> He said, "Legion is my name, because we are many."[803] He entreated him not to banish them from the region. There was a large herd of pigs grazing on the hill and the demons begged him, saying, "Send us into the pigs so that we can enter them." He gave them permission and the unclean spirits came out and entered the pigs and the herd of about two thousand pigs stampeded over the cliff and into the sea and drowned in the sea.[804]

---

[800] Hull, *Hellenistic Magic*, 165. The exceptional use of εξουσια is found in Mark 13:34, where the reference is apocalyptic.

[801] *Chaldean Magic: Its Origin and Development*, 60.

[802] ουδεις εδυνατο αυτον **δησαι**: "no one was able **to restrain** him..." (Mark 5:3). See below for discussion of the term δεω. The failure to "bind" the man may imply previous failed exorcisms as well as broken physical restraints.

[803] Horsley: "the ancient hearers of the Gospel, painfully aware of how they had been subjected by Roman military forces, would have recognized the identity of the demon immediately as 'Roman Legion,' i.e., a 'battalion' of Roman troops who were known to have wrought extreme violence against subjected peoples." *Experientia*, I, 55-56.

[804] Mark 5:2-13.

Mark's account has a number of points in common with the manipulation of demons and ghosts described in ancient sources —that the demons in question may have included ghosts is suggested by the report that the afflicted man "lived among the tombs."

The exorcisms of the New Testament are nearly identical in many details with an exorcism described by Lucian:

> Everyone knows of the Syrian from Palestine, the master of his art, and how he receives many moonstruck, frothing at the mouth and eyes rolling, and he sets them aright and sends them away sound of mind...standing beside them as they lie there, he asks from whence [the demons] have come into the body. The madman himself is silent, but the demon answers in Greek or barbarian from whence and how he entered the man. By adjuring, or if the spirit does not obey, threatening, he drives out the demon.[805]

The "Syrian from Palestine" is a Jewish exorcist.

The imagery of magically binding demons is very old. Regarding binding and the imagery of knots, Lenormant described this procedure: "...next he holds over this symbolical image a cord which he has prepared with this intention, making a knot in it to signify that he is acting with resolution and persistence, that at the moment when he spat he made a compact with the demon who acted as his associate in the operation..."[806]

The reference to a person as "demon-possessed"[807] is well known from the magical papyri: "If you say the name to the demon-possessed while putting sulfur and asphalt under his nose, instantly [the demon] will speak and go away..."[808]

---

[805] *The Lover of Lies*, 16.

[806] *Chaldean Magic*, 63.

[807] θεωρουσιν τον **δαιμονιζομενον** καθημενον: "they saw **the demon-possessed man** sitting..." (Mark 5:15).

[808] εαν **δαιμονιζομενω** ειπης το ονομα: "if you say the name **to the demon-possessed**..." *Papyri Graecae Magicae* XIII, 243-244.

The threat of torture[809] is also known from the magical papyri: "god of gods, king of kings, now compel a kindly demon, a giver of oracles, to come to me lest even more severe tortures be applied..."[810] "Accomplish what has been written here, demon, and after you have finished it, I will offer a sacrifice to you, but if you hesitate, I will heap upon you punishments you cannot endure..."[811]

...names to conjure with

The demand that the demon tell its name is standard magical procedure: "The invocation of angelic names in Jewish magic may be regarded as in part the parallel to the pagan invocation of many deities, and in part as invocation of the infinite (personified) phases and energies of the one God. Both Jewish and pagan magic agreed in requiring the accumulation of as many names of the deity or demon as possible, for fear lest no one name exhaust the potentiality of the spiritual being conjured."[812] The names of spirit entities are central to magical working, they function as "the reservoir of heavenly power."[813]

It is of interest that healing and raising people from the dead also involves calling them by name. Several examples can be cited, that of Aeneas, a paralytic,[814] Tabitha, who is dead,[815] and particularly, Lazarus.[816] In the case of Lazarus, who has been dead for four days, the miracle raises not only a corpse, but an interesting question: to whom or to what is the command to come forth addressed? To the body, which has begun to decay?[817] The soul? A ghost? A tentative answer to this question is proposed in Chapter 9.

The casting of the demons into a herd of swine represents another common magical procedure involving the transfer of an evil spirit into

---

[809] ορκιζω σε τον θεον μη με βασανισης: "I beg you in God's name **do not torture me!**" (Mark 5:7).

[810] ινα μη εις χειρονας βασανους ελθω: "lest even **more severe tortures be applied...**" *Papyri Graecae Magicae* II, 53-55.

[811] *Papyri Graecae Magicae* IV, 2095-2098.

[812] *Jewish Magic and Superstition*, 86-87.

[813] *Harvard Theological Review* 89: 52.

[814] Acts 9:33-34.

[815] Acts 9:40.

[816] John 11:43.

[817] John 11:17, 39.

an inanimate object or living subject, a technique sometimes known in the literature as *envoûtement*. "Sumerian incantations against evil demons describe how an animal, usually a goat or pig, was offered as a substitute for the sick person. The purpose of the ritual was the transference of the disease or demon from the man to the animal…the demon was conjured to leave him and take possession of the animal instead."[818]

…the centurion's boy

We are given some further insight into the nature of Jesus' authority by the story of the centurion's slave boy.

> As he entered Capernaum, a centurion came to him, entreating him, "Lord, my boy is lying at home paralyzed, suffering terribly."
>
> Jesus said to him, "I will come and heal him."
>
> The centurion replied, "Lord, I am not worthy for you to step under my roof, but say a word and my boy will be healed. For I too am a man with authority, having soldiers under my command, and I say to this one, "Go!" and he goes, and to another, "Come!" and he comes, and to my slave, "Do this!" and he does it."[819]

The point of the story is that the centurion intuitively understands Jesus' command of the spirits to be the same as his command of his soldiers,[820] and for this insight is rewarded with the healing of his boy. The wording of the pericope of the centurion and his boy is nearly identical to that of the Greek magical papyri: τω δουλω μου ποιησον τουτο και ποιει: "to my slave, '**Do this,' and he does it**" and λεγε αυτω ποιησον τουτο το εργον και ποιει παραυτα: "say to him, "**Do this task, and he does it** immediately…""[821] Or the following example:

---

[818] Marie-Louise Thomsen, *Witchcraft and Magic in Europe: Biblical and Pagan Societies*, 71-72.

[819] Matthew 8:5-9.

[820] Compare Matthew 26:53. Jesus can say the word and summon 12 legions of angels, 72,000! Elijah enjoyed similar angelic support in the form of heavenly armies (2 Kings 6:16-17).

[821] *Papyri Graecae Magicae*, I, 182.

No spirit of the air that is joined to a powerful assistant will draw back into Hades, for all things are subordinate to him, and if you wish to do something, merely speak his name into the air and say, "Come!" and you will see him standing near you. Say to him "Do this task," and he does it immediately, and having done it, he will ask, "What else do you wish, for I am hurrying into the sky." If you have no orders at that moment, tell him, "Go, Lord," and he will leave. In this way the god will be seen by you alone, nor will anyone except you alone hear his voice when he speaks.[822]

The text of Matthew reflects nearly identical imagery from the *Sepher Ha-Razim*: "...to declare the names of the overseers of each and every firmament...and what are the names of their attendants...and to rule over spirits and over demons, to send them (wherever you wish) so they will go out like slaves..."[823] Jennings and Liew conclude:

What is stunning is that both the centurion and the Pharisees are basically embracing the same assumptions: authority works only *within* chains of command. Just as a centurion can order the coming and going of soldiers and servants under his command, the ruler of demons can cast out demons under its rule. What then is the centurion implying about Jesus' identity? He believes that Jesus can order the coming and going of the demon that has been "torturing" his boy-love with paralysis, because he believes that Jesus is the commander or the ruler of that and other demons. In other words, not only are the centurion and the Pharisees in agreement about how authority operates, they further concur on the identity of Jesus as a commanding officer in the chain of demonic beings.[824]

"My boy," could also be translated "my servant," or even "my boyfriend." Luke completely recasts this story, inserting Jewish elders who make the plea on the centurion's behalf, and friends who speak for the centurion himself, thereby destroying the immediacy of Jesus' interaction with the centurion and his slave boy, who, as Gentiles, are ceremonially unclean. Nevertheless, one wonders, since Luke was writing *to* Gentiles, if there might have been another motivation. Luke also

---

[822] *Papyri Graecae Magicae* II,179-189.

[823] *Sepher Ha-Razim*, 17-18.

[824] *Journal of Biblical Literature* 123: 485-486. The article from which the citation is taken contains a complete discussion of the homoerotic possibilities of the text.

redescribes the boy as a "slave" (7:2) who was "precious" to the centurion (7:7), a valuation usually interpreted as merely financial. In John's account, the centurion becomes a "royal official," and the enigmatic boy is variously described as his "son" (4:46), as "my child" (4:49), and "his boy" (4:51). None of these accounts entirely succeed in clearing up the relationship between the centurion and his boy.

The word παιδιον (paidion) used of the enigmatic boy carried sexual connotations, and homosexual relations with slaves were apparently common. As noted by MacDonald, "Male and female slaves were quite simply sexually available to their masters at all times—whether children, adolescents or adults—and also available to those to whom their owners granted rights...In essence, a slave was excluded from the very category of manhood, perpetually retaining—despite his physical characteristics—the character of a child."[825] The slave, along with women and boys, is in "a catchall category that might best be labeled *unmen*..."[826]

In his classic study of childhood, deMause sketches the situation:

> The child in antiquity lived his earliest years in an atmosphere of sexual abuse...Boy brothels flourished in every city, and one could even contract for the use of a rent-a-boy service in Athens ...men kept slaves boys to abuse, so that even freeborn children saw their fathers sleeping with boys. Children were sometimes sold into concubinage.[827]

The story and its redaction give us a nearly perfect example both of the ambiguity of the Greek vocabulary and of the editing and rephrasing to which the New Testament material has been subjected. In any case it is clear that even if the *Sitz im Leben* of the story has been blurred, the point made about authority is retained.

...the stronger overcomes

---

[825] *New Testament Studies* 53: 95, 106.
   MacDonald also points out that from a Christian perspective *total* obedience of children and slaves was expected (Colossians 3:20, 22).
[826] Anderson and Moore, *New Testament Masculinities*, 69.
[827] *The History of Childhood*, 43.

The notion that superior authority encompasses the idea of superior strength agrees entirely with Jesus' own characterization of exorcism: the strong are overcome and bound by the stronger:

"How can Satan cast out Satan? If a kingdom divides against itself, that kingdom cannot stand, and if a house divides against itself, that house will not be able to stand. So if Satan rises up against himself and becomes divided, he cannot stand. To the contrary, his end has come."

"No one can enter the strong man's house[828] to plunder his possessions unless he first binds the strong man, and then he plunders his house."[829]

The claim being made is that Jesus is stronger than "the strong man," able to bind him and take away his possessions.[830] On this passage Grundmann commented:

The mission of Christ means that the ισχυτερος ["stronger," *my note*] comes, that he binds the ισχυρος ["strong"] when he has entered his house, and that He robs him of his spoil. This is how the exorcisms are to be understood.[831]

As Susan Garrett notes in connection with the metaphor of plunder, "whenever Jesus exorcises or heals, he takes spoil from Satan's kingdom and adds it to God's own...he as 'the stronger one' is entering and plundering the domain of the conquered Satan."[832] The gospels consistently represent Jesus as operating from a position of superior strength in regard to demons. Samson Eitrem: "The exorcist mentioned by Mark, ix.38-39, introduced the very name of Jesus into the stock of ισχυρα ονοματα ["powerful names," *my note*] and formulae which he—like other Jewish conjurors—probably had at his command for the expulsion of demons...This indeed very surprising concession on the part of the Lord implied that his ονομα ["name," my note] worked *ex opere operato*, like other 'strong names' of traditional

---

[828] την οικιαν του ισχυρου: "the **strong man's** house..." Regarding ισχυρος (ischuros), *mighty one*, as a description of a demon, compare εγω ειμι ο ακεφαλος δαιμων ισχυρος ο εχων το πυρ το αθανατον: "I am the headless demon...the mighty one who has the unquenchable fire..." *Papyri Graecae Magicae* V, 146-147.
[829] Mark 3:23-27.
[830] Compare Matthew 3:11, "The one coming after me is *stronger* than I..."
[831] *Theological Dictionary of the New Testament*, III, 401.
[832] *The Demise of the Devil*, 45.

magic."[833] The story of the Jewish conjuror, with its implication that Jesus' name *worked like magic*, was carefully omittted by Matthew and Luke. To the objection that these gospel accounts may not be literally historical, Reimer notes that accounts[834] of exorcists using Jesus' name "actually represents the rapid spread of a potentially powerful name or technique in activities such as exorcism."[835]

In keeping with his authority, the gospels speak of Jesus *rebuking* demons. The verb in question, επιτιμαω (epitimaō), is variously translated *rebuke*, *warn*, *reprimand*, or *reprove*, and it is used not only for exorcism, but for healing and for the performance of weather magic. In addition to demons,[836] Jesus "rebukes" the wind,[837] a fever,[838] and the apostle Peter —where the wording, "Get away from me, Satan,"[839] has the character of an exorcism. Horsley argues that the "term signifies something far stronger than a 'rebuke,' something more like 'vanquish' or 'destroy'"[840] and the question of the demons, "Have you come to destroy us?"[841] certainly supports that conclusion.

...the techniques

A brief account in the gospel of Mark reveals some additional magical elements of Jesus' healing technique:

> They brought a deaf mute[842] to him and they entreated him to lay his hand upon him. Taking him away from the crowd to a

---

[833] *Some Notes on the Demonology in the New Testament*, 4-5.

[834] Specifically Luke 9:49-50.

[835] *Miracle and Magic*, 75, note 81.

[836] **επετιμησεν** δε ο Ιησους τω πνευματι τω ακαθαρτω και ιασατο τον παιδια: "Jesus **rebuked** the unclean spirit and the boy was healed." Luke 9:42 (Compare Luke 4:41).

    Howard Kee emphasizes the notion of exorcism *as subjugation by force*, as in Mark 3:27. *New Testament Studies* 14: 232-246.

[837] και διεγερθεις **επετιμησεν** τω ανεμω: "and arising, he **rebuked** the wind." Mark 4:39.

[838] **επετιμησεν** τω πυρετω και αφηκεν αυτην: "he **rebuked** the fever and it left her." Luke 4:39.

[839] **επετιμησεν** Πετρω και λεγει **υπαγε οπισω μου σατανα**: "he rebuked Peter and said, 'Get away from me, Satan!'" Mark 8:33. Compare the language of Matthew 4:10: λεγει αυτω ο Ιησους **υπαγε σατανα**: "Jesus said to him, '**Get away, Satan!**'"

[840] *Experientia*, I, 53.

[841] Mark 1:24.

[842] Mute because the demon possessing him is mute (Matthew 9:32, Luke 11:14).

private place, he put his fingers in his ears, spit, and touched his tongue, and looking up into the sky, he groaned[843] and said, "Ephphatha!" that is, "Be opened!"

Instantly his ears were opened, and the bond that held his tongue was loosed[844] and he spoke normally.[845]

The several steps in this healing ritual —"he put his fingers in his ears, spit, and touched his tongue, and looking up into the sky, he groaned"— find very close parallels with similar rituals in the magical papyri: "Facing the sun, speak seven times into your hand, and spit once, and stroke your face..."[846] We note a similar observation on Egyptian magical procedure: "The healer would sometimes accompany these incantations with a ritual which involved carrying out a series of acts and gestures upon the patient..."[847] Hull: "Whilst healing this man, Jesus put his fingers into the man's ears...in other biblical contexts the finger appears as the symbol of God's power. In this latter use it may have connections with magic and exorcism, and there are many parallels in the magical literature."[848]

Spittle was a well-known magical substance. In the *Satyricon*, we are told how a witch used spit and dirt to cure Encolpius' erectile dysfunction: "The old woman pulled a string made from threads of different colors from her dress and tied it around my neck. Then she took some dirt, mixed it with her spittle, and with her third finger made a mark on my forehead..."[849]

Essentially the same technique is used by Jesus to cure blindness: "Spittle is used in three of the miracles. In John 9.6 paste is made from the spittle of Jesus and clay is smeared on a man's eyes; in Mark 8.23 and 7.33 spitting is used in cases of blindness and dumbness...All races of antiquity attached magical significance to spittle. The Pyramid Texts (late third millennium BC) speak of Atum spitting out Shu, the air, in the act of creation...The Epidaurus inscriptions describe mi-

---

[843] και αναβλεψας εις τον ουρανον **εστεναξεν**: "And looking up into the sky, he **groaned**..."

[844] και ελυθη ο **δεσμος** της γλωσσης αυτου: "and the **bond** that held his tongue was loosed..."

[845] Mark 7:32-35

[846] *Papyri Graecae Magicae*, III, 422-423.

[847] *Religion and Magic in Ancient Egypt*, 286.

[848] *Hellenistic Magic*, 82.

[849] Quoted by Luck, *Arcana Mundi*, 89.

raculous cures wrought by the lick of sacred snakes and dogs within the temples of Asclepius…"[850] And from Lenormant: "…at the moment he spat he made a compact with the demon…"[851] Achtemeier observes that "saliva…was effective in cures, especially of the eyes.."[852]

> Spittle, like every secretion of the body and, indeed, the πνευμα [spirit, *my note*] itself, is by itself a vehicle of δυναμις [power, *my note*] and ambivalent—in Palestine as elsewhere…On the whole the spittle of θειοι ανδρες [divine men, *my note*] was preeminently powerful.[853]

Tipei, a dogmatically apologetic writer, concedes, "The use of spittle in healing brings together medicine, miracle and magic. There are cases when the use of spittle has unambiguous magical functions." After presenting pages of references which support this observation, he nevertheless concludes, "Whatever its significance in the healing practice of Jesus, the use of spittle had no magical connotations."[854]

Regarding such similarities between Jesus' actions and the spells described in the papyri, John Dominic Crossan's words are particularly relevant:

> Finally, Jesus as a popular first-century Jewish magician in the tradition, say, of Elijah and Elisha, may well be different from the professional magicians who owned those magical papyri, but that should be established by comparing their actions, not presuming their motives.[855]

As far back as 1927, Campbell Bonner noted that "στεναζω ["groan," *my note*] and αναστεναζω ["cry out, wail" *my note*] are words which have mystical and magical associations, and that the action denoted by them may be considered as a conventional part of the mystical-magic technique."[856] Such details of magical technique are typically omitted by Matthew and Luke, who also chose to delete any mention of healings that take place in stages such as the healing of the blind man re-

---

850 *Hellenistic Magic*, 76-77.
851 *Chaldean Magic*, 63.
852 *Aspects of Religious Propaganda in Judaism and Early Christianity*, 153.
853 *Some Notes on the Demonology in the New Testament*, 56, 58.
854 *The Laying On of Hands in the New Testament*, 143-145.
855 *The Historical Jesus*, 310.
856 *Harvard Theological Review* 20: 172.

corded in Mark 8:22-26.[857] In the magical papyri, groaning or wailing is a technique for summoning the powers of the underworld:

> Having said these things, make sacrifice and back away, wailing loudly as you finish,[858] and [the goddess] will come immediately.[859]

As Wendy Cotter notes, "The redaction of Matthew and Luke on Markan exorcism stories removes features that might suggest a magical association for Jesus' miracles. The deep sighs of Jesus and his pronouncing of foreign phrases in Mark have been removed by these evangelists precisely because they seem to fit so well into a magical tradition of healing."[860] Using accepted canons of interpretation, it is evident that the gospel of Mark is the source closest to the historical Jesus, a source that —to the dismay of later writers— clearly records "a magical tradition" of exorcism and healing.

The stories of healing and exorcism recounted in the gospels of Mark and John reveal several well-known elements of magical practice including the use of spittle, a word of power or *vox magica*, as well as sighing and gestures:

> From other stories in the New Testament, Greco-Roman and rabbinic texts we can reconstruct a fairly standard repertoire of exorcistic techniques. These included looking upwards, sighing or groaning, making hand gestures (such as making the sign of the cross), spitting, invoking the deity and speaking "nonsense" words or letter strings. Sometimes the demon was commanded to speak as a way of demonstrating both his presence in the human body and the practitioner's control over him.[861]

The invocation Jesus uses as a part of his technique of exorcism also has close parallels in the magical papyri as the comparison below illustrates:

---

[857] Elijah raises a dead boy after lying on him three times (1 Kings 17:21).
[858] ἀναστενάξας αναποδιζων καταβηθι: "back away, **wailing loudly** as you finish …"
[859] *Papyri Graecae Magicae* IV, 2491-2492.
[860] *Miracles in Greco-Roman Antiquity: A Sourcebook*, 177.
[861] Janowitz, *Magic in the Roman World*, 39.

Seeing the crowd bearing down on him, Jesus rebuked the unclean spirit, saying to it, "I order you, speechless and deaf spirit,
get out of him,[862] and may you never come back into him!"[863]

Shrieking and convulsing him horribly, it came out and left him
like a corpse so that most of them said, "He's dead!" But Jesus,
taking him by the hand, raised him and stood him upright.[864]

Excellent ritual for casting out demons.
Spell to be recited over his head:
  [*Coptic gloss inserted into Greek text.*]
I order you, demon, whoever you are, by this god…Get out, de-
mon,[865] whoever you are, and stay away from [*Name*]! Now, now!
Quickly, quickly! Get out, demon…![866]

The procedure reflects a widely-known formula for exorcism used by
Jesus among others. The exorcist is supposed to fill in the name or
characteristics of the particular demon —"whoever you are"— in
question. In the case cited above from Mark 9:25-27, the "whoever"
you are is the "speechless and deaf spirit."

The textual history of this spell presents some difficulties: an Old
Coptic gloss has been inserted into the Greek text. The Coptic reads:
"Hail, God of Abraham; hail, God of Isaac; hail, God of Jacob; Jesus
Chrestos, the Holy Spirit, *etc*…"[867] The Greek χρηστος (chrēstos), —
not Χριστος (Christos), *Christ*— means *auspicious* or *true, trustworthy*.[868]
Auspicious for the working of magic. Morton Smith: "These uses of
Jesus' name in pagan spells are flanked by a vast body of material testi-
fying to the use of his name in Christian spells and exorcisms…The
attestations are confirmed by a multitude of Christian amulets, curse
tablets, and magical papyri in which Jesus is the god most often in-

---

[862] εξελθε εξ αυτου: "**get out** of him…"

[863] Geller: "Jesus' specific exorcism formula, 'Go out from him and never enter him
again' can also be identified in contemporary magical literature." *Journal of Jewish Studies*
28: 145.

[864] Mark 9:25-27

[865] εξελθε δαιμων οστις ποτ' ουν ει: "**get out**, demon, whoever you are…!"

[866] *Papyri Graecae Magicae*, IV, 1229-1246.

[867] *The Greek Magical Papyri in Translation*, 62.

[868] As pointed out by Twelftree, "even though 'Christos' (Christ) and 'Chrēstos' (excellent) were pronounced the same, in Coptic manuscripts of the classical period the
words were not generally confused, even though this was not the case among pagans."
In the Name of Jesus: Exorcism among Early Christians, 39.

voked..."[869] Several possibilities might be suggested: the formula re-presented a widely known Jewish exorcistic invocation which finds an echo in Mark and the Coptic gloss was interpolated to make it more "Christian," or the formula was derived from Mark or a Jewish source like that of Mark and adopted to pagan use after which the Coptic interpolation was added.

It is worth noting that in the accounts of both Matthew and Luke, the procedural details of the exorcism of the deaf and dumb spirit, as well as the description of the dramatic physical effects, have been stripped away, leaving us with these insipid versions:

> So Jesus rebuked the unclean spirit and the demon came out of him and the boy was healed in that very hour.[870]

> As the boy approached, the demon threw him down in convulsions, so Jesus rebuked the unclean spirit and healed the boy and returned him to his father.[871]

I propose that these are particularly clear examples of the way in which the exorcisms have been "edited" —*cleaned up* would be more accurate— to make them more "miraculous" and less "magical," thereby rendering Jesus more palatable to a sophisticated audience. Similar editorializing continued with the apocryphal gospels and acts following Jesus' death: "Almost as if to disprove any charge against the apostles as sorcerers or magicians, the apocryphal acts never describe their miracles in such as way as even to hint at the use of herbs or incantations, or magical devices...this is the most obvious example of anti-magical polemic in the way a miracle is performed, the intention is symptomatic of other accounts of miracles..."[872]

However, an alternative reading of Mark 9:25-27 must be acknowledged. According to this reconstruction of the history of the text, the core idea 'Jesus rebuked the demon and it left' was the basic form of the text of Mark from which Matthew and Luke copied. In short, the gospel of Mark used by Matthew and Luke lacked the exorcistic formula, "I order you, speechless and deaf spirit, get out of him, and may

---

[869] *Jesus the Magician*, 63.

[870] Matthew 17:18.

[871] Luke 9:42.

[872] Achtemeier, *Aspects of Religious Propaganda in Judaism and Early Christianity*, 169.

you never come back into him!" This reading of the texts assumes that the exorcistic formula represents a later addition to Mark, i.e., it could not have been deleted by Matthew and Luke since it was never in the edition of Mark from which they copied.

The pericope under discussion is one of a number of well-known instances in which Matthew and Luke differ from Mark at points where they appear to be using Mark as a source. It is possible that Matthew and Luke copied from a shorter form of the gospel of Mark which is now lost to us. This theory assumes that in the first century the text of Mark existed in two or more forms. Since we have no manuscript of any gospel from the first hundred years after their composition, the theory of multiple coexisting forms of the gospels cannot be confirmed, but it is not in any way inconsistent with the available evidence.

The plausibility of this reconstruction of events is supported by Koester's observation that the exorcistic formula does not really match the demonic manifestation: if specific demons were held responsible for specific diseases, then why is a demon of *deaf-mutism* being adjured in a case of *seizure*? "Apparently, the redactor shows little interest in the healing of the disease. Rather, he wants to describe the effect of a powerful exorcism and thus introduces the following action of Jesus which has no parallel whatever in Matthew and Luke."[873]

Regardless of how the history of the text is reconstructed, the textual evidence shows that early Christians could describe the details Jesus' exorcism in the same language as that of the magical papyri and that such a description became incorporated into the officially approved edition of the gospel. "Details of some of the healing stories in Mark indicate a magical context just as details of the exorcisms seem to. The healing of the deaf mute in Mark 7:32ff. is perhaps the clearest case."[874] In any event, the inclusion of the exorcistic formula is evidence that formulae of exactly this kind were already in use among Christians when the gospel was composed and that its insertion or retention in the gospel of Mark served to validate such use.

Although the healings and exorcisms are held up as evidence of Jesus' divine status, the details of their performance evidently became an

---

[873] *Gospel Traditions in the Second Century*, 24.
[874] *Hellenistic Magic*, 73.

embarrassment to elements within the later church —they portray a Jesus who might be regarded merely as one among many itinerant wonder-working holy men. By this point theology was already moving steadily away from the historical Jesus whose flaws, particularly his reputation as a magician, were being papered over even as his official résumé was being prepared. As Hull notes, "Matthew has a suspicion of exorcism. We have seen how though the messianic authority over the evil spirits is maintained, almost all details of techniques are omitted. This is because exorcism was one the main functions of the magician. The magic consisted in the method; Matthew retains the fact without the method, trying in this way to purify the subject."[875] Keck also notes "the Matthean reluctance to celebrate the signs of present salvation, which in Paul, Luke-Acts, and John are signaled by the enabling presence of the Spirit...if for Paul, Luke-Acts, and John the presence of the Spirit is characteristic of Christian life, for Matthew it is reserved for a truly exceptional situation."[876]

The author of Matthew anxiously eliminated all references to magical technique, including the *voces magicae*: "and he cast out the spirits *with a word*,"[877] but the *word* is never specified. It should be noted that λογος (logos), *word*, frequently occurs as a text heading in the magical papyri where it clearly means *spell*. It would be possible, though almost certainly incorrect, to translate the passage in Matthew as "he cast out the spirits *with a spell*." In fact, Matthew reports only one word spoken to a demon, and twenty-three words spoken by demons, whereas Luke records nine words spoken directly to demons, and three more indirectly, as well as thirty-four words spoken directly by demons to Jesus.[878]

It will come as no surprise that some modern Christian apologists draw the very conclusions that Matthew, the chief editor of the exorcism stories, intended:

> Mark reports Jesus' prayer consisting of a single word, "Eph-phatha (be opened)" (7:34) — which stands in the sharpest possible contrast with the extended invocations and formulas of the

---

[875] Ibid, 139.
[876] *The Social World of the First Christians*, 152-153.
[877] Matthew 8:16.
[878] Hull, *Hellenistic Magic*, 130.

magical texts...As in the first story, there is no hint of elaborate invocation of angelic powers or of therapeutic procedure.[879]

This line of argument, which seeks to exonerate Jesus of charges of magical practice, begins by assuming that Jesus' word was a "prayer," not an "invocation" or a "formula." The text of the gospel nowhere calls Jesus' words a "prayer," but does specify that Jesus groaned and looked up to the sky —behavior consistent with magical technique— and tells us that Jesus took the man aside, put his fingers into his ears, spit, and touched the man's tongue, all actions which are quite obviously "therapeutic procedure." Even if *ephphatha* had been specifically called a *prayer*, the magical element would still clearly exist. Spells in the magical texts are rather frequently called ευχαι (euchai), *prayers*.

Even those with strongly apologetic tendencies concede that the gospel accounts have been severely edited. Susan Garrett: "Matthew excised not only the more blatant thaumaturgical traits but even whole incidents, such as the stories of the healing of the deaf mute (Mark 7:31-37) and of the blind man near Bethsaida (Mark 8:22-26), both of which might lend themselves to magical interpretation...Luke seems to have made an intentional effort to distance Jesus and church leaders from magical notions."[880]

The brevity of the formula in no way diminishes its magical force. As Morton Smith noted, "That Jesus is not represented by the Gospels as using long spells is insignificant. Once a magician 'had' his spirit, he need only command it and it would instantly obey. Here too, the Gospels represent Jesus as a successful magician would have represented himself."[881] Brenk, in his discussion of the demonology of the imperial era, observes that "the holy man in the Graeco-Roman period disdains magical formula, such disdain being a sign of his power...he can accomplish his object with one wonder-working word."[882]

David Aune's observation on the question of *voces magicae* merits an extended quote:

---

[879] Howard Clark Kee, *Religion, Science, and Magic*, 136.
Further comment on Kee's criticism of Hull can be found in Cotter, *Miracles in Greco-Roman Antiquity*, 176.
[880] *Religion, Science, and Magic*, 143.
[881] *Clement of Alexandria*, 235.
[882] *Aufstieg und Niedergang der Römischen Welt*, II.16.3: 2113.

The brevity of [Jesus'] exorcistic formulae has led some scholars to contrast them with the long adjurations of the magical papyri ...Aside from the not unimportant observation that such a contrast is quantitative, not qualitative, it should be noted that most of the magical papyri come from the third through the fifth centuries A.D. during the great *Blütezeit* of Graeco-Roman magic; it appears the older the magical forms, the shorter and more precise are the formulas...The short authoritative commands of Jesus to demons in the gospel narratives are formulas of magical adjuration.[883]

There is no clear distinction between spell-casting and praying in the magical papyri: "To the Greeks, a magician not only uttered spells, he also prayed to the gods: Plato, for one connects the επωιδαι (spells) and the ευχαι (prayers) of the magician...I count five instances where ευχη [prayer, *my note*] occurs as an actual title of a spell..."[884] Rodney Werline points out that "the Dead Sea Scrolls contain a number of apotropaic prayers...The book of Tobit contains two prayers used as part of a 'spell' to drive away a demon..."[885] There is no clear distinction between religion and magic in the 1st century so there is correspondingly no clear difference between prayers and spells. The imposition of such a difference is a clumsy apologetic maneuver which does violence to the evidence.

Kee's first assumption is then followed by another: that in the few verses Mark allots to the story, he provides a complete description of *all that happened and all that Jesus said,* something that can never be taken for granted given the obvious manipulation of the texts. This selective apologetic reading of the evidence follows on the heels of the selective apologetic reporting of the evidence in the gospels themselves, and the foregone conclusion is that what Jesus did was in some way different *in substance,* if not in form, from what other miracle workers did. This sort of willful misreading of the text is unfortunately typical of believer scholarship, an approach to the texts that simply refuses to see what is inconvenient in the documents of the New Testament.

---

[883] *Aufstieg und Niedergang der Römischen Welt,* II.23.2: 1531-1532.
[884] *Magika Hiera,* 188, 189.
    Compare the following spell: ευχη προς Σεληνην επι πασης πραξεως ελθε μοι ω δεσποινα φιλη...: "**Prayer** to Selēnē [goddess of the moon, *my note*] for any matter. Come to me, O Beloved Mistress..." *Papyri Graecae Magicae* IV, 2785.
[885] *Experientia,* I, 68.

A second argument intended to dodge the charge of magic is the claim that the 'evangelists' carefully distinguish between exorcism and healing, so that whatever may be said about Jesus' exorcisms, Jesus' healings cannot be read as magical. This distinction is quite obviously false. The 'rebuke' of a fever in Luke 4:38 employs the vocabulary of exorcism. Wahlen, who tends toward the position that exorcism and healing are separate categories, nevertheless concedes it "is decisive that here we have a healing depicted in terms of an exorcism." In his discussion of the terminology of exorcism in Mark, Wahlen states, "The exorcisms in Mark, unlike in Matthew or Luke, are consistently distinguished from the healing of disease," but concedes that in Luke 9:42, based on the exorcism story in Mark 9:25-27, "by casting out the demon, Jesus is said to have healed (ιασθαι) the child…"[886] Matthew says of a man possessed by a demon that Jesus "healed him."[887] Richard Bell also concedes that exorcisms "can be difficult to distinguish" from healings and that the distinction is "not always clear."[888] In fact, not at all clear.

The remains of a incomplete amuletic papyrus from the 4th century shows that Christians of that era considered healing to include not only interventions against fever, chills and disease, but also possession and witchery:

> Christ was born from the Virgin Mary and was crucified under Pontius Pilate and was buried in a tomb and was raised on the third day and will come again from the heavens…Jesus that once healed every debility of the people[889] and every disease, Savior Jesus, we believe you went once into the house of Peter's mother-in-law who had a fever and touched her hand and cast the fever out from her[890] and now we call upon you, Jesus, heal also now

---

[886] *Jesus and the Impurity of Spirits in the Synoptic Gospels*, 88, 154, 164.

[887] εθεραπευσεν αυτον: "**he healed** him." Matthew 12:22.

[888] *Deliver Us from Evil*, 78.

[889] Ιησου οτι **εθεραπευσες** τοτε πασαν μαλακιαν: "Jesus that once **healed** every debility…"

[890] An example of an *historiola*, a short recitation of a biblical miracle designed to produce an analogous miracle. The practice is very common in both Jewish and Christian magic. See particularly Bohak, *Ancient Jewish Magic*, 413, and Meyer, *Magic and Ritual in the Ancient World*, 415, for *historiolae* invoking Mary.

και **αφηκεν** αυτην ο πυρετος: "and **cast** the fever **out** from her…" The language is that of exorcism.

your servant girl,[891] who wears your great name,[892] from every disease and from every fever, and from fever with chills and from migraine and from bewitchment[893] and from every wicked spirit[894] in the name of the Father, and the Son and the Holy Spirit, *etc.*[895]

Another papyrus amulet of Christian origin combines an invocation to Christ with *voces magicae*:

Amulet of Jesus Christ the Helper against fever:
    Quick, quick, heal John, son of Zoē.
    sarix, aorkach, rhougach, chiosnēch, koch[896]

Spellwork generally makes no distinction between demons, ghosts, diseases or other sources of suffering:

An amulet,[897] a bodyguard against demons, against ghosts, against every sickness and misfortune, inscribed on a leaf of gold or silver...[898]

There is likewise no clear distinction between healing and exorcism in either the New Testament, early Christianity, or Judaism of the era:

The book of Tobit contains two prayers used as part of a "spell" to drive away a demon named Asmodeus...in order to "heal" (ιασασθαι) both Tobit and Sarah (v.17). This healing takes the form of "setting her free" (λυσαι) from the demon (v.17).[899]

---

[891] Ιησου **θεραπευσον** και νυν την δουλην σου: "Jesus also now **heal** your servant girl..."

[892] i.e., who wears this magical amulet.

[893] και απο πασης **βασκοσυνης**: "and from every **bewitchment**..." The text uses a poetic form of βασκανια (baskania), *malign influence, witchery, the evil eye* which was understood to arise from envy of good fortune.

[894] και απο παντος **πνευματος** πονηρου: "and from every wicked **spirit**..."

[895] *Supplementum Magicum*, 31.

[896] *Supplementum Magicum*, 28.

[897] φυλακτηριον (phulaktērion): "An amulet," or protective spell, derived from φυλαξ (phulax), *guard* or *sentinel*.

[898] *Papyri Graecae Magicae* VII, 580.

[899] *Experientia*, I, 68.
    The references are to Tobit 3:17.

The evidence of the gospels is perfectly plain on this point: και γυν-αικες τινες αι ησαν τεθεραπευμεναι απο πνευματων πονηρων και ασθενειων: "and there were certain women who **had been healed** of evil spirits **and** infirmities..." The passage is purportedly by Luke,[900] a doctor,[901] who might be presumed qualified to have known the difference between exorcism and healing if there was one.

Rather less attention has been paid to the passage in John 20:22 which describes the magical technique by which the resurrected Jesus passed power on to his disciples:

And saying this, he blew and said to them, "Receive holy spirit."

The magical papyri contain very similar wording to that found in John: ενπνευματωσον αυτον θειου πνευματος, "**infuse** it **with spirit**, divine spirit..."[902] *Blowing* is a well-attested magical technique in our sources. Celsus compares Christian miracles, described by him as "the works of the sorcerers,"[903] to the arts of street magicians "who drive demons out of men, and blow away diseases[904] and call up the souls of heroes..."[905] "**He blew**" —ενεφυσησεν— in the gospel of John is exactly duplicated in the story told by Lucian about the "Babylonian" snake charmer who calls out all the vipers from a vineyard: "**he blew** on them —ενεφυσησε μεν αυτοις— and they were instantly burned up by the breath and we were amazed."[906] Lucian, who wrote satirical pieces for public performance, obviously considered it a given that his audience would be familiar with such magical techniques as blowing and the expectation that onlookers would be "amazed" by magical performances.

...binding and loosing, locking and unlocking

The story of the deaf mute introduces the metaphor of binding and loosing —"the bond that held his tongue was loosed."[907] The concept

---

[900] Luke 8:2. Compare Acts 10:38.
[901] Colossians 4:14.
[902] *Papyri Graecae Magicae* IV, 967.
[903] τα εργα των γοητων: "the works **of the sorcerers**..."
[904] και νοσους αποφυσωντων: "and **blow away** diseases..."
[905] *Contra Celsum* I, 68.
[906] *Lover of Lies*, 12.
[907] Mark 7:35.

of binding was basic to 1st century magical practice: the verb and noun set is δεω (deō), *bind*, and δεσμος (desmos), *bond*. A closely related set, καταδεω (katadeō), *tie down*, and καταδεσμος (katadesmos), *binding spell*, were used of magical incantations designed to restrain the actions or choices of others.

An early magical charm directed against a woman named Aristo says, "...I seized and bound her hands and feet and tongue and soul ...may her tongue become lead..."[908] The idea of magical binding is extensively attested: "Illness and death: it is these two elements of the magico-religious complex of 'binding' which have had the widest currency almost all over the world..."[909] "...running throughout all antiquity we find the idea that a man can be 'bound' or 'fettered by demonic influences. It occurs in Greek, Syrian, Hebrew, Mandaean, and Indian magic spells."[910] "In the book of Daniel (5:12, 16) the ability 'to loose knots' is listed as one of the magician's accomplishments."[911] Gager reports a curse tablet that refers to "this impious, accursed, and miserable Kardelos...bound, fully bound, and altogether bound..."[912]

These references hardly exhaust the discussion of knots and magical binding in the ancient Middle East.[913] The metaphor of binding is also used in Jesus' argument with the Pharisees regarding the source of his powers over the demons.[914] In Acts, Paul says, "I have been bound by the spirit."[915] Strelan observes, "Binding and loosing are common technical terms in magical practices in which people are bound by spirits or released from them."[916]

Because sickness and possession are not clearly differentiated in the gospels, identical language is often used in connection with both healing and exorcism:

---

[908] εγω ελαβον και **εδησα** τας χειρας και τους ποδας και την γλωσσαν και την ψυχην...η γλωσσα αυτης μολυβδος γενοιτο: "I seized and **bound** her hands and feet and tongue and soul...may her become lead..." *New Documents Illustrating Early Christianity* 4:45.
[909] Eliade, *Images and Symbols*, 92-124.
[910] *Light from the Ancient East*, 304.
[911] *Jewish Magic and Superstition*, 127.
[912] *Curse Tablets and Binding Spells from the Ancient World*, 71.
[913] *Witchcraft and Magic in Europe: Biblical and Pagan Societies*, 37-38.
[914] Matthew 12:22-32.
[915] Acts 20:22.
[916] *Strange Acts*, 94.

"And this woman, a daughter of Abraham, who Satan bound[917] for —just imagine! Eighteen years! Was it not fitting that she be loosed from this bond[918] on the Sabbath day?"[919]

The notion of binding and loosing is extended both in the New Testament and the magical books to *locking* and *unlocking,* particularly of the realm of the dead.

I will give you the keys of the kingdom of the heavens and whatever you bind on earth will be a thing which has been bound in the heavens and whatever you may loose on earth will be a thing loosed in the heavens.[920]

The risen Christ says to John, "Do not fear! I am the First and the Last, the Living One, and I died, and look! Now I am living for the ages of the ages and I have the key of death and of Hades."[921]

The *key* is a frequent topos in erotomagical charms[922] and the dead can be summoned up through the good offices of the chthonic gods: "O Anoubis, Keybearer[923] and Guardian, send up to me in this very hour these phantoms of the dead to be my attendants…"[924]

Such language finds a close parallel in this attraction spell:

I entrust this binding spell to you, gods of the underworld… Anubis the powerful, *pseriphtha,* who has the keys of Hades and divine demons of the underworld, men and women prematurely

---

[917] ην **εδησεν** ο σατανας: "who Satan **bound**…" Satan himself will be bound (Revelation 20:2): και **εδησεν** αυτον χιλια ετη: "and **bound** him for a thousand years."

Büchsel: "[δεω] is used of supernatural binding in L[uke] 13:16 and also in A[cts] 20:23." *Theological Dictionary of the New Testament,* II, 60.

[918] ουκ εδει λυθηναι απο του **δεσμου** τουτου: "Was it not fitting that she be loosed from this **bond**…?

[919] Luke 13:16.

[920] Matthew 16:19.

[921] Revelation 1:18.

David Aune's discussion of the chthonic goddess Hecate, who is called κληιδου-χος and κλειδοφορος —"key bearer"— in the magical papyri is especially recommended. *Apocalypticism, Prophecy, and Magic in Early Christianity,* 353-361.

[922] *Greek Magical Amulets,* 49.

[923] κλειδουχε: "Keybearer…"

[924] *Papyri Graecae Magicae* IV, 1469.

dead...I adjure you, demon of the dead Antinous[925]...do not ignore me, demon of the dead Antinous, but raise yourself for me
and go to every place...and bring me Ptolemais, born of Aias,
daughter of Horigenes...If you do this, I will release you.[926]

Antinous, the lover of the Emperor Hadrian, drowned in the Nile[927] in
130 CE, possibly in self-sacrifice for the ailing emperor. It is estimated
that he was by that time in his late teens, hence dead well before his
time and like others prematurely dead, available for the workings of
magicians. In this case, he is called upon to fetch a woman for a sexual
liaison. The murdered Osiris, like the executed Jesus, has the keys of
Hades, and therefore the power to release the ghost of Antinous. It is
evident that the Christian understanding of Jesus' powers shares much
common ground with Greco-Egyptian necromancy: resurrected gods
have the keys to the realm of the dead.

Jesus the Keybearer has joined the ranks of the chthonic deities like
those adjured in this erotic attraction spell:

> I entrust [this binding spell] to you, underworld gods and infernal
> goddesses,[928] Pluto Yesmigadōth, and Kourē Persephonē,
> Ereschigal and Adonis, also called Barbaritha, and chthonic
> Hermes Thoth and mighty Anoubis Psēriphtha who holds the
> keys down to Hades[929] and underworld ghosts of men and

---

[925] νεκυδαιμον Αντινοε: literally, "dead-demon Antinous," i.e., the ghost of
Antinous.

[926] *New Documents Illustrating Early Christianity*, I, 33-34.

[927] Necromancy using the famous dead was common in Egypt, and "extended to
nonroyal spirits as well, particularly those whose death by drowning assimilated them
to the god Osiris." Rittner, *Magic and Divination in the Ancient World*, 94.

According to Egyptian legend, Osiris, husband of Isis, the goddess of magic, was
drowned in the Nile by his brother Seth. Osiris, "the divine Drowned," (*Leyden Papyrus*
VI.12) therefore becomes a major chthonic god, a gatekeeper of the world of the dead,
and drowning results in magical identification with him. A scarab is to be drowned
before being bound to the body of a boy (IV.34,35), a hawk is drowned in a jar of
wine (XXV.33), a cat is drowned to create a spirit-empowered ghost (*Papyri Graecae
Magicae* III, 1-2, 50).

[928] θεοις καταχθονιοις και θεαις καταχθονιαις: "**underworld** gods and **infernal**
goddesses..." The adjective καταχθονιος (katachthonios), refers to the 'infernal' gods
of Hades who rule the 'underworld' of the dead.

[929] τας κλειδας εχοντι των καθ' Αδου: "who holds the **keys** down to Hades..."

women prematurely dead,[930] youths and virgins, year after year, month after month, day after day, night after night, hour after hour. I command[931] all the ghosts of this place, assist this daemon...[932]

As part of his praxis the magician may assume the identity of Hermes and control him through the manipulation of his cultic objects:

As Hermes, Chief of magicians, the Elder,[933] I am Father of Isis ...I have hidden this, your symbol, your sandal, and I hold your key...I speak the sign, the bronze sandal of the Tartaros Keeper, wreath, key, herald's wand,[934] iron magic wheel[935] and black dog...[936]

The metaphor of locking and unlocking, common in the magical papyri, is also prominent in Revelation, possibly the most overtly magical of the New Testament books. The risen Jesus is "The One who has the key of David, who opens and no one locks and who locks and no one opens."[937]

Other terms, such as φιμαω (phimaō), *muzzle, silence, shut* (the mouth) are used magically in both the New Testament and the papyri:

---

[930] και **δαιμοσι** καταχθονιοις αωροις τε και αωραις: "and underworld **ghosts** of men and women prematurely dead..." The 'daemons' in sight are clearly ghosts as indicated by the context.

[931] ορκιζω παντας τους **δαιμονας**: "I command all the **ghosts**..."

[932] *Supplementum Magicum*, 46.

[933] **μαγων αρχηγετης** Ερμης ο πρεσβυς: "**Chief** of magicians, the Elder..."

The word αρχηγετης (archēgetēs) can also mean *founder*, reflecting the legend that Hermes or Thoth was the inventor of magic.

[934] κηρυκιον or κηρυκειον (kērukeion), "herald's wand," the wand of Hermes, psychopomp and messenger of the gods, the *caduceus*.

[935] **ρομβος** σιδηρους: "iron **magic wheel**..." The ρομβος (rhombos), *magic wheel* or *bullroarer*, a device spun on cords or whirled to create the sound of wind, summons the numina.

[936] και κλειδα **κρατω**: "and **I hold** your key..." *Papyri Graecae Magicae* IV, 2290-2294, 2334-2337.

Holding magical symbols appears in the book of Revelation: ο **κρατων** τους επτα αστερας εν τη δεξια αυτου: "the One **holding** the seven stars in his right hand..." Revelation 2:1.

[937] Revelation 3:7.

And after he woke up, he rebuked the wind and said to the sea,
"Be silent! You have been muzzled!" [938]

This rather strange command finds close parallels in the spellwork of
the magical papyri:

> ...on the back of the sheet of metal [write]: eulamō sisirba-
> baiērsesi phermou chnouōr Abrasax utterly subject, completely
> enslave, muzzle the soul,[939] the breath of life of [Name] because I
> command you by the fearsome Necessity..."[940]

> Say the spell seven times. Ermallōth. Archimallōth. Muzzle the
> mouths[941] of those [who speak] against me..."[942]

> ...they will muzzle my adversary..."[943]

To "muzzle" in these contexts is to restrict the action of someone or
something, even as the oxen who turned the grindstone might be
muzzled to prevent them from eating the falling grain.[944] The prophets
who "stopped the mouths" of lions[945] were *restraining their actions*, not
silencing them. A spell designed to subject and restrain a victim[946] is
called a φιμωτικον, a *silencing spell*, as well as a υποτακτικον, "a charm
for bringing people into subjection."[947] Certainly both 'silencing' and
'restraining' were closely related in the minds of magical practitioners.

...the Beelzeboul controversy

---

[938] πεφιμωσο: **"You have been muzzled!"** Mark 4:39.

    Samuel Eitrem is one of the few commentators to have drawn attention to the
magical use of this term. *Some Notes on the Demonology in the New Testament*, 38.

[939] φιμωσον την ψυχη: **"muzzle** the soul..."

[940] *Papyri Graecae Magicae* IX, 8-10.

[941] φιμωσατε τα στοματα τα κατ εμου...: **"muzzle** the mouths..."

[942] *Papyri Graecae Magicae* XXXVI, 164-165.

[943] φιμωσουσιν τον αντιδικον εμου: **"they will muzzle** my adversary..." Audollent, *Defixionum Tabellae* (Insula Cyprus), 22:43.

[944] 1 Corinthians 9:9.

[945] Hebrews 11:33.

[946] *Papyri Graecae Magicae* VII, 396.

[947] Liddel & Scott, *A Greek-English Lexicon*, 1897.

In the 1ˢᵗ century it was well known that people with supernatural gifts often exhibited unnatural behavior, an observation reflected in this account from Mark:

> He came home and a crowd gathered again, so much so that they were not even able to eat a meal. His family went out to restrain him when they heard about it, because they were saying, "He's out of his mind!"[948]
>
> The scribes who came down from Jerusalem were saying, "He has Beelzeboul!"[949] "He casts out the demons by the ruler of the demons."
>
> Calling them together, he made an analogy: "How can Satan cast out Satan? If a kingdom divides against itself, that kingdom cannot stand, and if a house divides against itself, that house will not be able to stand. So if Satan rises up against himself and becomes divided, he cannot stand. To the contrary, his end has come."
>
> "No one can enter the strong man's house to plunder his possessions unless he first binds the strong man, and then he plunders his house."
>
> "Truly I say to you, every error and blasphemy will be forgiven the sons of men, but whoever blasphemes against the holy spirit will have no forgiveness for all ages, but is guilty of everlasting sin" —because they were saying, "He has an unclean spirit."[950]

The verb εξιστημι (existēmi) can refer to states of confusion or amazement or to insanity, but there is certainly nothing in the context to suggest that Jesus was either so confused or so amazed that his family felt they needed to restrain him. The related noun, εκστασις (ekstasis), which has already been mentioned, is commonly regarded as referring to a state of trance or frenzy. Concluding a discussion of the 'agitation' associated with Jesus' miracles and the probable textual tampering done at Mark 1:41 to conceal this feature of his healing, Eitrem says, "We have to interpret the cure of the leper as *originally* effected by an ecstatic Jesus by the expulsion of a demon or foul spirit."[951]

---

[948] ελεγον γαρ οτι εξεστη: "because they were saying, '**He's out of his mind!**'"

[949] Βεελζεβουλ εχει: "**He has** Beelzeboul."

[950] Mark 3:20-30.

πνευμα ακαθαρτον εχει: "He **has** an unclean spirit."

[951] *Some Notes on the Demonology in the New Testament*, 53.

To Jesus' family it may have appeared that he had taken leave of his senses, but the religious authorities saw it differently. They believed Jesus to be in control of a demon, a belief based on Jesus' erratic behavior. The claim that Jesus controlled demons led to his rejoinder concerning blasphemy against the holy spirit and his question, "If I cast out demons by means of Beelzeboul by what means do your sons cast them out?"[952] Significantly, Jesus nowhere denies being able to manipulate a spirit —which is after all the sine qua non of the miracle-working holy man— but replies that the spirit in question is the holy spirit, not an unclean spirit. The idea that spirits can perform miracles is reflected in the apocalyptic books of Jesus' time. "And I saw...out of the mouth of the false prophet three unclean spirits like frogs. They are spirits of demons that perform signs..."[953]

Jesus' success as an exorcist appears to have been beyond dispute. No one questioned it. "All they could do was cast doubt on the power behind such exorcisms."[954] However, Mark's reference to Jesus as being "out of his mind" was too extreme for both Matthew and Luke — there is no trace of this part of the story in either of their gospels and as noted elsewhere, exorcism itself proved too incriminating in nature for the writer of John. According to Twelftree, exorcism passes without mention in the gospel of John because "the Fourth Gospel portrays Jesus as relying on no other source of power-authority outside himself in performing miracles."[955] The last gospel thus evades the entire question raised by exorcism in the synoptics: "Tell us, by what authority are you doing these things?"[956]

Crossan underscores the tension that must have existed between Jesus and the temple authorities: "In all of this the point is not really Galilee against Jerusalem but the far more fundamental dichotomy of magician as personal and individual power against priest or rabbi as communal and ritual power. Before the Second Temple's destruction, it was magician against Temple, thereafter magician against rabbi...If a magician's power can bring rain, for what do you need the power of temple priesthood or rabbinical academy?"[957] But in this contest of authority, of exactly what did the accusation consist?

---

[952] Matthew 12:27.
[953] Revelation 16:13, 14.
[954] *Deliver Us from Evil*, 84.
[955] *In the Name of Jesus*, 193.
[956] Luke 20:2.
[957] *The Historical Jesus*, 157-158.

...'to have' Beelzeboul

That the expression "He has Beelzeboul" should be taken in the *active*, rather than passive sense, was pointed out by Kraeling:

> In the relations of men and demons there are two basic possibilities, either the demon has a man in his possession, or a man has a demon under his control...in the second the demon is the servant and the man a magician.[958]

Kraeling's observation is confirmed by the nearly identical wording of Revelation 3:1 where the glorified Christ is called "the One who has the seven spirits of God and the seven stars" —"stars" which are identified in the context as angels.[959] On the meaning of *having* the seven spirits, Hanse says,

> ...These seven spirits are thought of as autonomous beings, and they are to be equated with the seven angels which stand before God...What does it mean that Christ "has" them? It obviously means that He has authority over them, that He can command them...[960]

Yet Hanse interprets the identical expression in Mark 3:22 in a passive sense, that of possession *by* a demon, an inconsistency that seeks to avoid the implication that Jesus worked magic through the control of demons. David Aune: "...the rise of the Biblical theology movement was accompanied by a strong reaction against the notion that ancient Mediterranean magic could have influenced early Christianity in any substantial way. The authors of many of the articles in the 'Theologisches Wörterbuch zum Neuen Testament,' [the German predecessor of *The Theological Dictionary of the New Testament, my note*] most of whom consider themselves Biblical theologians, write as if they were involved in a conspiracy to ignore or minimize the role of magic in the New Testament and early Christian literature."[961]

---

[958] Kraeling, *Journal of Biblical Literature* 59: 153.

[959] Revelation 1:20. ο εχων τα επτα πνευματα του θεου: "**the One who has the** seven spirits of God..."

[960] "εχω" in *The Theological Dictionary of the New Testament*, II, 821.

The *Exegetical Dictionary of the New Testament* says of εχω in Revelation 3:1, "It probably means that [Christ] has sovereignty over these powers." (II, 95).

[961] *Aufstieg und Niedergang der Römischen Welt*, II, 23/2, 1508. See my further remarks in the *Preface*.

The accusation by the Jewish leaders is not that Jesus is possessed *by* a demon, but rather that he is the magician *par excellence* because he has bound Beelzeboul himself, the prince of demons, to his service and works his miracles as a result of exercising that control. It is nonsense to acknowledge that Jesus has authority over demons and in the next breath claim that he is *possessed* by one. Demonic possession means that the man is controlled by the demon, not that the demon is controlled by the man.

Nearly identical wording —"I *have* him"— is found in the magical papyri in a necromantic spell to retain power over the spirit of a man killed violently, a favorite category of ghost for working sorcery:

> I beseech you, Lord Helios, listen to me, [Name],[962] and grant me the power over this spirit of a man killed violently[963] from whose tent[964] I hold [a body part?]. I have him with me, [Name], a helper[965] and avenger for whatever business I desire.[966]

"I have him with me..." —εχω αυτον μετ' εμου— or in other words, "I control his spirit which serves me as a helper."

That *the demon is controlled by the magician* is the point of Jesus' question, "How can one enter a strong man's house and seize his belongings *unless one first binds the strong man?*"[967] Jesus is not only claiming to loose those bound by Satan, but to bind demons to his will, an authority he can transmit to others.[968] After a thorough review of the evidence intrinsic to the gospel accounts, Samain construed "to have a demon" in the active sense, i.e., *to have control of the demon:*

> ...Christ is the master of Beelzeboul and he controls him to the point of using him to perform his exorcisms...Christ is alleged to

---

[962] The name of the person using the spell is to be inserted as appropriate.

[963] τουτου του **βιοθανατου** πνευματος...: "this spirit of **a man killed violently**..."

[964] The "tent" —σκηνη (skēnē)— the body as the covering of the soul, hence a *corpse.* Compare 2 Corinthians 5:4, 'to be in the tent,' i.e., alive in a body.

[965] **βοηθον**: "a **helper**..." The word βοηθος, "helper," is used of a spirit entity, the Lord Jesus, in Hebrews 13:6 —Κυριος εμοι **βοηθος**: "the Lord [is] my **Helper**."

[966] *Papyri Graecae Magicae* IV, 1947-1954.

[967] εαν μη πρωτον **δηση** τον ισχυρον: "unless one first **binds** the strong man..." (Matthew 12:29).

[968] As at Luke 13:16. Compare Matthew 10:1, 16:19 (what is bound on earth is bound in heaven).

be a magician: joined with the ruler of the demons, he compels him, by using his name, to perform the miracles he wants, particularly exorcisms; no spirit, no demonic power can resist him… Δαιμονιον εχει ["He has a demon," *my note*] therefore means that Jesus is a false prophet, a magician."[969]

That having a demon under one's control is very different from being possessed by a demon is reflected both in the language of the New Testament and in the terminology of the magical papyri. A particular verb —δαιμονιζομαι (daimonizomai)— "to be possessed by a hostile spirit"[970] is consistently reserved for those tormented by demons and it is *never* applied to Jesus in the New Testament even by his opponents.[971] In response to the accusations that Jesus is employing an evil spirit to accomplish his miracles, the crowd correctly states, "These are not the words of a possessed man!"[972] Samain also noted, "It is true that δαιμονιζομενος [possessed by a demon, *my note*] is never used to describe a magician."[973] The verb is used of those under the control of a demon, not of a man in control of one.

This use is also noted by Paige: "The evangelists never use the familiar 'neutral' or good terms of religious possession known from Plato and other writers…They always use the verb δαιμονιζομαι in its very late (first century onwards) and probably Jewish/Christian sense, 'to be afflicted with or possessed by demons' (e.g., Mark 1:32-34), even when the evil entity is described in the pericope as a 'spirit'…"[974]

Spirit manipulation was standard magic praxis in the Middle East well before the time of Jesus. As Sorensen notes, "by associating itself with power over demons Christianity associated itself with magic in the

---

[969] My translation of: "le Christ est maître de Béelzéboul et le domine au point de l'employer pour opérer ses exorcismes…uni au chef des demons, il le forcerait, possédant son nom, à opérer les prodiges qu'il veut et spécialement les exorcismes; nul esprit, nulle puissance démoniaque ne lui résiste…Δαιμονιον εχει signifie donc encore que Jésus est un faux prophète magicien." *Ephemerides Theologicae Lovanienses* 15: 468, 470, 482.

[970] Danker's *Greek-English Lexicon*, 209.

[971] δαιμονιζομαι occurs 13 times in the gospels and nowhere else in the New Testament.

[972] ταυτα τα ρηματα ουκ εστιν δαιμονιζομενου: "These are not the words **of a possessed man!**"

[973] Samain: "Il est vrai que δαιμονιζομαι ne se rencontre jamais pour designer un magicien." *Ephemerides* 15:482.

[974] *Harvard Theological Review* 95: 427-428.

minds of its critics."[975] Ghosts of the dead were often invoked to accomplish magical acts as illustrated by this sample spell from the papyri:

> I command you, ghost of the dead,[976] by the powerful and implacable god and by his holy names, to stand beside me in the night to come, in whatever form you had, and if you are able, transact for me [named] deed, if I command you, now, now, quick, quick...
>
> ...and he will actually stand alongside you in your dreams throughout the night and he will ask you, saying, "Command what you wish and I will do it."[977]

It is essential to point out that Jesus is never represented as being among the demon-possessed, those who have lost control of themselves —"demon-possessed and epileptic and paralyzed."[978] Of such tragic figures Joshua Trachtenberg observed, "Demons who have taken possession of a human body exercise such complete control over it that the personality and the will of the victim are extinguished."[979] Such persons have most emphatically not been placed in command of spirits, whereas Jesus is everywhere presented in the gospels as operating from a position of superior strength vis-à-vis the demons. Jesus' authority —his *exousia*— "means a mysterious superhuman force whereby demons were controlled and afflictions miraculously healed."[980]

We should be perfectly clear on this point: *pace* Howard Clark Kee, the scribes nowhere "charge that [Jesus] can control the demons because he is himself controlled by their prince, Beelzebub," a situation that would for all intent make Jesus into a puppet of Satan.[981] To the contrary, their charge is that *Jesus is in control of Beelzeboul*: "He casts out demons *by the ruler of the demons*." The charge of the scribes is that Jesus is a magician so powerful that he can bind even the prince of demons

---

[975] *Possession and Exorcism in the New Testament and Early Christianity*, 179.

[976] εξορκιζω σε **νεκυδαιμον**...: "I command you, **ghost of the dead**..."

[977] *Papyri Graecae Magicae* IV, 2030-2053.

[978] **δαιμονιζομενους** και σεληνιαζομενους και παραλυτικους: "**demon-possessed** and epileptics [literally, "moonstruck"] and paralyzed" (Matthew 4:24).

[979] *Jewish Magic and Superstition*, 51.

[980] Joshua Starr, *Harvard Theological Review* 23: 303.

[981] *Religion, Science, and Magic*, 138.

to his service. Jesus even gives others authority to expel demons.[982] How could that happen if Satan had control of Jesus? As made clear by previously cited gospel references, Jesus controls the demons through *coercion*, a trait he shares with pagan magicians: "The fact that in the *corpus* of papyri magic operates through 'coercion' can be considered as a unifying element. The presence of 'coercive' elements needs no further justification than the real needs of the operator."[983]

Erratic or strange behavior was long associated with exorcistic ritual, prophecy, and wonder-working generally. In a hostile encounter with Jewish holy men, this very power was turned against Saul as described in the account of his hunt for his rival, David.

> Saul was told, "David is at Naioth in Ramah." Then Saul sent messengers to take David. When they saw the company of prophets in a frenzy, with Samuel standing in charge of them, the spirit of God came on the messengers of Saul and they also fell into a prophetic frenzy.
>
> When Saul was told, he sent other messengers, and they also fell into a frenzy. Saul sent messengers again the third time, and they also fell into a frenzy.
>
> Then he himself went to Ramah. He came to the great well that is in Secu; he asked, "Where are Samuel and David?" And someone said, "They are at Naioth in Ramah." He went there, toward Naioth in Ramah; and the spirit of God came upon him. As he was going, he fell into a prophetic frenzy, until he came to Naioth in Ramah. He too stripped off his clothes, and he too fell into a frenzy before Samuel. He lay naked all that day and all that night. Therefore it is said, "Is Saul also among the prophets?"[984]

The bizarre behavior that accompanied Jesus' own miracle working is the subject of this telling passage in the gospel of John:

> Again a division of opinion occurred among the Jews because of these words. Many of them were saying, "He has a demon and he's raving![985] Why listen to him?"

---

[982] Luke 9:1.
[983] Scibilia, *The Metamorphosis of Magic*, 74.
[984] 1 Samuel 19:20-24, *NRSV*
[985] δαιμονιον εχει και μαινεται: "He has a demon and he's **raving!**"

Others said, "These are not the words of a possessed man! Is a demon able to open the eyes of the blind?"[986]

In this text "raving" translates the verb μαινομαι (mainomai), and given the context, it is clear that Jesus' opponents are not simply accusing him of talking nonsense, but are pointing to Jesus' raving as evidence of magical ritual. The nominal form, μανια (mania), which occurs as a description of the frenzy of the Bacchic rites, refers specifically to violent behavior that accompanied possession.[987] In either case, it is important to note that the word simply designates behavior, and not its cause or motive. In point of fact, the ancients distinguished between different types of ecstatic experience; appearances were not necessarily accurate indicators of how ecstasy functioned.[988]

Raving as a magical technique is specifically addressed by Lucian in his biting exposé of Alexander of Abonutichos. Even allowing for the overtly hostile description of Alexander's actions, the reader can still detect the presence of a magical praxis: "feigning madness, he sometimes filled his mouth with foam..."[989]

At no point do Jesus' opponents deny that he casts out demons. It is only Jesus' method that is open to question, but whether accomplished by the spirit of God or by the spirit Beelzeboul, the prince of demons, the results are formally identical: the demons leave when commanded. It must also be emphasized, however, that for the exorcist —unlike the prophet— raving appears to function as a mimetic technique, not a symptom of passive possession. Whereas the prophet raves as a sign of possession, the magician raves to establish control. For the magician, raving is an enactment, sacred theater. Unlike the prophet, who courts possession through music, dance, and dream, the role of the magician is active —magic is about taking control of and manipulating power. Lewis, in his extensive discussion of possession phenomena,

---

[986] John 10:19-21.
[987] Burkert: "The words which the Greeks used to describe such phenomena are varied and inconsistent...These various expressions can neither be reconciled systematically nor distinguished in terms of an evolution in the history of ideas; they mirror the confusion in the face of the unknown. The most common term is therefore *mania*, frenzy, madness." *Greek Religion*, 109-110.
[988] See Shaw, *Theurgy and the Soul*, 231-236.
[989] μεμηνεναι προσποιουμενος ενιοτε και αφρου υποπιμπλαμενος το στομα: "feigning madness, he sometimes filled his mouth with foam..." Victor, *Alexandros Oder der Lügenprophet*, 90.

points out the distinction between involuntary possession and "a spirit possessed (voluntarily) by a person...controlled trance, the essential requirement for the exercise of the shamanistic vocation...the shaman 'possesses' his spirits ..."[990] This explanation accords completely with the New Testament description of Jesus: he is the *master*, not the slave, of spirits and ghosts.

..."Messianic secret" or secretive magic?

As Jesus' fame as an exorcist and healer spread across Galilee,[991] crowds of the sick and possessed assembled. So densely packed were the multitudes that a paralytic had to be lowered to Jesus through a hole broken in a roof and at one point he retreated to a boat offshore to avoid being crushed by the mob.[992] Yet Jesus repeatedly commanded that his activity and identity be kept secret, so admonishing a leper, demons he cast out, the family of a girl raised from the dead, a deaf mute, a blind man, and Peter.[993]

Why the command for secrecy when Jesus' reputation spread like wild-fire and drew people by the thousands? In actual practice, the command for silence may have functioned as a clever publicity ploy —the more Jesus commanded silence, the more loudly his works were proclaimed.[994] The gospel writer implies that Jesus sought to conceal his identity as the Messiah, having Peter say, "You are the Christ."[995] However, the author of the gospel never puts this declaration into the mouth of Jesus himself.

Modern attempts to explain why Jesus is never unambiguously self-identified as the Messiah in the gospel of Mark began with the German theologian William Wrede who proposed (in 1901) that Jesus' status was not recognized during his 'ministry' —hence the term "Messianic secret"— but became clear to his followers only after his resurrection. Since that time other solutions, several of them quite speculative, have been proposed. It is the consensus of scholarly opinion that Mark is the earliest of the gospels, and likely the most historically accurate. The

---

[990] *Ecstatic Religion*, 54-55.
[991] Mark 1:28; 2:2, 4; 3:7-10; 5:17; 6:14, 56; 7:24-25; 10:1.
[992] Mark 1:32-33; 1:45; 2:13; 3:20; 4:1; 5:24; 6:33.
[993] Mark 1:44; 3:12; 5:43; 8:26, 30.
[994] Mark 7:36.
[995] Mark 8:29.

gospel of Mark confronts us with a Jesus who is an outspoken apocalyptic prophet and wonder-worker of rapidly spreading fame. So why the early tradition of secrecy?

Without wishing to retrace the convoluted course of the whole "Messianic secret" argument, I would add a simple explanation for Jesus' insistence on secrecy: it is clear from the papyri that magic was secret, hence carried out under cover of darkness. The sacred names invoked by magicians were secret,[996] and certain spells are disclosed to the magician with the command "Keep it secret!"[997] That magic was generally illegal and magicians subject to prosecution is widely acknowledged. That magic was also mostly performed at night is evident from the texts.[998]

...the "son of David."

Jesus is frequently called the "son of David," a title usually interpreted as a reference to the kingdom of Israel of which Jesus is the promised heir.[999] However, a different explanation has been proposed.

It is notable that the term "son of David" is very frequently used in the context of healing and exorcism, particularly in the formula, "Son of David, take pity on me!"[1000] Jesus is so addressed by the Canaanite woman whose daughter he exorcises,[1001] and after the exorcism of a blind and deaf man, which exorcism is characterized as a healing, the crowd asks, "Can this be the son of David?" In response to this question, the Jewish leaders reply that Jesus *casts out demons* by the power of Beelzeboul, the prince of demons,[1002] i.e., he is not the "son of David." The final occurrence of the title is part of the acclamation of the crowds in the temple at Jerusalem, "Hosanna, Son of David," which is said in recognition that Jesus is a prophet, a wonder-worker who cures the blind and lame.[1003]

---

[996] *Papyri Graecae Magicae* I, 216.
[997] *Papyri Graecae Magicae* IV, 2514, 2519.
[998] *Papyri Graecae Magicae* II, 4; III, 224; IV, 435, 1329, etc.
[999] As at Luke 1:32-33.
[1000] Mark 10:47-48, Matthew 9:27, 20:30, Luke 18:38-39.
[1001] Matthew 15:22.
[1002] Matthew 12:22-24.
[1003] Matthew 21:11.

The context of the gospels firmly connects the "son of David" with exorcism. As has been noted by various scholars,[1004] the son of David was, in fact, *Solomon*,[1005] —"the great exorcist and magician of antiquity, the forerunner of the exorcistic activity of Jesus, and the genius of later Christian magic and divination."[1006] "David and Solomon, whose roles were not those of miracle workers in the canonical books of the O[ld] T[estament], came later to be regarded as exorcists. Whatever may have been the reason for the reinterpretation of the role of many ancient heroes—it seems *not* to have been the Greco-Roman influence—the Jewish traditions furnished a wealth of material of their own for such reinterpretations."[1007]

There is substantial evidence that Solomon's magical abilities were already celebrated in Jesus' lifetime. The *Wisdom of Solomon*, which was probably composed in the Jewish community in Alexandria, Egypt, a century or more prior to Jesus' birth, reflects the belief that Solomon's fabled wisdom consisted of both manifest and occult knowledge. Solomon's wisdom, extolled in 1 Kings,[1008] "surpassed...all the wisdom of Egypt," a land known in antiquity as the cradle of magic. Of Solomon the Septuagint reports, "and his songs were five thousand," a considerable improvement over the 1005 mentioned in the Hebrew bible. Regarding the possible purpose of these songs, it may be recalled that when Solomon's father David played the harp, the evil spirit sent from God left Saul.[1009]

The Σοφια Σαλωμων, the *Wisdom of Solomon*, was included among the apocryphal books of the *Septuagint*, the Greek translation of the Hebrew bible made in Alexandria, Egypt, for the Greek-speaking Jews of the Diaspora. That *Wisdom* was known to the earliest Christians is vir-

---

[1004] Recently by David Duling, whose article "Solomon, Exorcism, and the Son of David" provides a thorough summation of the evidence that *son of David* acknowledged Jesus' magical skills. *Harvard Theological Review* 68:235-252.

Roy Kotansky notes, "David, as an early Jewish exorcist himself anticipating Solomon of later lore, is able to ward off the spirit by singing and playing the kinnor." *Ancient Magic and Ritual Power*, 257.

[1005] Matthew 1:6.

[1006] Rainbow, *Harvard Theological Review* 100: 249.

[1007] Koskenniemi, *Journal of Biblical Literature* 117: 465.

See also Alexander in *The History of the Jewish People in the Age of Jesus Christ*, III, Part I, 375-379.

[1008] 1 Kings 4:29-34.

[1009] 1 Samuel 16:14-23.

tually certain: Romans 9:21 is very likely a close paraphrase of *Wisdom* 15:7. Of Solomon's many gifts, *Wisdom* has this to say:

> For he gave me faultless knowledge of the things that are, to know the structure of the world and the conjuring of elemental spirits,[1010] the beginning, end, and turning points of time, the manner of the change and transitions of the seasons of the year, the orbits and position of the stars, the natural qualities of animals and passions of beasts, the power of spirits[1011] and designs of men, the varieties of plants and powers of roots, I know both what is hidden and what is visible.[1012]

Solomon's accomplishments receive further elaboration in Josephus' *Antiquities of the Jews*, where it is said of him,

> God allowed [Solomon] to learn the art of casting out demons[1013] for the benefit and healing of men and the formulation of incantations[1014] by which sicknesses are healed and he left behind the ways of performing exorcisms…[1015]

In this brief passage from the *Antiquities*, the ωδαι, *songs*, of the *Septuagint* have become επωδαι, *incantations*, and Solomon's mastery of the demons is made explicit. It is from Josephus that we first hear of Solomon's signet ring —which Solomon received from Michael the archangel[1016] — the ring the exorcist Eleazar uses to expel a demon in the presence of no less a person than Vespasian, the future Caesar.[1017]

[1010] συστασιν κοσμου και ενεργειαν **στοιχειων**: "the structure of the world and the conjuring of the **elemental spirits**…"

The term στοιχειον (stoicheion), *elements*, in reference to superhuman spirit powers occurs several times in the writings of Paul and his school (Galatians 4:3, 9; Colossians 2:8).

[1011] **πνευματων** βιας: "the power **of spirits**…" Demonic spirits, as at Mark 1:27.

Georg Luck: "Some translators obscure these facts; they write, e.g., 'the power of the winds', when the context shows that daemons are meant. Josephus certainly understood the passage in this way." *Witchcraft and Magic in Europe: Ancient Greece and Rome*, 117.

[1012] *Wisdom* 7:17-21.

[1013] **την** κατα των δαιμωνιων **τεχνην**: "**the art** of casting out demons…" or literally, "the art against the demons…"

[1014] **επωδας** τε συνταξαμενος: "and the formulation of **incantations**…"

[1015] τροπους εξορκωσεων κατελιπεν: "he left behind the ways **of performing exorcisms**…" *Antiquities* VIII, 45.

[1016] *Testament of Solomon* I, 6.

[1017] *Antiquities* VIII, 46-49.

Solomon's fame is on a rising trajectory from the *Antiquities*, through the *Testament of Solomon* of late antiquity, to the well known grimoires of the present such as the 17th century *Clavicula Salomonis*.[1018] Morton Smith noted that "Solomon's control of demons was a matter of pride for Josephus…is often reported in Rabbinic literature, and is the subject of a romance preserved in several Greek versions, The Testament of Solomon."[1019]

A group of early apotropaic amulets depict a horseman, identified as Solomon, spearing a recumbent female figure, the demon Lilith. The iconography of Solomon the Cavalier spread beyond Jewish circles, becoming the Christian Saint George and the dragon.[1020]

The answer to the question, 'Who is this that he commands the winds and demons?'[1021] is answered when, *in the context of exorcisms*, the New Testament proclaims of Jesus, "Something greater than Solomon is here!"[1022] An early tradition related to the control of demonic power, rather than kingship, is probably in sight and the title "Son of David" is a thinly veiled reference to Jesus' success as an exorcist and healer. The identification of the title with the Messiah who comes from the line of David may be a latter interpretive gloss which shifts the focus away from magical practice.

It is possibly for this reason that Mark, who also used the title, felt no need to concoct a story placing Jesus' birth in Bethlehem, the city of David. For the primitive tradition that Mark represented, "son of David" means simply "successor to Solomon" with all that implies.

[1018] A thorough description of the Solomonic tradition in magical texts is given in Davies' *Grimoires: A History of Magic Books*, 12-15.
[1019] *Jesus the Magician*, 79.
[1020] Alexander, *The Cambridge History of Judaism*, III, 1076-1078.
[1021] Matthew 8:27, Mark 1:27, Luke 8:25.
[1022] Matthew 12:22-32, 42, Luke 11:14-23, 41.

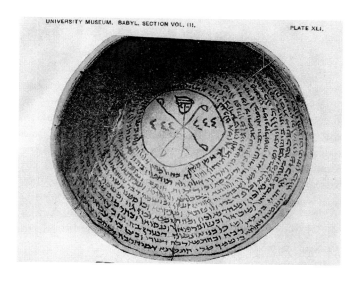

Bowls used for cursing

Chapter 8: A Darker Sorcery

Given the Christian view that connects sorcery with all that is evil, it is quite surprising to find Jesus performing acts that incorporate dark magical elements. It is even more surprising to find some of these accounts clustered in the gospel of John, widely held to be the most theologically evolved gospel.

> As he passed by, he saw a man blind from birth. His disciples asked him, "Rabbi, who sinned, this man or his parents, so that he was born blind?"[1023]
>
> Jesus answered, "Neither this man nor his parents sinned, but it happened so that the works of God might be manifest in him. We must perform the works of the one who sent me while it is day. A night approaches when no one can act. While I am in the world, I am the light of the world."
>
> When he had said this, he spit on the ground, made a paste from the spittle, and smeared the paste on the man's eyes and said to him, "Go wash in the pool of Siloam," which interpreted means Sent. Then he went and washed and came back seeing.
>
> Consequently the neighbors and those who had previously seen that he was a beggar said, "Isn't this the man who sat and begged?" Others said, "That's him!" But others were saying, "No, it's someone like him." The man was saying, "It's me!" So they said to him, "So how were your eyes opened?"
>
> The man answered, "The man called Jesus made a paste and smeared it on my eyes and said to me, 'Go to Siloam and wash,' and then I went and washed and received my sight."[1024]

This episode, like the version in Mark which differs from it in that it requires *two* applications of spit to be effective,[1025] is not conventionally miraculous. Indeed, it fairly reeks of magic: one must do *this*, then *this*, and next *this* to accomplish *that*. The common perception is that

---

[1023] One must wonder exactly when the man sinned, if his punishment was to be *born* blind. The question probably reflects a belief in prenatal demonic attack.
[1024] John 9:1-11.
[1025] Mark 8:22-26. Compare 1 Kings 17:21: Elijah lays on a dead child three times to resuscitate him.

Jesus simply speaks and his miracles occur, but as this account shows, that is not the case. These accounts describe exactly the sort of ritual-istic *step-by-step* procedure typical of the performance of magic.

Regarding the healing of the blind man, Crossan notes: "The magic features of that process are also emphasized by the private nature of the cure 'out of the village.' The concluding injunction not to reenter the village may well be Markan redaction, another of those injunctions to silence that indicate the danger of misunderstanding Jesus' miracles. But the opening separation is part of the traditional story, and it un-derlines the dangerously deviant nature of magical healing."[1026]

So powerful is Jesus' magic that even his clothing takes on talismanic power:

> There was a woman who had suffered from a flow of blood for twelve years, and she had endured many treatments by many doctors and spent everything she had and received no benefit, but had become even worse off.
>
> Having heard about Jesus, she came up from behind him in the crowd and touched his clothing, for she kept saying, "If I just touch his clothes, I will be healed." And immediately her flow of blood dried up and she perceived in her body that she was healed of the affliction.
>
> Suddenly realizing in himself that power had gone out of him, Jesus turned around in the crowd and said, "Who touched my clothes?" His disciples said to him, "You see the crowd pressing in on you and yet you say 'Who touched me?'"
>
> He looked around to see who had done it, but the woman, knowing what had happened to her, came trembling with fear and fell down before him and told him the whole truth. But he said to her, "Daughter, your confidence has healed you. Go in peace and be healed of your affliction."[1027]

Predictably, Matthew's reworking of the story shortens it by excising details, with the net result that the healing is no longer impersonal, i.e., magical, in nature. In Matthew's version Jesus knows he has been touched and turns and heals the woman.[1028] But as Graham Twelftree

---

[1026] *The Historical Jesus*, 325.
[1027] Mark 5:25-34.
[1028] Matthew 9:20-22.

points out, "δυναμις [power, *my note*] works immediately and imper-
sonally, responding to the contact of any believing person without the
knowledge or approval of Jesus."[1029]

Both Matthew and Luke are careful to specify that the bleeding
woman, who was ritually unclean,[1030] touched only the fringe or tassel
of Jesus' garment.[1031] The tassel on the four corners of the garment
marked the wearer as an observant Jew,[1032] —longer tassels signified
greater holiness.[1033] That whoever touched the tassels of Jesus' robe
were healed *ex opere operato*[1034] indicates the impersonal nature of the
healing. Even a scholar who leans toward the apologetic must admit
the 'automatic' nature of this healing, a trait which marks it as magical.[1035]

Similar magical healing became a prominent feature of later Christianity:

> Cures were effected by...contact with the saint, living or, more
> often, dead. So people touched the saint's clothes, the ground on
> which he had stood, the straw on which he had slept, his tomb,
> his relics, his images. Tombs were scraped or chipped and the
> dust or fragments consumed, and the same was done to statues,
> crosses, walls and floors of shrines...Water was drunk that had
> been used to wash the saint's corpse or relics or tomb. At the
> shrine of St Anthony, wine was poured over the relics and ad-
> ministered to patients in tiny amounts.[1036]

This story of the woman with a hemorrhage has provoked some very
interesting observations by John Hull which may be summarized as
follows:

1. the woman exhibits no particular interest in or knowledge of
   Jesus' mission or his person,

[1029] *In the Name of Jesus*, 137.
[1030] Leviticus 15: 25-27.
[1031] Matthew 9:20, Luke 8:44.
[1032] Numbers 15:25-27.
[1033] Matthew 23:5.
[1034] Mark 6:56.
[1035] *Medicine, Miracle and Magic in New Testament Times*, 118.
[1036] *Saints and Their Cults*, 19.

2. she knows the healing power is available independent of Jesus' will,

3. the impersonal nature of Jesus' power is known to himself, the woman, and the evangelist,

4. the power, like electricity, flows automatically to anothers if their touch is deliberate and they have confidence in its efficacy,

5. the power in Jesus is also in the garment,

6. Jesus notices the flow of power, not the touch, and

7. Jesus does not find the woman's action blameworthy.[1037]

Jesus' power is such that other exorcists, unknown to him or his disciples, cast out demons using his name[1038] —"clearly an example of a professional magical use"[1039]— a practice which continues after his death.[1040] Matthew has Jesus himself predict that lawless men will cast out demons, prophesy and perform miracles in his name,[1041] almost certainly in response to the fact that after Jesus' death disreputable men were in fact doing those very things. Regarding the unknown exorcist of Mark 9:38, Schäfer notes that "the magical use of the name of Jesus worked automatically, no matter whether or not the magician believed in Jesus."[1042]

These accounts reveal an attitude toward working miracles that shares the same basic assumption as working magic: power is value-free and available to those who master the techniques required to access it. Such techniques could be taught to an aprentice and power transferred from one practitioner to another. In fact, the gospel of Mark specifies that Jesus taught his disciples —including Judas?— the techniques of exorcism,[1043] and it was the understanding of the impersonal nature of the energy involved that motivated Simon to offer to pay Peter for his miraculous powers.[1044]

[1037] *Hellenistic Magic*, 109-110.

[1038] Mark 9:38-39.

[1039] *Hellenistic Magic*, 72.

[1040] Acts 19:13.

[1041] Matthew 7:21-22.

[1042] *Jesus in the Talmud*, 60.

[1043] Mark 9:28-29.

[1044] Acts 8:18-19. The details of this failed transaction are examined in a subsequent chapter.

Any magical operation presupposes that some sort of energy is available in the universe which can be used by the operator. The modern anthropologists call it *mana*, the Greeks called it *dynamis* [δυναμις, *my note*], "power," or *charis* [χαρις, *my note*[1045]], "grace," or *arete*, [αρετη, *my note*[1046]] "effectiveness." In a polytheistic society, it was only natural that the one Power took on the forms and names of many powers —gods, daemons, heroes, disembodied souls, etc— who were willing, even eager, to work for the *magos*.[1047]

..."the powers are at work in him"

And Herod heard of it, for [Jesus'] name became known and they were saying, "John the Baptist has been raised from the dead and because of this the powers are at work in him.[1048]
    But others said, "He is Elijah," but others, "A prophet, like one of the former prophets." But when Herod heard, he said, "John, the one who I beheaded, has been raised."[1049]

Since Greek does not depend on sentence inversion to indicate a question, the text at Mark 6:16 could also be translated, "But when Herod heard, he said, 'Has John, the one who I beheaded, been raised?'" Various suggestions have been offered for why John was beheaded, including Antipas' desire to see the head as proof of John's death. However, Ross Kraemer has proposed that the gospels emphasize the method of John's death —decapitation— precisely to counter the rumor that Jesus was John raised from the dead:

Why is Jesus not John resurrected from the dead? The Gospel narratives are clear that this identification has been suggested...Jesus is not John raised from the dead because John's body and head were severed: only his body was buried by his disciples, while the

---

[1045] From which χαρισμα, *charisma*, "gift," from whence *charismatic*.
[1046] Hence *aretology*, *a list of virtues*, or in a magician's case, *miracles*.
[1047] *Witchcraft and Magic in Europe: Ancient Greece and Rome*, 105.
[1048] Ιωαννης ο βαπτιζων εγηγερται εκ νεκρων και δια τουτο **ενεργουσιν** αι δυ-ναμεις εν αυτω: "John the Baptist has been raised from the dead and because of this the powers **are at work** in him."
[1049] Mark 6:14-16.

whereabouts of his head, given to Herodias, are unknown, thus, implicitly, making his bodily resurrection impossible.[1050]

From a superficial reading of the gospel text, a person might assume that people were speculating that John the Baptist had been resurrected from the dead in much the same way that Lazarus and others were raised. However, a much different reading, one not only in accord with the circumstances of the times, but with the vocabulary of the passage, was proposed by Carl Kraeling:

> Between demons as the servants of magicians, and spirits of the dead used in a similar way there is no basic distinction. Both are beings of the spiritual order, not limited by time or space, and endowed with supernatural powers...What the people and Herod originally said about Jesus' relation to John was that Jesus was using the spirit of John brought back from the dead to perform his miracles for him.[1051]

The broader context of the story establishes that Herod Antipas not only knew and feared John the Baptist as a holy man, but that he had previously protected him. Furthermore, Herod obviously knew John was dead —Herod himself had ordered John's execution and had seen his head delivered on a platter.[1052]

Whoever "they" were that claimed John the Baptist had been raised from the dead, it is clear that they had known John. Why else would they mention him unless they had been in the crowds that went out to be baptized by him and considered him a prophet?[1053] And they must certainly have known Jesus and seen him in action. What else would explain their animated speculation about the source of his powers? Why, therefore, should we suppose that the crowds who first flocked to hear John the Baptist and later witnessed the wonders performed by Jesus could not tell that John the Baptist and Jesus of Nazareth were two different people? The gospels agree that John attracted large crowds and that he became very well known. John's fame was such that Jesus used it to trap the temple authorities,[1054] and John sent out

---

[1050] *Journal of Biblical Literature* 125: 343.

[1051] Kraeling, "Was Jesus Accused of Necromancy?" *Journal of Biblical Literature* 59: 154-155.

[1052] Mark 6:20, 26-28.

[1053] Mark 1:5. Compare Matthew 3:5, Luke 3:7-15, John 1:20-26.

[1054] Matthew 21:24-26.

disciples to question Jesus.[1055] It strains credibility to suppose that any-one familiar with either man's career thought Jesus could literally have been John raised from the dead, although such confusion may have occurred among people who were *not* eyewitnesses to either man's career, people alive at the time the gospels were being composed.

Note carefully how the common people explained Jesus' powers: "John the Baptist has been raised from the dead *and because of this* the powers are at work in him." The people did not mean that John had been resurrected, but that his ghost had been raised up for magical purposes. The unquiet ghost —the νεκυδαιμων (nekudaimōn)— fell into several categories: the αωρος (aōros), the *untimely dead*, the βιαιο-θανατος (biaiothanatos), the *dead by violence*, the αγαμος (agamos), the *unmarried*, the αταφος (ataphos), the *unburied*, as well as the αγυναιος (agunaios), *wifeless* and the απαιδης (apaidēs), *childless*.[1056]

The power of the "untimely dead" would have lasting repercussions in later Christianity. Legends arose of child saints and confessors, in-cluding Pancras, Agnes, Vitus, Goswin and Donninus, and their cult was spread by the "translation" of their "relics," or body parts from place to place. During the Middle Ages their legends were still con-nected to magic: "In several instances the children were suspected by their persecutors of being magicians rather than saints, and of practic-ing magical arts...The charge may indicate an attempt to reduce the beliefs of Christians into something more understandable to the Ro-mans..."[1057]

In Jesus' day it was widely believed that the ghosts of those who had died before achieving life's goals, particularly by meeting with a violent end or dying without issue, were earth-bound sources of enormous power. Jacob Rabinowitz vividly describes such restless dead: "Needy and dangerous figures waiting in the shadows of existence...particu-larly those who died young or violently, the unhappy and unsatisfied dead with their restless energy and free-floating rage."[1058] Or as Ver-

---

[1055] Matthew 11:2-6.

[1056] For the last two categories see *Papyri Graecae Magicae* IV, 2734.

[1057] *Martyrdom, Murder, and Magic*, 57.

[1058] *The Rotting Goddess: The Origin of the Witch in Classical Antiquity*, 104

See also *Arcana Mundi*, 165-168; *Magic, Witchcraft, and Ghosts in the Greek and Roman Worlds*, 146-152.

The νεκυια (nekuia), the rite by which ghosts are raised, is pre-Homeric.

meule expresses it, "...no living person has the power of even a minor
nameless hero, whose power flows simply from the fact that he is dead
and angry about it, and cannot sleep still...many heroes die angry
...waiting to be avenged for their murders; these are potential actors in
ghost stories, dangerous and partly wakeful."[1059] The ghosts of these
dead are "the typical instruments of malign magic."[1060] I will attempt
to make the case that the 'raising' of John the Baptist described in
Mark is the earliest Christian record of necromancy, the attempt, in the
memorable phrase of Peter Brown, "to join Heaven and Earth at the
grave of a dead human being."[1061] The argument that a form of necromantic practice became central to the function of early Christian miracle and continued in the guise of adoration of martyrs is made in the
next chapter.

That necromancy was known among the Jews of Jesus' era is certain,
as these spells from the *Sepher Ha-Razim* make clear:

These are the angels that obey (you) during the night (if you
wish) to speak with the moon or the stars or to question a ghost
or to speak with the spirits...

If you wish to question a ghost; stand facing a tomb and repeat
the names of the angels of the fifth encampment...I adjure you,
O spirit of the ram bearer [Hermes, *my note*], who dwell among
the graves upon the bones of the dead...[1062]

The "ghost" of the *Sepher Ha-Razim* that one might wish to question is
the familiar אוב (ōb) of the Old Testament.[1063]

Regarding the unburied, "The ατελεστοι [atelestoi, "not completed," *my note*] are
the dead that have not received the due rites. Such spirits, like the ones of those that
have died by violence or before their time, cannot achieve rest..." *Witchcraft and Magic
in Europe: Ancient Greece and Rome*, 22.

For similar concerns about the unquiet dead in Mesopotamia, see *Witchcraft and Magic
in Europe: Biblical and Pagan Societies*, 79-82.

[1059] *Aspects of Death in Early Greek Art and Poetry*, 7, 27.

[1060] Richard Gordon: "a biaiothanatos, those who have been killed by violence, part of
the wider class of the restless dead, who came to be thought of as the typical instruments of malign magic." *Witchcraft and Magic in Europe: Ancient Greece and Rome*, 176.

[1061] *The Cult of the Saints: Its Rise and Function in Latin Christianity*, 1.

[1062] *Sepher Ha-Razim*, 36, 38.

[1063] *Aspects of Religious Propaganda in Judaism and Early Christianity*, 133.

Regarding a possible motive for why Jesus might have selected the ghost of John the Baptist above all others as a source of power, this observation by Daniel Ogden bears careful note:

> How significant were these categories of dead for necromancy in particular? Often the prime criterion in selecting a ghost for necromancy was the relevance of the individual ghost to the matter at hand. Hence, the ghost exploited was often a dear one...A further category that may have been particularly valued for necromancy was that of the exalted ghost.[1064]

Who could have been more relevant to Jesus' career than John the Baptist? He is Jesus' forerunner, "the voice of one crying in the wilderness," even a relative according to Luke, and of those born of women, who was greater than John?[1065]

Because the people believe that Jesus has raised the ghost of John, they conclude that "the powers are at work in him" —the powers of darkness.[1066] In several New Testament passages "powers" make a clear reference to spirit entities,[1067] and of the verb translated "be at work in" —ενεργεω (energeō)— Bertram notes that in the New Testament "theological or demonological use is predominant."[1068] Both the verb and corresponding noun, ενεργεια (energeia), from whence *energy*, are used in the magical papyri for working sorcery.[1069]

In the process of redacting his version of the story, Matthew has Herod say, "This man is John the Baptist. He was raised from the dead and that is why the powers are working in him."[1070] The text makes Herod identify Jesus as John, interpreting Jesus as John redivivus, but this gloss does not fully address the question of *why* the powers would be working in someone because they had been raised from the dead —

[1064] *Greek and Roman Necromancy*, 226-227.

Kraeling cites the fact that John was a *biaiothanatos* in his article and observes that the verb used of raising John is also used in the Greek magical papyri for conjuring spirits of the dead.

[1065] John 1:23, Luke 1:36, Matthew 11:11.

[1066] Compare Colossians 1:13.

[1067] As at Romans 8:38, 1 Peter 3:22.

[1068] *Theological Dictionary of the New Testament*, II, 653.

[1069] *Léxico de magia y religión en los papiros mágicos griegos*, 39.

[1070] Matthew 14:2: ουτος εστιν Ιωαννης ο βαπτιστης αυτος ηγερθη απο των νεκ-ρων και δια τουτο αι δυναμεις ενεργουσιν εν αυτω: "This man is John the Baptist. He was raised from the dead and that is why the powers **are working** in him."

no person raised by Jesus is reported to have had supernatural powers as a result— nor does it contemplate what sort of powers were thought to be involved.

Even Matthew clearly indicates that the 'Herod' of his muddled version of events is mistaken, by no means intending to leave his reader with the impression that Jesus might have been John raised physically from the dead. To clarify the point, he has John's disciples come and take the now headless body away, bury it, *and tell Jesus about it.* Jesus then temporarily retires from the scene.[1071]

Luke, on the other hand, produces a Herod who is "completely perplexed,"[1072] at a seeming loss how to even begin to explain Jesus' famous powers. Apologist scholars such as Susan Garrett admit that Luke rephrases "the most damaging part of the account," to avoid the charge of necromancy, but next claims that the evangelists "did not share modern readers' frequent assumption that identity of appearance implies actual identity."[1073]

Garrett does not explain *how* she knows what assumptions the "evangelists" shared, or explains how else one might establish an identity *based on performance.* The gospel writers apparently assumed that 'trees are known by their fruit.'[1074] Indeed, the frequent alteration and omission of incriminating details by Matthew and Luke indicate that the writers of those gospels shared *exactly* the assumption that appearances imply "actual identity" and knew that their readers would also assume that appearances define identity. Why report Jesus' healings and exorcisms at all if their performance was not thought to establish something about his identity? And why change or delete Mark's reports of Jesus' performance unless the identity established by Mark was not to the liking of Matthew and Luke?

Garrett's argument also ignores the historical evidence of Jesus' reputation among non-Christians —Gentiles regarded Jews as accomplished exorcists and Jesus the Jew as a magician. Evidently his early critics also shared our "modern" assumption that appearances tell us something about identity:

[1071] Matthew 14:12-13.
[1072] Luke 9:7-9.
[1073] *The Demise of the Devil*, 3.
[1074] Matthew 7:20.

The charge that Jesus was a magician has been preserved outside the New Testament in both Jewish and pagan traditions…The church fathers, among them Irenaeus, Arnobius, Justin Martyr, Lactantius, and Origen, were keenly aware of the charge —made by Jew and Gentile alike— that Jesus was a magician. In reply to this assertion, these early Christian writers made no effort to distinguish Jesus' actions from those of a wonder-worker…It was a question not of the form of the wonders, but of the relationship of the purported doer to the person speaking or writing.[1075]

Those pondering the source of Jesus' power, then as now, are torn between two possibilities: he is a prophet like one of the prophets of old and his powers come from the spirit of God, or he is a necromancer and the powers at work in him include the ghost of John the Baptist. Herod Antipas appears to lean toward the latter conclusion: "John, the one who I beheaded, has been raised." Little wonder that the origin of Jesus' authority remains an issue up to the end of his life.[1076] The possibility that Jesus may have fit the description of a אוב בעל (baal ōb), *ghost-master*, or a שאל אוב (shoel ōb), *one who calls up ghosts*, is raised in a previous chapter. In any case, it seems clear enough from the gospel of Mark that the ghost Jesus was accused of calling up was not the Holy Ghost.

…cursing opponents.

That Jesus controlled demons is everywhere acknowledged, even by his enemies, but the fact that he could send unclean spirits into animals and men has received far less attention.

After saying this, Jesus became disturbed in spirit and declared, "Most certainly I tell you, one from among you will betray me!"

The disciples looked around at one another, uncertain about whom he was speaking. One of the disciples —the one that Jesus loved— was lying up against Jesus. Simon Peter motioned him to ask him about whom he was speaking, so the disciple leaning against Jesus' chest said to him, "Lord, who is it?"[1077]

[1075] Steven Ricks, *Ancient Magic and Ritual Power*, 141.
[1076] Matthew 21:23, Mark 11:28, Luke 20:2.
[1077] The disciple Jesus loves is εν τω κολπω του Ιησου: "lying up against Jesus." The term κολπος (kolpos), which is often translated "bosom," can mean "lap" when

Jesus answered, "It is the one I give the morsel of bread that I dip. Then he took the morsel and dipped it and gave it to Judas, the son of Simon Iscariot. And after the morsel, then Satan entered into him.

Jesus said to him, "Do what you are doing more quickly."[1078] But none of those reclining with Jesus knew why he said that to him.[1079]

As soon as John tells us that Jesus "became disturbed in spirit" we are put on notice of an impending supernatural event. Such "disturbances" in the gospel of John always precede miraculous occurrences. When the water of the pool of Bethzatha is "stirred" by an angel, the first sick person in is healed —a sort of divinely-sponsored 'race for the cure'— and when Jesus' soul is "troubled" a heavenly voice is heard. Jesus becomes similarly "disturbed" on first encountering the mourners at Lazarus' tomb and again as he stands before the tomb itself —the raising of the beloved Lazarus quickly follows.[1080]

In the case of the final meal with his disciples, Jesus' disturbance of spirit again signals a preternatural event, two of them to be exact. First, Jesus foresees Judas' betrayal —that Jesus has the power to read thoughts is everywhere stated in John (John 1:47-48; 2:24-25; 4:16-18; 5:42; 6:61, etc.). John 6:64 even says that Jesus foreknew which of his disciples did not believe and which would betray him (compare Mark 2:8). It should nearly go without saying that the power to read others' intentions is a frequent preoccupation of the magical books: "let me foresee today the things in the soul of each person…"[1081]

---

applied to humans (Luke 6:38), or can refer to the fold of a garment, or to a bay where it "folds" into the land. It is the hollow formed where the trunk of the body bends at the waist. The picture John presents is that to two men lying close enough to "make spoons."

John also uses the imagery of the pre-existent Word who is "in the bosom of the Father" (John 1:18), an expression meant to pointedly emphasize intimate association and the knowledge that flows from it.

[1078] As noted by Morton Smith, this comparative use of ταχυς, *quickly*, appears to echo a frequently attested conclusion to magical spells, ηδη ηδη ταχυ ταχυ: *now, now, quick, quick. Jesus the Magician*, 111.

[1079] John 13:21-28.

[1080] John 5:7. The longer text found in the *King James Version*, which explains the agitation of the water as the result of an angel, likely originated as a marginal gloss which was later copied into the body of the text.

John 12:27-29, 11:33, 38.

[1081] *Papyri Graecae Magicae* III, 265, to cite one of many examples.

Next Jesus hands Judas over to Satan so that Satan can destroy him. There is a clear precedent for this action: he has previously handed a herd of swine over to the horde of demons that drove the pigs over a cliff to their death —as previously noted, "transference of the disease or demon from the man to the animal" is a well-attested magical technique in the ancient Middle East.[1082] As Davies noted over a century ago,

> Demons were among the later Jews supposed to be capable of being transferred from one individual to another, or from human beings to animals. We come across this formula in the Talmud: "May the blindness of M, son of N, leave him and pierce the eyeballs of this dog."[1083]

As pointed out by Strelan, the use of animals, particularly dogs, for cleansing and healing was common: "a dog, through contact with an ill person, was thought to contract the disease...Rubbing people with the dead bodies of puppies was thought to cause all harmful and polluting substances to be absorbed by the animal, and thus remove them from the person."[1084] Magical transference might be accomplished through words, gestures, spells, or even ensorcelled food.

Tzvi Abusch: "There need not always be a lack of proximity between victim and witch...she causes her victim to incorporate witchcraft by means of food, drink, washing, and ointment."[1085]

The piece of bread that Jesus dips in the bowl and hands to Judas is the equivalent of Judas' kiss of betrayal: it is the sign to the Adversary to approach and take control. Morton Smith: "The notion that a demon can be sent into food so as to enter anyone who eats the food is common."[1086] Jesus betrays Judas to Satan before Judas betrays Jesus to the temple police. In so doing, Jesus is merely following the example set in the Old Testament where God regularly sends evil spirits into those of whom he disapproves.[1087] Regarding "masters of spirits,"

[1082] *Witchcraft and Magic in Europe: Biblical and Pagan Societies*, 71-75.
[1083] *Magic, Divination, and Demonology Among the Hebrews and their Neighbors*, 104, Kessinger (reprint).
[1084] *Biblical Theology Bulletin* 33:149.
[1085] *Mesopotamian Witchcraft: Toward a History and Understanding of Babylonian Witchcraft Beliefs and Literature*, 7.
[1086] *Jesus the Magician*, 110
[1087] Judges 9:23, 1 Samuel 16:15, 16, 23, 18:10, 19:9.

Lewis asked, "if their power over the spirits is such that they can heal the sick, why should they not also sometimes cause what they cure?"[1088]

The gospel admittedly does not say the morsel of bread was offered *to* Satan, only that "after the morsel, then Satan entered into him."[1089] The magical papyri record this attraction spell, used to call up the gods of the underworld, that utilizes morsels of bread:

> Leave a little of the bread you did not eat, and breaking it apart, make seven morsels and go where heroes and gladiators and men who died violently were slaughtered. Say the spell into the morsels[1090] and throw them.
> This is the spell to be pronounced into the morsels…[1091]

Apparently after the spell goes "into the morsels," the infernal deities eat the pieces of bread now imbued with the spell, and the spell is activated.

The notion that powerful entities, good or bad, can be transferred into or out of a subject is the very basis for exorcism as well as hexing a victim. As Ann Jeffers points out,

> The magical principle behind the treatment of diseases can be identified as that of correspondence or symbolic magic, the more important effect being the transfer of the illness into a concrete thing, liquid, person or animal through various rituals. We should also note that the means used to heal a person can be used to harm him, showing that the forces used in rituals are fundamentally neutral.[1092]

The magical papyri and curse tablets supply us with many examples of black magic. The verb used in the New Testament which is translated "hand over," παραδιδωμι (paradidōmi), is commonly used in magical curse tablets —known as a καταδεσμος (katadesmos) or 'tie down' in

---

[1088] *Ecstatic Religion*, 33.

[1089] και μετα το ψωμιον τοτε εισηλθεν εις εκεινον ο Σατανας : "and after the **morsel**, then Satan entered into him." John 13:27.

[1090] λεγε τον λογον **εις** τους ψωμους: "Say the spell **into** the morsels…"

[1091] *Papyri Graecae Magicae* IV, 1392-1395.

[1092] *Magic and Divination in Ancient Palestine and Syria*, 235.

Greek and as a *defixio* or 'nail down' in Latin— to send a person's soul to the gods of the underworld. For example, we find this curse, carved on a tombstone, directed against anyone who might disturb the man's grave: "...I hand him over to the gods of the underworld."[1093]

That Jewish magicians in the time of Jesus used techniques of cursing opponents is certain. The *Sepher Ha-Razim* preserves this spell: "I deliver to you, angels of anger and wrath, N son of N, that you will strangle him and destroy him and his appearance, etc..."[1094]

Specific references to Jesus cursing people to death, if such events occurred, have been removed from the gospels, but the fact that Jesus could curse something to death is supported by the story of the withered fig tree.[1095] The anonymous author of the *Infancy Gospel of Thomas* had no trouble imagining that Jesus could curse people to death. He has Jesus killing other children by magic starting when he is only five years old, as well as crippling and blinding the objects of his infantile temper.[1096]

However, an example of an indirect form of cursing to death is given in Matthew 26:24: "Woe to that man through whom the son of man is handed over! Better for him if that man had not been born!"[1097] In response to this proleptic countercurse, Judas hangs himself.[1098] As Myllykoski notes, "The horrible death of Judas [Acts 1:18-19, *my note*] can also be considered a divine *Strafwunder*, even though there is no agent mentioned."[1099]

The attitude of early Christians toward their opponents, particularly toward nonconformists arising from within their midst, was from the very first one of intense opposition. Even as Jesus handed Judas over to the Adversary, Jesus' followers exercise the power both to strike people dead on the spot, as well as hand them over to Satan.[1100] The

---

[1093] παραδιδωμαι αυτον θεοις καταχθονιοις: "**I hand** him **over** to the gods of the underworld..." *New Documents Illustrating Early Christianity* 4:165.
[1094] *Sepher Ha-Razim*, 27.
[1095] Mark 11:13, 21-24.
[1096] *Infancy Gospel of Thomas* 3:3, 4:1-4, 8:3.
[1097] ουαι δε τω ανθρωπω εκεινω δι ου ο υιος του ανθρωπου παραδιδοται: "Woe to that man through whom the son of man **is handed over**..."
[1098] Matthew 27:5.
[1099] *Wonders Never Cease*, 156.
[1100] Acts 5:1-11. Compare the response of James and John in Luke 9:54.

process of "handing someone over" to demonic forces is a well documented technique in the magical papyri:

> Next, take [the curse written on papyrus] off to the tomb of one dead before his time,[1101] dig down four fingers deep and put it in [the hole] and say:
> "Spirit of the dead, whoever you may be, I hand [Name] over to you[1102] so that he may not accomplish [named] action." Then, after burying it, go away. Better you do it when the moon is waning...[1103]

Of this procedure Deissmann remarks,

> "A person who wished to injure an enemy or to punish an evildoer consecrated him by incantation and tablet to the powers of darkness below...The only difference between Jewish and pagan execrations probably lay in the fact that Satan took the place of the gods of the lower world."[1104]

In his letter to the Corinthians regarding a man in an incestuous relationship, Paul commands the congregation "to hand such a person over to Satan for the destruction of the flesh."[1105] And in the pseudo-Pauline 'pastoral' epistle, two more miscreants are similarly "handed over" to Satan.[1106] As noted by Adela Yarbro Collins, "The tradition of Greek magic helps explain why the procedure advocated by Paul took the form it did and how the process was expected to work...the passage is quite similar to the thought of the magical papyri. The recalcitrant opponents are to be consigned to a demonic power which will prevent them from doing a type of deed."[1107]

Paul's correspondence even contains curses pronounced upon those who deviate from his gospel:

[1101] εις αωρου μνημα: "to the tomb **of one dead before his time**..."
[1102] **παραδιδωμι** σοι τον δεινα: "**I hand** [Name] **over** to you..."
[1103] *Papyri Graecae Magicae*, V, 332.
[1104] *Light from the Ancient East*, 302.
[1105] 1 Corinthians 5:5: **παραδουναι** τον τοιουτον τω σατανα εις ολεθρον της σαρκος: "**to hand** such a person **over** to Satan for the destruction of the flesh..."
[1106] 1 Timothy 1:20: Υμεναιος και Αλεξανδρος ους **παρεδωκα** τω σατανα: "Hymenius and Alexander, whom **I handed over** to Satan..."
[1107] *Harvard Theological Review* 73: 256, 258.

> For even if we, or an angel from heaven, proclaim a gospel different from the gospel we preached to you, a curse on him![1108]
> As we have said before, even now I repeat, if anyone proclaims a gospel contrary to what you received, a curse on him!...Oh foolish Galatians, who bewitched you?[1109]

As Betz notes in his commentary, "Galatians begins with a conditional curse, very carefully constructed, cursing every Christian who dares to preach a gospel different from that which Paul had preached...What does this imply for the literary function of the letter? It means that as the carrier of curse and blessing the letter becomes a 'magical letter.' This category is well-known from ancient epistolography."[1110]

Regarding the bewitching of the Galatian Christians —τις υμας εβασκανεν: "who bewitched you"— Neyrey says, "It is my hypothesis that Paul is using it [the term for casting the evil eye, *my note*] in its formal sense as an accusation that someone has bewitched the Galatians." In an extended analysis, he goes on to note "evidence of an intense sense of rivalry, competition, and even jealousy...Galatians fairly bristles with a sense of rivalry and competition."[1111]

So the short answer to Paul's question, "Who bewitched you?" is *other Christians*. In the world of the early Christians βασκανια (baskania), *jealousy* or *envy*, was thought to be the driving force behind the βασκανος οφθαλμος or *evil eye*. By extension *baskania* also designated *bewitchment*, and βασκανος (baskanos) meant both *slanderer, envious* (one) and *sorcerer*. Christians considered envy as a basic component of the personality of Satan. In the apocryphal *Acts of Thomas*, the demon is addressed as "O **Jealous One** who never rests" —ο βασκανος ο μηδεποτε ηρεμων.[1112]

[1108] αναθεμα εστω: literally, "Let him be **accursed**!"
[1109] Galatians 1:8-9; 3:1.
[1110] *Galatians*, 25.
[1111] *Catholic Biblical Quarterly* 50: 72, 97.
[1112] *Acts of Thomas*, 44.

Regarding the common fear that success would attract not only human, but supernatural envy, Dickie remarks, "men were afraid lest their good fortune would draw envy on their heads. They might fear it would come from their fellow men, demons, the gods, fortune, the fates, and a malign supernatural power they called simply φθονος or *invidia*. *Byzantine Magic*, 12.

In summary, Paul is accusing other Christians of witchery driven by envy and the book of Galatians functions as a kind of countercurse against their malign influence. The possibility that Paul himself had a reputation for sorcery is raised by the apocryphal *Acts of Paul* which records the reaction of the people when Paul is hauled into court for preaching sexual abstinence: απαγαγε τον μαγον διεφθειρεν γαρ ημων πασας τας γυναικας: "Away with **the magician**! He has corrupted all our wives!"[1113]

In the account about Ananias and his wife Sapphira, the apostle Peter performs a "punitive action, which is a typical feature of magic,"[1114] causing the death of both. Ananias, confronted with his dishonesty, drops dead on the spot. Three hours later his wife arrives, reiterates their lie, and is told, "Why did you conspire to test the spirit of the Lord? Now look! The feet of the men who buried your husband are at the door and they will carry you out! Instantly she fell at his feet and expired."[1115]

> In contrast to the gospels, *Strafwunder* occupy a very prominent position in the 'Acts of the Apostles' where they are performed by both Peter and Paul. In the story of Ananias and Sapphira, Peter presides over the death of Ananias (Acts 5:5), who dies without the invocation of a curse, while the death of his wife Sapphira (5:10) is preceded by a curse (5:9) which becomes immediately effective...Elymas the magician is struck blind in consequence of an imprecation pronounced by Paul...In early Christian apocryphal literature, the incidence of *Strafwunder* attributed to both Jesus and the apostles exhibits a marked increase in frequency...[1116]

Meyer notes "the express authorization for the disciples to curse cities and individuals,"[1117] and the use of magic against opponents continues long after the death of the apostles: "An unworthy woman was paralyzed when she received the eucharist at Paul's hands...and an unworthy lad's hands withered when he took the elements from Thomas

---

[1113] *Acts of Paul*, 15.
[1114] *Medicine, Miracle and Magic in New Testament Times*, 118.
[1115] Acts 5:9-10.
[1116] David Aune, *Aufstieg und Niedergang der Römischen Welt*, II.23.2: 1552-1553.
  Strafwunder refers to a miracle of punishment. The German *straf* is the basis of the English word *strafe*.
[1117] *Ancient Christian Magic*, 185.

...As a result of slapping Thomas, a man dies, as Thomas had predicted he would...Simon is struck dumb when a baby speaks to him with a man's voice, and Simon kills a boy by whispering in his ear...At Peter's prayer, the flying Simon falls and breaks his leg in three places."[1118] Within the canonical gospels and Acts, ritualistic magical behavior is also in evidence: "shake the dust from your feet,"[1119] and "he shook out his clothing."[1120]

The apocryphal Acts both continue and enlarge upon this rich tradition of magical cursing. When Drusiana raises Fortunatus from the dead, the young man denounces her act (of necromancy?) and flees, provoking this curse of incandescent malignancy from the apostle:

> Be thou destroyed from among those who trust in the Lord, from their thoughts, from their mind, from their souls, from their bodies, from their affairs, from their life, from their conversation, from their death, from their business, from their counsel, from the resurrection unto God, from the fragrance of fellowship you share, from their fasts, from their prayers, from the holy bath, from the Eucharist, from food for the body, from drink, from clothing, from love, from abstinence, from self-control, from righteousness, from all these, may you be profaned before God! Hated Satan! Jesus Christ our God will destroy you and those who share your character![1121]

The apostle soon announces, "Brothers, some spirit in me[1122] foretold that Fortunatus is about to die from the blackness of a snake bite." The young men run in search of him and find him dead as John has described. Triumphant, the apostle declares, "Your child is delievered, O Devil!"[1123]

The posture of Christianity was one of active aggression directed toward opponents, an attitude that crystallized into summary executions once the Roman state had embraced the new religion. As Paul himself

---

[1118] *Aspects of Religious Propaganda in Judaism and Early Christianity*, 166.
[1119] Matthew 10:11-15, Luke 9:5, 54.
[1120] Acts 18:6.
[1121] *Acta Ioannis*, 84.
[1122] πνευμα τι εν εμοι εμαντευσατο: "**some spirit** in me foretold..."
[1123] *Acta Ioannis*, 86.

MAGIC IN THE NEW TESTAMENT

so correctly observed about the Christian response to opposition, "The kingdom of God is not about speech, but about power."[1124]

Occasionally the bargain was explicit: acknowledge God or be punished. So an ascetic of Hermoupolis in Egypt reduces a procession of non-Christian worshippers to frozen immobility, right in the middle of the road, through spells; and they cannot regain the use of their limbs until they 'renounce their error.' Or you might defy the ascetic—in this case, Aphraates, in a Syrian city—and by no mere coincidence, straightway you died a horrible death. From that, people 'realized the strength of Aphraates' prayer.'[1125]

It should come as no surprise that Christian curses appear in surviving magical texts. The offended Sabinos prays regarding his daughter, "Let her body wither away in bed..." and ends his curse with "strike [my] enemies with your hard hands! Do justice, Emmanuel, do justice!"[1126] Or to take another example: "Holy God, Gabriel, Michael...smite Phēradelphēs and her children, Lord, Lord, Lord, God, God, strike her down with Jesus Christ! Have mercy on me and hear me, Lord."[1127]

...necromantic sortilege

In earliest Christianity we find another strong parallel with pagan practice: as the apostles attempted to select a replacement for the traitor Judas, they engaged in a séance. They first pray to Jesus to designate a successor and then cast lots —κλῆρος (klēros), lot— which fall to Mathias.[1128] This is a straightforward example of necromantic sortilege:

Sanctuaries where divination was exercised regularly, as part of the cult of the god, are known as oracles (L. oracula, Gk. manteia or chresteria). But as noted earlier, an oracle is also the response of the god to a question asked by a visitor to the shrine.

[1124] 1 Corinthians 4:20.
[1125] *Christianizing the Roman Empire*, 62.
[1126] *Supplementum Magicum*, 59.
[1127] *Supplementum Magicum*, 61.
[1128] Acts 1:23-26.

The method of divination varied from shrine to shrine. Sometimes the will of the god was explored by the casting or drawing of lots (*kleroi, sortes*) —for example, dice or sticks or bones. The word *sortilegus* originally designated a soothsayer who practiced this particular method of divination (*sortes legere* 'to pick up lots'); later by extension, it referred to any type of prophecy or sorcery.[1129]

...the Christian 'busybodies' —sorcery in action

The early Christians were accused of being "evildoers" and "meddlers" and the charge of "meddling" was serious enough to warrant execution:

Nor may any of you suffer death as a murderer, or an evildoer, or a thief, or as a meddler in others affairs...[1130]

The Greek term αλλοτριεπισκοπος (allotriepiskopos), which I've translated "meddler in others affairs" merits extended comment. The word occurs only in this passage in the New Testament. It is a compound word composed of αλλοτριος (allotrios), meaning *foreign*, or *belonging to another*, and επισκοπος (episkopos) *inspector, overseer, guardian*. That being said, it should be noted that the *etiology* of a word is not the *definition* of a word, so knowing the elements from which the word was formed does not tell us much about how the recipients of the epistle of 1 Peter may have interpreted the term.

Various attempts, all speculative, have been made to discern the meaning of this word both in the context of the letter of 1 Peter — written pseudonymously decades after Peter's death— and in the context of the society of the day. Whatever the meaning of such "meddling," it was a capital offense, on par with theft and murder. It seems unlikely that such punishment, however well deserved, was meted out to the local neighborhood busybody or even to officious Christians who then like today considered themselves society's moral guardians. It has been claimed that "It is unnecessary...to propose a

---

[1129] Luck, *Arcana Mundi*, 244.
[1130] 1 Peter 4:15.

ως φονευς η **κακοποιος** η κλεπτης η ως αλλοτριεπισκοπος: "as a murderer, or an **evildoer**, or a thief or as a meddler in others affairs..."

more serious form of activity than the one suggested by the English translation equivalents 'meddler' or 'busybody'" which, it is said, was "considered by some to be subversive to the fabric of society."[1131] It seems that to substantiate this assertion one would have to produce some evidence that the Roman authorities actually executed busybodies with anything approaching the frequency with which murderers and brigands were dispatched.

The term "meddler" is linked in the passage with the term "evildoer," the same charge brought against Jesus at his trial. It has been argued (Chapter 4) that the evil Jesus was accused of doing was sorcery. Elsewhere in the epistle, the writer notes of Christians that "they slander you as evildoers."[1132] Like murder and theft, the practice of magic was considered a crime punishable by death and the Romans credited both Jews and Christians —who were not clearly distinguished from Jews— with the practice of magic. As noted by Selwyn, Tertullian translated κακοποιος in 1 Peter 4:15 with the Latin *maleficus*, meaning *magician*.[1133]

That the Roman government sometimes prosecuted people engaged in magical practice with a ferocity that approached caricature is clear from the report of the historian Ammianus Marcellinus, who records such an episode of violent persecution: "...for if anyone wore on his neck an amulet against the quartan ague, or was accused by the testimony of the evil-disposed of passing by a grave in the evening, on the ground that he was a dealer in poisons,[1134] or a gatherer of horrors of tombs and the vain illusions of the ghosts that walk there, he was condemned to capital punishment and so perished."[1135]

When Marcus Aurelius speaks of τερατευμενοι (terateumenoi), *miracle-mongers*, and γοητες (goētes), *sorcerers*, it is thought likely that he had Christian exorcists in mind.[1136] The term γοης, meaning *fraud* or *sor-*

[1131] *Journal of Biblical Literature* 125: 549.

[1132] 1 Peter 2:12: καταλαλουσιν υμων ως **κακοποιων**: "they slander you as **evildoers**."

[1133] *The First Epistle of St. Peter: The Greek Text with Introduction, Notes and Essays*, 225.

[1134] *ut veneficus.* "a dealer in poisons," i.e., a sorcerer who might gather body parts for necromantic rites during which ghosts were summoned and questioned about the future.

[1135] *Ammianus Marcellinus* XIX, 14.

[1136] *Meditations* I, 6.

cerer, or both, occurs only once in the New Testament: "Evil men and *frauds* will give ever worse offense, misleading and being misled."[1137]

The case that γοης in 2 Timothy 3:13 might be translated "sorcerer" —although no English translation does so— based on the context has been made by Lloyd Pietersen, who points out that the close context of the letter compares the writer's opponents to Jannes and Jambres (3:8),[1138] magicians who engaged in a magical duel with Moses.[1139] Further favoring this interpretation of *goēs* is the nearly parallel phraseology used by Philo of those who employ "enchantments and charms,"[1140] and "transform rods into real serpents."[1141] Philo's magicians "are ever more deceived while thinking they are deceiving others"[1142] like pseudo-Paul's evil men who are "misleading and being misled."[1143]

Julian, a Christian who converted to a theurgic form of paganism prior to becoming emperor, said, "I will point out that Jesus the Nazarene, and Paul also, outdid in every respect all the sorcerers and tricksters."[1144] Celsus also described Jesus as a sorcerer. In short, Roman officials regarded Christians as more than merely obnoxious and meddlesome; they were widely suspected of performing nocturnal magical rites. Suetonius said that Christianity was "a new and evil superstition" —"*superstitio nova et malefica*"— a charge which carried "connotations of magical practices and sorcery."[1145] As noted previously in the discussion of the Beelzeboul controversy, Jesus' wonder-working undermined authority, a charge also leveled against his followers. Indeed,

---

A number of Christians were executed under his generally benign rule, including the relentless busybody, Justin Martyr.

[1137] 2 Timothy 3:13: πονηροι δε ανθρωποι και **γοητες** προκοψουσιν επι το χειρον πλανωντες και πλανωμενοι: "Evil men and **frauds** will give ever worse offense, misleading and being misled."

[1138] *Magic in the Biblical World*, 166.

[1139] Exodus 7:10-12.

[1140] τους επαοιδους και φαρμακευτας: "enchantments and charms"

[1141] τας βακτηριας εις δρακοντων μεταστοχειουσι φυσεις: "transform rods into real serpents"

[1142] συναυξοντες απατον δοκουντες απατωναι: "are ever more deceived while thinking they are deceiving others," *De migratione Abrahami*, 83.

[1143] πλανωντες και πλανωμενοι: "misleading and being misled," 2 Timothy 3:13.

[1144] *Against the Galileans*, I, 100. τους πωποτε **γοητας** και απατεωνας: "the **sorcerers** and tricksters..."

[1145] *Pagan Rome and the Early Christians*, 20-21.

early Christianity not only redefined the *faithful*, it radically redefined authority itself.[1146]

Paul was known for works of power, "in word and deed, by the power of signs and wonders, in powerful works of the spirit"[1147] to quote his own boast, so it comes as little surprise that the apocryphal Acts recall accusations of practicing sorcery leveled against Paul. As Bremmer notes of Paul's influence in *The Acts of Paul and Thecla*, "Thecla, as the mother vividly described her, 'sticks to a window like a spider...bound by a new desire and fearful passion' [2.9]. The term 'bound' [δεδεμενη, from δεω, *my note*], as used by Theoclia, recurs later when Thamyris finds Thecla 'bound with him [συνδεδεμενεν, a compound of δεω, *my note*] in affection' [2.19]. These recurring references to 'binding' suggest a case of erotic magic; they prepare the reader for the later accusation of Paul as a performer of erotic magic."[1148] The words of Paul weave a spell over the women of the town. Thecla, who is betrothed, renounces marriage, and her fiancé, Thamyris, brings a complaint against the apostle with the following result:

> And the whole crowd shouted: "Away with the sorcerer! For he has corrupted all our wives."[1149]

One of the several editions of the *Acts of Paul* contains the freakish story of Paul and the "baptized lion," an elaboration of Paul's claim to have fought with the beasts in Ephesus.[1150] When Paul's encounter with the lion in the arena fails to end in his dismemberment, the crowd screams, "Away with the magician! Away with the sorcerer!"[1151]

There are several Greek synonyms for αλλοτριεπισκοπος which refer to prying into what is off limits. A more common synonym is the adjective περιεργος (periergos) and the related verb περιεργοζομαι (periergazomai) which occur in three places in the New Testament.

[1146] *Medicine, Miracle and Magic in New Testament Times*, 73.

[1147] εν δυναμει σημειων και τερατων εν δυναμει πνευματος: "by the power of signs and wonders, in powerful works of the spirit..." Romans 15:18.

[1148] *The Apocryphal Acts of Paul and Thecla*, 42.

[1149] *New Testament Apocrypha*, II, 357.

[1150] 1 Corinthians 15:32.

[1151] αραι τον **μαγον**, αραι τον **φαρμακον**: "Away with the **magician**! Away with the **sorcerer**!" *Hellenistic Greek Texts*, 129.

In two cases the context links snooping with an excess of leisure: "We hear that some among you are conducting themselves in a disorderly way, not working, but meddling in others affairs."[1152] The writer does not specify in what the disorderly behavior consisted, nor does he indicate in what exactly the reprimanded subjects were meddling, but there is no suggestion that the meddling was overtly magical in nature.

The second case, part of an advisory on enrolling young widows in congregationally sponsored assistance programs, is part of an early Christian version of *kinder, küche, kirche*: "...they learn to gallivant around from house to house, not only lazy, but prattling and meddlesome, talking about what is not proper..."[1153] Although the writer is sure that such young women with too much time on their hands are up to no good, he does not appear to be accusing them of witchcraft.

It is in the next occurrence of περιεργος that we find a meaning pertinent to the text of 1 Peter 4:15. In Acts 19:19 we are told of Christian converts, many of whom were "dabbling in the magical arts,"[1154] who brought their books out and burned them. It is worth asking if the burning of a book might not be considered a sort of countercurse in itself, but the point being made is the use of the fixed expression τα περιεργα (ta perierga), *things about which one should not inquire*, that is, *magical arts*. That *periergos* is a synonym for *magos, magician*, is clear from the apocryphal *Acts of Andrew*, where the apostle clearly equates the terms περιεργος, μαγος and αλλοτριος: "God, who harkens not to magicians,[1155] God, who submits not to sorcerers,[1156] God, who remains far from those foreign to him..."[1157]

In this context, an extended quote from an official circular of the 2nd century, published in Roman Egypt, sheds some light on what was covered by the term:

[1152] μηδεν εργαζομενους αλλα **περιεργαζομενους**...: "not working, but **meddling in others affairs**..." 2 Thessalonians 3:11.
[1153] φλυαροι και **περιεργοι**...: "prattling and **meddlesome**..." 1 Timothy 5:13.
[1154] ικανοι δε των **τα περιεργα** πραξαντων...: "many of those dabbling in **the magical arts**..."
[1155] **μαγοις** μη επακουων: "who harkens not **to magicians**..."
[1156] **περιεργοις** μη παρεχων εαυτον: "who submits not **to sorcerers**..."
[1157] ο **των αλλοτριων** αφισταμενος θεος: "God, who remains far from **those foreign** to him..." *Acta Andreae*, 447.

[Since I have come across many people] who consider themselves to be beguiled by the means of divination [immediately I thought it essential], so that no risk should follow from their foolishness, to state explicitly here to all to abstain from this misleading curiosity.[1158] Therefore neither through oracles, viz., written documents ostensibly emanating in the presence of the divinity, nor by the means of procession of images or similar trickery, let anyone lay claim to have knowledge of the supernatural, or give himself out as an expert about the obscurity of future events...if anyone is discovered sticking to this undertaking, let him be sure that he will be handed over for capital punishment..."[1159]

In short, there is considerable circumstantial evidence to suggest that the "meddling" against which the readers of 1 Peter were being warned were accusations of practicing magic. In Plutarch's essay on being a busybody, he refers to the goals and activities associated with meddling, goals identical in many cases to those achieved through magic: "... but if meddling in degraded things,[1160] like a maggot in dead matter, proves altogether necessary...seductions of women... compounding of potions[1161]...insinuate themselves into forbidden assemblies, behold sacred rites it is not lawful to see, trample holy ground, and pry into the actions and words of rulers."[1162] A magical spell to induce a woman to have sexual relations —known as an αγωγη (agōgē), a *spell for attraction*— was a common enough form of magic, and to foretell the death of a ruler through divination, a capital crime. Charges of malicious sorcery continued to circulate against Christians for centuries: "Christian miracle was cruel and destructive: the saints burned a palace with its inhabitants and murdered the magician...the pagan magician was here a provider of food, and the disciples of St. Paul arsonists and killers."[1163]

[1158] της επισφαλους ταυτης **περιεργιας**: "this misleading **curiosity**..."
Perhaps better translated, "this dangerous curiosity," since its practice would lead to execution.

[1159] *New Documents Illustrating Early Christianity*, I, 47-48.

[1160] **το περιεργον** εν φαυλοις τισιν: "**meddling** in degraded things..."

[1161] παρασκευαι **φαρμακων**: "compounding of **potions**..." The reference would also cover the preparation of poisons.

[1162] *Moralia* VI, 486-514.

[1163] Kazhdan, *Byzantine Magic*, 79.

It is primarily through the holes in the narrative seams of the gospels that we catch a fleeting glimpse of Jesus the man, the man condemned to stand forever in the shadow of the Christ. To the office of apocalyptic prophet we may now add a second, that of ecstatic wonder worker. Jesus would likely have been regarded by the pagan population of his day as a γοης (goēs), or "wailer," a sorcerer, a necromancer, or merely as a charlatan, a fraud. The ancient world was a full of wonderworkers —θαυματουργος (thaumatourgos), *thaumaturge*, is only one of many terms we have inherited from it. Magicians were the faith healers and televangelists of their day, and like their modern counterparts, the religious actors of Jesus' day were received with responses that spanned the spectrum from bug-eyed credulity to smirking derision.

It is initially surprising how easily exorcism, magic, and apocalyptic speech flow together in the person of Jesus, breaking through the artificially imposed categories laid down by centuries of theology. In point of fact, we see little distinction in our texts between religion and magic, or between healing and magic. In both Mark and John, the magical details of Jesus' workings are reported quite ingenuously, with little awareness of a difference between magic and miracle, whereas Matthew and Luke carefully filter the same details out of their accounts, attempting at every turn to distinguish Jesus from other itinerant healers who prophesy and cure blindness with spittle and dirt. But as Mark and John reveal, at the level of the earliest, most primitive tradition, it is a distinction without a difference.

Chapter 9: Christian Necromancy

The degree to which the worlds of the living and the dead intersected in the ancient world can hardly be overestimated. As Betz remarks in his introduction to the magical papyri, earthly life as seen through the lens of the magical texts "seems to consist of nothing but negotiations in the antechamber of death and the world of the dead."[1164] The people of antiquity were familiar with the face of death. Many children died in infancy, many women died in childbirth, nearly all people died at home and the responsibility for the washing, dressing, carrying out and burial of bodies fell to family members. In times of plague and famine, death was literally in the streets, a visitor in every house. Against this background of day-to-day mortality were superimposed violent crime, domestic abuse, political assassinations, wars that swept up civilian populations, infanticide, public executions, brawling, and fighting to the death as entertainment.

Yet despite the proximity of the living and the dead, normative religious practice dictated that certain boundaries between their worlds be enforced, and transgression of those limits was the very mark of black magic. With the advent of Christianity, however, pagan religious practice was overturned and the boundary between the living and the dead utterly breached.

...calling up Lazarus

I have attempted to make the case elsewhere[1165] that some within early Christianity saw the raising of Lazarus, the beloved disciple,[1166] as an enacted parable of Jesus' own rising from the dead, an identification which I believe may go back to the time of Jesus himself. That identity was reinforced through the use of various markers, including the im-

---

[1164] *The Greek Magical Papyri in Translation*, xlvii.

[1165] *Jesus the Sorcerer*, 231-256.

[1166] There are six references to the beloved disciple, all occurring late in the gospel of John: 13:23, 19:26, 21:7, 20 in which he is ον ηγαπα: "the one **he loved**," and John 20:2 in which he is ον εφιλει: "the one **he loved**."

age of linen grave clothes. Jesus is wrapped in linen prior to burial in a garden tomb[1167] sealed with a stone[1168] and Lazarus, raised from a tomb sealed with a stone,[1169] appears in Jerusalem during Passover[1170] and in the garden at Gethsemane where Jesus is arrested. Lazarus eludes arrest,[1171] still wearing the sign of his resurrection, his linen shroud.[1172]

Morton Smith may have come close to this reconstruction of events. He noted the several parallels between the raising of Jesus and the raising of Lazarus, and in his comments on περιβεβλημενος σινδονα επι γυμνου, "wearing a linen cloth over his naked body" in Mark, he said, "Verbatim in Mk. 14.51...the subject is νεανισκος τις ["a certain young man," *my note*] —the young man in a sheet who was with Jesus at the time of his arrest and who, on being seized, fled naked (an episode both Mt. and Lk. chose to omit)...the occurrence of the phrase both in the longer and the canonical texts of Mk. can hardly be explained as an accident of free composition. Either the phrase was a fixed formula in the life of some early church (a baptismal rubric?) or its presence in both texts *is evidence of some historical connection* [emphasis added]."[1173] How much of the Lazarus story is "historical" we cannot know, but I believe it is nearly certain that Lazarus was a real person of pivotal importance in Jesus' later career and that his 'raising' was thought to presage that of Jesus.

In any case, the resurrection of Lazarus is presented in John as proof of Jesus' divine calling.[1174] Like the figure of Lazarus, who appears late in John's gospel, "a certain young man" appears late in the gospel of Mark —και νεανισκος τις συνηκολουθει αυτω: "and a certain young man **had gone along with** him..."[1175] The verb συνακολουθεω (sunakoloutheō), *to accompany*, is used also in Mark 5:37 in the following passage: ουκ αφηκεν ουδενα μετ' αυτον συνακολουθησαι ει μη τον Πετρον: "he allowed no one except Peter...**to go along with** him." That the verb marks an inner circle of

---

[1167] John 20:15.
[1168] Mark 15:46.
[1169] John 11:38-39.
[1170] John 12:9.
[1171] John 12:9-11.
[1172] Mark 14:51-52.
[1173] *Clement of Alexandria*, 116.
[1174] John 12:9-11.
[1175] Mark 14:51.

disciples is shown by the fact that it is again Peter, James and John who accompany Jesus to the garden of Gethsemane.[1176] Lazarus has joined this inner circle: he is the beloved who at Peter's behest asks who will betray Jesus,[1177] the one to whom Jesus entrusts his mother,[1178] the first male witness of the resurrection,[1179] and the first to identify the risen Jesus in Galilee.[1180] Based on an analysis of the footwashing ceremony of the gospel of John, Neyrey notes that the 'beloved disciple' is "the consumate insider, a true elite" who even "acts as Peter's broker or mediator."[1181]

That Lazarus, like Jesus, was unmarried is suggested by the observation that it is his *sisters* —not his wife and children— who send for Jesus when Lazarus falls sick and are his chief mourners when he dies.[1182]

Van Hoye noted the similarity between the *young man*, νεανισκος (neaniskos), in the garden of Gethsemane and the young man who appears in the empty tomb.[1183] The same verb, περιβαλλω (periballō), *wrap up in*, is used to describe the wearing of the linen garment by the youth in the garden, and the wearing of the white robe by the youth in the tomb.[1184] Van Hoye concluded, "There is therefore reason to think that the numerous verbal correspondences which we have noted are not the result of pure chance, but manifest an intention."[1185]

The numerous parallels point to a specific individual, known to the primitive community, who remains unnamed in Mark, but is identified by name in John: Lazarus. The enigmatic young man in the garden who escapes arrest[1186] is Lazarus, still dressed in his linen burial

---

[1176] Mark 14:33.
[1177] John 13:23-25.
[1178] John 19:26-27.
[1179] John 20:4.
[1180] John 21:17.
[1181] *The Social World of the First Christians*, 208.
Neyrey does not, however, identify the beloved disciple as Lazarus.
[1182] John 11:3.
[1183] Mark 14:51, 16:5.
[1184] Mark 14:51, 16:5.
[1185] My translation of: "Il y a donc lieu de penser que les nombreaux contacts verbaux que nous avons relevés ne sont pas un pur effet du hazard, mais manifestent une intention" in "La fuite du jeune homme nu (Mc 14,51-52)," *Biblica* 52:406.
[1186] Mark 14:51.

shroud. To my knowledge, both Miles Fowler and Michael Haren have separately suggested this identification. Fowler asks,

> How would a crowd recognize which person standing among the numerous followers of Jesus is Lazarus? Mark 14:51 provides the answer that there could be no more impressive identification of Lazarus, nor any more vivid symbol of his resurrection, than his wearing a burial shroud.[1187]

To this Haren adds,

> The question must arise whether the manifestation of the glory was to be confined to Bethany or whether it was contemplated presenting Lazarus, dramatically and dressed so that he would instantly proclaim the miracle, in Jerusalem itself. Alternatively or concurrently, if, as the Gospels insist, Jesus was reconciled to or intent upon his own sacrifice, the prospect that Lazarus would be presented in Jerusalem as a sign of God's power might have been a central part of the mechanism by which the Jewish authorities were utterly drawn to act.[1188]

The raising of Lazarus raises questions as well. Was Lazarus' emergence from the tomb understood by the first Christians to be a mere 'resusitation' or a true resurrection? If a resurrection, what was thought to have been raised? A body four days dead and in the process of decay?[1189] A soul? A ghost?

That Lazarus' raising was understood as a true example of resurrection, and not merely a resusitation, is supported by the text of John:

> Jesus said to her, "Your brother will be raised."
> Martha said to him, "I know that he will be raised in the resurrection on the last day."
> Jesus said to her, "I am the resurrection and the life. Those who believe in me will live even if they die."[1190]

[1187] Fowler, *Journal of Higher Criticism* 5/1: 3-22.
[1188] Haren, *Biblica* 79: 525-531.
[1189] John 11:49.
[1190] John 11:23-25.

The whole point of the dialogue is to establish that Jesus is more than 'the resusitation and the life' and as proof of this claim Lazarus is resurrected. In that case, one might suppose that the conditions of those resurrected would apply to Lazarus:

"For in the resurrection neither do they marry, nor are they given in marriage, but they are like angels in heaven."[1191]

"Nor can they still die,[1192] for they are like angels and are sons of God, being sons of the resurrection."[1193]

The case has been made in Chapter 6 that Jesus' post mortem appearances are apparitions consistent with a supernatural entity that retains traces of its previous life such as premortem wounds,[1194] but is also polymorphic[1195] and able to appear and disappear at will.[1196] The text of John may preserve a faint trace of a similar tradition in regard to Lazarus:

And saying these things, he shouted out with a loud voice, "Lazarus, come out here!"[1197]

In calling up Lazarus —Λαζαρε δευρο εξω: "Lazarus, **come** out **here!**"— the text of the gospel preserves a remarkable parallel to spells used to summon spirit beings:

Because all fear your great grace-name, your great power, give me the good things...come to me, Kupris,[1198] every day..."[1199]

I call you, Fawn Slayer, Trickstress, Infernal One, Many Formed,[1200] come, Hekate Trivia who has fire-breathing ghosts...[1201]

[1191] Matthew 22:30.

[1192] Compare 1 Corinthians 15:42, 44.

[1193] Luke 20:36.

[1194] John 20:25-27.

[1195] John 20:15; 21:4.

[1196] Luke 24:31.

[1197] John 11:43.

[1198] δευρο μοι, Κυπρις: "**come to** me, Kupris..." *Kupris* (Cyprus), a common name for Aphrodite.

[1199] *Supplementum Magicum*, 63.

[1200] πολυμορφε: "Many Formed..."

[1201] *Papyri Graecae Magicae* IV, 2726-2728.

Come hither to me,[1202] He of the four winds, almighty god, who blows the spirits of life into men[1203]...[1204]

The evocation of polymorphous Hekate —δευρ' Εκατη τριοδιτι: "**come**, Hekate Trivia"— is similar to the invocation of an aerial spirit[1205] which is to possess a boy medium: δευρο μοι κυριε επι τω αχραντω φωτι οχουμενος: "**Come** to me, O Lord, borne upon the pure light..."[1206] Citing another example of the formula found on a divination bowl —δευρο μοι ο αυτογεννητωρ θεε: "Hither to me, O self-begotten god"— Daniel and Maltomini note, "The phrase δευρο μοι is very common in prayers in the magical papyri."[1207] The phraseology of John 11:43 suggests that Lazarus' *spirit* was being summoned back from the underworld. If that was the case, was the resurrected Lazarus a revenant, a corporeal ghost? Did the youth in the linen shroud slip from the grasp of his would-be captors[1208] because he was agile or because he was immaterial? Was he, in another form, the youth in the tomb?[1209] There was speculation about *the mortality* of the beloved disciple: "So word spread among the brothers that that disciple would not die."[1210]

That raising the dead by magic was thought possible is clear:

Raising of a dead body: I command you, spirit winging in air, come in, instill spirit, be empowered, raise up this body by the power of the eternal god and let it walk around this place because I am the one who acts with the power of Thauth, the holy god. Say the name![1211]

[1202] δευρο μοι: "Come hither to me..."

[1203] ο ενφυσησας πνευματα ανθρωποις εις ζωην: "who **blows** the spirits of life into men..."

Compare the remarkably similar language of John 20:22, discussed in more detail in Chapter 8.

[1204] *Papyri Graecae Magicae* XII, 237.

[1205] το πνευμα το αεροπετες: "the spirit that flies in the air..."

[1206] *Papyri Graecae Magicae* VII, 560, 571.

[1207] *Supplementum Magicum* II, 74. The divination bowl is their item number 65.

[1208] Mark 14:51-52.

[1209] Mark 16:5.

[1210] John 21:23.

[1211] *Papyri Graecae Magicae* XIII, 278-282.

Among the many works of magicians, Lucian mentions "leading up ghosts and calling up the putrid dead."[1212]

Jesus, who has the keys to death and the grave,[1213] has *released* Lazarus —"Unbind him[1214] and let him go."[1215] If the raising of Lazarus was thought to presage the (self) resurrection of Jesus, and if the youth in Jesus' tomb[1216] was Lazarus, an interesting circularity appears: the reality of Jesus' resurrection is announced by the disciple Jesus has raised from the dead:

"You are seeking Jesus of Nazareth who was crucified. He was raised. He is not here. Look at the place where they laid him."[1217]

The resurrected Lazarus thus becomes both the harbinger of Jesus' resurrection as well as its first witness.[1218] Given the various parallels in their accounts, it would appear that Mark and John drew upon a common source for the Lazarus story. Although the Lazarus story is incompletely preserved in the gospels, it was apparently an early tradition, rich both in symbolic detail and emotional resonance.

...a culture of relics

Borrowing a phrase from theology, various commentators have remarked that the miracles of both Jesus and other exorcists and healers appear to work *ex opere operato*, i.e., by the mere fact of performance, not due to the merit of the performer. It is this feature of Jesus' performance of miracles that permits strangers to use his name effectively.[1219] In a fashion similar to the function of a sacrament, efficacy depends upon willingness to receive the benefit, not on the status of the one performing the ritual. And because of the impersonal nature

---

[1212] δαιμονες αναγων και νεκρους εωλους ανακαλων: "leading up ghosts and calling up the putrid dead ..." *Lover of Lies*, 14.

[1213] Revelation 1:18.

[1214] λυσατε αυτον: "**unbind** him..." The magical use of λυω (luō), to *unbind, release,* is considered in Chapter 8.

[1215] John 11:44.

[1216] Mark 16:5.

[1217] Mark 16:6.

[1218] In Matthew's redaction, the young man in white has become an "angel" (Matthew 28:5). The term might still have been understood as applying to a resurrected person (Matthew 22:30).

[1219] Matthew 7:22; Mark 9:38.

of the action, objects and places once in contact with a person, as well as substances —including the body, its parts, or even blood— could continue to transmit their magical power. "There is pow'r, pow'r, wonder working pow'r in the precious blood of the Lamb,"[1220] the hymn proclaims.

Discussing motives for theft of Jesus' body, Richard Carrier says,

> One general motive we know of is that the body parts (especially, it seems, of a holy or crucified man), along with such things as crucifixion nails, were valuable for necromancy…people of the time believed corpses had to be guarded to prevent theft by witches, who used body parts in their magic…Thus sorcerers would have a motive to steal any body, and perhaps an even greater motive to steal the body of a holy man, possibly a miracle worker, who was certainly untimely dead.[1221]

As one of the 'untimely dead,' Jesus became a potent source of power. A curse from the magical papyri stipulates "Osiris will grant your request because you are untimely dead and childless and wifeless[1222] …"[1223] The best evidence suggests that Jesus was unmarried, childless, prematurely deceased and executed as a criminal, all factors thought to produce a restless and powerful ghost. Jesus may have been considered *unburied* as well if left hanging on the cross or tossed into a lime pit by the Romans without benefit of proper rituals. The ancient traditions of 'ascent from the cross' and/or the 'empty tomb' may reflect a fate that resulted in a missing body. Shantz notes the connection between texts "colored by and filled with the phenomena of religious ecstasy…identified as signs of possession" and "the arresting image of carrying the death of Jesus in the body" of the believer.[1224]

According to Matthew 27:64-66, the Jewish leaders arranged to place guards at Jesus' tomb to prevent his disciples from coming by night to steal his body. But is it plausible to suppose that the disciples would have made themselves ritually unclean through contact with a corpse

---

[1220] "Power in the Blood" (1899)
[1221] From "The Plausibility of Theft" in *The Empty Tomb*, 350-351.
[1222] αωρος και ατεκνος και αγυναις: "untimely dead and childless and wifeless…"
[1223] *Supplementum Magicum*, 52.
[1224] "The Confluence of Trauma and Transcendence," *Experienta*, I, 195, 197. The reference is to 2 Corinthians 4:10.

during Passover? Or is it rather more likely to consider the story a later invention designed to address the problem of a missing body?

That their power continues to adhere to inanimate things associated with miracle workers provides an obvious motive for the preservation of relics associated with saints, particularly pieces of bodies —"keeping them safely under the control of the church."[1225] Regarding the habit of collecting such relics, Lane Fox says: "The new Christian attitude to the dead and their relics marked a break in previous religious life. Before long, church leaders were digging up corpses and breaking them into fragments, a type of grave robbery which pagans had never countenanced."[1226] This observation, while true of *official* pagan religions, does not hold for necromantic sorcerers or specialists in love spells who, like early Christians, "naturally focused their attention on those objects which afforded immediate contact with the source of [supernatural] powers; the most convenient objects were relics."[1227]

Faraone has made a convincing case that fear of prosecution caused necromancers to conceal the use of body parts in ritual, skull necromancy in particular, by substituting σκυφος (skuphos), meaning *cup*, or *pail*, as a code word for *skull*, and σκηνος (skēnos), *tent*, for *corpse* in necromantic spells. Nevertheless, a close reading of the text reveals "that the author of the recipe...has no scruples about recommending a form of graveside ritual that involves grasping part of the corpse in ones' hands."[1228] It is clear from pagan sources the Christian exorcist was seen as just another magical practitioner, and a necromantic one at that.

The use of personal possessions was basic to spell casting. Regarding the items required by "an effective witch, a Syrian by race," the courtesan Bakchis tells her girlfriend Melitta,

> "...You'll also need something belonging to the man himself, like clothes or boots or a few hairs or something of that sort."
> "I have his boots."[1229]

[1225] Kolenkow, *Aufstieg und Niedergang der Römischen Welt*, II.23.2, 1497.
[1226] *Pagans and Christians*, 448.
 See particularly Bentley's work, *Restless Bones: The Story of Relics*, for a full (to say nothing of entertaining) account of the Christian obsession with the relics of saints.
[1227] *Furta sacra: Thefts of Relics in the Central Middle Ages*, 35.
[1228] *Mantikē: Studies in Ancient Divination*, 256-265.
[1229] Μελιττα και Βακχις (Melitta and Bakchis), 4. *Dialogues of the Courtesans*, 376.

Ancient literature is replete with references to the theft of body parts for magical working. The newly dead had be guarded from witches in search of ears and noses, and the literature of the era describes them grubbing around in graveyards and scouring battlefields and places of execution in search of gruesome trophies.[1230] The *Leyden Papyrus* describes the concoction of a potion: "You take a little shaving of the head of a man who has died a violent death, together with seven grains of barley that has been buried in a grave of a dead man…"[1231]

The magical value of a piece of 'the true cross' would have been instantly appreciated by any necromancer of antiquity who read a spell that advised,

> …and take wood from a gallows and carve a hammer and strike the eye while saying the spell, "I command you by the holy names…"[1232]

Lucian's Eucrates says, "The Arab gave me the ring made from the iron [nails] of crosses[1233] and taught me the spell of many names."[1234] —demons and ghosts were thought to be afraid of iron. The substance of the nails became magically charged by association with violent death.

It has been observed of the early Christian saints that people came seeking "a transfer of supernatural power…as if [the saint] were a talisman…the only thing believed in was some supernatural power to bestow benefits."[1235] Geary notes that "devotion to the remains of saints can be traced to two fundamental antecedents: the pagan cult of heroes, and the Christian belief in the resurrection of the body."[1236] The ηρως (hērōs), *hero*, is the ghost of a powerful figure, such as the founder of a city, that has been elevated to the rank of a minor diety.

The cult of martyrs quickly became an organizational principle in the early church. The gifting of body parts established chains of patronage

---

[1230] *Magic, Witchcraft, and Ghosts in the Greek and Roman Worlds*, 140ff.

[1231] *Leyden Papyrus* XV,1, 2.

[1232] *Papyri Graecae Magicae* V, 75-76.

[1233] τον δακτυλιον σιδηρου του εκ των σταυρων πεποιημενον: "the ring made from the iron [nails] of **crosses**…"

[1234] *Lover of Lies*, 17.

[1235] *Christianizing the Roman Empire*, 3-4.

[1236] *Furta Sacra*, 33.

that united Christian communities. The "Holy Innocents," as Herod's legendary victims were later called,[1237] were a potent source of material "since the number of children was unknown, a limitless supply of relics was thereby made available." Relics "found many commercial applications beyond the initial gift or sale" within medieval Christianity since they drew pilgrims with money to sites where bones and other saintly bric-a-brac were venerated.[1238]

Indeed, the relationship between miracles and dead martyrs brought Christianity much closer to the attitude of necromantic sorcery than to anything in normative pagan religious belief.

> Not only did former cemeteries become centres of population and worship, but a degree of intimacy was sought with the relics of saints that was horrifying to a Roman pagan with traditional ideas about the pollution of death...It is clear that in establishing this new intimacy with the dead, and in fact using it as a basis for public worship, the Christian Church had overthrown a great tabu, and its subsequent success shows that it had gained strength from doing so. A deep well of psychological power may have been tapped...[1239]

The deep well of power that had been tapped through evocation of the dead would have been instantly recognizable to any pagan sorcerer, and accounted in part for the suspicion with which pagans regarded Christians in their midst, a suspicion which was founded on a strong element of fact. Smith noted this similarity: "Christianity was allied with another type of magic, that by which the recalled spirits (*not* resurrected bodies) of executed criminals and of persons who had died unmarried or childless were invoked by the magician. Jesus belonged to all three of these categories."[1240]

[1237] Matthew 2:16.

[1238] *Martyrdom, Murder, and Magic*, 30-31, 39.

[1239] *The Archaeology of Ritual and Magic*, 81-82.

[1240] *Harvard Theological Review* 73: 243.

Premature death was a powerful motive for the creation of 'martyrs' who did not die due to persecution. Wasyliw notes of Gelasius, a child who died at the beginning of the 5th century, long after persecution of Christians had ceased, "his cult was justified on the grounds of his innocence and untimely death." *Martyrdom, Murder, and Magic*, 35.

...crucified —raising the spirit of Jesus

The spirit of a person who had suffered a violent or untimely death, particularly execution, was considered to be a source of tremendous power, an assumption basic to the performance of both necromantic sorcery and primitive Christian miracle. "For Paul, to know Jesus Christ is to manifest the power of Jesus' crucifixion in one's body through spirit possession and performance characterized by possession phenomena."[1241] It was common knowledge among pagans that "the souls of those dead by violence" could be raised by sorcerers —"one beheaded or one who has been crucified"[1242] serving as paradigmatic examples. I hope to have made the case that the fact that John the Baptist and Jesus conspicuously fit this description is anything but co-incidental.

Pagan magical praxis included calling upon both *gods* and *ghosts* of the dead to achieve a goal:

> I deposit this binding spell with you, underworld gods, Pluto and Kore and Persephone and underworld ghosts,[1243] men and women dead before their time, virgins and youths, help this de-mon, whoever he may be. Kamēs, ghost of the dead,[1244] raise yourself for me, from the repose that holds you fast. For I com-mand you by the holy name...[1245]

Christian apotropaic spells combine *angels*, *god*, and *the dead*:

> I command you, Michael, archangel of the earth[1246]...the Al-mightly Sabaōth[1247]...I command you and the dead, release Taiollēs...[1248]

[1241] Mount, *Journal of Biblical Literature* 124: 319-320.

[1242] Lucian, *The Lover of Lies*, 29.

[1243] δεμονες καταχθονιοις: literally, "underworld demons," understood to mean "ghosts," as stipulated by the next words. Kamēs, the name of the deceased, should appear where the placeholder "whoever he may be," occurs, but the careless scribe copied it in addition to the dead man's name.

[1244] νεκυδαιμων: *nekudaimōn*, a term compounded from νεκυ-, *dead*, and δαιμων, *demon* or *ghost*. It is often translated "corpse demon." The νεκυια (nekuia) is the rite by which ghosts are raised.

[1245] *Greek Magical Amulets*, 50.

[1246] ορκιζω σε **Μιχαηλ αρχαγγελε** γης: "I command you, **Michael, archangel** of the earth..."

[1247] τον παντοκρατορα Σαβαωθ: "the Almighty Sabaōth..."

"...the invocation of the dead on the part of a Christian is noteworthy, especially in the light of the often-discussed relationship between pagan and Christian cults of the dead..."[1249]

Another spell against fever invokes Michael the archangel, Yahweh under the name Sabaoth, the dead, Abraham, Isaac and Jacob as well as Solomon, and tosses in a few biblical quotations, including a garbled rendition of the Lord's Prayer! Although Kotansky, the translator, regards it as "syncretistic rather than distinctively Christian" due to "the incoherent manner by which the [biblical] verses are quoted,"[1250] it is as perfect an example as could be wished for of the notion that *power resides in names of the dead.* But we need not go outside the New Testament for confirmation of this linkage: when Peter and John are arrested their inquisitors ask, "By what power or what name did you do this?"[1251] The answer has already been given: 'God raised his servant, Jesus...'[1252]

It is clear that early Christians, like their pagan contemporaries, credited the dead with magical δυναμις, but Christianity rapidly made public what until that time had been most secret, the use of the dead as conduits of supernatural power. Peter Brown:

> To gain this advantage, further ancient barriers had to be broken. Tomb and altar were joined. The bishop and his clergy performed public worship in a proximity to the human dead that would have been profoundly disturbing to pagan and Jewish feeling.[1253]

As an illustration of how thin this barrier quickly became, note how the suffering, death, and resurrection of Jesus figure in this healing spell, likely derived from primitive liturgy:

Sabaōth is the Greek transliteration of the Hebrew "Lord of armies." "Holy, holy, holy is the Lord of Hosts" (Isaiah 6:3) is frequently used in Christian magical spells. As a further example, a Christian spell of protection against fever begins, IXς νικα — "J[esus] Ch[rist] conquers"— and ends with αγιος αγιος αγιος κς Σαβαοτ — "holy, holy, holy, L[ord] Sabaot." *Supplementum Magicum,* 25.

[1248] ορκιζω σε και νεκρους απαλλαξατε Ταιολλης: "I command you and the **dead**, release Taiollēs..." *Supplementum Magicum,* 29.

[1249] Ibid, I, 80.

[1250] *The Greek Magical Papyri in Translation,* 2nd edition, 300.

[1251] Acts 4:7.

[1252] Acts 3:26.

[1253] *The Cult of the Saints,* 9.

241

> Christ foretold,
> Christ appeared,
> Christ suffered,
> Christ died,
> Christ raised,
> Christ ascended,
> Christ reigns,
> Christ saves Ouibius, who Gennaia bore, from all fever, from all
> shivering, daily, quotidian, now, now, quickly, quickly![1254]

The connection between Jesus' *violent death* by crucifixion and the *power* that derived from his rising is everywhere presupposed in the authentic writings of Paul and Luke. Reimer observes that the apostles testify to Jesus' resurrection with "with great power (δυναμει μεγαλη)":

> If δυναμις is understood here as 'miracle working power', that is, the sort of power that works δυναμεις ('miracles'), then the apostles' role in testifying to the resurrection is not just oral, but linked directly to their miracle-working.[1255]

In short, the risen Jesus provides the power for miracles which authenticate the message of his resurrection. Myllykoski notes that the raising of Jesus "is the foundation miracle for the whole narrative of Acts."[1256] The book of Acts, purporting to tell the story of the beginning of the Christian movement, consistently connects the performance of signs and wonders with the risen Jesus, "nailed up and killed by the hands of lawless men."[1257] The gospel of John, which specifies that the spirit will not be given until Jesus is "glorified,"[1258] implies that future spirit possession was contingent on Jesus' death.

[1254] *Supplementum Magicum*, 35.

The Greek text: ΧΣ προεκηρυχθη, ΧΣ εφανη, ΧΣ επαθεν, ΧΣ απεθανεν, ΧΣ ανηγερθη, ΧΣ ανελημφθη, ΧΣ βασιλευει, ΧΣ σωζει Ουιβιον, ον ετεκεν Γενναια, απο παντος πυρετου και παντος ριγους αμφημερινου καθημερινου **ηδη ηδη ταχυ ταχυ**. Note that the incantation ends as do nearly all *pagan* spells, **"now, now, quickly, quickly!"**

ΧΣ is a *nominum sacrum*, an abbreviation for Χ[risto]Σ, *Christ*.

[1255] *Miracle and Magic*, 91.
[1256] *Wonders Never Cease*, 162.
[1257] Acts 2:23, 43.
[1258] John 7:39.

Having come proclaiming "the mystery of God," Paul is determined to know nothing "except Jesus Christ and him crucified" and backs up his preaching "by demonstrations of spirit and power[1259] so that your faith might not be in the wisdom of men, but in the power of God."[1260] In the letter to the "bewitched" Galatians, "Jesus Christ crucified" supplies both "the spirit" and the resulting "performance of powerful works."[1261] The Ephesian Christians will know "the surpassing greatness of his power among us who believe, according to the working[1262] of the power of his might, which he put into operation[1263] by raising Christ from the dead..."[1264] The same pattern of evocation is carried over into the apocryphal Acts: εγω Ιωαννης εν ονοματι Ιησου Χριστου του σταυρωθεντος επιτασσω σοι: "I, John, command you in the name of **Jesus Christ the crucified**..."[1265]

In Romans 8:9-10, Paul's language is the terminology of spirit possession: "If anyone does not **have** the **spirit** of Christ,[1266] he does not belong to him" —ει δε τις πνευμα Χριστου ουκ εχει ουτος ουκ εστιν αυτου— and "if Christ is **in** you" — ει δε Χριστος εν υμιν— duplicates the language of Mark 1:23, "a man **in** [the power of] an unclean **spirit**" — ανθρωπος εν πνευματι ακαθαρτω.

Just as Jesus 'raised' John the Baptist from the dead and "because of this the powers are working in him,"[1267] so has the spirit promised by the risen Jesus[1268] come to empower his followers. The παρακλητος (parakletos), the Christian "Paraclete," the one summoned to assist, becomes the Christian version of the παρεδρος (paredros), the 'assis-

---

[1259] εν αποδειξει πνευματος και δυναμεως...: "by demonstrations of spirit and power..."

[1260] 1 Corinthians 2:1-5.

[1261] Galatians 3:1, 5.

[1262] κατα την ενεργειαν: "according to the **working**..." The same noun — ενεργεια— used in the magical papyri for the working of magical rites.

Of the use of ενεργεια in the magical papyri, Kotansky observes that it "generally refers to the (activated) power of magic...the actual 'activating' of a magic spell." *Greek Magical Amulets*, 241.

[1263] ενεργησεν εν Χριστω εγειρας αυτον εκ νεκρων: "which **he put into operation** by raising Christ from the dead."

[1264] Ephesians 1:19-20.

[1265] *Supplementum Magicum*, I, 95, quoting the apocryphal *Acts of John*.

[1266] Like Jesus "has" Beelzeboul (Mark 3:20-30).

[1267] Mark 6:14.

[1268] John 14:16-17.

tant' of the magical papyri.[1269] The παρακλητος, or *helper* —who is a *spirit*[1270]— functions in much the same way as the παρεδρος, the magical helper, who is a spirit. Significantly, the spirit cannot *arrive* until after Jesus *leaves*.[1271] Eitrem: "The death of Christ set the Pneuma free ..."[1272]

It is commonly claimed that παρακλητος means *advocate* in a legal sense, but in a survey of the occurrences of this uncommon word, Grayston found scant evidence for such a meaning. "...the universal conviction in antiquity...that in approaching an important person, for whatever reason, you need an influential person or group of supporters...the Paraclete is, as it were, an eminent person through whom the petitioner gains favorable access to the Father."[1273] In a later century, the Christian martyrs would become "invisible friends" —αορατος φιλος— and "intimate companions" —γνησιος φιλος— of the faithful like the personal δαιμων or *numen* ('guardian angel') of paganism,[1274] and with the passage of time functioned "as advocates pleading causes before a stern divine judge, as mediators, as go-betweens, as intriguers or wire-pullers at the court of Heaven,"[1275] the Christian equivalent of the magician's παρεδρος.

Most of the spirits called upon by pagan magicians "are the disembodied former inhabitants of [people]...the δαιμονες [ghosts, *my note*] of the deceased," which are also called "an αεριον πνευμα, an 'aerial spirit'" in the magical papyri.[1276] In Acts, the "holy spirit" is used synonymously with "the spirit of Jesus"[1277] who had been raised from the dead. Pagan sorcerers raised ghosts by incantations. How did early Christians raise the spirit of Jesus in order to perform powerful works?

[1269] παρακλησις, a *calling upon*, or *summoning*, is linked in several places to the gift of prophecy (1 Corinthians 14:3, 1 Timothy 4:13-14), a possession phenomenon.

[1270] The παρακλητος is το **πνευμα** της αληθειας —"the **spirit** of truth" (John 16:13).

[1271] John 16:7.

[1272] *Some Notes on the Demonology in the New Testament*, 69.
  Compare Luke 23:46; John 19:30.

[1273] *Journal for the Study of the New Testament* 13: 72, 80.

[1274] Brown, *The Cult of the Saints*, 50-68.

[1275] Wilson, *Saints and Their Cults*, 23.

[1276] *Ancient Magic and Ritual Power*, 286.

[1277] Acts 16:6,7.

Justin Martyr, describing the expulsion of demons in his day, says, "they are exorcized in the name of Jesus Christ, crucified under Pontius Pilate."[1278] As pointed out by Lietaert Peerbolte, Justin often links the *power* of the name of Jesus with his *crucifixion*.[1279] For the purposes of Christian magic, Jesus' power is raised through the recitation of his 'name,' *Jesus-Christ-crucified*.

There existed such a strong relationship between ghosts and magic, that the connection was frequently alleged to have led to ritual murder to create ghosts for necromantic use.[1280] Pagans likely saw something which to them seemed very similar to necromancy in Christian rituals such as the eucharist, the talismanic use of relics, and the symbol of the cross, an instrument of execution.[1281]

...relics as "ousia."

Whether a piece of the 'true cross,' the Shroud of Turin, the Church of the Nativity in Bethlehem, the purported place of Jesus' birth, or the Holy Sepulcher, the supposed site of his burial, Christian fascination with objects and places once in contact with Jesus is of ancient vintage. The merest association with Jesus could render a site magical; a fountain where Jesus washed his feet "consequently possessed the ability to remove all forms of disease from both people and animals."[1282] Jesus' disciples possess such power that not only can contact with articles of their clothing heal, but *even their shadow falling across the sick effects a cure*.[1283] It is certainly worth mentioning that one's *shadow* could function as a *paredros* or magical assistant.[1284]

The cult of the martyrs is a direct continuation of such magical belief:

[1278] εξορκιζομενα κατα του ονοματος Ιησου Χριστου του σταυρωθεντος επι Ποντιου Πιλατου: "they are exorcized in the name of Jesus Christ crucified under Pontius Pilate." *Iustini Martyris Dialogus cum Tryphone*, 118.
[1279] *Wonders Never Cease*, 190-192.
[1280] *Night's Black Agents: Witches, Wizards and the Dead in the Ancient World*, 158-160.
[1281] *Pagan Rome and the Early Christians*, 60-63, 118-124.
[1282] Trzcionka, *Magic and the Supernatural in Fourth-Century Syria*, 131.
[1283] Acts 5:12-16, 19:11-12.
[1284] *Papyri Graecae Magicae* III, 612-632. See Gordon, *Envisioning Magic*, 73.

The rise of the Christian cult of saints took place in the great cemeteries that lay outside the cities of the Roman world: and, as for the handling of dead bodies, the Christian cult of saints rapidly came to involve the digging up, the moving, the dismemberment—quite apart from much avid touching and kissing—of the bones of the dead, and, frequently, the placing of these in areas from which the dead had once been excluded.[1285]

As already noted, only one other group besides the Christians was strongly identified in antiquity with the practice of digging up and dismembering corpses, namely *witches*.

But along with these pieces of corpses, certain objects which had been in contact with the body at the moment of death are also in high demand among the sorcerers...[Apuleius] provides us with specific information regarding their origin: these nails come from gallows, so they have been in contact with a particular category of the dead, those condemned and tortured. That is not without importance; these can form a part of those *biaithanatoi*, the dead who have perished from a violent death...Everything that has been in contact with death and its realm, be it part of a corpse or an object, has, in the final analysis, a special interest for the sorcerer. These materials really represent the *ousia*, magical materials that still have a link with the soul of the deceased from which they come.[1286]

The importance of *ousia* —from ουσια (ousia), *substance, essence, material* or merely *stuff*—for working sorcery is everywhere attested in the magical papyri. Of a spell recorded on a papyrus fragment from the 3rd century, Daniel notes, "A lock of hair (the *ousia* of the beloved) was originally attached to the papyrus, and some of it still remains on the

---

[1285] Brown, *The Cult of the Saints*, 4.

"[Lucilla] had owned a bone of a martyr, and had been in the habit of kissing it before she took the Eucharist..." Ibid, 34.

[1286] My translation of: Mais à coté de ces morceaux de cadavres, certains objets ayant été en contact avec le corps au moment du trépas se trouvent tout aussi recherchés par les sorcières...Une precision quant à leur origine nous est fournie par [Apulée]: ces clous proviennent de gibets, donc ont été au contact d'une catégorie particulière de morts, les condamnés et les suppliciés. Cela n'est pas sans importance; ceux-ci peuvent faire partie de ces biaithanatoi, ces morts qui ont perí de mort violent...Tout ce qui a été en contact avec la mort et son royaume, que ce soit une partie du cadavre ou un objet, a, en fin de compte, un intérêt particulier pour le sorcière. Michaël Martin, *Magic et magicians dans le monde gréco-romain*, 223.

verso."[1287] An αγωγη (agōgē) or erotic spell[1288] aimed at a certain "Matrona who Tagenēs bore," summons the "underworld gods, Pluto and Kore and Persephone, and ghosts of the underworld, the dead, maidens and youths dead before their time" to assist the magicians spirit helper. The spell must work because "you have the hairs of her head...you have the material"[1289] the magician has obtained from her body.

> Ουσια μαγικη, 'magical material', are things taken from the body or clothing of the victim, hair, nail clippings, bits of cloth; some of the actualizations of the recipe [from the magical papyri, *my note*] show that it was a lock of hair which was used in its application. In the same sense, the sorcerer later has to take ousia of the dead in his hand in order to direct the attention of Helius to this specific nekydaimon; ousia, 'being, essence' thus is a sort of pointer which points to its owner.[1290]

It is clear that body parts were handled during necromantic ritual, a practice much like intimate contact with Christian relics of the dead:

> Petition related to the magical operation:
> Facing the setting sun while holding material from the tomb,[1291] say:
> ...I summon the Ruler of heaven and of earth, Chaos and Hades, and the ghosts of men[1292] slain, who once looked upon the light, and even now I beg you, Blessed One, Immortal Master of the world, if you enter the hidden places of the earth, the Land of the Dead, send this ghost to [Name], from whose corpse I hold the remains in my hands.[1293]

[1287] *Supplementum Magicum* I, 128.
  The practice of conserving items once in contact with a person in order to perform sorcery is also known as "the doctrine of [magical] contagion" or "the law of contact," a theory still very much in use.
[1288] *Greek Magical Amulets*, 50.
[1289] εχις τας τριχες της κεφαλης αυτης...εχις την ουσιαν: "you have the hairs from her head...you have the **material**."
[1290] Graf, *Envisioning Magic*, 98.
[1291] εχων ουσιαν του μνημειου: "while holding **material** from the tomb..."
  Literally "while *having* the matierial from the tomb..."
[1292] δαιμονες ανθρωπων: "the **ghosts** of men..."
[1293] *Papyri Graecae Magicae* IV, 435, 443-449.

Although the terminology is altered, Christian miracle is not a clean break from pagan necromancy. Christian miracle inhabits the same mental world as pagan magic and understands the basis for performing powerful works in a very similar way. *Ousia* makes the ghost of the one dead before his time magically present, even as the relic of a saint, "such as a blood-soaked handkerchief,"[1294] makes the saint miraculously present, hence the burial of Christian relics beneath altars[1295] where 'miracles' such as transubstantiation occur. The magical use of cloth which has come in contact with the relics of a martyr exactly replicates such use in pagan magic: "bind it up in piece of cloth from one who has died violently."[1296]

In his brief history of the religious fraud Peregrinus, Lucian describes how following his suicide by fire, some came "absolutely set on seeing the actual spot and finding some relic left by the fire."[1297]

Lucian's account may be compared to the earliest record of Christians collecting relics which comes from *The Martyrdom of Saint Polycarp*. The writer describes what happened after Polycarp's body was burned:

> So later we collected his bones, more valuable than the most precious stones, more excellent than gold, and put them aside for ourselves in a suitable place.[1298]

It is clear from this account, written in the 2nd century, that Christians had already developed a devotion to corpses that bordered on necrophilia. Pilgrimages to the graves of saints could also involve sleeping by the tomb, a continuation of the ancient practice of incubation.

[1294] *Furta Sacra*, 34.

[1295] *The Cult of the Saints*, 37.

Relics are often divided into two categories: *bodily relics*, which are bodies or pieces of bodies, and *brandea*, ordinary objects or substances such as cloth or water, that have come into contact with the bodies of saints or with holy places. *Brandea* were frequently worn around the neck as talismans. Corpses of saints were often moved or "translated," sometimes by theft, and were also broken into pieces, or "partitioned," and the parts distributed, a magical version of 'trickle-down' economics.

See particularly Brown, *The Cult of the Saints*, 86-105.

[1296] περιειλησας ρακει απο βιοθανατου: "bind it up in **a piece of cloth** from one who has died violently." *Papyri Graecae Magicae* II, 49.

In another text, a lamp wick is fashioned from *a piece of cloth* —ρακος— once in contact with a man who has met a violent end. *Papyri Graecae Magicae* II, 145.

[1297] *On the Death of Peregrinus*, 173.

[1298] *The Martyrdom of Saint Polycarp, Bishop of Smyrna*, XVIII, 2.

Stroumsa: "Among the Christians, incubation is done at the shrine of holy men or martyrs. Among many examples: a Jew suffering from sciatica dreamed in the basilica of Saint Dometius in Syria; the saint appeared to him and healed him."[1299] In his biting satire of superstition, Lucian of Samosata recounts a cure of snake bite achieved by a "Chaldean" magician through the use of a spell and "a piece of rock chipped from the tombstone of a dead girl."[1300]

That an attitude toward miracle which was never far from pagan necromancy pervaded early Christianity was noted by Morton Smith:

> The later Christian collection of the remains of martyrs' bodies was suspiciously like magicians' collection of the remains of bodies of executed criminals (the martyrs were legally criminals) whose spirits they wished to control. We have many ancient stories of thefts of dead bodies for magical purposes; the practice was evidently common and may explain the disappearance of Jesus' body and the empty tomb. Be that as it may, the Christians' frequent gatherings around tombs and in catacombs must have seemed to most pagans an indication of necromancy.[1301]

The revulsion with which many pagans viewed this Christian practice is captured by the 4th century writer Eunapius:

> Next they imported the men called "monks" into the holy places, men in appearance, but living like pigs.[1302] They publicly engaged in countless evil and unspeakable acts and considered it righteous to despise divine things. Every man in a black robe, resolved to disgrace himself publicly, possessed tyrannical authority, to such an extreme of virtue had humanity been driven...They also settled these monks in Canobus, chaining humanity to the service of worthless slaves instead of the real gods. They gathered up the bones and heads of those apprehended for numerous crimes, men the courts had condemned, and proclaimed them to be gods, wallowed around their tombs, and declared that being defiled by graves made them stronger. The dead were called "mar-

---

[1299] *Barbarian Philosophy: The Religious Revolution of Early Christianity*, 199.
[1300] *The Lover of Lies*, 11.
[1301] *Studies in the Cult of Yahweh*, II, 211.
[1302] In the *Odyssey* X, 234-240, the witch Circe turns Odysseus' men into pigs. Eunapius seems to imply that conversion to Christianity resulted in a similar transformation.

tyrs," and some kind of "ministers," and "ambassadors" of the gods, these degraded slaves, eaten alive by whips, their ghosts carrying the wounds of torture.[1303]

Rittner: "Contemporary veneration of saintly relics—with invocations, visions and healings—is 'necromancy' by definition, but not by name."[1304]

The witch goddess Hecate, who holds the key to the grave, "is portrayed as leading packs of dead souls through the night" and Persephone, "the queen of the dead, could release souls when she wished to."[1305] In the new Christian spiritual economy, Jesus, "the firstborn from the dead" as well as "the firstborn of all creation,"[1306] holds the key to the abyss.[1307] Regarding Lazarus he commands, "Unbind him, and let him go."[1308] Jesus, who has "the name above every name"[1309] becomes the new Christian god of resurrection and magic.

[1303] Eunapius, *Lives of the Philosophers and Sophists*, 473.
[1304] *Magic and Divination in the Ancient World*, 96.
[1305] Johnston, *The World of Ancient Magic*, 86.
[1306] Colossians 1:15, 18.
[1307] Revelation 20:1.
[1308] John 11: 25, 44.
[1309] Philippians 2:9-10.

Chapter 10: Cults of Possession

At times the obvious bears pointing out: the sources on which we rely for information about magical practices were not written for our instruction. They were written by people of antiquity for other people of antiquity, for people who regularly saw processions of pagan priests, participated in annual festivals in honor of the dead, were initiated into mystery cults, witnessed the performances of itinerant miracle workers, wore amulets and trusted in their powers, and walked in temples that were not yet ruins, but places of active worship and service of the transcendent.

Most people of antiquity made no clear distinction between religion and magic, or between magic and medicine, and to impose such distinctions on records from the past is not only anachronistic, but precludes real comprehension of what rituals of healing, exorcism, cursing, and divination may have meant for the participants: "…the neat distinctions we make today…did not exist in antiquity except among a few intellectuals."[1310] "In Republican Rome, as in Archaic Greece, magic was never thought as something special and radically different from religion or medicine."[1311]

Of religious wonder-workers and his decision to call them *magicians*, Crossan says, "The title *magician* is not used here as a pejorative word but describes one who can make divine power present *directly through personal miracle* rather than *indirectly through communal ritual*…magic renders transcendental power present concretely, physically, sensibly, tangibly, whereas ritual renders it present abstractly, ceremonially, liturgically, symbolically…*Magic*, like *myth*, is a word and a process that demands reclamation from the language of sneer and jeer."[1312]

With this caveat in mind, the reader should understand that *magic* might apply to any ritual behavior that involves speaking or perfor-

---

[1310] Betz., *The Greek Magical Papyri in Translation*, xli.
[1311] *Ancient Magic and Ritual Power*, 41.
[1312] *The Historical Jesus*, 138.

mance, and that when a term like *sorcery* is used, it means something like "religion that works."

The sources of our very incomplete knowledge deserve a brief comment. The oldest magical texts known to us are the pyramid and coffin texts from Egypt, but to what extent these texts still reflected any popular practice in the time of Jesus is uncertain. Something of the magic of ancient Mesopotamia is also known to us, and the Old Testament contains numerous references to sorcery, a few of which have been considered. That leaves the Greek magical papyri which are roughly contemporaneous with Jesus' era and have the added advantage of preserving traces of the magic performed by and for common people.

Most of our historical sources, however, were critical of magical practice and may have been preserved down through the *Christian* centuries partly for that very reason. Even in pre-Christian times magicians were regarded with suspicion and their books were considered dangerous, and under the Christian regime, the persecution of practitioners of magic intensified. As Betz observes, "the systematic destruction of the magical literature over a long period of time resulted in the disappearance of most of the original texts by the end of antiquity."[1313]

Moreover, the official histories were composed by members of the upper echelon of a stratified society that regarded the magic of the lower classes much as they regarded the people themselves, with a mixture of condescension, fear, and contempt. As Frederick Cryer notes, "In hierarchically ordered societies there is vastly more magic at the bottom of society than there is at the top...It is also full of the elite disdain for the welter of popular superstition that the masses below advocate."[1314] However, it would be a mistake to suppose that belief in the efficacy of magic was confined to the lower rungs of society. The ruling class generally regarded magic as real and as dangerous and passed laws against it. As Greenfield observes, members of the higher social strata "who took magic seriously or who actually wanted to practice it themselves, people who would have been able to record it if they wished, had compelling reasons for not doing so, since it was

---

[1313] *The Greek Magical Papyri in Translation*, xl.
[1314] *Witchcraft and Magic in Europe: Biblical and Pagan Societies*, 116-117.

generally considered illegal and association with it could bring ruinous, if not actually fatal, consequences."[1315]

The implications of these negative attitudes toward magic for an understanding of the New Testament are potentially enormous. As has already been noted, Jesus, his disciples, and the majority of those to whom he preached, were drawn from the rural laboring class, a class known to be susceptible to the machinations of sorcerers. Moreover, the evening celebrations of the Christians were identified by pagan critics as "secret and nocturnal rites," conducive to conspiracy, for that reason alone suspicious.[1316] So when the time finally came to present Jesus and his wonder working to the greater Greco-Roman world, there would be plenty of incentive to downplay the magical elements of Jesus' performances. And that, as we have seen, is exactly what we find when examining certain gospel accounts.

...the sorcerer and his works

Several terms were used of magicians during the period in which the New Testament was being composed. Fritz Graf defines the αγυρτης (agurtēs) as "an itinerant and beggar priest"[1317] associated particularly with the worship of Cybele —in response to which I would merely point out that Christian religious orders, such as the Dominicans and Franciscans, that lived by collecting alms are typically known as *mendicants*, not as beggars. The role of gender variance and homoeroticism in connection with the priests of Cybele is well established,[1318] additional motivation for itinerant wonder-working Christian missionaries to distance themselves from their pagan counterparts.

The term μαγος (magos), encountered in previous chapters, is one of the most generally used and hence one of the least specific words for *magician*. It is the obvious source of our word in English. Of these men Luck notes, "It seems the *magos* had a bit of everything —the bacchantic (i.e. ecstatic) element, the initiation rites, the migratory life, the nocturnal activities."[1319]

[1315] Greenfield, *Byzantine Magic*, 122.
[1316] *Pagan Rome and the Early Christians*, 11.
[1317] Fritz Graf, *Magic in the Ancient World*, 22. The noun is derived from a verb meaning *to collect*.
[1318] Randy Conner, *Blossom of Bone*, 99-131.
[1319] Luck, *Witchcraft and Magic in Europe: Ancient Greece and Rome*, 104.

A complete description of the γοης (goēs) and the nature of his type of sorcery —γοετεια (goeteia), "the invocation of the dead"— has been given by Sarah Iles Johnston. The *goēs* is a man who raises the dead through wailing, a typically female role as indicated by depictions on funeral vases, but is also associated by ancient writers with initiation into mystery cults, protecting the living from the wrath of angry ghosts, and enchantments and incantations, both written and sung.[1320] Graf defines the *goēs* as "a man who combines healing, weather magic, and the calling up of dead souls..."[1321] The *goēs* "attracts the attention of the dead through songs and spells, exchanges messages with them, temporarily resurrects them; the necromantic counterpart of the poet."[1322] But as pointed out by Greenfield, there are "no Greek terms that correspond precisely to the distinction that has been drawn between sorcery and witchcraft, while quite a number of Greek words are employed to indicate the general activity which may be included in...the single English word 'magic.'"[1323]

Other terms for magicians include the ριζοτομος (rhizotomos), or "rootcutter," the forebear of the herbalist or 'kitchen witch,' and the more sinister φαρμακος (pharmakos), which could mean *sorcerer* or *poisoner*, or both. Lest the latter term be completely misunderstood, however, it should be pointed out that the term φαρμακον (pharmakon) means both *medicine* and *potion*. That most substances used as remedies are also potent poisons comes as no great surprise —even modern over-the-counter medications are lethal if taken in sufficient quantity as many have learned to their dismay. The case in antiquity was little different: "...references to *veneficium* throughout Roman literature, and to φαρμακον in Greek literature, are often ambiguous. The potions were powerful; whether that power was for good or for evil depended on the outcome of each specific case."[1324]

The intimate connection in the ancient mind between medicine, magic, and the art of writing is exemplified by this reference in a Greek magical papyrus:

[1320] *Restless Dead*, 103, 105-123. Johnston's is an indispensable reference for the cultural background and practice of goeteia.
[1321] Graf, *Magic*, 33.
[1322] *Aspects of Death in Early Greek Art and Poetry*, 17.
[1323] *Byzantine Magic*, 120.
[1324] *Magic in the Roman World*, 12.

I am Thoth, inventor and creator of spells and writings...[1325]

in which the word translated "spells," φαρμακον (pharmakon), covers both magical potions and medicines. "Thoth was said to be the inventor of both magic and writing and he was the patron deity of scribes... Thoth was linked in myth with two potent images of power used in magic, the sun eye and the moon eye...The image of the Thoth baboon beside a *wedjat* eye occurs on magic wands as early as the twentieth century BC."[1326] Indeed, the connection between magic and writing is commemorated in the double meaning of the English word "spell," to say nothing of *gospel*, literally "good spell."

None of the terms for magician necessarily excludes other functions. Graf therefore describes the γοης-αγυρτης-μαγος as "the itinerant specialist who practices divination, initiation, healing, and magic."[1327] It is unlikely that these terms were used in any consistent way by the people of the era to distinguish between "specialists" in magical practice,[1328] all of whom were working in what Hans Dieter Betz has felicitously called "the energy jungle,"[1329] the human dependency on universal forces conceived under the rubric of divinities of varying rank.

...to enter the inner circle

Of the many forms of religious experience current in the days of Jesus, the practices of at least five mystery cults are still known to us in some detail. The Eleusinian mysteries, located at Eleusis,[1330] a small town about fourteen miles west of Athens, were held in high regard even by skeptics. The cult of Mithras, in which the membership was restricted to males, was popular among the Roman legions. The cult of Isis and Osiris (Serapis) enjoyed a wide popularity, particularly among women. The ecstatic cults of Dionysus and Cybele, or Mater Magna, finish out our brief list.

[1325] Εγω ειμι Θωυθ **φαρμακων** και γραμματων ευρετης και κτιστης: "I am Thoth, inventor and creator of **potions** and spells..." *Papyri Graecae Magicae* V, 249.

[1326] *Magic in Ancient Egypt*, 28-29.

[1327] Graf, *Magic*, 49.

[1328] *Magic and Magicians in the Greco-Roman World*, 12-15.

[1329] Betz, *Papyri*, xlvii.

[1330] The sanctuary at Eleusis —ελευσις, *arrival*— was destroyed in 394 CE by the troops of Alaric, a Goth who had converted to Arian Christianity.

Μυω (muō), the Greek verbal base from which *mystery* and its cognates are formed in both Greek and English, means *to shut*, in the case of mystery cults, *the mouth*. The initiate's lips were sealed and the oath of secrecy was taken seriously. Rather little is known with any certainty about the inner life of these cults, but it is clear that they shared broad characteristics: initiation, reenactment, personal transformation following the revelation of secret knowledge —often called *rebirth*— and particularly in the cults of Dionysus and Mater Magna, ecstatic possession by the god.[1331] Meyer: "…the mysteries emphasized an inwardness and privacy of worship within closed groups."[1332] The mystery religions were vehicles of salvation: "Isis was a mistress of magic and a saviour goddess who initiated human beings into the mysteries of everlasting life."[1333]

Mystery cults shared one other noteworthy trait: a close association with magic. Luck: "*Mystes*…applies also to the sorcerer who has reached a certain level. *Mysterion* or *telete* [τελετη, *my note*] could designate a high degree of magical knowledge, while telesma [τελεσμα, *my note*] (hence 'talisman') also means 'amulet,' sometimes also *alexikakon*, [αλεξικακον, *my note*] 'averter of evil.'"[1334] On the connection between magic and the mystery cults, Graf notes, "It must be concluded that there existed, at the level of ritual, affinities between the mystery cults and magic…Magic in general, as a combination and linked series of different rites, is called *ta musteria* or *hai teletai*, 'mysteries'…the *musterion* also designates magical objects or tools, like a ring or ointment."[1335]

The vocabulary of the mystery cults proved irresistible to Hellenistic Judaism and to primitive Christianity —both assimilated mystery cult terminology to describe the inner workings of their respective faiths.[1336] Nevertheless, as Devon Weins has pointed out, it is a mistake to look for an exact correspondence between the pagan mystery cults and Christianity. In spite of shared characteristics such as symbolism, redemption, rebirth, death and rising of a deity, sacramental drama, eschatology, and focus on the fate of the individual, the details

---

[1331] A discussion of the phenomenon of induced ecstasy, written by Georg Luck, can be found in *Religion, Science, and Magic*, 185-217.
[1332] *Ancient Mysteries*, 4.
[1333] *A History of Pagan Europe*, 23.
[1334] *Witchcraft and Magic in Europe: Ancient Greece and Rome*, 1001
[1335] Graf, *Magic*, 92, 97.
[1336] Betz, *Magika Hiera*, 250-251.

of the Judeo-Christian and pagan mysteries were based on different frames of reference.

> Alongside the venerators of Isis, Mithra, Cybele, Attis, and company, existed the adherents of a thousand and one other cults and philosophical belief-systems, in a veritable "rush hour of the gods." This manifold complexity, this bewildering plethora of religions makes it extremely difficult to reconstruct the actual situation.[1337]

The μυστης (mustēs), the *initiate* into a mystery cult, was typically introduced to the rites by a sponsor, the μυσταγωγος (mustagōgos), or *mystagogue*. The body of secret knowledge revealed to the initiate was usually called τα μυστερια (ta musteria), *the mysteries*. In the cults of Dionysus and Cybele, *possession* by the god was a regular feature of the rites, resulting in εκστασις (ekstasis) or ενθουσιασμος (enthousiasmos) —the obvious sources of our *ecstasy* and *enthusiasm*— altered states of consciousness associated with visions, oracular speech, and frenzied behavior. For the Greeks, the oracle at Delphi with its "pythoness" speaking in a trance exemplified oracular possession.[1338] In the case of the Bacchic rites associated with the worship of Dionysus, the god of wine, the participants entered a state of μανια (mania), a condition of violent frenzy in which live animals were ripped apart and their raw flesh consumed. Female participants in the rites of Dionysus were called *maenads*, which roughly translated, means "crazies." A similar inspired frenzy is recorded of Samson: "and the Spirit of the LORD came mightily upon him, and he tore the lion asunder as one tears a kid; and he had nothing in his hand."[1339]

The Greeks distinguished between four categories of divinely inspired madness: *mantic*, or prophetic, associated with Apollo, the god of prophecy, *poetic*, associated with the Muses, *erotic*, linked to Aphrodite, and *telestic*, from τελεστικος (telestikos), *initiatory*, or *mystical*, having to do with τελετη (teletē), *initiation* into the mysteries, particularly those connected to Dionysus.

[1337] "Mystery Concepts in Primitive Christianity and its Environment," *Aufstieg und Niedergang der Römischen Welt*, II, 23.2, 1265.

[1338] On the recent archeology, see the recent discussion by John Hale, *et al*, *Scientific American* 289/2: 66-73.

[1339] Judges 14:6, *RSV*.

It has been claimed that the water-to-wine miracle at Cana echoes similar wonders performed by Dionysus. One of Dionysus' many miracles connected with wine were the εφημεροι αμπελοι, "one-day vines" that flowered and bore grapes in the space of a single day,[1340] a pagan miracle which may have incited the Christian claim, εγω ειμι η αμπελος η αληθηνη: "I am the true vine."[1341] The cult of Dionysus must therefore be the false one.

The roots of modern theater trace back to the Bacchic initiation rites, the Dionysia held in Athens in honor of Dionysus, at which performances were given by actors speaking from behind masks. "The theatrical use of the mask presumably grew out of its magical use: Dionysus became in the sixth century the god of theatre because he had long been the god of masquerade."[1342]

Our word *tragedy* —τραγωδια, *goat ode*— comes from this source, as does *thespian* —θεσπις, *inspired*, having words from the gods. Accompanied by flutes, drums, and cymbals —associated variously with altered mental states, gender variance and homoeroticism[1343]— a chorus of men dressed as satyrs, half-man and half-goat, chanted the dithyramb in unison as the dancing celebrants tossed their heads in a violent, whirling motion, entering a state of ecstatic frenzy. "The pandemonium in which Dionysus himself, and his divine entourage make their entry —that pandemonium which the human horde, struck by his spirit, unleashes— is a genuine symbol of religious ecstasy."[1344]

Dionysus was an ecstatic god of paradox, often portrayed as effeminate,[1345] yet whose symbols included the φαλλος (phallos), a likeness of the erect penis, a symbol of the generative power of nature, and the θυρσος (thursos), the Bacchic wand wreathed with ivy with a pine cone at the tip. The wand, an obvious phallic image, doubled as a tool of magic and as a weapon. "The priest in female clothes is typical of

---

[1340] Otto, *Dionysus*, 98.

[1341] John 15:1.

[1342] *The Greeks and the Irrational*, 94.

[1343] *Blossom of Bone*, 114-122.

Deissmann quotes from a letter written in Greek during the 3rd century BCE: "And send us also Zenobius the effeminate, with tabret, and cymbals, and rattles." *Light from the Ancient East*, 164.

[1344] *Dionysus: Myth and Cult*, 92.

[1345] ο μαινολας Διονυσος και γυναικεια περιβεβλημενος: "the raving Dionysus and his womanly attire..." *Contra Celsum* III, 23.

trance religion...in eastern shamanism the male shaman also cross-dresses as a sign of his separateness from normal life."[1346]

The *wand* or *staff* —ραβδος (rhabdos)— is a very old magical tool,[1347] well attested in both the magical papyri and in the Greek translation of the Hebrew Old Testament, where, in the story of the confrontation between Aaron and Moses and the magicians of Egypt, Aaron is told: "take your staff[1348] and cast it on the ground before Pharoah."[1349] The magical papyri allow Jesus the use of a magical staff or wand,[1350] as does the book of Revelation where he "is destined to shepherd all the nations with a staff of iron."[1351] The iron staff —κατεχων ραβδον σιδηραν: "who possesses an iron **staff**"— is both a symbol of authority and a phallic reference in an erotomagical spell addressed to the god Min.[1352]

The power of music to inspire ecstatic speech is reported in the Old Testament. Elisha, asked to foretell the fate of the army of Judah, requests a musician and, as the instrument is played, is seized "by the hand of the Lord" and begins to prophesy.[1353] The connection between prophecy and possession is made again when Elisha sends a young prophet to anoint Jehu as king. The prophet calls Jehu aside, gives him the message, and flees.

> When Jehu came back to his master's officers, they said to him, "Is everything all right? Why did that madman come to you?" He answered them, "You know the sort and how they babble."[1354]

The Greek Old Testament labels the young "madman" with a revealing term: επιληπτος (epileptos), source of *epileptic*, one *seized* —even as was Elisha— by the hand of God. The connection between song and magic, and between "seizure" and prophecy is evident in Greek culture: the term for *enchantment* (which itself means *to chant in*) —επωδη

[1346] *History of Pagan Europe*, 118.
[1347] See particularly the wands in the Egyptian collection of The Metropolitan Museum of Art illustrated in Brier's *Ancient Egyptian Magic*, 49.
[1348] λαβε την ραβδον: "take your staff..."
[1349] Exodus 7:9, *Septuagint*.
[1350] *Supplementum Magicum*, I, 32.
[1351] εν ραβδω σιδηρα: "with **a staff** of iron." Revelation 12:5.
[1352] *Papyri Graecae Magicae* XXXVI, 109.
[1353] 2 Kings 3:13-15.
[1354] 2 Kings 9:11, *NRSV*.

(epōdē)— is literally a *song*——ωδη (ōdē)— chanted *over* —επι (epi)—
the subject of a spell. From this comes the term επαοιδος (epaoidos),
enchanter, a close associate of the *magos*.[1355] Similarly, we find
πυθοληπτος (putholēptos), literally *seized by the python* —the python is
a symbol of Apollo, god of prophecy— to describe the ecstatic state
entered by the priestess of the god as she utters oracles. However, that
the ecstatic utterance of the Pythoness was not the same as the glossolalia of early Christianity is now generally acknowledged.

The transcultural nature of this general method of divination can be
appreciated from the following quotation regarding the Scottish Celts:

> The Dingwall Presbytery Records tell of the *derilans* who appear
> to have been officiating priests on the island. Dixon suggests that
> this title comes from the Gaelic *deireoil*, "afflicted," inferring that
> the priesthood was composed of people enthused by "divine
> madness" in the manner of shamans the world over."[1356]

The mystery cults incorporated three fundamental types of obser-
vances: (1) *invocations* —the λεγομενα (legomena), or "things said," (2)
performances —the δρωμενα (drōmena) or "things enacted," and (3) the
δεικνυμενα (deiknumena) or "things shown." The New Testament
contains several sacred formulas —known in the mystery cults as
συμβολα (sumbola)— confessions of faith sometimes called *Christ
hymns*, as well as cultic invocations to which some verbal response was
probably expected:

> For everything that is brought to light is light. Therefore it is
> said, "Awake, O sleeper, and rise from the dead and the Christ
> will shine upon you!"[1357]

...magical dreaming

Pilgrims to the temples of Asklepius, the god of healing, hoped for
εγκοιμησις (enkoimēsis), the manifestation of the god in a healing or

---

[1355] As at Daniel 2:2, 4:7, for example.
[1356] *History of Pagan Europe*, 107.
[1357] Ephesians 5:14.

και επιφαυσει σοι ο Χριστος: "and the Christ **will shine upon** you," or alternatively, "**will enlighten** you." The double meaning was obviously intentional.

prophetic dream. The temple area where sleepers awaited dreams was the κοιμητηριον (koimētērion) or *sleeping room*, the source of our *cemetery*.[1358] To achieve a dream, the patient might have to sacrifice a sheep and sleep on its fleece, a practice known as *incubation* from Latin *incubare*, "to lie down on," the source of the English *incubus*. "Incubation must involve, somehow, a magic procedure, for a god is conjured or summoned by some ritual, but it is performed within a religious context, under the supervision of priests who may have had some medical knowledge."[1359] Again one observes the melding of magic, religion, and medicine.

The practice of incubation "continued at some Christian shrines in the East. Western examples may be cited, too, in which patients slept on or by tombs and shrines, or in which the healing saint appeared to them in dreams." The custom of bringing *ex-votos*, models of body parts that have been healed, "a tradition dating back to Neolithic times," continued at Christian shrines.[1360]

Consulting ghosts, or necromancy —νεκυομαντεια (nekuomanteia)— was also an important function of dreams. Daniel Ogden: "It is not surprising that ghosts should have been sought in dreams, since they often visited the living spontaneously in this way," and notes that various Greek characters return to visit the living in their dreams.[1361] As mentioned in a previous chapter, the Israelites "who sit in tombs, and spend the night in secret places"[1362] were likely using graveyards to provoke necromantic visions. Incubation also is a cross-cultural phenomenon: the calling of a "man of high degree" in the Australian aboriginal cultures "may be deliberately sought by sleeping in an isolated place, particularly near the grave of a medicine man or some other enchanted spot."[1363] And of the Scandanavian people: "The *Flateyjarbók* tells of a man who was inspired with the gift of poetry by a dead *skald* on whose howe he slept."[1364]

[1358] "in the patient's dream the god came with an attendant carrying mortar, pestle and medicine chest, mixing a potion, applying a plaster, using the knife or summoning a sacred serpent to lick the afflicted part." *Cure and Cult in Ancient Corinth: A Guide to the Asklepieion*, 13-15.

[1359] Luck, *Arcana Mundi*, 141.

[1360] Wilson, *Saints and Their Cults*, 20-21.

[1361] *Greek and Roman Necromancy*, 76.

[1362] Isaiah 65:4.

[1363] *Aboriginal Men of High Degree*, 17.

[1364] *History of Pagan Europe*, 142.

In Matthew's infancy narrative, prophetic warning dreams are sent to Joseph (1:20), to the magi (2:12), again to Joseph a second (2:13), third (2:19), and fourth time (2:22), and later to Pilate's wife (27:19). As noted by Hull, "No less than five dreams surround the divine birth and Messiah goes to his death in the ominous mystery of Pilate's wife's dream...The parousia of the Messiah is also to be accompanied by warning portents. The reference to 'the signal of your coming' and 'the sign that heralds the Son of Man' (24:3, 30) are unique to this gospel. So the birth, death and reappearance of Jesus Christ are all authenticated by signs."[1365] Prophetic dreams are likewise common in the Old Testament.[1366]

Whether through dreams, visions, necromancy, or ecstatic rites, the participants sought γνωσις (gnōsis), *knowledge* based not on empirical observation, but on revelation. Could the contents of such revelations ever have been adequately expressed in mere words?[1367]

..."I will pour out my spirit..."

"The form of early Christianity associated with Paul can be characterized as a spirit-possession cult. Paul establishes communities of those possessed by the spirit of Jesus."[1368] Paul assures the Corinthians, "because you are devotees of spirits,"[1369]

> On that account I reveal to you that no one speaking by a spirit of God[1370] can say "Anathema Jesus!" and no one is able to say "Lord Jesus!" except by a holy spirit.[1371]

[1365] *Hellenistic Magic and the Synoptic Tradition*, 116-117.

[1366] As at Genesis 3:5-8, 41:7-41, or Daniel 2:1-30 to cite a few examples.

[1367] Compare 2 Corinthians 12:4.

[1368] Christopher Mount, *Journal of Biblical Literature* 124: 316. (This is an essential reference.)

[1369] υμεις επει ζηλωται εστε **πνευματων**: "because you are devotees **of spirits**" (1 Corinthians 14:12).

Primitive Christianity evidently believed in the *plurality of spirits* (1 John 4:1-3).

[1370] ουδεις εν **πνευματι θεου** λαλων λεγει: "no one speaking **by a spirit of God**..."

[1371] 1 Corinthians 12:3.

ουδεις δυναται ειπειν κυριος Ιησους ει μη εν **πνευματι αγιω**: "no one is able to say 'Lord Jesus!' except **by a holy spirit**."

For a discussion of the connection between spirit possession and apocalypticism, see Lietaert Peerbolte, *Experientia*, I, 159, ff.

When Paul spoke of wanting to share "some spiritual gift,"[1372] he was referring to a miraculous manifestation of divine power for which early Christians used the word χαρισμα (charisma), a word absorbed into English unchanged in form but altered in meaning. To the early Christians the word had little to do with personal magnetism; it described gifts bestowed by God, the supernatural gifts of the spirit, "a flourish of ecstatic effervescence."[1373] For the Greeks the gifts of the gods were music and dance, theater and oracular utterance, poetry and love, for the Christians, healing and exorcism, tongues and prophesying, visions and discernment of spirits.

Davies is undoubtedly correct when he points out that spirit possession was "the defining characteristic" of primitive Christianity and that *"Christology grew out of pneumatology. Pneumatology originated from possession experience."*[1374] Paul's first letter to the Corinthians completely supports this assessment.

Among the earliest Christians the spirit manifested its power through portents, signs, and miracles:

> Men, Israelites, hear these words: Jesus the Nazarene, a man attested to you by God through powerful works and portents and signs which God performed through him in your midst, just as you yourselves know..."[1375]

The New Testament uses a number of words for powerful works: δυναμις (dunamis), *power*, from which *dynamite* was coined, and by extension, *powerful work, miracle*. Δυναμις is what flows like current from Jesus when a miracle is performed: "I felt the power leaving me..."[1376] Referring to Acts 1:8 where Jesus tells his disciples they will "receive power" when "the holy spirit comes upon you,"[1377] Strelen notes, "Clearly what Jesus was promising was something overwhelming and radical in its effect."[1378]

[1372] χαρισμα...πνευματικον: "spiritual...**gift**" (Romans 1:11).
[1373] *Ecstatic Religion*, 132.
[1374] Davies, *Jesus the Healer*, 186-187.
[1375] Acts 2:22.
[1376] Luke 8:46.
[1377] επελθοντος του αγιου πνευματος εφ' υμων: "when the holy spirit **comes upon** you..."
[1378] *Strange Acts*, 59.

There is also τερας (teras), *portent*, *omen*, or *prodigy*, the basis for our medical term *teratology*, the study and classification of birth defects. The ancient Mediterranean cultures considered the birth of deformed animals and humans to be ill-omened and employed priests —the τερατοσκοπος (teratoskopos), *omen inspector*— who specialized in the interpretation of such dark events. Regarding the impending plagues upon Egypt, the *Septuagint* has Yahweh say to Moses, "Behold all the portents I have placed in your hands!"[1379]

The most common word for a work of wonder in the gospel of John is σημειον (sēmeion), *sign*, of which there are a magical seven: water into wine, healing a fever, a healing at Bethzatha, feeding a multitude, the translocation of a boat, healing a blind man, and the raising of Lazarus.[1380] In addition to its seven signs, the gospel also records seven witnesses that say Jesus has been sent from God or is "the Son of God": John the Baptist, Nathanael, Peter, Jesus himself, Martha, Thomas, and the author of the gospel.[1381] There are also seven "I am" sayings: "I am the bread of life," "the light of the world," "the good shepherd," "the resurrection and the life," "the way, the truth, and the life," "the true vine," and "before Abraham, I am".[1382]

"I am..." sayings are frequent in the spells of the magical papyri:

> I am the Great One, the One who sits in heaven...[1383]
> I am the One upon the lotus, having the power, the holy god ...[1384]
> I am Abrasax...[1385]

Or this slightly different version:

> "Come to me, Isis, because I am Osiris, your male brother ..."[1386]

[1379] Exodus 4:21.

[1380] John 2:1-11, 4:46-54, 5:1-48, 6:1-14, 6:15-21, 9:1-41, 11:1-57.

[1381] John 1:34, 1:49, 6:69, 10:36, 11:27, 20:28, 20:31.

[1382] John 6:35, 8:12, 10:11, 11:25, 14:6, 15:1, 8:58.

[1383] **Εγω ειμι ο μεγας ο εν ουρανω καθημενος**:"**I am** the Great One, the One who sits in heaven..." Kotansky, *Greek Magical Amulets*, 183-184.

[1384] **Εγω ιμι** [sic] **ο επι του λωτου την δυναμιν εχων ο αγιος θεος**: "**I am** the One upon the lotus, having the power, the holy god..." *Supplementum Magicum*, I, 18.

[1385] Ibid, I, 36.

[1386] **Ελθε προς εμε Ισις οτι εγω ειμι Οσιρις ο αρρην αδελφος σου**: "Come to me, Isis, because **I am** Osiris, your male brother..." *Greek Magical Amulets*, 362.

"I am" sayings occur in late Egyptian religion,[1387] in the Septuagint, and are exceedingly common in the magical papyri. Since the composition history of the gospel of John is a matter of conjecture and the exact dating of formulas of the magical papyri is insecure, it is not possible to establish a dependent relationship.[1388] Nevertheless, the similarity is remarkable.

Interestingly, *exorcisms*, which are central to Jesus' miracle working in the synoptics, are completely ignored by John. Eric Plumer has made a strong case that the absence of any mention of exorcism as well as the substitution of σημειον, *sign*, for incriminating terms such as δυναμις, "work of power," represent editorial changes made by the author of John to counter charges of sorcery.[1389]

Other terms include αποδειξις (apodeixis), *display*,[1390] and θαυμα (thauma), *wonder*.[1391] The apparent avoidance of *thauma* and its cognates may signal a reticence to associate Jesus with *thaumaturgy*, or "wonder-working" which was common in the pagan world.

Paul's first letter to the Corinthians, which contains the single most complete account of the charismatic gifts, is a book written early in the history of the church. The nearness of Jesus' return is everywhere assumed in this letter:

> ...so that you are not lacking any of the gifts while you eagerly await the revelation of our Lord Jesus Christ...therefore do not judge anything before the appointed time, until the Lord comes, who will shine a light on the things hidden by the darkness and expose the motives of men's hearts...consequently, because of the impending tribulation, I consider it desirable for a man to remain just as he is...the appointed time is growing shorter...the

---

[1387] "for I am Horus, son of Isis" (*Leyden Papyrus* IX. 22-23), for example.

[1388] See Ball, *'I Am' in John's Gospel*, 24-27.

[1389] *Biblica* 78: 356-357.

As noted elsewhere in this work, σημειον, *sign*, occurs with some frequency in magical texts.

[1390] Not common: "in a *display* of spirit and power" (1 Corinthians 2:4).

[1391] Used only once in the New Testament in an exclamation: "And no *wonder!*" (1 Corinthians 11:14).

The related adjective, θαυμασιος (thaumasios), is used once as a collective noun: "When the chief priest and scribes saw *the wonderful things* that he did..." (Matthew 21:15).

ways of this world are passing away...on whom the end of the ages has arrived...if anyone does not love the Lord, let him be cursed. Lord, come![1392]

For the early Christians, the gifts of the spirit are proof that the world is about to end:

"It will be in the last days," God says, "that I will pour out my spirit on all flesh and your sons and daughters will prophesy and your young men will see visions...the sun will be turned to darkness and the moon to blood before the great and glorious Day of the Lord comes."[1393]

The primitive church was both apocalyptic and charismatic. In his letter to the church in Corinth Paul enumerates the major charismatic gifts:

To each is given the manifestation of the spirit for the common good. To one, speech of wisdom is given through the spirit, but to another, speech of knowledge according to the same spirit. To another, faith by the same spirit, but to another gifts of healing[1394] in the spirit, but to another, works of power.[1395] To another, prophecy, but to another, distinguishing between spirits,[1396] to yet another, kinds of tongues, and to another, interpretation of tongues. But all this operates through one and the same spirit, apportioned to each as it chooses.[1397]

The phrase translated "works of power" in the passage above — ενεργηματα δυναμεων (energēmata dunameōn), "miraculous powers"[1398] —duplicates the terminology used in the magical papyri where it means *magical powers*:

[1392] 1 Corinthians 1:7; 4:5; 7:26, 29, 31; 10:11; 16:22.

[1393] Acts 2:17, 20.

[1394] **χαρισματα ιαματων**: "**gifts** of healing." The *charismata* may also refer to the spiritual gifts collectively.

[1395] αλλω δε **ενεργηματα δυναμεων**: "but to another, **works** of power..."

[1396] **διακρισεις πνευματων**: literally, "**discernment** of spirits," apparently the *ability to differentiate* (διακρισις) between works done through the power of God and those done through the power of demons.

Note, for example, 1 John 4:1, on "testing the spirits."

[1397] 1 Corinthians 12:7-11.

[1398] Danker, *Greek-English Lexicon*, 335.

The mighty assistant[1399] will gladly accomplish these things. But impart them to no one except your own true and worthy son when he asks you for the magical powers.[1400]

However often you want to command the greatest god Ouphora, speak and he will comply. You have the ritual of the greatest and most divine magical working.[1401]

..."tongues of men and angels..."

Paul's discourse on the gifts of the spirit is specifically directed to people who had once worshipped the pagan deities —"You know that when you were serving speechless images"— and who were therefore already familiar with such manifestations of spirit possession as ecstatic oracular speech, particularly during rites accompanied by music.[1402] Regarding such ecstatic speech, Paul adds:

> ...for tongues are a sign, not for believers, but for unbelievers, and prophecy, not for unbelievers, but for those who believe. In the same way, if the whole church comes together and all speak in tongues, and strangers or unbelievers enter, will they not say you are possessed?[1403]

Tongues are a sign for unbelievers because ecstatic speech, already familiar to pagans, is proof that Christians have a spirit —"that religious trances and ecstasy were the manifestation of possession by a god was one of wide currency in Greek and Near Eastern religions."[1404]

The pagan who enters a Christian gathering and finds a house full of agitated Christians all raving incomprehensibly will come to the conclusion that the speakers are *possessed*, the meaning of μαινομαι (mainomai) in this context. Given Paul's legendary lack of precise expres-

---

[1399] ο κραταιος **παρεδρος**: "the mighty **assistant**," i.e., a magical assistant.

[1400] τα...**ενεργηματα**: "the **magical powers**..." *Papyri Graecae Magicae*, I, 193-194.

[1401] την τελετηον του μεγιστου και θειου **ενεργηματος**: "...the ritual of the greatest and most divine **magical working**." *Papyri Graecae Magicae*, XII, 316-317.

[1402] 1 Corinthians 12:2. Note the mention of the flute and lyre in the same letter (14:7).

[1403] 1 Corinthians 14:22-23.
ουκ ερουσιν οτι **μαινεσθε**: "will they not say **you are possessed?**"

[1404] Esler, *The First Christians in their Social Worlds*, 46.

sion, whether pagans were expected to regard possession positively or negatively is uncertain.[1405] Nevertheless, Stephen Chester has made a strong case for a positive reading of 1 Corinthians 14:23, pointing out that in the 1st century cultural context, "Speaking in tongues would then function as a sign for unbelievers by alerting them to the presence of divine activity among the Corinthians."[1406] This opinion receives some support from the magical papyri: powerful divine names, "living, immortal, honored names," are not "uttered in articulate speech by the human tongue nor in mortal speech or mortal sound."[1407]

Elsewhere Paul mentions his own spiritual transports: "if we are in ecstasy, it is for God, if in our right mind, for you"[1408] and reminds the blabbering mass that he speaks in tongues more than all of them.[1409]

Confronted with raving Christians, the response of the unbeliever, "God is truly *in* you!"[1410] —translated "God is really *among* you" by the *Revised Standard Version*— reflects the ancient notion of possession, ενθεος (entheos), *entered by the god*. The act of spirit possession is consistently described by the metaphor of filling a container: God "will pour out" his spirit[1411] and fill the disciples even as sound fills a house;[1412] their "extravagance of divine power" is contained "in clay vessels."[1413] In the Old Testament, Yahweh promises to 'pour out' the spirit like water,[1414] 'pour it out' on all flesh.[1415]

A description of divine possession from a contemporary of Jesus is found in Philo:

Whenever [the light of the mind] dims, ecstasy and possession naturally assail us, divine seizure and madness.[1416] For whenever

---

[1405] An exhaustive discussion of this and many other aspects of such speech can be found in Forbes' *Prophecy and Inspired Speech In Early Christianity and its Hellenistic Environment*, 175, ff.

[1406] *Journal for the Study of the New Testament* 27: 417, 430.

[1407] *Papyri Graecae Magicae* IV, 605-610.

[1408] 2 Corinthians 5:13.

[1409] 1 Corinthians 14:22.

[1410] οντως ο θεος εν υμιν εστιν: "God is truly **in you**" (1 Corinthians 14:25).

[1411] Acts 2:17.

[1412] Acts 2:2, 4.

[1413] 2 Corinthians 4:7.

[1414] Isaiah 44:3.

[1415] Joel 2:28, quoted in Acts 2:17.

[1416] κατοκωχη τε και μανια: "divine seizure and madness..."

the light of God shines upon us, human light is extinguished and when the divine sun sets, the human dawns and rises. This is what is apt to happen to the guild of the prophets. At the arrival of the divine spirit our mind is evicted. When the spirit departs, the wandering mind returns home, for it is well established that that which is subject to death may not share a home with that which is deathless. Therefore the eclipse of the power of reason and the darkness which envelopes it begets ecstasy and inspired madness.[1417]

Philo's characterization of possession is aggressive: εικος εκστασις και η ενθεος επιπιπτει: "ecstasy and possession naturally **assail** us." The verb επιπιπτω (epipiptō), like other verbs of magic, is a power verb. It means *to fall upon* or *attack*, and is used of disease, accidents and storms. The New Testament equivalent, επερχομαι (eperchomai), "when the holy spirit *comes upon* you,"[1418] likewise has violent connotations. The Jews "came down" from Antioch and provoked the stoning and eviction of Paul,[1419] and Simon prays that the curses uttered by Peter "may not come upon me."[1420] The holy spirit "will come upon"[1421] Mary and "the power of the Most High will overshadow" her. In short, Mary will be *taken, overpowered, seized.*

The verb επερχομαι and its simplex is also used in the papyri for magical attacks: φυλαξατε με απο παντος πραγματος επερχομενου μου: "defend me from all troubles **coming upon** me..."[1422] An amulet for the protection of Sophia, aka Priscilla, an amulet which may represent "yet another instance of Christians resorting to the use of pagan magic," says (twice), "Put an end to the One coming against little Sophia,[1423] called Priscilla, if shivering, restrain it, if a phantom, restrain it, if a demon, restrain it..."[1424]

[1417] εκστασιν και θεοφορητον μανιαν εγεννησε: "begets ecstasy and inspired madness." *Quis rerum divinarum heres*, 264-265.

[1418] Acts 1:8.
See particularly *Strange Acts*, 59-63.

[1419] Acts 14:19.

[1420] Acts 8:24.

[1421] πνευμα αγιον επελευσεται επι σε: "holy spirit **will come upon** you..." Reiteration of the preposition, a characteristic of koine Greek, heightens the notion of 'falling upon.'

[1422] *Papyri Graecae Magicae* XXXVI, 176.

[1423] καταργησον τον ερχομενον της μεικρας Σοφια: "Put an end to **the One coming against** little Sophia ..."

That 'an eclipse of the power of reason' resulted in something close to chaos during meetings of the house churches Paul makes explicit when setting out rules that will rein in the wild enthusiasm of the Corinthians:

> So if anyone speaks in a tongue, do so two at a time, or three at most, and in turn, and let one interpret. But if there is no interpreter, keep silent in church. Let each speak to himself and to God. Let two or three prophets speak and let others evaluate what they say. But if another receives a revelation while seated, let the first person be silent. For all can prophesy in turn so that all may learn and all be encouraged. The spirits of the prophets are subject to the prophets, for God is a God, not of pandemonium, but of harmony.[1425]

The translation of ακαταστασια (akatastasia), —*disorder* or *insurrection* as in Luke 21:9, where it is paired with *war*— as "pandemonium" seems justified given the context. The descriptions of spirit manipulation are strikingly similar: πνευματα προφητων προφηταις υποτασσεται: "the spirits of the prophets **are subject** to the prophets" as are the demons: τα δαιμονια **υποτασσεται** ημιν εν τω ονοματι σου: "the demons **are subject** to us in your name."[1426] In Corinth, as in some modern Christian sects, spirit possession, not message, had become the mark of the supposed spiritual elite. "Paul is gentle, but not uncritical of the babbling contests that threaten to displace the gospel in Corinth (1 Cor. 14:2-4)."[1427]

There are substantial differences between the "tongues" described by Paul and the phenomenon described by Luke in the book of Acts. According to Paul, "the open display of the spirit"[1428] in Christian gatherings could take various forms including "speech of wisdom"[1429] and "speech of knowledge," both of which are listed separately from

---

The verb καταργεω, *to render useless, come to nothing*, used in Christian writings (e.g., 1 Corinthians 2:6) is otherwise unknown in the Greek magical papyri.

[1424] *Supplementum Magicum*, 13.

[1425] 1 Corinthians 14:27-32.

[1426] Luke 10:17.

[1427] Hoffman, *Jesus Outside the Gospels*, 33.

[1428] 1 Corinthians 12:7: η **φανερωσις** του πνευματος: "the **open display** of the spirit..."

[1429] 1 Corinthians 12:8: λογος σοφιας; "speech of wisdom"; λογος γνωσεως: "speech of knowledge..."

"kinds of tongues."[1430] The related spiritual gift of "interpretation of tongues"[1431] as well as the context makes clear that tongues conveyed neither wisdom nor knowledge. In fact, Paul's discussion of the gift makes clear that "tongues" were unintelligible:

> The one speaking in tongues speaks, not to men, but to God, for he speaks mysteries by means of the spirit...for if the trumpet sounds but is not clearly heard, who will prepare himself for war? And so with you: if through tongues[1432] you are given unintelligible speech, how will it be known what is said? You will be talking into the air...but in church rather I speak five words with my mind, that another be taught, than a thousand words in a tongue.[1433]

By the time Luke composes Acts —*mirabile dictu*— the tongues have become recognizable languages, not an utterance of unknown meaning to either speaker or listener.[1434] Regarding speaking while possessed, Esler observes, "[Luke's] presentation of what happened at Pentecost does not encourage confidence in this phenomenon having been current among the group or groups for whom he was writing...Luke is portraying xenoglossy, not glossolalia."[1435]

The sound of rushing wind[1436] that accompanied the gift of languages in Acts has parallels with other forms of paranormal phenomena, a point explored by Greg Taylor in an interesting and provocative essay.[1437] The sound of the wind, which indicates the active presence of the numina, was produced by spinning the ρομβος (rhombos), or *bullroarer*, during magical rites of mystery initiation, a technique of spirit raising known to several cultures. The clearest example from Greco-Egyptian magic was the rustling sound produced by the shaking of the sistrum.[1438] From a spell addressed to the goddess Selene: "give heed

---

[1430] 1 Corinthians 12:10: γενη γλωσσων: "kinds of tongues…"

[1431] 1 Corinthians 12:10: ερμενεια γλωσσων: "interpretation of tongues…"

[1432] δια της γλωσσης: literally "through the tongue…"

[1433] 1 Corinthians 14:2, 9, 19.

[1434] Acts 2:4-13. See particularly Forbes, *Prophecy and Inspired Speech In Early Christianity and its Hellenistic Environment*, 47-49.

[1435] *The First Christians in their Social World*, 49.

[1436] Acts 2:2.

[1437] "Her Sweet Murmur: Exploring the Aural Phenomenology of Border Experiences," *Dark Lore*, 15-37.

[1438] See *The Greek Magical Papyri in Translation*, 142, footnote 146.

to your sacred symbols, give a whizzing sound, give a holy angel or magical assistant..."[1439]

Of course no one knows of what *glossolalia* —the *tongues* of early Christianity— actually consisted since no one transcribed it. It was almost certainly not the *voces magicae* such as we find in the magical books, ritual language which "appears always to have been directed toward the accomplishment of particular religious objectives."[1440] Nor does glossolalia appear to have been precisely the same as the επικλησις (epiklēsis), the *invocation* of the theurgist who used "unintelligible names"[1441] likely derived from real languages: "the gods have shown that the entire dialect of the sacred peoples such as the Assyrians and Egyptians is appropriate for religious ceremonies."[1442] However, it has been suggested that the exclamation, "Abba!"[1443] —a palindrome like many of the *voces magicae*— was the Christian equivalent of "the ecstatic cry ευαν by devotees of Dionysos."[1444] Paul stipulates that by such cries, "the spirit itself bears witness with our spirit that we are children of God,"[1445] a reference that would have been easily understood by any 'child' of Bacchus.

From the magical papyri come these instructions for an initiate:

> ...and with sustained bellowing, stare at the god and greet Him thus: "Welcome, Lord, Master of water, welcome, Lord, Founder of earth...O Lord, while being reborn, I am dying, growing and already grown, I die. Being born from a quickening birth, I am released to death...I am *Pheroura Miouri*..." After you say these things, you will receive an oracular answer...and should you attempt the things revealed by the god, you will speak as in ecstasy..."[1446]

[1439] δος ροιζον δος ιερον αγγελον η παρεδρον: "give a **whizzing sound**, give a holy angel or magical assistant..." *Papyri Graecae Magicae*, VII, 884.

[1440] *Aufstieg und Niedergang der Römischen Welt*, II.23.2, 1551.

[1441] τα ασημα ονοματα: "unintelligible names..." *De mysteriis*, VII, 4.

[81] Clarke, *Iamblicus: De mysteriis*, 297.

[1443] Roman 8:15.

[1444] *Aufstieg und Niedergang der Römischen Welt*, II.23.2, 1550.

[1445] Romans 8:16.

[1446] *Papyri Graecae Magicae* IV, 711-739.
     Compare Matthew 10:20.

A pagan who encountered a group of jabbering Christians reborn could hardly have reached any other conclusion than that they were possessed.

Although Paul chides former pagans for having worshipped "speechless images," he conveniently forgets that unless the God of the church speaks through the mouth of some intermediary,[1447] he is just as dumb as the idols Paul despises.

Given the ecstatic visions and séances of the early church, what need had it of a written gospel? In this turbulent spiritual milieu, in the living presence of the Lord's first associates, and the expectation that Jesus might return at any moment to exalt his followers, what possible interest could there have been in compiling a record of the Lord's doings? The first Christians likely had no more interest in Jesus' personal history than a toddler has in assembling a photo album of its parents.

> ...but regarding visions and revelations of the Lord, I know a man in Christ who, fourteen years ago, whether in the body I do not know, or out of the body I do not know —God knows— such a man was snatched away to the third heaven. And I know such a man, whether in the body or out of the body I do not know —God knows— that was snatched up to paradise and heard ineffable words which are not permitted a man to speak.[1448]

The connection between ecstasy and music has now been mentioned several times and there is evidence that this technique was also familiar to primitive Christians. The *Acts of John*,[1449] a work of the late 2nd century, describe how the disciples join in a circle, holding hands, and chant "Amen" in response to Jesus:[1450]

"Glory be to thee, Logos.
  Glory be to thee, Grace.   "Amen."
  Glory be to thee, Spirit.
  Glory be to thee, Holy One.

[1447] As at Acts 2:16-17, for example, where Yahweh is said to speak through angels, prophets, visions, and dreams —pretty much like any other deity.
[1448] 2 Corinthians 12:1-4.
[1449] *Acta Ioannis*, 94-96.
[1450] I have used Barbara Bowe's translation without strictly following her punctuation. *Journal of Early Christian Studies* 7: 84-85.

Glory be to thy Glory.	"Amen."
We praise thee, Father,	
We thank thee, Light,	
In whom darkness does not reside.	"Amen."
And why we give thanks I tell you:	
I will be saved and I will save.	"Amen."
I will be loosed and I will loose.	"Amen."
I will be wounded and I will wound.	"Amen."
I will be born and I will bear.	"Amen."
I will eat and I will be eaten.	"Amen."
I will hear and I will be heard..."	"Amen."
etc.	

It is likely that this chant, which is quite a bit longer than the section reproduced, employed an increasing tempo, and it would seem quite natural for those in the circle to begin to sway in unison or move together in a circular direction. Bowe notes "that its choreography and antiphonal chorus describe a circle dance performed by Jesus and his disciples on the night before his death."[1451] There is no need to reproduce Bowe's extensive analysis of the form of this text; for my purposes its function is of greater interest:

> To each statement the chorus answers "Amen." The repeated affirmation of "Amen" to the speaker's will ($\theta\epsilon\lambda\omega$) creates a staccato rhythm in this section which becomes almost mesmerizing...The hymn, therefore, can rightly be understood as a celebration of the mystery of the union between the Lord as revealer, the Godhead, and those who dance their way into this mysterious divine presence.[1452]

Examples of similar *confession-response*, which were adapted to clearly magical ends, can be cited:

> Christ was born. Amen.
> Christ was crucified. Amen.
> Christ was buried. Amen.
> Christ was raised. Amen.

[1451] The canonical gospels refer to singing as part of the 'Last Supper' (Mark 14:26; Matthew 26:30). It is tempting to think that this story may preserve a trace of historical memory.

[1452] *Journal of Early Christian Studies* 7: 97, 100.

He has awakened to judge the living and the dead.
You, too, fever with chills,
flee from Kalē who wears this magic charm.[1453]

Any claim that only Christians sought possession by 'the holy spirit' or that the notion of a 'holy spirit' was a Judeo-Christian invention could not be further from the truth:

This [is] the spell: "Come to me, lord...holy spirit..."[1454]

...and let the holy spirit breathe in me...[1455]

Hail, spirit that enters into me and convulses me and leaves me[1456] according to the will of god...[1457]

...continue revealing, truthfully, lord, a waking vision of every action by the command of the holy spirit, the angel of Phoibos ...[1458]

...and immediately the divine spirit enters...[1459]

..."I tell you a mystery..."

The Epicurean and Stoic philosophers who encountered Paul and listened to his arguments regarded him as a σπερμολογος (spermologos), a *seed-picker*, a person who, like a bird randomly gathering seeds, picks up scraps of information and terminology here and there and cobbles them together in an unsystematic, extemporaneous way that everywhere betrays a lack of understanding.[1460] Paul conforms to a standard figure of the ancient world: "This type of wandering craftsman seems keen to adopt and adapt every religious tradition that ap-

---

[1453] απο Καλης της φορουσης το **φυλακτηριον** τουτο: "from Kalē who wears this **magic charm**." *Supplementum Magicum*, 23.

[1454] κυριε...**αγιον πνευμα**: "lord...**holy spirit**..." *Papyri Graecae Magicae* III, 392-393.

[1455] **και πνευση εν εμοι το ιερον πνευμα**: "and let **the holy spirit** breathe in me..." *Papyri Graecae Magicae* IV, 510.

[1456] "leaves me" as the soul leaves the body (compare Liddel & Scott, *Greek-English Lexicon*, χωριζω, 2016).

[1457] *Papyri Graecae Magicae* IV, 1121.

[1458] *Papyri Graecae Magicae* III, 288-289.

[1459] **εισερχεται το θειον πνευμα**: "**the divine spirit** enters..." *Papyri Graecae Magicae* I, 284.

[1460] Acts 17:18.

peared useful to him, while the knowledge and understanding of what he adopted was characterized by a certain superficiality."[1461] As Charles Freeman observes, "Paul appears to have known very little of the philosophical tradition which he was attacking."[1462]

There is much in Paul's confirmed writings to support such an assessment; not only does Paul contradict himself, his style of argumentation is often a mixture of clashing metaphors and illogical rhetorical flourish. When it suits him —and it often does— Paul becomes suddenly vague about details. His correspondence veers erratically from boasting, to accusing, to cajoling, to pious condemnation. Paul embodied fundamentalism: he was fanatical, irrational, and *slick*, concerned only with convincing. "Paul's contempt for 'human' standards of wisdom and authority is deep-seated: His unsystematic theology, arising mainly from self-defensive diatribes against rival preachers, is characterized by a dislike of learning and philosophy that blends ill with the legend that he was a pupil of the famous Rabbi Gamaliel."[1463]

Nowhere is this more evident than in Paul's treatment of the parousia: "Behold! I tell you a mystery: we will not all fall asleep, but we will all be changed in an instant, in the blink of an eye at the sound of the last trumpet. For the trumpet will sound and the dead will be raised incorruptible and we will be changed."[1464] The language is still very much apocalyptic, as at 1 Thessalonians 4:15-17, but Paul is now trying to integrate the Jewish apocalyptic vision of the resurrection of the body with the pagan belief in the immortality of the soul by conjuring up spiritual bodies. Burton Mack: "The argument is only a bizarre assortment of metaphors strung together by ad hoc associations, this time in order to create the impression of 'spiritual body.'"[1465]

In a subsequent letter, Paul mixes metaphors of shelter and clothing: "For we know that if our earthly house, our tent, be destroyed, we

---

[1461] *The Greek Magical Papyri in Translation*, xlvi.
[1462] *The Closing of the Western Mind*, 341, n. 3.
[1463] *Jesus Outside the Gospels*, 32.

In the *Preface* to his lengthy defense of Christianity, Origen says, "Better yet the man, who encountering Celsus' composition, thinks nothing of the contents of his book, nor makes a defense, but sensibly rejects it all because of the faith acquired in Christ and the spirit which is in him." *Contra Celsum*, Præfatio, VI.

In short, the most "Christian" response to intellectual challenge was blind fideism.
[1464] 1 Corinthians 15:51-52.
[1465] *Who Wrote the New Testament?* 133.

have a building from God, a house not made by hand, everlasting in the heavens...for while we are still in this tent we sigh because we do not want to be unclothed, but to put on an additional garment so that what is mortal may be swallowed up by life."[1466] At no point does Paul succeed in explaining himself in any consistent way. Remarking on Paul's slippery exegesis, the emperor Julian said, "He changes his ideas about God according to his situation —just as a polypus changes his colors to match the rocks."[1467]

For better or worse, it was Paul and his school of followers who framed Christianity's "orthodox" theology, and it is preeminently their writings which survive —Paul's letters and those writing pseudonymously in his name account for over half the books in the New Testament. It should be pointed out that Paul's interpretation of Christianity was merely one of many, and that it was neither particularly persuasive nor understandable to many early Christians.[1468]

Many scholars have noted within the New Testament both the terminology of the mystery religions and of Gnosticism. It was inevitable that in their travels Christian missionaries came into contact with multiple cults and philosophical systems, and that they borrowed terms and phrases that had cultural currency. As we have seen, Paul does not commit to a particular position even in regard to the parousia; like all apocalyptic opportunists, his explanations change to fit circumstances. To seek a clear correspondence, therefore, between primitive Christianity and another, equally amorphous, system like 'gnosticism' is largely an exercise in futility. It is not my purpose to draw attention to the many ways in which the language of the Pauline school mirrors that of gnosticism, a project which has been carried forward to great effect by Elaine Pagels.[1469]

From the response of some of Pagel's bible college detractors, one might conclude that she has simply hallucinated the remarkable similarity between Paul's language and that of gnostics. However, regarding the vocabulary of Colossians, the grammarian A.T. Robertson, whose Christian credentials I would assume are impeccable, remarked

---

[1466] 2 Corinthians 5:1-4.
[1467] *Julian's Against the Galileans*, 101.
[1468] 2 Peter 3:15-16.
[1469] See particularly *The Gnostic Paul: Gnostic Exegesis of the Pauline Letters*.
   Whatever gnosticism's origins, the early Christian communities appear to have included gnostic factions.

(in 1934): "The Christians did not shrink from using these words in spite of the debased ideas due to emperor-cult, Mithraism, or other popular superstitions. Indeed, Paul (cf. Col.2:1 f.) often took the very words of Gnostic or Mithra cult and filled them with the riches of Christ…The mass of the N.T. vocabulary has been transfigured."[1470] To what extent the vocabulary of gnosticism had been filled with riches, transfigured, or otherwise improved upon by Christians would have been debatable even in Paul's day, but that Christians plagiarized terminology and ideas from gnosticism there is no disputing.

Christianity bears additional striking similarities to both the language and theory of the mystery religions. Hans Dieter Betz: "Expansion of mystery cult terms and ideas is evidenced also by the early Christian literature. Paul frequently employs μυστηριον (mystery) as a term designating the revelation of the transcendental realities of the divine world and of wisdom, prophecy, history, the afterlife and, by implication, the sacraments of baptism and the eucharist as well. Ephesians extends the usage, calling the Gospel itself μυστηριον (mustērion, *mystery*), something Paul himself did not do. The *agape* relationship between the heavenly Christ and his church on earth is called το μυστηριον μεγα (the great mystery). In all probability, Ephesians received this language from Colossians, which more closely reflects Paul's usage. 1 Timothy (3:9, 16) speaks of το μυστηριον της πιστεως (the mystery of faith) and το της ευσεβιας μυστηριον (the mystery of religion)."[1471]

Paul, one of the "assistants of Christ and stewards of the mysteries of God,"[1472] often employs such language:

> We speak wisdom among the initiated[1473]…the wisdom of God in a mystery that has been hidden away…[1474]

Samuel Angus:

[1470] *A Grammar of the Greek New Testament*, 116.

[1471] *Magika Hiera*, 251.

[1472] 1 Corinthians 4:1.

[1473] εν τοις **τελειοις**: "among the **initiated**…"

[1474] 1 Corinthians 2:6.

θεου σοφιαν εν μυστηριω την αποκεκρυμμενην: "the wisdom of God **in a mystery** that has been hidden away…"

Common to the Mysteries and Gnosticism were certain ideas, such as pantheistic mysticism, magic practices, elaborate cosmogonies and theogonies, rebirth, union with God, revelation from above, dualistic views, the importance attaching to names and attributes of the deity, and the same aim at personal salvation. As Gnosticism took possession of the field East and West, the Mysteries assumed an increasingly Gnostic character. The dividing line is sometimes difficult to determine.[1475]

Christian metaphors such as rebirth,[1476] being a new creation,[1477] the importance attaching to the name of Christ[1478] and claims of special revelation —including being snatched away to heaven[1479] — are common knowledge and certainly need no reiteration here. "Every serious *mystes* [initiate into a mystery cult, *my note*] approached the solemn sacrament of Initiation believing that he thereby became 'twice born,' a 'new creature,' and passed in a real sense from death unto life by being brought into a mysterious intimacy with the deity."[1480]

By the end of the first century, the apocalyptic belief of the first generation was rapidly fading into a harsh austerity that would soon lead to an ascetic condemnation of the world, a state of mind predicted by Paul's declaration:

May I never brag except about the cross of our Lord Jesus Christ through which the world has been crucified to me, and I to the world.[1481]

Hand in hand with the retreat from the early apocalyptic expectation, the initial charismatic ebullience becomes muted, and the Christian experience is increasingly described in the terms of the mystery cults:

For it was not by following cleverly contrived tales that we revealed the power and the presence of our Lord Jesus Christ to you, but by becoming witnesses of that majesty.[1482]

[1475] *The Mystery Religions*, 54.
[1476] As at John 3:3.
[1477] 2 Corinthians 5:17, Galatians 6:15.
[1478] For example Ephesians 1:20-21, Philippians 2:9.
[1479] Galatians 1:11-12, for example.
[1480] *The Mystery Religions*, 95-96.
[1481] Galatians 6:15.
[1482] 2 Peter 1:16.

The word I have translated *witness* in this passage, εποπτης (epoptēs), is a technical term borrowed from the vocabulary of the mystery cults. It refers specifically to "those who have been initiated into the highest grade of the mysteries."[1483] Pagan writers described from three to five stages in the initiatory process, the final one of which was the εποπτεια (epopteia), the *ecstatic vision.*

The "majesty" to which the writer refers is to the transfiguration of Jesus, of which Mark says και **μεταμορφωθη** εμπροσθεν αυτων: "and **he was transformed** before them."[1484] In Mark's version, Jesus' clothing becomes dazzlingly white, Moses and Elijah appear, and a voice from a cloud identifies Jesus as the beloved Son of God. Matthew's account characterizes the transformation as "the vision"[1485] and drops the verb from which *metamorphosis* is derived, possibly because of its association with the shape-shifting of the pagan gods.

In fact, the true vision of the new sect was near to fruition, nearer indeed than anyone living in the 1st century could have guessed. Within the space of a few centuries the majesty of Christ would supplant the majesty of Rome itself.

The early gifts of the spirit are a perfect illustration of the law of unintended consequences. As the Church would soon discover, claims to status by virtue of direct revelation could cut both ways, Paul or no Paul. The issue reached crisis proportions with the appearance of Montanus, who initiated a movement of ecstatic prophesying in the late 2nd century. Claiming possession by the Holy Spirit in a manner reminiscent of modern Pentecostalism, Montanus represented himself to be the Paraclete foretold in the gospel of John, and began to foretell the end of the world.

John Chrysostom (347-407) said of the spiritual gifts, "the present church is like a woman who has fallen from her former prosperous days and in many respects retains the symbols only of that ancient prosperity; displaying indeed the repositories and caskets of her golden ornaments, but bereft of her wealth."[1486] James Dunn made the following oservations regarding the waning of the spiritual gifts:

[1483] *The Mystery Religions,* 77.
[1484] Mark 9:2.
[1485] Matthew 17:9.
[1486] Quoted by Thiselton, *The Holy Spirit and Christian Origins,* 221.

If Paul's vision of charismatic community under the control of the Spirit of Christ was translated into reality *it was a reality which does not appear to have outlived him*...In the Pastorals *charisma* has lost its dynamic character. It is no longer the individual manifestation of grace...the vision of the charismatic community has faded, ministry and authority have become the prerogative of the few, the experience of the Christ-Spirit has lost its vitality, the preservation of the past has become more important than openness to the present and future. *Spirit and charisma have become in effect subordinate to office, to ritual, to tradition*...the present becomes in effect only a channel whereby the religion of the past can be transmitted to the future in good order.[1487]

Whereas Paul had successfully challenged the central Christian authority in Jerusalem, Montanus did not prove as successful with the ecclesiastical powers in Rome. As Lewis noted in his classic work, "the religious enthusiast, with his direct claim to divine knowledge, is always a threat to the established order...Christianity and Islam likewise must have appeared initially as cults of peripheral spirits which the entrenched religious establishments of their times were ultimately unable to destroy or control."[1488] One might propose as a corollary that as established religion begins to fail, cults of possession and splinter sects may reassert their influence.

To rein in the Montanist outbreak of enthusiasm, the Church moved to make written texts, not private revelations, the final arbiter of Christian teaching, hastening "the invention of scripture"[1489] by the formation of a canon of accepted books. The collection of an approved body of writings, the interpretation of which the Church could control, signaled that henceforth inspired prophets would be appearing more often in paintings than in person.

[1487] *Jesus and the Spirit*, 346-349.
[1488] *Ecstatic Religion*, 34, 131-132.
[1489] *Lost Christianities*, 238.

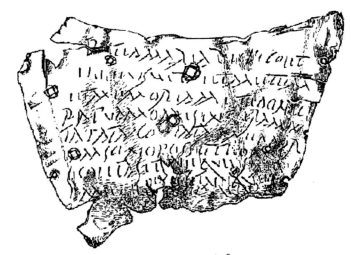

FIG. 24. INSCRIPTION NO. II. (¼ ⅞)

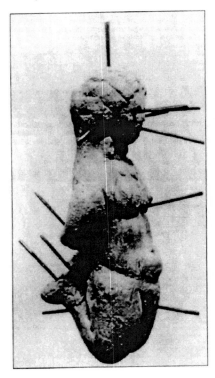

Above: Curse tablet (tabellae defixionum)
Below: Poppet used for magical cursing

Chapter 11: Spirit Versus Spirit

The book of Acts records several encounters between Christian missionaries and pagan miracle workers, and it comes as no surprise that the accounts demonstrate the superiority of the power of the apostles over the powers of their pagan contemporaries —pagan accounts of Christian miracle working were equally dismissive. The stories preserve a wealth of information about the role of magic in primitive Christianity, and it is to an examination of them that we will turn next.

In Acts we encounter a ploy which would be used to great effect by Christians against both pagan opponents and other Christians: the accusation of magic. Klauck: "When systems competed against each other, this accusation regularly provided a handy instrument: one party would accuse the other of black magic, hurling its entire available arsenal of abuse and polemics. As for one's own group, it practiced magic of the older, unreservedly positive kind—unless one preferred a priori to avoid the risk of even the remotest connection between one's own side and the concept of magic."[1490]

The distinction was particularly essential to Christians who "either made or presupposed one central, crucial point: that magic is the work of demons, while miracles are the work of God. What this amounted to, of course, was the claim that the Christian God is true and the pagan gods are false...unlike the pagans and the Jews, Christians had no ethnic cohesion, and they asserted their group identity not only by using mysterious rituals (like the mystery religions) but also by emphasizing strongly the distinctiveness of their God and their teachings about him...for them it was first of all a truth and secondly the sole basis for their existence as a group."[1491] Hull: "The argument is simply: God works miracles, demons work magic...Magic may look the same but (because it is done by devils) it cannot possibly be the same. The only conclusion is that it is deceptive. The similarity is a fraud."[1492] The ploy of charging opponents with practicing magic, a tactic still in use

---

[1490] *Magic and Paganism in Early Christianity: The World of the Acts of the Apostles*, 17.
[1491] *Magic in the Middle Ages*, 35-36.
[1492] *Hellenistic Magic and the Synoptic Tradition*, 61.

by Christian fundamentalists, "was used to undermine the ancient and venerated cults of Greece and Rome...[and] functioned to marginalize and alienate other Christians who followed teachings or practices that certain writers rejected."[1493]

Differentiating between miracle and magic in the New Testament is everywhere a matter of perspective. Miracles "are open to misunderstanding, and can even turn against the author; the apostolic word must then control their interpretation...What separates the magus from the gospel is neither the belief in supernatural powers, nor a charismatic performance, but the positioning of the human being before God."[1494] "Luke insults [Bar-Jesus] by describing him as a magician, because he sees his Christian preachers confronted with a situation of acute competition. There existed a wide spectrum of religious 'special offers,' often with a whiff of the exotic. The external appearance of the itinerant Christian missionaries was very similar to the 'men of God' of every shade who wandered from place to place, and they risked being evaluated against this background and absorbed into this spectrum."[1495]

...Simon Peter versus Simon Magus.

Now those who had been scattered went through the region spreading the word. Phillip went down to the city of Samaria and preached Christ to them. Everyone in the crowd was paying close attention to the things Phillip said; while listening to him they also saw the signs he performed. Unclean spirits, screaming with a loud voice, were cast out of many of the possessed, and many who were paralyzed and crippled were being healed. There was great joy in that city.

A certain man by the name of Simon, claiming to be someone great, had formerly practiced magic[1496] in the city and had amazed the people of Samaria. Everyone followed him eagerly, from the least to the greatest, saying, "This man is the Power of God, the Power called Great!" They followed him for quite some

---

[1493] Stratton, *Naming the Witch*, 107.

[1494] Marguerat, *Magic in the Biblical World*, 100, 120.

[1495] *Magic and Paganism*, 51-52.

[1496] μαγευω (mageuō), *to practice magic*, the only occurrence of this verb in the New Testament.

time because he had amazed them with his magical feats.[1497] But when they believed Phillip, who was preaching about the kingdom of God and the name of Jesus Christ, baptizing men and women, Simon himself believed and was baptized. He followed Phillip around constantly, astonished as he watched the signs and great miracles that occurred.

When the apostles in Jerusalem heard that Samaria had embraced the word of God, they sent Peter and John to them. They went down and prayed for them so that they might receive the holy spirit because up to that point it had not fallen upon any of them. They had only been baptized in the name of the Lord Jesus.

Then they laid their hands on them and they received the holy spirit. When Simon saw that the spirit was given by the application of the apostles' hands, he offered them money, saying, "Give me this power too so that anyone on whom I lay my hands may receive the holy spirit."

But Peter said to him, "To hell with you and your silver! You intended to buy the gift of God with money! There is no part or share for you in this proclamation, for your heart is not upright before God. So repent of this wickedness of yours and pray to the Lord that you may be forgiven the intention of your heart, for I see in you the gall of bitterness and the shackle of unrighteousness!"

Simon answered, "You must pray for me to the Lord so that nothing you have said may befall me!"[1498]

The "**laying on** of the hands," επιθεσις των χειρων, was a technique of passing the spirit from believer to believer.[1499] This is a set phrase in the Christian vocabulary, pointing to an early ritual that probably went back to the person of Jesus. Of the application of hands in Egyptian magic, Pinch notes, "The gesture of laying a hand on the patient is sometimes linked with sealing. One spell to safeguard a child promises, 'My hand is on you, my seal is your protection.' In another spell, the goddess Hathor is described as laying her hand on a woman suffering in childbirth. Ivory rods ending in hands represented

---

[1497] μαγεια (mageia), *magical art*, the only occurrence of this noun in the New Testament.

Samaria's connection with magic leads the Jews to accuse Jesus of being a Samaritan (John 8:48).

[1498] Acts 8:4-24.

[1499] 1 Timothy 4:14, 2 Timothy 1:6, Hebrews 6:2.

the divine hand and were part of a magician's equipment. A figure wearing an animal or Bes mask seems to be holding such a hand rod in a relief dating to the twenty-fourth century BC."[1500]

The intercession of the apostles indicates that Phillip did not have the authority to bestow supernatural gifts, therefore their intervention becomes necessary, a detail designed to support the emerging "apostolic fiction" that traces the transfer of power from Jesus to the apostles to the church.

The story of Simon —who will be known henceforth to history as Simon Magus— is the origin of *simony*, the purchase of church offices. Although Acts does not tell us what became of Simon, the church fathers lost no time creating a substantial legend around him and his heresies, and his memory is excoriated in the *Acts of Saint Peter*, as well as by Justin Martyr, Irenaeus, Epiphanius, Hippolytus, and Pseudo-Clement.

Simon's offer of money was probably customary in his circles. If magical power is a commodity, then payment for it was quite naturally in order: "The power can be passed from one person to another. It is not a moral quality nor a learned skill but an acquisition, a property which can be conveyed either with the will of the donor, as in Luke 9.1, or without it, as in 8.46."[1501] And it was precisely the value-free nature of magical power that posed a critical problem for Christianity: "an objective consideration will note a suspicious similarity between the public appearance and working of Philip and of Simon; it is to some extent a question of interpretation, whether a successful healing is attributed to a miracle or to sorcery...most religious phenomena were ambiguous and required interpretation. Without interpretation, the phenomena have no value; this is what makes it so difficult to distinguish the working of miracles from magical activity."[1502] There are wonder-workers of every stripe in the Hellenistic world, the circumstance that motivates the temple rulers to ask, "By what power or *by what name* did you do this?" to which Peter replies, "in the name of Jesus Christ of Nazareth."[1503] There are obviously *other* effective names.

[1500] *Magic in Ancient Egypt*, 84.
[1501] *Hellenistic Magic*, 107.
[1502] *Magic and Paganism*, 18-19.
[1503] Acts 4:7-10.

As will be seen in the case of Paul, apostles tended to become shrill when their authority was challenged, but Peter's response to Simon's offer borders on hysteria. The apostolic diatribe contains what may be a single telling point: "There is no part or share for you in this proclamation," literally "in this word," i.e., "the word of God" the Samaritans had embraced. Simon had attached himself to Phillip, been baptized as a Christian convert, and in all likelihood had begun to preach the word himself, to spread "the word." Simon, who had formerly amazed the Samaritans with his "magical feats," now sought to perform "signs and great miracles" in the name of Jesus. That was too much for Peter. A turf war promptly ensued.

The point of the story is not as much Simon's magic as it is Peter's apostolic authority. Luke-Acts, written relatively late in the first century, long after Peter's death, reveals yet another step in the evolution of the Christian movement: the filling of an administrative vacuum. Jesus, who believed he was living on the very cusp of history, passed miraculous powers to his disciples but made no provision for the continuity of administrative authority. "The twelve are the bearers of personal continuity, guaranteeing and handing on to future generations everything that had happened from the baptism of Jesus until his apparitions after Easter. In this special function, they are irreplaceable..."[1504]

At first this lack of continuity posed no problem; the early Christians expected the quick return of the Lord and set about preparing themselves for it. But the Lord did not return. The Jews grew weary of Christians proselytizing in their synagogues and kicked them out, while Gentiles began to join the movement in real numbers. Who now had the authority to decide what constituted true Christian practice? Who would determine the doctrinal content of the new religion? In the stories of magicians recounted in Acts we are witnessing the emergence of a new Christian pecking order, the establishment of apostolic authority as the beginning of a continuous chain of command that culminates in the creation of a line of bishops that starts with the apostles.

[1504] *Magic and Paganism in Early Christianity*, 7.

...Paul versus Bar-Jesus

When they had gone through the whole island as far as Paphos, they encountered a certain man, a magician,[1505] a false prophet,[1506] the Jew named Bar-Jesus, who was with the proconsul Sergius Paulus, a man of discernment, who summoned Barnabas and Saul because he wanted to hear the word of God. But Elymas[1507] the magician —for that is how his name is translated— resisted them, trying to turn the proconsul away from the faith.

But Saul, also known as Paul, filled with the holy spirit, stared at him intensely and said, "O you who are full of every treachery and every kind of fraud, son of the Devil, enemy of all righteousness, will you not stop making crooked the straight paths of the Lord? Now look! The hand of the Lord is upon you[1508] and you will be blind, not seeing the sun for a time."

Immediately mist and darkness fell on him and he wandered around searching for someone to lead him by the hand. When the proconsul saw what had happened, he believed, having been overwhelmed by the teaching of the Lord.[1509]

The false prophet Bar-Jesus was hardly the end of the problem for the early church which was also plagued by false brothers,[1510] false teachers,[1511] false apostles,[1512] and even false christs.[1513]

A thorough analysis of this passage has been done by Rick Strelan,[1514] who observes that "false prophets" arise from the *Christian* ranks,[1515] as do the "false brothers."[1516] "The narrator wants it understood that the charismatic power of miracle is in danger of being hijacked, as

---

[1505] μαγος (magos), *magician*, like the magi in Matthew's infancy narrative.

[1506] ψευδοπροφητης (pseudoprophētēs), *false prophet*.

[1507] Possibly derived from Aramaic *haloma*, an interpreter of dreams. *A Kind of Magic*, 106. See also L. Yaure, *Journal of Biblical Literature* 79: 297-314.

[1508] χειρ κυριου επι σε: "the hand of the Lord is upon you," like the "finger of God," (Luke 11:20) is a threat.

[1509] Acts 13:6-12.

[1510] Galatians 2:4.

[1511] 2 Peter 2:1.

[1512] 2 Corinthians 11:13.

[1513] Mark 13:22.

[1514] *Biblica* 85: 65-87.

[1515] Matthew 7:15, 24:11, 24, 2 Peter 2:1, 1 John 4:1.

[1516] 2 Corinthians 11:26, Galatians 2:4.

much as those who covet this force from the outside, as by the followers of Jesus."[1517]

Paul addresses Bar-Jesus —which means "Son of Jesus"— as a "son
of the Devil" and pronounces a classic slander spell against him, a
διαβολη (diabolē), "a spell that ascribes unholy actions to an opponent,[1518] causing the offended divinity to avenge itself: Bar-Jesus is
struck temporarily blind even as was Paul himself for his opposition to
Jesus.

As Strelan points out, Sergius Paulus "wanted to hear the word of
God," and it is over the interpretation of the "word" that Paul and
Bar-Jesus are fighting. Neither Simon nor Bar-Jesus can lay claim to
"the word." They are outside the prophetic circle which —as Luke is
eager to show us— consists only of the apostles and their immediate
associates. The conflict in sight in this passage is over true versus false
representations of Christianity. Bar-Jesus, as his name strongly implies,
is within or at the margins of the 'Jesus community,' and Paul accuses
him not of denying Jesus, but of "making crooked the straight paths of
the Lord," i.e., of *twisting* the gospel. Brown observed of Roman political infighting, "resentments and anomalous power on the edge of the
court could be isolated only by the more intimate allegation—sorcery."[1519] An accusation of magical practice as a tool for political control was already a standard rhetorical device.

The Jewish magicians like Bar-Jesus often attended Roman officials is
nearly certain: "It is of some significance that the author of Acts can
take it for granted that his readers will not have been puzzled by the
presence of a Jewish magician and seer in the entourage of a high Roman official. That suggests that Jewish magicians and magicians who
were part of the court of Roman administrators were in their eyes familiar figures."[1520] All the more reason for the Christian missionaries
to differentiate themselves.

Luke hastens to assert that Sergius Paulus is astonished by the "teaching" of Paul lest we assume that it is Paul's power alone that has
"overwhelmed" him. However, it is "primarily as a miracle worker"

[1517] *Magic in the Biblical World*, 122-123.
[1518] *Magika Hiera*, 196.
[1519] *Religion and Society in the Age of Saint Augustine*, 125.
[1520] *Magic and Magicians in the Greco-Roman World*, 223.

that Jesus attracts attention, and his disciples' success "arose from their deeds, above all, in healing."[1521] It is noteworthy that we again encounter the term *teaching* as code word for performing magic. As noted previously, *astonishment* is the expected reaction to *magic*, not teaching.

The purpose of the book of Acts —the Acts of the *Apostles*— is to establish the myth of apostolic authority in the face of competing gospels. The proclamation of the true gospel belongs to the inner circle and to them alone. Henceforth the conflict between Christian sects will be characterized as a front in the universal war between the Lord and his agents of light and Satan and his army of darkness:

> Each side is represented visibly on earth by a set of human lieutenants. To the prophets correspond the false prophets, to the apostles, false apostles, to the Christ, the Antichrist. And as God empowers his "saints" to accomplish miracles that authorize their mission, Satan and his underlings enable their fiends to perform powerful works that are, or so they would seem, equivalent. These "sons of the devil" who perform such marvels are magicians.[1522]

...in re: Paul and Silas.

It so happened that as we were going to the place of prayer a certain servant girl who had a spirit of divination met us.[1523] She used to turn a tremendous profit for her masters by making predictions. She kept tagging along after Paul and the rest of them, saying, "These men who are proclaiming a way of salvation to you are servants of the Highest God!"

She went on doing this for many days. Finally at the end of his patience, Paul turned and said to the spirit, "I command you in the name of Jesus Christ to come out of her!" It came out of her

---

[1521] *Christianizing the Roman Empire*, 22.

[1522] My translation of: "Chaque parti est représenté visiblement sur terre par une série d'hommes-lieutenants. Aux prophètes respondent de faux prophètes, aux apôtres, de faux apôtres, au Christ l'Antéchrist. Et comme Dieu donne à ses 'saints' d'accomplir des miracles accréditant leur mission, Satan et ses satellites donnent à leurs suppôts de faire des prodiges qui sont, ou du moins paraissent, équivalents. Ces 'fils du diable' qui opèrent des merveilles sont les magiciens." *Ephemerides Theologicae Lovanienses* 15: 455.

[1523] παιδισκην τινα εχουσαν πνευμα πυθωνα: "a certain servant girl who had a spirit **of divination**..."

that very hour. When her masters saw that their hope of profit had fled them, they seized Paul and Silas and hauled them to the marketplace to appear before the authorities.[1524]

The girl who follows Paul and Barnabas has "a spirit of divination" — πνευμα πυθωνα, "a spirit of the python." This curious terminology derives from the myth of Apollo,[1525] the god of prophecy, who slew the dragon Python that lived in the caves of Delphi at the foot of Mount Parnassus. As a mark of his victory over the serpent, Apollo appointed a priestess, the Pythia, or Pythoness, who spoke oracles when she was possessed by the spirit of the god,[1526] the Pythonic spirit or spirit of divination.

The Delphic oracle, which spoke continuously through its priestess for nearly 2000 years, thus became synonymous with female mediums of a type known as an εγγαστραμυθος (engastramuthos), or 'belly talker.' Such mediums, like the priestess of Apollo and the slave girl who tailed after Paul, were typically women "with little education or experience of the world,"[1527] and their presence in the ancient world is well attested. There were male "pythons" as well, but regardless of sex, possession was held to occur most readily in the "young and somewhat simple."[1528] Iamblichus described such seers as ευηθικος (euēthikos), *good-hearted*, or speaking bluntly, *simpletons*. Of such persons he remarks, "In this way, through those utterly deprived of knowledge, [the god] reveals understanding that surpasses all knowledge."[1529] This description is in substantial agreement with the Christian understanding of divine revelation through possession: to the rational mind it is folly and foolishness.[1530]

By far the most famous biblical medium is the witch of Endor. Identified in the *Septuagint* as an *engastramuthos*, she is more correctly an evocator, or "soul-drawer" —a ψυχαγωγος (psuchagōgos)— as the account shows:

[1524] Acts 16:16-19.
[1525] Απολλων, *Slayer*.
[1526] πυθολητος (putholēptos), *seized by the python*, like the επιλητος (epilēptos), *seized by the god* like the young prophet (2 Kings 9:11).
[1527] Dodds, *The Greeks and the Irrational*, 72.
[1528] *Pagans and Christians*, 208.
[1529] *Iamblichus: De mysteriis*, 162-165.
[1530] 1 Corinthians 1:18-25.

When Saul saw the army of the Philistines, he was afraid and his heart trembled greatly. When Saul inquired of the Lord, the Lord did not answer him, not by dreams, or by Urim, or by prophets. Then Saul said to his servants, "Seek out for me a woman who is a medium, so that I may go to her." His servants said to him, "Behold, there is a medium at Endor."

So Saul disguised himself and put on other garments and went, he and two men with him; and they came to the woman by night. And he said, "Divine for me by a spirit, and bring up for me whomever I shall name for you." The woman said to him, "Surely you know what Saul has done, how he has cut off the mediums and wizards from the land. Why then are you laying a snare for my life to bring about my death?" But Saul swore to her by the Lord, "As the Lord lives, no punishment will come upon you for this thing." Then the woman said, "Whom shall I bring up for you?" He said, "Bring up Samuel for me." When the woman saw Samuel, she cried out with a loud voice; and the woman said to Saul, "Why have you deceived me? You are Saul!" The king said to her, "Have no fear; what do you see?" The woman said to Saul, "I see a god coming up out of the earth." He said to her, "What is his appearance?" She said, "An old man is coming up; and he is wrapped in a robe." And Saul knew that it was Samuel, and he bowed with his face to the ground, and did obeisance.

Then Samuel said to Saul, "Why have you disturbed me by bringing me up?" Saul answered, "I am in great distress, for the Philistines are warring against me, and God has turned away from me and answers me no more, either by prophets or by dreams; therefore I have summoned you to tell me what I shall do."[1531]

Although we know of the evocation of ghosts by female mediums, it is not possible to tell what was thought to have possessed the girl who followed Paul. In any case Paul makes it clear that the 'proclamation of a way of salvation' will not be shared with disembodied entities, whatever their nature. The spirits of the prophets are subject to the prophets, as are also demonic spirits —not even an angel from heaven can contradict the apostolic gospel.[1532]

[1531] 1 Samuel 28:5-15 (RSV).
[1532] 1 Corinthians 14:32, Galatians 1:8.

Christ's human officers, led by His apostles, are now especially alerted to the possibility of demonic wickedness in all those who try to oppose them by supernatural means. Put in another way, humans who manifest objectionable traits and behaviour may now be *expected* to have demonic helpers..."[1533]

The account of the servant girl again raises the issue of the role of women in magical practice, a point previously touched upon in the discussion of the angelic Watchers of *1 Enoch*. There is a clear tendency to regard black magic as preeminently the work of women. "The prime model for witchcraft is the female practitioner in Exodus 22:18. In other instances the charge of witchcraft is combined with charges of prostitution and illicit sexuality. Prophetic texts associate harlotry and magical charms (Nah. 3:4) while historical texts denounce women as harlots who engage in sorcery (Jezebel in 2 Kings 9:22)."[1534]

In addition to the Old Testament account of the ghost mistress of Endor, female necromancers are also known in Egyptian magic: "A few personal letters from the late second millennium BC preserve references to women who were called *rekhet*—'knowing one.' These wise women were consulted as seers who could get in touch with the dead."[1535] Daniel Ogden also notes the "tendency to associate a specialization in necromancy with aliens—Persians, Babylonians, and Egyptians—and with women or witches," a tendency which may reflect "cultural distancing."[1536]

Paul acknowledges that he and his fellow travelers are treated "as deceivers"[1537] —ως πλανοι— a word already noted to carry the added weight of *magician*. Although Paul says nothing to illuminate the meaning of *planos*, the charges brought against him by the Roman slaveholders following the exorcism of their girl medium are suggestive:

These men, being Jews, are creating a disturbance in our city and they advocate rites[1538] which are not lawful for us, as Romans, either to view with approval or to perform.[1539]

[1533] Valerie Flint, *Witchcraft and Magic in Europe: Ancient Greece and Rome*, 298.
[1534] *Magic in the Roman World*, 87.
[1535] *Magic in Ancient Egypt*, 56.
[1536] *Greek and Roman Necromancy*, 95.
[1537] 2 Corinthians 6:8.
[1538] καταγγελλουσιν εθη: "they advocate **rites**..."

The context of the accusation makes clear that rituals peculiar to Jews —namely *exorcism*, a form of magical practice— are being distinguished from Roman rites, which are legal to perform. Reimer notes, "The customs (εθος) that Paul is thus accused of promoting are economically disruptive magical practices, which as the two slave-owners correctly point out are illegal for Romans to practice in any way, shape, or form."[1540] A powerful case for this understanding of the text has also been made by de Vos:

> In practical terms magic only became magic when someone was accused of it...Why would Paul and Silas have been labeled as magicians? Their actions had resulted in harm to the slave-girl's owners, namely, property damage (to their slave) and the loss of their means of livelihood...the Jews were perceived to be magicians by many Romans, and exorcism was probably the main type of magic associated with Jews in this period."[1541]

...a demon versus the sons of Skeva

God was doing uncommonly powerful works through Paul's hands, so that when handkerchiefs and aprons that had touched his skin were placed upon the sick, they were set free from their diseases and the evil spirits came out of them. Some of the itinerant Jewish exorcists[1542] pronounced the name of the Lord Jesus

---

[1539] Acts 16:20-21.

[1540] *Miracle and Magic*, 217.

[1541] *Journal for the Study of the New Testament* 74: 51, 57, 60.

[1542] εξορκιστης (exorkistēs), *exorcist*, the only occurrence of the word in the New Testament. The related verb εξορκιζω (exorkizō), *to put under oath*, is used of the high priest putting Jesus under oath to answer his question (Matthew 26:63). The simplex form of the verb is used by the demon to "adjure" Jesus, "I adjure you by God, that you not torture me" —ορκιζω σε τον θεον μη με βασανισης (Mark 5:7).

Garrett points out that *exorcist* occurs nowhere else in the New Testament "perhaps because it too had magical connotations, as did the closely related verb 'adjure.'" *The Demise of the Devil*, 92.

The formula of adjuration —(εξ)ορκιζω σε, "I adjure you" or "I conjure you"— very common in the magical papyri, "is regularly used of compelling netherworld demons to perform aggressive or malicious tasks; or, in protective contexts, of actual 'exorcisms' of possessing demons." Kotansky, *Greek Magical Amulets*, 281.

over those having evil spirits,[1543] saying, "I command you by the Jesus Paul proclaims…"

There were seven sons of Skeva the Jewish high priest doing this. The evil spirit said to them by way of reply, "I know Jesus and I am well aware of Paul, but who are you?" With that, the man in whom the evil spirit was leaped upon them, overcoming them all, and so overpowered them that they fled from the house naked and wounded.

This became known among all the Jews as well as Greeks who were living in Ephesus and fear fell on all of them and the name of Jesus was exalted. Many of those who had believed came forward, confessing and publicly disclosing their practices. A good number of those who were dabbling in such matters collected their books together[1544] and burned them before everyone and when their value was calculated, it came to fifty thousand silver coins.[1545]

It is widely acknowledged that there was no Jewish High Priest named Skeva, another bit of Lukan pseudo-history. The name was probably concocted from the Latin *scaevus, left-handed,* or from *scaeva,* an *omen.* The diminutive, *scaevola,* often referred to a phallic good luck charm. Further analysis of the possibilities is given by Strelan.[1546]

The Christian use of amulets —or *relics of the saints* if so preferred— is obviously very ancient. Like Jesus' robe, Paul's aprons and sweat cloths are known to transmit magical power: "According to Acts xix.12, evil spirits were driven out by the aid of pieces of cloth which have been impregnated with Paul's superior power, his δυναμις."[1547]

[1543] τους **εχοντας** τα πνευματα τα πονηρα: "those **having** evil spirits…" (Acts 19:13). In this case the context indicates that "to have" an evil spirit is to be possessed by one.

[1544] Magical books were clearly gathered into collections: Μεγαλη Ισις η κυρια, αντιγραφον ιερας βιβλου της ευρετισης εν τοις του Ερμου ταμιοις: "Great is Lady Isis. **Copy of a sacred book** found in the Hermetic archives…" P. Oxy. 886, *Selections from the Greek Papyri,* 110, Cambridge University Press, 1910.

[1545] Acts 19:11-19.

"Lots of magic was practiced in the early churches: Acts 19.19 suggests the extent of it in Ephesus (the magical books of those Christians who could be persuaded to burn them were valued at about $320,000)." *Jesus the Magician,* 94.

[1546] *Strange Acts,* 109-110.

[1547] *Some Notes on the Demonology in the New Testament,* 6.

"Such cloths were indeed amulets (φυλακτηρια),[1548] and though not engraved with magic words, there is little to detract from the prospect that the cloths, once used effectively, would have been deployed again and again. These magically-charged reliquaries would have no doubt been reapplied with the necessary prayers or incantations: the young Christian community at Ephesus, it seems, adhered tenaciously to their magical beliefs, in some cases for up to two years after conversion (Acts 19:10)."[1549] And regarding the "apostle's laundry," Klauck observes, "it appears that the miraculous power is thought of in material terms, so that it can be 'tapped' from the person of the wonder-worker and stored for subsequent use. The cloths take on the function of amulets and talismans which were so common in the magic of antiquity."[1550] Jesus' name also takes on magical power, featuring fairly commonly in the magical papyri where it is particularly efficacious for exorcism: ορκιζω σε κατα του θεου των Εβραιων Ιησου: "I cast you out by the god of the Hebrews, Jesus..."[1551]

The *seven* Jewish exorcists reflects the wide-spread belief in magical numbers. The *Sepher Ha-Razim* contains this spell:

> Take water from seven springs on the seventh day of the month, in the seventh hour of the day, in seven unfired pottery vessels ...Expose them beneath the stars for seven nights; and on the seventh night take a glass vial, *etc.*...[1552]

An apologetic reading might assume that Luke merely meant to parody magical practice by portraying seven exorcists driven out by a demon —the demon demands to know the names of the exorcists before casting them out, a surprise role reversal— but that seven was thought significant is clear. The apocryphal ending of Mark tells of seven demons driven from Mary Magdalene[1553] and Revelation has seven churches and seven spirits,[1554] seven stars and seven lampstands,[1555]

[1548] φυλακτηριον (phulaktērion), *safeguard* or *outpost*, from whence *phylactery* or *tefillin*, a small leather box containing scriptural passages worn by Jewish men during prayer, formerly used as amulets.
[1549] *Ancient Magic and Ritual Power*, 244.
[1550] *Magic and Paganism*, 98.
[1551] *Papyri Graecae Magicae*, IV, 3019.
[1552] *Sepher Ha-Razim*, 26.
[1553] Mark 16:9.
[1554] Revelation 1:4.
[1555] Revelation 2:1.

and seven torches which are identified with seven spirits,[1556] to cite but a few examples from a book riddled with magical sevens. Magical sevens are also common in the *Leyden Papyrus*: "utter these charms seven times...take seven new bricks...seven palm sticks...seven clean loaves...seven lumps of salt...stamp on the ground with your foot seven times...pronounce these spells over the lamp again another seven times...call down into the middle of his head seven times..."[1557] A spell against fever specifies that the magician is to take oil in his hands and say "Sabaōth" seven times.[1558]

The magical papyri record multiple examples of prolonged vocalization of the **seven vowels** along with other vowel strings: "IŌĒ MIMIPSŌTHIŌŌPH PHERSŌTHI **AEĒIOYŌ**[1559] IŌĒ EŌ CHARI PHTHA, come out from NN...This is the conjuration: 'I conjure you by the god of the Hebrews, Jesus...'"[1560] The seven vowels were thought to "signify the seven planets, the seven spheres and their ruler, the Αναγκη ["Fate," or "Destiny," *my note*]. They signify the whole κοσμος ["order," *my note*], ultimately the creator and leader of the κοσμος...Magicians, pagans as well as Christians, had, however, been impressed by the mysterious powers of these letters..."[1561] As is obvious from the quotation above which combines the seven vowels with a conjuration in the name of Jesus, early Christians were well aware of the magical powers of the seven vowels, τα επτα φωνηεντα (ta hepta phōnēenta). Eusebius said that "the combination of the seven vowels" was the equivalent of the "four letters" which the Hebrews "apply to the supreme power of God,"[1562] i.e., the tetragrammaton, יהוה, the name of Yahweh which is so holy it must not be pronounced.

An exorcism attributed to Athanasius reads in part:

[1556] Revelation 4:5.
[1557] *Leyden Papyrus*, II, 14-15; III, 5, 8-9; V, 1, 6; X, 16-17.
[1558] *Papyri Graecae Magicae*, VII, 211-212.
[1559] The seven Greek vowels: α,ε,η,ι,ο,υ,ω: a,e,ē,i,o,u,ō.
[1560] *The Greek Magical Papyri in Translation*, 96. The referenced spell is IV, 3010-3020.
   Εστιν δε ο **ορκισμος** ουτος ορκιζω σε κατα του θεου των Εβραιων Ιησου ...: "This is the **conjuration**: 'I conjure you by the god of the Hebrews, Jesus'..."
[1561] *Some Note on the Demonology in the New Testament*, 26-27.
[1562] Gifford, *Preparation for the Gospel*, 558.
   επι της **ανωτατω** του θεου **δυναμεως**: "apply to the **supreme power** of God ..." *Praeparationis Evangelicae*, XI, 6.36.

I command you, all evil and unclean spirits, by the seven letters[1563] written in the heart of Helios and no one deciphers them except the Lord God...[1564]

Acts 19:19, the *locus classicus* of Christian book burning, reveals that the Ephesian Christians were dabbling in matters "pert[aining] to undue or misdirected curiosity,"[1565] i.e., magic, the meaning of περιεργος (periergos) in this context. "Concerning the burning of the magical books at Ephesus, described in Acts 19.19, Deissmann points out that *ta perierga* and *prassein* are technical terms in the vocabulary of magic and that the papyrus codices may in general be similar to those burnt by the Christians."[1566] Regarding the charges brought up against Simon Magus by the church father Irenaeus, Dickie notes, "The list begins with exorcisms and incantations and moves on to amatory spells and spells that draw a person and ends with the use of familiar spirits and the sending of dreams and whatever other curious and excessive practices (*periergia*) they pursue...Now excessive or curious practices in this context mean interfering in what ought to be left undisturbed, which is to say, practicing magic."[1567]

It was essential that the apostles distinguish themselves early and clearly from the other wonder-workers of the day: "The manhandling of demons—humiliating them, making them howl, beg for mercy, tell their secrets, and depart in a hurry served a purpose quite essential to the Christian definition of monotheism: it made physically (or dramatically) visible the superiority of the Christian's patron Power over all others."[1568]

The Christian exorcists are everywhere at a disadvantage compared to professional orators —"of rude speech" as the church historian Eusebius freely admits— and they "proclaimed the knowledge of the kingdom of heaven only by the display of the divine spirit working in them and by what the wonder-working power of Christ accomplished

---

[1563] τα επτα γραμματα: "the seven **letters**..."
[1564] Delatte, *Anecdota Atheniensia*, 231.
[1565] *Greek-English Lexicon of the New Testament*, 800.
[1566] *Hellenistic Magic*, 17.
[1567] *Magic and Magicians*, 231-232.
[1568] *Christianizing the Roman Empire*, 28.

through them."[1569] In short, Eusebius attributed the success behind Christian preaching to *thaumaturgy*, not doctrine.

Guy Williams has proposed that Paul's claim to have fought wild animals in Ephesus[1570] is a reference to confrontation between himself and other magicians:

> Paul viewed the confrontations and physical threats that he experienced in Ephesus as instigated by the evil spirits, or 'beasts', at work in the demon-possessed, sorcerers, and idolaters of the city...in the vocabulary of magic, magicians summoned various spirits through the imagery of wild animals...The book of Acts remembers Paul's time in Ephesus as characterized by exorcisms, magical rivalries, and violent controversies regarding idolatry, while the epistle to the Ephesians also presupposes that evil spirits gravely challenged the early Christian community there.[1571]

In the lifetime of Paul, Ephesus was the capitol of Asia Minor and the site of the temple of Artemis,[1572] the ever virgin goddess of childbirth. In Asia, however, Artemis was assimilated to the ancient Mother Goddess, Cybele, a fertility deity. It was here that Christian converts, "many of those who had believed," came forward with their books of magic and burned them. With magic, as with all life's endeavors, success is copied, and given the cultural context, one might fairly ask if the Ephesian Christians regarded themselves as having truly *discarded* magic along with their books, or instead to have simply traded up.

Evidence that the Christians from Ephesus had, in effect, basically exchanged one magical system for another even more potent comes from the epistle to the Ephesians itself which invokes an impressive string of magical 'power words':

[1569] και τη δι' αυτων συντελουμενη **θαυματουργω** του Χριστου δυναμει: "and what the **wonder-working** power of Christ accomplished through them." *Ecclesiastical History*, III, 24, 3.

[1570] 1 Corinthians 15:32.

[1571] *Journal of Theological Studies* 57: 45.

[1572] One of the seven wonders of the ancient world, some 260 feet wide, 430 feet long, and 60 feet high, with 127 columns. The central cella, or sanctuary, contained the famous Διοπετης (Diopetēs), *fell-from-Zeus*, in all probability a meteorite seen as a heaven-sent cultic object. Likewise, "the primary image of Aphrodite was aniconic. It was...a black meteoric stone kept in her temple at Kouklia (Old Paphos), Cyprus." *A History of Pagan Europe*, 21.

...and what is the surpassing greatness of his power[1573] for the use of us believers, according to the operation of the power[1574] of his might which he put into effect when he raised Christ up from the dead and seated him at his right in the heavens above, far above all rulership and authority and power and lordship and every name named, not only in this age, but that to come.[1575]

Regarding this passage, Arnold writes,

The writer introduces the power of God in an extremely emphatic fashion. He uses the adjectival participle of υπερβαλλω combined with the adjective μεγεθος to emphasize in bold relief the incredibly mighty power of God. Both of these rare terms may have been chosen by the author to communicate especially to those converted from magic in Asia Minor. They both appear in the magical papyri and also in a number of inscriptions from Ephesus...The author provides still another expression to emphasize the comprehensive scope of Christ's supremacy. "Every name that is named" (πας ονομα ονομαζομενος) is encompassed in the mighty reign of the Lord Jesus Christ. This particular phrase is loaded with significance for exorcism and magical incantation both in Judaism and the pagan world. Every conceivable name of both known and unknown deities and supernatural "powers" is called upon in at least one of the magical papyri. In fact, the very term ονομα is so important in the magical papyri that in the index to his collection, Preisendanz lists close to 400 occurrences of it.[1576]

Consistent with the necromantic focus of magical power, the writer does not fail to mention Christ "raised...up from the dead."

[1573] της δυναμεως αυτου: "of his power..."

[1574] κατα την ενεργιαν του κρατους: "according to the **operation** of the power..." ενεργεια, *working*, a word common in the magical papyri, is the application of δυναμις, *power* which is latent.

[1575] Ephesians 1:19-21.

[1576] *Ephesians: Power and Magic*, 54, 72-73. Arnold's is by far the most comprehensive discussion in English of the many references to magic in the epistle to the Ephesians.

Schnackenburg: "[Christ] has overthrown and put under his authority the 'powers' which operate in the lower heavenly regions...Through the Crucifixion-event they have been deprived of their power...The victory Christ achieved over every dark power guarantees victory for his Church also...all the powers named and whatever else may have a 'name' —i.e. might and influence— are all subjected to Christ." *Ephesians: A Commentary*, 77-78.

Except for later writings which quote it, the dimensional terms "the breadth and length and height and depth"[1577]

> ...never occur in succession except for their appearance in PGM IV.965, ff. This text twice uses the *four* dimensions—and appears to use the combination as an expression of supernatural power. The expression occurs in the context of a magical formula for the obtaining of a vision while awake...It is doubtful that the Ephesian passage influenced the magical texts I have cited. The two spells betray no sign of Christian influence, much less any influence by the Ephesian epistle...If the recipients of the epistle had come from a background of magical practices it is likely that the dynamic significance of the four dimensions would be readily intelligible to them.[1578]

The portion of magical text referenced by Arnold reads, "I conjure you, holy light, holy radiance, breadth, depth, length, height, radiance, by the holy names..."[1579]

Public manifestations of repentance notwithstanding, Christian miracles and pagan magic would exist in an uneasy alliance for centuries to come as proven by the survival of magic spells used by Christians:

> Ablanathamala...Akrammachamari
> kaicha k aia, Lord God,
> Lord of all gods, heal Thaēsas! ...
> Release [him] in the name of Jesus!
> (*a row of written magical symbols follows*)
> Heal Thaēsas, now, now, quickly, quickly![1580]

[1577] Ephesians 3:18.

[1578] *Ephesians: Power and Magic*, 91-92.

Other commentators are in broad agreement about the meaning of 'powers' intended in this passage. They are demonic powers of evil (Schnackenburg, *Ephesians: A Commentary*, 77-80), "angelic and also evil in character." The term κοσμοκρατωρ, *cosmic ruler* (6:12), "may well have been a term used in the first or second century A.D. of magical or astrological traditions. In fourth-century magical papyri it is used as one of the magical titles of Helios, Hermes, and Sarapis..." (Hoehner, *Ephesians: An Exegetical Commentary*, 276-288, 826-827).

[1579] *Papyri Graecae Magicae* IV, 978-979.

[1580] *Supplementum Magicum*, I, 55-56.

The relevant Greek text: Αβλαναθαμαλα...Ακραμμαχαμαρι καιχα κ αια κυριε θεε κυριαι θεων παντων θεραπευσον Θαησαν...απολυσον ονοματι Ιησου Χριστου...θεραπευσον Θαησαν ηδη ηδη ταχυ ταχυ.

As late as the mid-4ᵗʰ century, the church council of Laodicaea prohibited the practice of magic by the Christian clergy, a prohibition repeated in 398 at the council of Carthage, and in 667 the council of Toledo threatened to excommunicate clergy who said requiem masses for the living to induce "death by sorcery."[1581] Indeed, Christians, like Jews, used passages from their scriptures as incantations.[1582] It is known, for example, that the Latin *Iesus autem transiens per medium illorum ibat*: "Jesus passed through their midst"[1583] and *Et verbum caro factum est*: "And the Word became flesh"[1584] were used as talismans.[1585] Plus ça change…

> …in practice probably a very substantial percentage of contemporary Christians wore amulets of some kind or other. If this were not so, this part of [Chrysostom's] homily would not make sense, any more than similar condemnations by other Christian authors, for Chrysostom's preaching is addressed to Christians, not to pagans…That some kind of specifically Christian magic had in fact developed is clear from rulings of the Synod of Laodicea in the middle of the century when it was found necessary to forbid Christian clerics in major or minor orders to be magicians, charmers, soothsayers, or astrologers, or to fabricate amulets; wearers of such amulets were to be banned from the Christian community. Incidentally, this same Council of Laodicea had to forbid the exaggerated cult of angels, which had apparently assumed the form of magic.[1586]

Of the early church Brown says, "Such a group pullulated saints and sorcerers…St. Ambrose, to name only one saint, was associated with twelve deaths—more deaths than stand to the credit of any Late Roman *maleficus*."[1587]

As noted elsewhere, "now, now, quickly, quickly" is a very common ending of magical spells in the papyri. Volume One of the *Supplementum Magicum* gives examples of other Christian spells which use magical "holy characters" —αγιοι χαρακτηρες— sigil-like symbols of uncertain significance, as well as crosses and swastikas.

[1581] *Witchcraft and Magic in Europe: The Middle Ages*, 181.
[1582] *Priscillian of Avila*, 2-3.
[1583] Luke 4:30.
[1584] John 1:14.
[1585] *Magic in the Middle Ages*, 77-78, 102-103.
[1586] Barb, *The Conflict Between Paganism and Christianity in the Fourth Century*, 106-107.
[1587] *Religion and Society in the Age of Saint Augustine*, 129-130.

Regarding a papyrus spell (P.Lund IV 12), Daniel and Maltomini note, "The magical names and words in this text are clearly pagan, but two considerations suggest that the amulet may stem from a Christian milieu: the name of the patient, Sophia alias Priscilla, appears to be Christian...We may have yet another instance of Christians resorting to the use of pagan magic..."[1588]

The talismanic SATOR-AREPO magic square, believed to have originated as an anagram of the opening words of the Lord's Prayer, first came to light in a Christian house in Pompeii, and it was in Ephesus —where else?— that an ecumenical council, convened in 430 to decide the status of Mary in the Christian pantheon, declared that "the Holy Virgin is the Mother of God."[1589]

Under Theodosius II (423 CE), pagan rites were finally declared to be sacrifices to demons. Morton Smith observed, "With this the reversal is complete. Christianity which previously, by Roman law, was magic, has become the official religion, and the official religion of ancient Rome has become, by Roman law, magic. The notion that magic has no history could hardly be more conspicuously refuted.[1590]

[1588] *Supplementum Magicum*, I, 35.
[1589] θεοτοκος (theotokos), *god-bearing*. Madonna and child icons are still called *theotokos* icons in the Greek Orthodox Church.
[1590] Morton Smith, *Studies in the Cult of Yahweh*, 215.

Chapter 12: The Christian Mysteries

...Clement of Alexandria

Titus Flavius Clemens, known as Clement of Alexandria (died circa 215 CE), may have been initiated into one or more of the mystery cults before converting to Christianity.[1591] Clement attempted a synthesis of Christian theology with pagan philosophy —a subject of his *Exhortation to the Greeks*— and revealed how easily Christian doctrine could be expounded in the imagery of the pagan mysteries, as well as how closely magic and mystery cults must have intertwined:

> Let us sweep away then, sweep away forgetfulness of the truth, the ignorance and the darkness, the obstacle which like a film[1592] slips down over our sight. Let us see a vision[1593] of what is really and truly divine, first of all singing out to Him this cry, Welcome, Light! Light for us from heaven![1594] For us who lie buried in darkness and wrapped up in the shadow of death!

> If, on the one hand, those who have trusted in the sorcerers[1595] receive amulets and enchantments[1596] merely purported to bring deliverance, do you not rather resolve to put on the heavenly

---

[1591] "Christian writers converted from paganism may, of course, have been initiated in their youth: and on this ground the evidence of Arnobius and Clemens is *a priori* suprior..." Farnell, *The Cults of the Greek States*, II, 128.

[1592] αχλυς (achlus), *mist*, or if the reference is to Homer —for Clement was well read— the *film* that forms on the eyes of the dying. The term αχλυς had a magical and specifically theurgic connotation in Neoplatonic thought. See Collins, *Magic in the Ancient Greek World*, 128.

[1593] εποπτευσωμεν: "**let us see a vision**," from εποπτευω, *to be admitted* into the highest grade of the mysteries, to become an εποπτης (epoptēs), one who has achieved the final grade of the mysteries and seen all that is to be revealed. Similar terminology is used in 2 Peter 1:16.

[1594] χαιρε φως φως ημιν εξ ουρανου: "Welcome, Light! Light for us from heaven!" The Light/Darkness dichotomy was central to the mystery cults as it was to Christianity (John 1:5).

[1595] Ειθ' οι μεν τοις γοησι πεπιστευκοτες: "If, on the one hand, those who have trusted in the **sorcerers**..." As noted elsewhere, the term γοης also meant *deceiver*, a double meaning Clement clearly intended.

[1596] τα **περιαπτα** και τας **επαοιδας**...αποδεχονται: "receive **amulets** and **enchantments**..." An amulet, περιαπτον (periapton) —the term was derived from the fact that it was suspended from or hung around the neck.

[amulet], the Word that saves, and trusting in the enchantment of God,[1597] be delivered from passions…[1598]

O the truly holy mysteries![1599] O pure light! Holding my torch aloft,[1600] I am initiated into the highest mysteries of the heavens and of God![1601] I become holy by being initiated![1602]

The Lord reveals the mysteries[1603] and places his seal upon the initiate when he has believed, and lighting his way, conducts him to the Father, where he is protected for all ages.

These are my mysteries, my Bacchic revelries![1604] If you desire, be initiated yourself and you will dance with angels around[1605] the unbegotten and undying and only true God as the Word of God chants along with us.[1606]

Clement quite ingenuously refers to the heavenly Christ as an *amulet* and salvation as an *enchantment*, describing his Christian faith in the terms of a mystery celebration. His imagery of dancing with the angels deliberately recalls ecstatic rites. MacMullen describes the difficulty the church faced in banning dancing from ritual: "Ambrose of Milan…

[1597] τη **επωδη** του θεου **πιστευσαντες**: "trusting in the **enchantment** of God…"

[1598] *Clement of Alexandria: The Exhortation to the Greeks*, XI (Loeb, 242, 244-246).

Johnston: "In accord with theurgy's Platonizing tendencies, these demons were interpreted by the theurgists as the inflictors of corporeal passions that would lure the soul away from its proper pursuits…" *Restless Dead*, 137.

[1599] Ω των αγιων ως αληθως **μυστηριων**: "O the truly holy **mysteries!**"

[1600] **δαδουχουμαι**: "Holding my torch aloft…" The δαδουχος (dadouchos), *torch bearer*, was an official in the Eleusinian mysteries.

[1601] τους ουρανους και τον θεον **εποπτευσαι**: "**I am initiated into the highest mysteries** of the heavens and of God!"

[1602] αγιος γινομαι **μυουμενος**: "I become holy **by being initiated!**"

[1603] **ιεροφαντει** δε ο κυριος: "the Lord **reveals the mysteries**…" To be the ιεροφαντης (hierophantēs), the *hierophant*, the revealer of the mysteries, derived from ιερος (hieros), *holy*, and φαινειν (phainein), to *show, bring to light*. The hierophant is an initiator who reveals what is holy as Clement's next words make clear.

[1604] ταυτα των εμων **μυστηριων** τα **βακχευματα**: "These are my **mysteries**, my **Bacchic revelries!**" The βακχευμα (bakcheuma), the frenzied nocturnal rites of Bacchus.

[1605] και **χορευσεις** μετ' αγγελων: "and **you will dance** with angels **around**…" From χορευω (choreuō), *dancing in the round*, used of religious rites, particularly of the Bacchic chorus.

For an analysis of similar mystery cult language in Clement's *Stromateis*, see Deutsch, "Visions, Mysteries, and the Interpretive Task: Text Work and Religious Experience in Philo and Clement," *Experientia*, I, 83, ff.

[1606] *Clement of Alexandria: The Exhortation to the Greeks*, XII (Loeb, 256)

συνυμνουντος ημιν του θεου λογου: "as the Word of God **chants along with** us." To chant a υμνος (humnos), *hymn* or *festal song* in honor of the god *with*, συν (sun), the rest of the Bacchic chorus.

witnessed his congregation dancing during times of worship. (He seems to mean right inside the churches, but he does not supply details.) He was shocked. Such conduct was pagan."[1607] That Clement could speak of Christ in frankly magical terms reflected contemporary Christian thought: "An amulet intended to provide protection against illness and the power of evil" preserves this wording: "for the seal of Jesus Christ is written upon my forehead…"[1608] During Clement's life, it is probable that the Christian movement in Alexandria consisted of "a number of esoteric groups"[1609] in which *gnosis* or divinely revealed knowledge led eventually to perfection.

Although Clement, the head of the catechetical school in Alexandria, was no minor figure, during the 16th century his feast day, December 4th, was dropped from the calendar after his writings came to be viewed as doctrinally tainted, an event which reflected the tendency of the Catholic Counter-Reformation to distance itself from anything that emitted the slightest whiff of heresy or magic. As indicated by the brief excerpt from Clement given above, the forces of Catholic orthodoxy may have been on to something. Clement's writings seem clearly to reflect an age in which the line between Christian teaching and mystery cult was fuzzy, at the very least so as far as Clement was concerned. It is, however, richly ironic that Clement, one of the earliest Christian apologists, should later be declared heretical by the very religion he sought to defend.

…Carpocrates, magic, and early Christianity

Very little is known about Carpocrates, and what little information we have comes to us from his enemies. Aside from a brief mention in Clement, the church father Irenaeus is our only other original source.[1610] We do not know what Christian books the Carpocratians may have used. Irenaeus lumps Carpocrates together with the Gnostics, but the teachings he attributes to him, reincarnation and reminiscence of previous lives, are derived from Platonism.[1611] And though Irenaeus considered him to be a Christian heretic, we don't know how

---

[1607] *Christianizing the Roman Empire*, 74.
[1608] *Ancient Christian Magic: Coptic Texts of Ritual Power*, 113, 115.
[1609] Klijn, *The Roots of Egyptian Christianity*, 173.
[1610] Hippolytus (2nd century) and Eusebius (early 4th century) refer to Carpocrates, but they are almost certainly using Irenaeus as their reference.
[1611] See *Gnosticism, Judaism, and Egyptian Christianity*, 205-206.

Carpocrates might have defined himself; the church saw to it that none of his writings survived. Clement records a small portion of a philosophical tract written by Carpocrates' son, Epiphanes, who died at age seventeen. Aside from its radical egalitarianism, there is nothing particularly scandalous about it.

Like Clement himself, Carpocrates taught in Alexandria, Egypt, his career overlapping the reigns of Hadrian (117-138) and Antonius Pius (138-161). His teachings are awarded six paragraphs in the polemic *Adversus Haereses* (*Against Heresies*), written about 180 by Irenaeus (130-202), the bishop of Lyon, considered to be the most important theologian of the 2nd century.[1612]

Subtracting the venom and libel, Irenaeus' sketch of the Carpocratians leaves us with a picture of a dualistic antinomian philosophy that regarded the material world as fallen and escape from the cycle of reincarnation as possible only by experiencing all human conditions, which apparently included all sexual behaviors. Pansexuality, whatever its value for any given individual, was justified as *ritually* necessary to escape the prison of the lower world and gain the reward of ascent into heaven.

The heterogeneous mix of sects grouped together as *Gnostics*, a label which includes various Christian groups, evidently shared a belief in "a cosmos filled with semi-divine beings displaying a wide array of sexual characteristics"[1613] including androgyny.

A certain amount of evidence for primitive Christian antinomianism survives in quotations from pagan critics. Hoffman's explanation for a tendency toward libertine behavior warrants an extended quote:

> Eschatological thinking thus seems to have bred both an ascetic form of piety, best represented in Paul's letters and stemming from the conviction that, as the present order is corrupt, one ought to defy the world through self-mortification and disregard the flesh, and an antinomian enthusiasm, one aspect of which

---

[1612] *Against Heresies* was originally composed in Greek —Ελεγχος και ανατροπη της ψευδονομον γνωσεως, *Detection and Refutation of Falsely-called Knowledge*— but largely survived in the form of an early Latin translation. Some Greek fragments of the original survive in the form of quotations.
[1613] *The Manly Eunuch*, 222.

was sexual self-indulgence. These responses to the eschaton, in turn, correspond to rival theological outlooks in the early church: the antinomian emphasis, favored especially by some of Paul's converts, took its cue from Paul's (and doubtless other missionaries') stance against the law. Without the constraints of the Jewish law, such Christians reasoned, anything is possible; and as the Christian is saved by grace and faith rather than by works, anything is permissible.[1614]

Two characteristics of Carpocratian practice really pertain to our discussion: the elements of mystery and magic. On these two points at least, Irenaeus is clear: the Carpocratians taught that Jesus "spoke privately in mystery to his disciples"[1615] and performed various types of magic. Morton Smith: "The claim to have apostolic traditions was common in the ancient church and, since new apostolic traditions were discovered to settle new disputes as they arose, it must have been believed that the traditions had been secret before the times of their fortunate discovery. Therefore, this common method of doctrinal argument presupposes a general belief in a considerable body of secret apostolic traditions to which privileged members of clergy had access."[1616]

If Irenaeus was vague about what "speaking in mystery" involved, he is much more specific about magic. Fortunately for us, the pertinent section is preserved not only in Latin, but also in Greek in the form of quotations by other church officials:

> They also perform magical arts and enchantments,[1617] potions and erotic spells,[1618] use magical assistants and messengers of dreams,[1619] and other such evil works, alleging they already have

---

[1614] *Celsus on the True Doctrine*, 14.

[1615] Iesum dicentes in mysterio discipulis suis et apostolis seorsum locutum...: "saying Jesus spoke privately in mystery to his disciples and apostles..." *Against Heresies* I, 25, 5.

[1616] *Clement of Alexandria and a Secret Gospel of Mark*, 29.

[1617] τεχνας...μαγικας...επαοιδας: "magical arts...enchantments..."

[1618] φιλτρα και χαριτησια: "potions and erotic spells..."

[1619] παρεδρους και ονειροπομπους: "magical assistants and messengers of dreams ..."

authority to be the masters of the princes[1620] and creators of this world...[1621]

A φιλτρον (philtron) —*potion*— is a spell for controlling the actions or emotions of others, used of horses it means *the bit*. A φιλτροκαταδεσ-μος (philtrokatadesmos) is an erotic binding spell. In the magical papyri, as in Carpocratian Christianity, spells and prayers may have intersected: "religion and magic, at least with regard to prayer, are coterminus."[1622] "A *philtron* or *amatorium* [the Latin equivalent, *my note*] may then be the substance put into food or drink to induce sexual passion in the person who consumes or imbibes it; it may be a substance used as an ointment; it may be a substance accompanied by a spoken spell designed to elicit the same result; and it may be a spoken spell intended to provoke sexual desire."[1623]

The term χαριτησιον (charitēsion) —*erotic spell*— "covered not only prayers and amulets but more directly material technologies for stimulating and managing sexual feelings, such as penis ointments and love potions...if you can throw your handkerchief over lizards copulating it will be a χαριτησιον μεγα (a great spell to produce charm); the tail worn as an amulet promotes erection..."[1624] That the Greek terms had become technical terms in magic is suggested by the fact that the Latin version simply transliterates them.

The Greek word for magical assistant —παρεδρος— is also carried over into Latin as *paredros*. "The 'assistant,' as one of the many spirits or stellar angels or daemons of the dead, may contribute anything, including dream transmissions and revelations by dreams."[1625] *Oneiropompos*, "dream sender," also a technical term, is likewise simply transposed into Latin. The complex interrelationship between sex magic and dreams is briefly discussed by Winkler who notes Celsus' charge that "Mary Magdalene's encounter with the risen Jesus was only the ονειρωγμος ["wet dream," *my note*] of a sexually excited woman."[1626]

[1620] φασκοντες εξουσιαν εχειν...των αρχωντων: "alleging they...have **authority**...of the princes..." Here, as in Mark, *authority* is connected with the power to perform magic.

[1621] *Against Heresies*, I. 25, 3.

[1622] *Magika Hiera*, 194.

[1623] *Magic and Magicians in the Greco-Roman World*, 17.

[1624] *Magika Hiera*, 220.

[1625] Ibid, 180.

[1626] Ibid, 230.

"Sorcerers offered spells for conjuring up prophetic dreams and considered the arts of 'dream-seeking' and 'dream-sending' to be a central part of their business."[1627] The ritual of dream sending, ονειροπομ-πεια (oneiropompeia), is multiply attested in the Greek magical papyri.[1628]

The "princes" over which the Carpocratians had authority were likely demonic entities like those referred to in Mark where the scribes accuse Jesus of expelling demons by his authority over "the prince of demons."[1629]

Irenaeus thus confronts us with clear evidence for varied magical practice in the primitive church, with a sexual component being preserved among some factions. It is against this background that Justin Martyr's *Apology* must be read, and it is to that early document we now turn.

...Justin Martyr

Justin, a student of several schools of philosophy, was born in Samaria (present-day Palestine) around the year 100 and was executed early in the reign of Marcus Aurelius, probably about the year 165. He converted to Christianity around 130 and wrote his protest against the persecution of Christians shortly after 150 CE. Justin's work, although poorly and incompletely preserved, is nevertheless a valuable window into the practices of early Christians, particularly as perceived by their pagan contemporaries. Justin's writings are of particular relevance because he was a near contemporary of Carpocrates and his followers.

Justin's argumentation is muddled and his writing discursive in the worst sense. There are two overriding assumptions in the *Apology*: the mere antiquity of the Old Testament is its guarantee of truth and that because Jesus fulfilled the prophecies of the Old Testament —which Justin quotes exhaustively— he must be the promised Messiah. Greco-Roman culture regarded religious novelty with deep suspicion while equating truth with antiquity, so the appeal to Jewish scripture, widely acknowledged to be of great age, possessed a certain apologetic inevi-

---

[1627] *Pagans and Christians*, 151.
[1628] *Léxico de magia y religión en los papiros mágicos griegos*, 94.
[1629] Mark 3:22.

tability. However, Christians of Justin's era went much further. Some denied that the Jewish scriptures had anything to do with the Jews, but rather pointed forward in anticipation to the Christians as the true Israel of God.

I have reproduced only those portions of Justin's discourse that deal with charges that Jesus and his disciples practiced magic. In fact, it is not until the thirtieth section of his tract that Justin finally manages to come to the crux of this issue, posing the question much as pagans undoubtedly did:

> What prevents him we call Christ, a man born of men, having performed what we call powerful works by magical art[1630] and by this means appear to be a son of God?

Like his Christian contemporaries, Justin is not only familiar with magicians and their practices, but apparently includes many of his coreligionists as formerly among their number:

> ...and we who once employed magical arts have now consecrated ourselves to the good and unbegotten God...[1631]

> For even necromancy and haruspexy using uncorrupted children,[1632] and calling up human souls, and those who among the magicians are called senders of dreams and familiars, and all things done by those with such skills, may these persuade you that even after death souls are sentient and men seized and thrown down by souls of the dead, who everyone calls demon-possessed[1633] and madmen, and which is known to you as "prophesying," Amphilochus and Dodona and Pytho and whatever others there are...[1634]

Munier, whose Greek text I have used, translates the passage on haruspexy, "les divinations faites sur les entrailles d'enfants innocents..." or

---

[1630] *Apology* 30.1.

μαγικη τεχνη ας λεγομεν δυναμεις πεποιηκεναι: "having done what we call powerful works by **magical art**...?"

[1631] *Apology* 14.2.

[1632] και αι αδιαφθορων παιδων **εποπτευσεις**: "and **haruspexy** using uncorrupted children..."

[1633] δαιμονοληπτος, literally "demon-seized." Justin appears to be arguing that the pagan oracles are possessed by the souls of dead humans, that they are necromantic.

[1634] *Apology* 18. 3-4.

"divination using the entrails of innocent children…"[1635] Since Justin is adducing the evocation of souls of the dead as proof of a conscious afterlife, this translation, which imputes the murder of children to pagans, is almost certainly correct. The verb Justin uses, εποπτεω, is used (as previously noted) in the mystery cults for revelation of ultimate truth, and if by such usage Justin implies that the ultimate revelation for pagans was to be glimpsed in the guts of dead children, it comes as little surprise that he finally managed to get himself executed.

It would appear that many Christians were still practitioners of magic. Justin says as much, citing the sect of Simon the Samaritan, who "by the art of working with demons performed feats of magic" and noting that "all who belong to his sect are, as we have said, called Christians." It is against this sect that the following accusations are leveled:

> Whether those legendarily evil works they perform —overturning the lamp,[1636] unrestrained intercourse, and feasting on human flesh— are true we do not know, but they are neither persecuted nor put to death by you on account of the doctrines they hold…[1637]

Justin returns to the subject of sexual license to reiterate that "promiscuous intercourse is not a mystery of ours."[1638] From the foregoing it is plain that Justin not only knew of accusations that Christian ritual included sexual free-for-alls, he joins in with the chorus of accusers by stipulating which sects he thought engaged in such practices.

Are such charges to be taken seriously? Christians charging other Christians with gross sexual indecency was certainly not new in Justin's day: the later books of the New Testament claim that non-conforming Christians behaved like "irrational animals"[1639] and generally portray the members of competing Christian sects as prisoners of unbridled lust. To these charges later writers added cannibalism and the ritual ingestion of semen and menstrual blood.[1640] Making allowances for

---

[1635] *Saint Justin Apologie pour les Chrétiens*, 60.
[1636] "Overturning the lamp" so that the participants could engage in intercourse under the cover of darkness.
[1637] *Apology* 26. 2,6,7.
[1638] *Apology* 29.2.
[1639] 2 Peter 2:1-2, 12-14, Jude 10, 18.
[1640] *Lost Christianities*, 197-202.

rhetorical exaggeration, the charges involving debauchery and murder are possibly false, whereas those of dabbling in magic are almost certainly true.

Eusebius reports that Christians were repeatedly accused of cannibalism: *Ecclesiastical History* IV, 7.11, V, 1.14, 52.

Chapter 13: The Son of Horus

Origen, whose name means "son of Horus," (185-254 CE) was a controversial figure both in life and death. While still in his late teens he replaced Clement as chief catechist in Alexandria, and early in his adult life, according to the historian Eusebius, he made himself a eunuch for the kingdom of heaven.[1641] Although regarded as one of the most important pre-Nicene Christian intellectual figures, his teachings included several ideas that were heretical by the standards of later theology.

I have reproduced several short sections from Origen's apologetic magnum opus, *Contra Celsum*, a paragraph-by-paragraph refutation of an extensive critique of Christianity by Celsus, an early pagan opponent of Christianity. Origen composed his rebuttal around 248 CE, years after Celsus, who wrote the Αληθης Λογος (*True Doctrine*), had already died. The curious result of Origen's delayed refutation was the nearly complete preservation of Celsus' polemic, a text which has been reconstructed by Joseph Hoffman.[1642]

Besides the unintended consequence of preserving Celsus' arguments nearly in their entirety, *Contra Celsum* records a number of crucial observations about the Christianity of Origen's day by one of its most highly educated insiders. By far the most interesting material for the purpose of this study concerns Origen's explanation of Christian miracles.

> After these things, through what motivation I do not know, Celsus says that Christians appear to exercise powers by using the names of demons and by incantations, hinting, I presume, at those who drive out demons by incantations. For not by incantations do Christians appear to have power over demons, but by the name of Jesus, combined with recitals of the accounts about

---

[1641] Matthew 19:12.
[1642] *Celsus On the True Doctrine.*

him,[1643] for recitation of these things has often succeeded in having driven the demon from men, and especially so when those reciting them speak with a healthy attitude and a believing frame of mind. Indeed, the name of Jesus is so powerful against the demon that now and then it is effective even when named by unworthy men, just as Jesus taught when he said, "Many will say to me in that day, we cast out demons and performed powerful works in your name."[1644] Whether Celsus overlooked this from intentional malice or lack of understanding, I do not know.

Next he even accuses the Savior of having performed wonders by practicing sorcery[1645] and, foreseeing that others are destined to acquire the same knowledge[1646] and brag about doing the same things by the power of God, Jesus banishes such men from his kingdom. Celsus' accusation is that if such men are justly banished, while Jesus himself does the same things, then he is morally base and subject to the same punishment, but if Jesus is not evil for performing such works, neither are they who do as he does. On the other hand, even if it is conceded to be beyond demonstration how Jesus did these things, it is clear that Christians reject the practice of using incantations. Rather they accomplish it by the name of Jesus together with other words in which they have faith[1647] according to the divine Scripture.[1648]

Even from this brief passage it is clear that Christian exorcists used the name of Jesus together with *other words in which they had faith*, which included "recitations of accounts about him." Although Origen did not consider such performances to be magical, the present-day scholar would classify such "recitations" as examples of *historiolae* —what Origen calls ιστορια (historia)— "short stories recounting mythical

---

[1643] της απαγγελιας των περι αυτον **ιστοριων**: "recitals **of the accounts** about him..."

[1644] Origen quotes from the form of the saying recorded at Matthew 7:22. The parallel saying in Luke 13:27 has Jesus call the miracle workers "workers of wickedness."

[1645] ως **γοητεια** δυνηθεντος α εδοξε παραδοξα πεποιηκεναι: "of having performed wonders by practicing **sorcery**..."

[1646] μελλουσι και αλλοι τα αυτα **μαθηματα** εγνωκοτες: "others are destined to acquire **the same knowledge**..."

[1647] μετ' **αλλων** λογων πεπιστευμενων: "together with **other words** in which they have faith..."

[1648] *Contra Celsum*, I, 6.

themes"[1649] that were a part of the ancient magical repertoire. Elsewhere Origen mentions το του Ιησου ονομα μετα της περι αυτου ιστοριας: "the name of Jesus and **stories** about him" as the source of healing power.[1650]

The recitations Origen mentions were probably very similar to this spell from a Christian magical amulet:

Christ born from the Virgin Mary and crucified under Pontius Pilate[1651] and buried in a tomb and raised on the third day and taken up into the heavens...[1652]

Concerning the power to convert sinners, Origen says of Christian preaching, "we consider it just like charms which have been filled with power."[1653] The integration of the names of Yahweh (Iaō) and Jesus into the magical papyri, where they function as "words of power," is a perfectly natural extension of their use both in Christianity and in Judaism. Space would not permit a tally of the similarities between the names in Revelation and the names in other magical texts, so I will cite a single example, the "king of kings and lord of lords" of the magical papyri,[1654] an expression also found on a magical amulet —ο βασιλευων των βασιλεων: "the king who rules over kings"[1655] — and compare it to the familiar title given to the glorified Jesus in Revelation 19:16, the "King of kings and Lord of lords."

It is obviously true that Christian exorcism did not employ magic *as Origen understood it* —συν ουδενι περιεργω και μαγικω η φαρμακευτικω πραγματι: "without any of the works of curious art and

---

[1649] Kotansky, *Magika Hiera*, 112. The author elsewhere mentions "the problem that one faces when presented with prayers for salvation that seem embedded in an indisputable magical context" (123).

See particularly Frankfurter's discussion in *Ancient Magic and Ritual Power*, 457-476 and Jørgen Podeman Sørensen, *Acta Orientalia* 45:5-19.

[1650] *Contra Celsum* III, 24.

[1651] **εσταυρωθη** υπο Ποντιου Πιλατου: "**crucified** under Pontius Pilate..." Jesus' crucifixion is still central to the performance of Christian magic.

[1652] *Supplementum Magicum*, 31.

[1653] επωδας δυναμεως πεπληρωμενους: "charms which have been filled with power." *Contra Celsum* III, 68.

[1654] επικαλουμαι σε **βασιλευ βασιλεων**...δαιμων δαιμονων: "I invoke you, **king of kings**...demon of demons..." *Papyri Graecae Magicae* XIII, 605.

[1655] *Greek Magical Amulets*, 36. See particularly the commentary on page 188, 191-193, 196-201.

magic or bewitchment"[1656] to use Origen's own specific claim. But as noted by David Aune, "...early Christianity rapidly developed a distinctive form of magic which cohered with its reality construction; early Christian writers unwittingly mapped the contours of Christian magic in their apologetic program developed in rebuttal to pagan and Jewish charges that Christians practiced sorcery."[1657]

> According to the belief of these first Christians the efficaciousness of the exorcism pronounced in the name of Jesus had nothing to do with Jesus himself; it was from the five letters J-E-S-U-S arranged in that particular order that the curative action proceeded![1658]

The point is that these "recitations," undoubtedly combined with prayers and gestures which may have included the laying-on of hands,[1659] would have been indistinguishable from incantations, for Celsus and other pagans at any rate, regardless of how the actions were interpreted by Christians. Oesterreich is almost certainly correct when he claims that exorcism "was accompanied by the laying on of hands, the breath of the Spirit was breathed on the possessed, and signs of the cross made."[1660]

As Stephen Benko observes, "it is clear that when Christians accepted the existence of demons who inhabited the air and discussed their influence on human life, they were really talking in the context of contemporary pagan magic, which was based on the assumption that demons can be made to obey the will of the person who knows how to approach them properly."[1661]

By quoting Matthew 7:22, Origen tacitly admits that the performance of exorcism was considered knowledge —μαθημα (mathēma), "that which is learned," from which we derive *math*— and that such knowledge not only could, but would *inevitably* be acquired by others: "fore-

---

[1656] *Contra Celsum* VII, 4.

[1657] *Aufstieg und Niedergang der Römischen Welt*, II, 23.2, 1520.

[1658] *Possession Demoniacal and Other Among Primitive Races*, 168.

[1659] The church historian Eusebius (3rd century) has the disciple Thaddeus tell Abgar, τιθημι την χειρα μου επι σε εν ονοματι αυτου: "**I lay my hand** on you in his name..." *Ecclesiastical History*, I, 13, 17. The implication is that the laying on of hands was not uncommon.

[1660] *Possession Demoniacal and Other*, 166.

[1661] *Pagan Rome and the Early Christians*, 121.

seeing that others are destined to acquire the same knowledge." The "others" in question are those "unworthy men" who Origen admits were even then using Jesus' name to perform exorcisms. As noted by Achtemeier, "the name of Jesus was understood to have power of its own (e.g., Mark 9:38; Acts 3:6; 16:8; in a negative context Matt. 7:22-23; Acts 19:15)."[1662]

One might fairly ask why, *if even unworthy men could learn to perform successful exorcisms using Jesus' name*, exorcisms performed by *anyone* in Jesus' name should not be considered magical since their performance did not depend on religious merit, but worked *ex opere operato* as previously noted. Origen's description of the performances by Christian exorcists has in common the basic assumption of the Jewish magicians of whom the Christians were the direct religious descendents: magic is "an *acquired body of technical knowledge*."[1663]

> Moreover, seeing that [Celsus] often speaks of "the secret doctrine,"[1664] in this also he stands accused —nearly everyone in the world knows the preaching of the Christians better than those things that tickle the fancy of the philosophers. For who does not know that Jesus was born of a virgin, and was crucified, and that his resurrection has been believed by many, and that the judgment of God has been proclaimed in which the wicked will be punished in keeping with their sins, but the righteous correspondingly rewarded? Yet not having discerned the mystery of the resurrection, it is chattered about derisively among unbelievers.
>
> So on this basis, to speak of "the hidden doctrine" is entirely out of place. But that certain doctrines not revealed to the majority are attained after the public ones[1665] is not unique to the teaching of Christians only, but also to that of the philosophers for whom some things were public teachings, but others private.[1666] Even some of Pythagoras' listeners accepted his statements without proof, whereas others were taught about those

---

[1662] *Aspects of Religious Propaganda in Judaism and Early Christianity*, 151.

[1663] *Ancient Jewish Magic: A History*, 27.

[1664] ονομαζει **κρυφιον** δογμα: "speaks of the **secret** doctrine..."

[1665] μετα **τα εξωτερικα**: after **the public ones**..." εξωτερικος (exōterikos), from whence *exoteric*, pertaining to *the outer*, i.e., those teachings revealed to those *outside* the inner circle, the public.

[1666] ετεροι δε **εσωτερικοι**: "but others **private**..." εσωτερικος (esōterikos), *esoteric*, pertaining to *the inner*, i.e., the teachings revealed to insiders.

things not to be spoken[1667] to profane and insufficiently worthy ears. All the mysteries everywhere, the Greek and the non-Greek, although being secret have not been slandered, therefore it is in vain that Celsus misrepresents what is secret in Christianity.[1668]

Origen nowhere denies that the Christianity of his day —in common with the Greek mystery cults to which he alludes— had *inner teachings*, esoteric doctrines not for public consumption, and though he condemns Celsus for misrepresenting what was secret about Christianity, he leaves unrevealed just what those secrets were. In another reversal of fortune, Origen, like Clement was a stalwart defender of the faith, was himself subsequently declared to be heretical due to his belief in the subordination of the Son and the pre-existence of human souls.

In short, the earliest extracanonical writers on Christian doctrine use the language of the mystery cults to describe their faith, and concede that secret doctrine was taught privately to an inner circle. A probable reference to such private revelations survives in the text of Colossians where the ambiguous phrase α εορακεν εμβατευων, which from the evidence of ancient inscriptions should be translated "entering an oracle for interpretation of what he has seen,"[1669] is more often rendered "taking his stand on visions,"[1670] thus saving early Christianity from an overt association with mystery cults.

Lane Fox: "Among the Colossians, by contrast, there were people who trusted other visions, worshipping angels and 'vaunting the things which they have crossed the threshold and seen'...Paul's word for 'crossing the threshold' is the word for visitors who 'entered' a temple like Claros and penetrated its tunnels."[1671]

As pointed out repeatedly in this work, Christian rite and wonderworking shared the presumptions, processes and procedures of Jewish and pagan magic. It was, in fact, inevitable that pagan authorities

---

[1667] εν απορρητω διδασκομενοι: "taught about those things **not to be spoken**..." απορρητος (aporrhētos), *secret*. The neuter form of the adjective can mean "state secret."

[1668] *Contra Celsum* 1.7.

[1669] Danker, *Greek-English Lexicon*, 321.

[1670] Colossians 2:18, *Revised Standard Version*.

[1671] *Pagans and Christians*, 380.

Claros was an oracular shrine of Apollo.

would see Christianity in terms of magical practice as described by Stratton:

> The Christians met in secret and at night. They took oaths to each other, worshipped an executed criminal, and shared a sacred repast consisting of their hero's flesh and blood. Furthermore, the invocation of someone who had died violently (*aōros*) figures prominently in ancient curse tablets (*katadesmoi*); Christian invocation of Jesus' name, therefore, would have resembled magic to most people living in the ancient world. Additionally, the Bacchanal and other nocturnal rites were associated with women in Roman tradition and were, on this account, especially suspect. No doubt, the fact that female slaves held leadership positions in this new religion, combined with its nighttime assemblies, triggered long-held fears of hysterical women, unrestrained promiscuity, and the violation of traditional patriarchal codes. Christianity thus smacked of magic, superstition, and possible treason from the viewpoint of an ancient Roman.[1672]

To these observations may be added the refusal of Christians to participate in the state cult, to acknowledge the *numen* of the emperor, and their accusation that the gods of the pagan religions were evil forces. To the Roman mind, their attitudes openly invited the wrath of the very gods that protected the continuity of the Roman state. In the apocryphal Acts, "magic discourse functions to attack Roman values and institutions."[1673] The Roman populace despised the Christians in their midst for a reason; Christians were traitorous and subversive.

Origen clearly believed that divine names were invested with miraculous power, a claim which formed the very basis for Greco-Egyptian magic.[1674] His defense of Christian exorcism explains the rationale for such belief:

> If, in reference to what has been mentioned, we are able to call attention to the nature of effective names,[1675] some of which are

---

[1672] *Naming the Witch*, 118.

[1673] Ibid, 135.

[1674] Stroumsa: "Origen, for instance, takes magic very seriously indeed. For him, the theory of language and the ontological value of letters and words, which lie at the basis of sympathetic magic, are to be taken with the utmost seriousness." *Barbarian Philosophy: The Religious Revolution of Early Christianity*, 197.

[1675] ονοματων ενεργων: "...of effective names"

used by the wise men of the Egyptians, or by the Persian magi, or the Indian philosophers called Brahmins, or by the Samaneans, and others from different nations, we will establish that magic so-called is not, as Epicurians and Aristotelians suppose, a totally incoherent affair, but as those of great skill prove, organized, having words known but to exceedingly few. Now we say that the name Sabaoth and Adonai, and others handed down and uttered with great reverence by the Hebrews, treat not of ordinary engendered things, but belong rather to a secret theology which refers to the Maker of everything.[1676] Accordingly, these names, pronounced in a way appropriate to their nature, are effective, but others, spoken in the Egyptian language, work against certain demons capable of only certain things, others in the Persian dialect, and so on for each of the nations as appropriate. And so it will be found that to the demons rooted in various places, there correspond appropriate names according to region and national dialect.[1677]

Origen's explanation for the use of particular power words to expel demons explains the concern to preserve Jesus' words of power verbatim: demons, like people, are native to various regions and accordingly respond to different languages. Ancient tongues constitute a sort of lingua franca recognized by demons. The exorcist must use the correct regional dialect in order to make himself understood. According to Lucian of Samosata, Alexander of Abonutichos "spewed out some unintelligible sounds, which might have been Hebrew or Phonician"[1678] in preparation of the faked discovery of a miraculous egg. Getting the language right was an essential element of magical practice.

Origen's understanding of how powerful names worked coincides exactly with surviving magical texts:

Yea, to you, lord, god in heaven, all things have been made subject, and not one of the demons or the spirits will oppose me because I have invoked your great name for the magical rite. And again I call on you according to the Egyptians, phnō eai iabōk,

---

[1676] τον των ολων δημιουργον: "the Maker of everything." The δημιουργος, the Demiurge of gnostic fame, the *craftsman*, Maker of the lower material world. The term is likely used here simply in the Christian sense of *Creator*.
[1677] *Contra Celsum* I, 24.
[1678] *Alexandros Oder der Lügenprophet*, 90.

according to the Jews, adōnaie sabaōth, according to the Greeks, ho pantōn monoarchos basileus,[1679] according to the high priests, "hidden, unseen, overseer of all things," according to the Parthians, ouertō pantodunasta.[1680] Accomplish and empower this object for me, for all the span of my glorious life. The names engraved on the back of the stone are these: IAŌ SABAŌTH ABRASAX.[1681]

Origen knew that the names of God which were used by Christian exorcists also appeared in magical books:

Combined with the name of God, so great are the names [of the Jewish patriarchs] that not only do the people of the nations employ them in their prayers to God, even to subdue demons by charms, "The God of Abraham, and the God of Isaac, and the God of Jacob" is used by nearly all those engaged in casting spells and doing magic. Such an invocation to God will be found in many places in the magical books,[1682] using the name of God as appropriate by these men who expel demons.[1683]

Regarding the use of Jesus' name, Origen says:

A similar philosophy of names also applies to our Jesus, in whose name, in fact, innumerable demons are seen already driven out of souls and bodies, so effective it was on those from whom [the demons] were driven. And on the topic of names, we have mentioned that those who are experts in the use of incantations relate that the spell pronounced in the appropriate dialect achieves the very thing commanded, but said in another tongue becomes weak and capable of nothing. Therefore it is not the things signified, but the qualities and peculiar properties of the words that have a certain power for this or that.[1684]

Origen provides the modern reader with a sketch of 'magic in theory and practice,' which completely overturns his apologetic intentions.

[1679] ο παντων μονοαρχος βασιλευς: "the king, sole ruler of all…"

[1680] παντοδυναστα: "master of all…"

[1681] *Papyri Graecae Magicae* XII, 261-266.

[1682] εν τοις **μαγικοις συγγραμασι** πολλαχου: "in many places in the **magical books**…"

[1683] *Contra Celsum* IV, 33.

[1684] *Contra Celsum* I, 25.

Instead, he demonstrates that Christian miracle workers shared exactly the same world view as pagan magicians, worked from identical presuppositions, and obtained similar results: cures can be achieved "by holy names."[1685] His words confirm the suspicion that the difference between *miracle* and *magic* was, and is, semantic and that the spirit of Jesus worked no differently than the ghost of any powerful prematurely dead man. In fact, the description of Jesus in Revelation could have been written about any of the chthonic deities: "His eyes are a flame of fire, and on his head are many bands,[1686] having a name written which no one knows but he himself."[1687] Parallels from the magical papyri are numerous.[1688]

[1685] Lucian, *The Lover of Lies*, 10.

υπο ιερων ονοματων: "by holy names."

[1686] Και επι την κεφαλην αυτου **διαδηματα** πολλα: "and on his head are many **bands**..." The διαδημα (diadēma), *fillet*, or jeweled *headband*, originally used by Persian royalty, a custom adopted by Alexander of Macedon.

[1687] Revelation 19:12.

[1688] *Papyri Graecae Magicae* IV, 637, 1338, 2273, 2336, etc.

Chapter 14: Last Rites

In the book of *First Enoch*, angels look down from heaven on the daughters of men, lust after them, and plan to have children with them. In the gospel of Luke, an angel announces a miraculous birth which will result from the union of the spirit and human realms. In the magical papyri, sorcerers raise the ghosts of executed men to work magic. In his letters, Paul describes a cult of spirit possession centered on the crucified Christ. The New Testament language of oaths, exorcisms, dreamsending and curses pronounced against enemies mirrors the language of the magical spell books, and the names of Jesus and Yahweh (Iao) are incorporated into the magical recipe books following Jesus' death. Both the Jewish authorities and pagan opponents of Christianity see Jesus and early Christians as practitioners of magic. Even the competing Christian sects accused one another of sorcery.

It is quite clear that the New Testament authors shared the same mental world with the magicians who were their contemporaries and their competition, a world in which the dead can transmit miraculous power to the living, words in another language are efficacious regardless of the merit of one who utters them, and angels (or demons) can be summoned and sent on errands.

The New Testament is a book of magic. *Christian* magic, it is true, but magic all the same.

By the end of the 1st century, Christians were in open warfare with each other. Their writings speak of little else than doctrinal perversion and matters of internal discipline, and in keeping with well established apocalyptic style, the spats between the various sects are characterized as the final battle between Light and Darkness, between God and Satan:

> ...in the last times some will fall away from the faith, misled by deceptive spirits and teachings of demons...for some have al-

ready turned away to follow Satan...having a sick craving for controversies and fights about words.[1689]

The one who sins is from the Devil because the Devil has been sinning from the beginning. That is why the Son of God was made manifest, to destroy the works of the Devil.[1690]

Even as there were false prophets among the people, so also there will be false teachers among you who will introduce destructive heresies.[1691]

The beleaguered flock, hemmed in on all sides by wicked powers, is warned "not to fight about words...to the utter ruin of those listening," "nor to be misled by Jewish myths," but to "reject the heretical man."[1692] "Those who do not remain in the teaching of Christ do not have God. The one who remains in the teaching has both the Father and the Son," but of the man who deserts the fold: "This is the imposter and the Antichrist."[1693] The Antichrist arises from the *Christian* ranks: "now there have come to be many Antichrists...they went forth from *us*."[1694]

The religious turmoil of Christianity's first century could hardly be overstated. The newly emerging faith broke from its parent, Judaism, during the same period that Judaism suffered a terrible defeat at the hands of the Roman army, losing the temple of Herod, the central symbol of the Jewish religion, in the process. At the same time, as the letters of Paul reveal, the fledgling religion began to splinter into rival sects. In 64 CE, a wave of persecution instigated by Nero was directed specifically at Christians, and according to tradition it was during this persecution that both Peter and Paul were martyred.

Romans considered *pietas, piety,* to be a core religious value, which in the Roman mind conspicuously included loyalty to the state in the person of the emperor and the gods who watched over the state. From the Roman point of view, Christianity was a *superstitio,* or *superstition,* by

---

[1689] 1 Timothy 4:1, 5:15, 6:4.
[1690] 1 John 3:8.
[1691] 2 Peter 2:1.
[1692] 2 Timothy 2:14, Titus 1:14.
[1693] 2 John 7, 9.
[1694] 1 John 2:18-19.
Or in the immortal words of Pogo, "We have met the enemy and he is us."

which Romans primarily meant a new and *subversive* cult. As such, Christians were regarded as a menace and became targets of sporadic persecution under the rule of Nero, Trajan and Marcus Aurelius. In 202 CE, the emperor Septimus Severus issued the first general edict designed to prevent the spread of Judaism and Christianity. At that point, gruesome death in the public arena became an increasingly common Christian fate. Adversity honed both Judaism and Christianity to a sharp edge; both became increasingly militant. In the case of Christianity, that militancy turned inward, directed toward those who denied the faith either through collaboration with the Roman state or through apostasy, deviation from the emerging orthodoxy.

Pseudo-Paul's "some **will fall away from** the faith" —αποστησονται τινες της πιστεως— employs the verbal form of αποστασια (apostasia), *apostasy, defection* from the faith, a new category of thought crime that led untold numbers to the rack and stake under the rule of totalitarian Christianity in the centuries to follow. As Julian, the last pagan emperor of Rome prophetically remarked, "no wild beasts are as dangerous to man as the Christians are to one another."[1695] Not long after he wrote, leaving the church became a capital offense.

By the end of the 1st century, Christianity had become rabidly anti-Semitic. As James Carroll, following Elaine Pagels, points out: "The Jews, which occurs 16 times in Matthew, Mark, and Luke combined, is found 71 times in John where *the Jews* has become synonymous with all that is in opposition to God."[1696] In Revelation, the Jews are called "the synagogue of Satan"[1697] and by the Middle Ages Christian anti-Jewish sentiment had escalated to the point that a Christian woman who had sexual relations with a Jew could be burned alive as punishment. It is no coincidence that conventicles of witches were called *sabbaths* or even *synagogues*, "a sign of anti-Semitism" by which the church conflated its murderous opposition to both Judaism and sorcery.[1698]

[1695] *Julian's Against the Galileans*, 32.

    Christian violence became so commonplace that the emperor Theodosius II passed a law, the Theodosian Code of 438, that said, "[Christians] shall not abuse the authority of religion and dare to lay violent hands on Jews and pagans..." *The Closing of the Western Mind*, 212.

[1696] *Constantine's Sword*, 92.

[1697] Revelation 3:9.

[1698] *Magic in the Middle Ages*, 197.

In 1144, a 12 year old boy, William of Norwich, was discovered dead in the woods. A monk, Thomas of Monmouth, accused local Jews of William's murder, claiming "the child had been crucified in imitation of Christ."[1699] The boy's body was subsequently exhumed, made an object of veneration, and the accusations of ritual murder against Jews entered the arsenal of Christian rhetoric. Accusations of ritual murder surfaced again in the 1980s; this time Christian fundamentalists directed the charge against non-existent Satanic cults.

Christianity spread a second category of crime. *Heresy* —from αιρεσις (hairesis), *sect*, the nominal form of αιρετιζω, to *choose*— entered the Christian lexicon and sealed the fate of millions. Deviation from the teaching of a particular sect also became a capital crime. As Guy Stroumsa notes, after the 4th century, religious violence could "draw new theological justification, or at least latent encouragement, from a religion claiming a new, total, and universal grasp on truth." As Stroumsa points out, this is not a novel insight; Edward Gibbon proposed that "the historical strength of Christianity stems from its innate fanaticism."[1700]

If for Jesus the apocalypse marked the rescue of the world *from* Satan, for the primitive church the failure of the apocalypse marks the abandonment of the world *to* Satan, who has become, in the words of Paul, "the god of this age."[1701] But few accused of following Satan would ultimately celebrate cruelty with a frenzy that matched that of the Christians.

Perhaps the greatest weakness of Christianity came from an apocalyptic predisposition to see the world as inherently evil, and to exchange the fantasy of the apocalypse for the New Jerusalem, declaring that the citizenship of its members is in heaven, in a city built by God.[1702] Pagan writers of antiquity voiced this objection to Christian belief: "The Christians, Celsus complains, inherit from the Jews the notion that the world was made solely for the benefit of mankind. When it does not conspicuously serve this purpose, they immediately call for a new or-

---

[1699] *Martyrdom, Murder, and Magic*, 110.
[1700] *Barbarian Philosophy: The Religious Revolution of Early Christianity*, 10, 18.
[1701] 2 Corinthians 4:4.
[1702] Revelation 3:12, 21:2, Philippians 3:20, Hebrews 11:10.

der that suits them, ascribing their failures to an increase of evil ordained by their god."[1703]

The moral failure which contemplates the destruction of the world as a thing most devoutly to be wished —I am dead to the world and the world is dead to me— represents also a failure of imagination, a spiritual second death. It is a failure that has produced, in the words of Thomas Berry, "an extinction spasm...a kind of ultimate manifestation of that deep inner rage of Western society against its earthly condition."[1704]

Two modes of thought emerged as hallmarks of Christianity, intolerance of contrary opinion and the rejection of the world as flawed. Contrary to the claims of Christian apologists, neither is inconsistent with Jesus' message which was emphatic in its claim that the world, particularly as embodied in the religious and social status quo, was soon to disappear. Indeed, the Christian religion unleashed an apocalypse of sorts upon the knowledge of the ancient world:

> The invasion of the barbarians who conquered the Roman Empire has destroyed infinitely less than did the Christian hatred and persecution of the heathen. Never in the world's history has so vast a literature been so radically given over to destruction. Nor is its historical value the only thing involved: the influence of antiquity on the present would have been still greater had more of the literature of its later times been preserved.[1705]

It is a principle claim of this book that public understanding of what the New Testament says about primitive Christianity has if anything *receded*, not advanced, and that this failure of comprehension is partly due to what passes for New Testament scholarship. It is inevitable that the majority of students of the New Testament come to the subject armed with a previously established belief in the truth of Christianity and its founding texts, and that their course of study in seminaries and departments of religion is largely designed to reinforce that belief, prepare them to proselytize, and to serve as pastors. It is also quite common that the professoriate in such schools teach and interact within a

---

[1703] *Celsus On the True Doctrine*, 40.
[1704] *The Chaos Point: The World at the Crossroads*, 124-125.
[1705] Oesterreich, *Possession Demoniacal and Other*, 160.

shallow pool,[1706] an intellectually incestuous tendency that actively discourages investigation while promoting a large measure of orthodoxy. Critical study of the New Testament within the ranks of sectarian colleges is in many cases little more than an interminable Sunday school for overachievers.

The era in which Christianity was born has receded so far from modern consciousness as to be nearly unreachable. As this review of the evidence suggests, it is only by sustained effort that a person living today can approach the mental world in which Christianity first appeared. It is time to hear once again the wisdom of Schweitzer in this regard:

> The study of the Life of Jesus has had a curious history. It set out in quest of the historical Jesus, believing that when it had found Him it could bring Him straight into our time as a Teacher and Saviour. It loosed the bands by which He had been riveted for centuries to the stony rocks of ecclesiastical doctrine, and rejoiced to see life and movement coming into the figure once more, and the historical Jesus advancing, as it seemed, to meet it. But He does not stay; He passes by our time and returns to His own. What surprised and dismayed the theology of the past forty years was that, despite all forced and arbitrary interpretations, it could not keep Him in our time, but had to let Him go. He returned to His own time, not owing to the application of any historical ingenuity, but by the same inevitable necessity by which the liberated pendulum returns to its original position. [1707]

It is time we let Jesus, liberated from theology, return to his era at last and there remain.

[1706] With a bit of research, the interested reader may find that the professors of most conservative departments of religion are themselves graduates of affiliated schools, and in more than a few cases, graduates of the very religious studies programs in which they teach.

[1707] *The Quest of the Historical Jesus*, 399.

References

Abusch, Tzvi. *Mesopotamian Witchcraft: Toward a History and Understanding of Babylonian Witchcraft Beliefs and Literature*, 2002, Brill.

Achtemeier, Paul J. "Jesus and the Disciples as Miracle Workers in the Apocryphal New Testament," in *Aspects of Religious Propaganda in Judaism and Early Christianity*, Elisabeth Schüssler Fiorenza, ed, 1976, University of Notre Dame Press.

Aland, Barbara & Kurt. *Novum Testamentum Graece*, 27th edition, 1993, Deutsche Bibelgesellschaft.

Alexander, Philip S. "The Demonology of the Dead Sea Scrolls," in *The Dead Sea Scrolls After Fifty Years*, II, Peter W. Flint & James C. Vanderkam, eds, 1999, Brill.

——. "Jewish elements in gnosticism and magic c. CE 70—c. CE 270," in *The Cambridge History of Judaism*, III, William Horbury, W.D. Davies & John Sturdy, eds, 1999, Cambridge University Press..

Anderson, Janice Capel & Stephen D. Moore. "Matthew and Masculinity," in *New Testament Masculinities*, Stephen D. Moore & Janice Capel Anderson, eds, 2003, Society of Biblical Literature.

Angus, Samuel. *The Mystery Religions: A Study in the Religious Background of Early Christianity*, 1975 (reprint of 1928 edition), Dover Publications.

Arnold, Clinton E. *Ephesians: Power and Magic*, 1989, Cambridge University Press.

Audollent, Augustus. *Defixionum Tabellae quotquot innotuerunt tam in Graecis Orientis quam totius Occidentis partibus praeter attias*, 1904, Luteciae Parisiorum: Alberti Fontemoing.

Aune, David E. "Magic in Early Christianity," *Aufstieg und Niedergang der Römischen Welt*, II, 23.2, 1507-1557, Hildegard Temporini & Wolfgang Haase, eds, Walter de Gruyer.

——. "The Apocalypse of John and Graeco-Roman Revelatory Magic," in *Apocalypticism, Prophecy, and Magic in Early Christianity*, 2006, Baker Academic.

——. "Magic in Early Christianity," in *Apocalypticism, Prophecy, and Magic in Early Christianity*, 2006, Baker Academic.

Avalos, Hector. *The End of Biblical Studies*, 2007, Prometheus Books.

Ball, David Mark. *'I Am' in John's Gospel: Literary Function, Background and Theological Implications*, 1996, JSNT Supplement Series 124.

Barb, A.A. "The Survival of Magical Arts" in *The Conflict Between Paganism and Christianity in the Fourth Century*, Arnaldo Momigliano, ed, 1963, Clarendon Press.

Barton, Stephen C. *Discipleship and Family Ties in Mark and Matthew*, 1994, Cambridge University Press.

Becker, Jürgen. *Jesus of Nazareth*, 1998, Walter de Gruyter.

Becker, Michael. "Μαγοι—Astrologers, Ecstatics, Deceitful Prophets: New Testament Understanding in Jewish and Pagan Context" in *A Kind of Magic: Understanding Magic in the New Testament and its Religious Environment*, Michael Labahm & Bert Jan Lietaert Peerbolte, eds, 2007, T&T Clark.

Bell, Richard H. *Deliver Us from Evil: Interpreting the Redemption from the Power of Satan in New Testament Theology*, 2007, Mohr Siebeck.

Benko, Stephen. *Pagan Rome and the Early Christians*, 1986, Indiana University Press.

Bentley, James. *Restless Bones: The Story of Relics*, 1985, Constable.

Bergman, J. "ידע" in *Theological Dictionary of the Old Testament*, G. Johannes Botterweck & Helmer Ringgren, eds, 1986, William B. Eerdmans.

Bernhard, Andrew E. *Other Early Christian Gospels: A Critical Edition of the Surviving Greek Manuscripts*, 2006, T&T Clark.

Berry, Thomas & Ervin Laszlo. "Thomas Berry…on the historical mission of our times" in *The Chaos Point: The World at the Crossroads*, 2006, Hampton Roads.

Bertram, Georg. "ενεργεω" in *Theological Dictionary of the New Testament*, Gerhard Kittel, ed, 1964,William B. Eerdmans.

Betz, Hans Dieter. *Galatians: A Commentary on Paul's Letter to the Churches in Galatia*, 1979, Fortress Press.

—. "Magic and Mystery in the Greek Magical Papyri" in *Magika Hiera: Ancient Greek Magic and Religion*, Christopher A. Faraone & Dirk Obbink, eds, 1991, Oxford University Press.

—. "Introduction to the Greek Magical Papyri," in *The Greek Magical Papyri in Translation: Including the Demotic Spells*, 2nd edition, 1992, University of Chicago Press.

—. "Secrecy in the Greek Magical Papyri," in *Secrecy and Concealment: Studies in the History of Mediterranean and Near Eastern Religions*, Hans G. Kippenberg & Guy G. Stroumsa, eds, 1995, E. J. Brill.

Bohak, Gideon. *Ancient Jewish Magic*, 2008, Cambridge University Press.

Bompaire, Jacques. *Lucien: Œuvres*, I, 2003, Les Belles Lettres.

Bonner, Campbell. "Traces of Thaumaturgic Technique in the Miracles," *Harvard Theological Review* 20: 171-181.

—. "The Technique of Exorcism," *Harvard Theological Review* 36: 39-49.

Borg, Marcus J. and John Dominic Crossan. *The Last Week: The Day-by-Day Account of Jesus's Final Week in Jerusalem*, 2006, Harper San Francisco.

Boswell, John. *Same-Sex Unions in Premodern Europe*, 1994, Vintage Books.

Bowe, Barbara E. "Dancing into the Divine: The Hymn of the Dance in the *Acts of John*," *Journal of Early Christian Studies* 7: 83-104.

Bremmer, Jan N. "Magic, martyrdom and women's liberation in the Acts of Paul and Thecla" in *The Apocryphal Acts of Paul*, Jan N. Bremmer, ed, 1996, Kok-Pharos.

Brenk, Frederick E. "In the Light of the Moon" in *Aufstieg und Niedergang der Römischen Welt*, II, 16.3, 2068-2143, Hildegard Temporini & Wolfgang Haase, eds, Walter De Gruyter.

Brenton, Lancelot C.L. *The Septuagint with Apocrypha: Greek and English*, 2003, Hendrickson Publishers.

Breyfogle, Todd. "Magic, Women, and Heresy in the Late Empire: The Case of the Priscillianists," in *Ancient Magic and Ritual Power*, Marvin Meyer & Paul Mirecki, eds, 2001, Brill Academic Publishers.

Brier, Bob. *Ancient Egyptian Magic*, 1981, Quill.

Brown, Jeannine K. "Just a Busybody? A Look at the Greco-Roman Topos of Meddling for Defining αλλοτριεπισκοπος in 1 Peter 4:15," *Journal of Biblical Literature* 125: 549-568.

Brown, Peter. *Religion and Society in the Age of Saint Augustine*, 1972, Faber & Faber.

—. *The Cult of the Saints: Its Rise and Function in Latin Christianity*, 1981, University of Chicago Press.

—. *The Body and Society: Men, Women and Sexual Renunciation in Early Christianity*, 1988, Columbia University Press.

Büchsel, Friedrich. "δεω" in *Theological Dictionary of the New Testament*, Gerhard Kittel, ed, 1964, William B. Eerdmans.

Burkert, Walter. *Greek Religion*, 1985, Harvard University Press.

—. *Ancient Mystery Cults*, 1987, Harvard University Press.

Butterworth, G. W. *Clement of Alexandria: The Exhortation to the Greeks*, 1982 (reprint), Harvard University Press.

Cameron, Ron. *The Other Gospels: Non-Canonical Gospel Texts*, 1982, The Westminster Press.

Carmichael, Joel. *The Unriddling of Christian Origins: A Secular Account*, 1995, Prometheus Books.

Carrier, Richard C. "The Plausibility of Theft" in *The Empty Tomb: Jesus Beyond the Grave*, Robert M. Price & Jeffery Jay Lowder, eds, 2005, Prometheus Books.

Cary, Earnest. *Dio's Roman History*, 1960, Harvard University Press.

Cavin, Robert Greg. "Is There Sufficient Historical Evidence to Establish the Resurrection of Jesus?" in *The Empty Tomb: Jesus Beyond the Grave*, Robert M. Price & Jeffery Jay Lowder, eds, 2005, Prometheus Books.

Chadwick, Henry. *Priscillian of Avila: The Occult and Charismatic in the Early Church*, 1976, Oxford University Press.

Chancey, Mark A. *The Myth of a Gentile Galilee*, 2002, Cambridge University Press.

—. "How Jewish was Jesus' Galilee?" *Biblical Archaeology Review*, 33: 42-50.

Chester, Stephen J. "Divine Madness? Speaking in Tongues in 1 Corinthians 14:23, *Journal for the Study of the New Testament* 27: 417-446.

Ciraolo, Leda Jean. "Supernatural Assistants in the Greek Magical Papyri" in *Ancient Magic and Ritual Power*, Marvin Meyer & Paul Mirecki, eds, 1991, Brill Academic Publishers.

Clarke, Emma C., John M. Dillon & Jackson P. Hershbell. *Iamblichus: De mysteriis*, 2003, Society of Biblical Literature.

Cohn, Norman. *Europe's Inner Demons: An Inquiry Inspired by the Great Witch Hunt*, 1975, Basic Books.

Collins, Derek. *Magic in the Ancient Greek World*, 2008, Blackwell.

Comfort, Philip W. & David P. Barrett, eds. *The Text of the Earliest New Testament Greek Manuscripts*, corrected and enlarged edition, 2001, Tyndale House Publishers.

Conner, Randy P. *Blossom of Bone: Reclaiming the Connections between Homoeroticism and the Sacred*, 1993, Harper San Francisco.

Conner, Robert. *Jesus the Sorcerer*, 2006, Mandrake.

Cosaert, Carl. P. *The Text of the Gospels in Clement of Alexandria*, 2008, Brill.

Cotter, Wendy. *Miracles in Greco-Roman Antiquity*, 1999, Routledge.

Crossan, John Dominic. *The Historical Jesus: The Life of a Mediterranean Jewish Peasant*, 1991, Harper San Francisco.

——. *Four Other Gospels: Shadows on the Contours of Canon*, 1992, Polebridge Press.

Cryer, Frederick H. "Magic in Ancient Syria-Palestine and in the Old Testament," in *Witchcraft and Magic in Europe: Biblical and Pagan Societies*, Bengt Ankarloo & Stuart Clark, eds, 2001, University of Pennsylvania Press.

Daniel, Robert W. & Franco Maltomini (eds), *Supplementum Magicum*, Volume I (1990) & Volume II (1992), Westdeutscher Verlag.

Danker, Frederick William. *A Greek-English Lexicon of the New Testament and Early Christian Literature*, 3rd edition, 2000, University of Chicago Press.

David, Rosalie. *Religion and Magic in Ancient Egypt*, 2002, Penguin Books.

Davies, Owen. *Grimoires: A History of Magic Books*, 2009, Oxford University Press.

Davies, Stevan L. *Jesus the Healer: Possession, Trance, and the Origins of Christianity*, 1995, Continuum.

Davies, T. Witton. *Magic, Divination, and Demonology among the Hebrews and Their Neighbors*, 1897, Kessinger (reprint).

Deissmann, Adolf. *Light from the Ancient East: The New Testament Illustrated by Recently Discovered Texts of the Graeco-Roman World*, 4th edition, 1922, Harper & Brothers.

Delatte, Armand. *Anecdota Atheniensia*, 1927, Édouard Champion.

de Mause, Lloyd. *The History of Childhood*, 1974 Harper & Row.

de Vos, Craig S. "Finding a Charge That Fits: The Accusation Against Paul and Silas at Philippi (Acts 16.19-21), *Journal for the Study of the New Testament* 74: 51-63.

Deutsch, Celia. "Visions, Mysteries and the Interpretive Task: Text Work and Religious Experience in Philo and Clement," in *Experientia*, I, *Inquiry into Religious Experience in Early Judaism and Christianity*, Frances Flannery, Colleen Shantz & Rodney A. Werline, eds, 2008, Brill.

Dickie, Matthew W. "The Fathers of the Church and the Evil Eye." in *Byzantine Magic*, Henry Maguire, ed, 1995, Harvard University Press.

——. *Magic and Magicians in the Greco-Roman World*, 2001, Routledge.

DiZerega, Gus. *Pagans & Christians: The Personal Spiritual Experience*, 2001, Llewellyn Publications.

Dodds, E.R. *The Greeks and the Irrational*, 1951, University of California Press.

Duling, Dennis C. "Solomon, Exorcism, and the Son of David," *Harvard Theological Review* 68: 235-252.

Dunn, James D. G. *Jesus and the Spirit: A Study of the Religious and Charismatic Experience of Jesus and the First Christians as Reflected in the New Testament*, 1975, The Westminster Press.

Ehrenreich, Barbara. *Blood Rites: Origins and History of the Passions of War*, 1997, Henry Holt & Company.

Ehrman, Bart D. *The Orthodox Corruption of Scripture: The Effect of Early Christological Controversies on the Text of the New Testament*, 1993, Oxford University Press.

—. "The Neglect of the Firstborn in New Testament Studies," Presidential Lecture, Society of Biblical Literature, 1997.

—. *Jesus: Apocalyptic Prophet of the New Millennium*, 1999, Oxford University Press.

—. *Lost Christianities: The Battles for Scripture and the Faiths We Never Knew*, 2003, Oxford University Press.

—. *The New Testament: A Historical Introduction to the Early Christian Writings*, 3rd edition, 2004, Oxford University Press.

Eitrem, Samson. *Some Notes on the Demonology in the New Testament*, 2nd edition, 1966, Symbolae Osloenses, 12.

—. "Dreams and Divination in Magical Ritual," in *Magika Hiera: Ancient Greek Magic and Religion*, Christopher Faraone & Dirk Obbink, eds, 1991, Oxford University Press.

Eliade, Mircea. *Images and Symbols: Studies in Religious Symbolism*, 1969, Sheed and Ward.

Elkin, Adolphus P. *Aboriginal Men of High Degree: Initiation and Sorcery in the World's Oldest Tradition*, 1977, Inner Traditions International.

Epp, Eldon Jay. "The Multivalence of the Term 'Original Text' in New Testament Textual Criticism," *Harvard Theological Review* 92: 245-281.

Epstein, Louis M. *Sex Laws and Customs in Judaism*, 1967, Ktav Publishing House.

Ericksen, Robert P. *Theologians Under Hitler: Gerhard Kittel, Paul Althaus and Emanuel Hirsh*, 1985, Yale University Press.

Esler, Philip F. *The First Christians in their Social Worlds: Social-scientific approaches to New Testament Interpretation*, 1994, Routledge.

Faraone, Christopher A. "The Agonistic Context of Early Greek Binding Spells" in *Magika Hiera: Ancient Greek Magic and Religion*, Christopher Faraone & Dirk Obbink, eds, 1991, Oxford University Press.

—. *Ancient Greek Love Magic*, 1999, Harvard University Press.

—. "The construction of gender in ancient Greek love magic" in *The world of ancient magic*, David R. Jordan, Hugo Montgomery & Einar Thomassen, eds, 1999, Bergen.

—. "Necromancy Goes Underground," in *Mantikê: Studies in Ancient Divination*, Sarah Iles Johnston & Peter T. Struck, eds, 2005, Brill.

Farnell, Lewis Richard, *The Cults of the Greek States*, 1977, Caratzas Brothers Publishers.

Felton, Debbie. *Haunted Greece and Rome: Ghost Stories from Classical Antiquity*, 1999, University of Texas Press.

Finucane, Ronald C. *Ghosts: Appearances of the Dead and Cultural Transformation*, 1996, Prometheus Books.

Flint, Valerie. "The Demonization of Magic and Sorcery in Late Antiquity: Christian Redefinitions of Pagan Religions" in *Witchcraft and Magic in Europe: Ancient Greece and Rome*, Bengt Ankarloo & Stuart Clark, eds, 1999, University of Pennsylvania Press.

Forbes, Christopher. *Prophecy and Inspired Speech In Early Christianity and its Hellenistic Environment*, 1997, Hendrickson Publishers.

Fowler, Miles. "Identification of the Bethany Youth in the Secret Gospel of Mark with Other Figures Found in Mark and John," *The Journal of Higher Criticism* 5/1: 3-22.

Frankfurter, David. "Narrating Power: The Theory and Practice of the Magical *Historiola* in Ritual Spells," in *Ancient Magic and Ritual Power*, Marvin Meyer & Paul Mirecki, eds, 2001, Brill Academic Publishers.

Freeman, Charles. *The Closing of the Western Mind: The Rise of Faith and the Fall of Reason*, 2002. Vintage.

Freyne, Sean. *Galilee, Jesus and the Gospels*, 1988, Fortress Press.

Gager, John G. *Curse Tablets and Binding Spells from the Ancient World*, 1992, Oxford University Press.

García Martínez, Florentino. "Magic in the Dead Sea Scrolls," in *The Metamorphosis of Magic from Late Antiquity to the Early Modern Period*, Jan N. Bremmer & Jan R. Veenstra, eds, 2002, Peeters.

Garrett, Susan R. *The Demise of the Devil: Magic and the Demonic in Luke's Writings*, 1989, Fortress Press.

——. "Light on a Dark Subject and Vice Versa: Magic and Magicians in the New Testament" in *Religion, Science, and Magic: In Concert and in Conflict*, Jacob Neusner, Ernest S. Frerichs & Paul Virgil McCracken Flesher, eds, 1989, Oxford University Press.

Geary, Patrick J. *Furta Sacra: Thefts of Relics in the Central Middle Ages*, 1978, Princeton University Press.

Geller, Markham J. "Jesus' Theurgic Powers: Parallels in the Talmud and Incantation Bowls," *Journal of Jewish Studies* 28: 141-155.

Gifford, Edwin Hamilton (tr). Eusebius' *Preparation for the Gospel*, II, 1981, Baker Book House.

Goldin, Judah. "The Magic of Magic and Superstition," in *Aspects of Religious Propaganda in Judaism and Early Christianity*, 1976, Elisabeth Schüssler Fiorenza, University of Notre Dame Press.

Gordon, Richard. "Reporting the Marvellous: Private Divination in the Greek Magical Papyri" in *Envisioning Magic: A Princeton Seminar and Symposium*, Peter Schäfer & Hans G. Kippenberg, eds, 1997, Brill

——. "Imagining Greek and Roman Magic" in *Witchcraft and Magic in Europe: Ancient Greece and Rome*, Bengt Ankarloo & Stuart Clark, eds, 1999, University of Pennsylvania Press.

Grabbe, Lester L. *Judaism from Cyrus to Hadrian*, II, "The Roman Period," 1992, Fortress Press.

—. *Priests, Prophets, Diviners, Sages: A Socio-Historical Study of Religious Specialists in Ancient Israel*, 1995, Trinity Press International.

Graf, Fritz. *Magic in the Ancient World*, 1997, Harvard University Press.

—. "How to Cope with a Difficult Life: A View of Ancient Magic" in *Envisioning Magic: A Princeton Seminar and Symposium*, 1997, Peter Schäfer & Hans G. Kippenberg, eds, Brill Academic Publishers.

—. "Excluding the Charming: The Development of the Greek Concept of Magic" in *Ancient Magic and Ritual Power*, Marvin Meyer & Paul Mirecki, eds, 2001, Brill.

Grant, Michael. *The Jews in the Roman World*, 1973, Charles Scribner's Sons.

—. *Jesus*, 1977, Rigel Publications.

Grayston, Kenneth. "The Meaning of Paraklētos," *Journal for the Study of the New Testament* 13: 67-82.

Greenfield, Richard P.H. "A Contribution to the Study of Palaeologan Magic," in *Byzantine Magic*, Henry Maguire, ed, 1995, Harvard University Press.

Griffith, F. & Herbert Thompson, eds, *The Leyden Papyrus*, 1974, Dover Publications.

Grundman, Walter. "ισχυω" in *Theological Dictionary of the New Testament*, 1964, Gerhard Kittel, ed, William B. Eerdmans.

Haart, Robert. *Gnosis: Character and Testimony*, tr. J.F. Hendry, 1971, E.J. Brill.

Hale, John R., et al. "Questioning the Delphic Oracle," *Scientific American* 289/2: 66-73.

Hanse, Hermann. "εχω" in *Theological Dictionary of the New Testament*, 1964, Gerhard Kittel, ed, William B. Eerdmans.

Hansen, William. *Phlegon of Tralles' Book of Marvels*, 1996, University of Exeter Press.

Hanson, K. C. & Douglas E. Oakman. *Palestine in the Time of Jesus: Social Structures and Social Conflicts*, 1998, Fortress Press.

Haren, Michael J. "The Naked Young Man: A Historian's Hypothesis on Mark 14,51-52," *Biblica* 79: 525-531.

Harmon, A. M. *The Works of Lucian*, III, 1921, G.P. Putnam's Sons.

Harvey, Graham. *Contemporary Paganism: Listening People, Speaking Earth*, 1997, New York University Press.

Heinichen, Frederick A. *Eusebii Pamphili: Praeperationis Evangelicae*, II, 1842, Lipsius.

Hennecke, Edgar. *New Testament Apocrypha*, II, 1964, The Westminster Press.

Hester, J. David. "Eunuchs and the Postgender Jesus: Matthew 19.12 and Transgressive Sexualities," *Journal for the Study of the New Testament* 28:13-40.

Hoehner, Harold W. *Ephesians: An Exegetical Commentary*, 2002, Baker Academic.

Hoffman, R. Joseph. *Jesus Outside the Gospels*, 1984, Prometheus Books.

——. *Celsus: On The True Doctrine, A Discourse Against the Christians*, 1987, Oxford University Press.

——. *Julian's Against the Galileans*, 2004, Prometheus Books.

Hoffner, Harry A. "אוב" in *Theological Dictionary of the Old Testament*, 1974, J. Johannes Botterweck & Helmer Ringgren, eds, William B. Eerdmans.

Holmes, Michael W. "Reasoned Eclecticism in New Testament Textual Criticism" in *The Text of the New Testament in Contemporary Research: Essays on the Status Quaestionis*, Bart D. Ehrman & Michael W. Holmes, editors, 1995, William B. Eerdmans.

Horsley, G.H.R. *New Documents Illustrating Early Christianity*, 1981, Macquarie University Press.

Horsley, Richard A, with John S. Hanson. *Bandits, Prophets and Messiahs: Popular Movements in the Time of Jesus*, 1999, Trinity Press International.

——. "'My Name is Legion': Spirit Possession and Exorcism in Roman Palestine", in *Experientia, I, Inquiry into Religious Experience in Early Judaism and Christianity*, Frances Flannery, Colleen Shantz & Rodney A. Werline, eds, 2008, Brill.

Hull, John M. *Hellenistic Magic and the Synoptic Tradition*, 1974, SCM Press Ltd.

Hutton, Ronald. "Modern Pagan Witchcraft" in *Witchcraft and Magic in Europe: The Twentieth Century*, Bengt Ankarloo & Stuart Clark, eds, 1999, University of Pennsylvania Press.

——. *Witches, Druids and King Arthur*, 2003, Hambledon Continuum.

Isbell, Charles D. *Corpus of the Aramaic Incantation Bowls*, 1975, Scholars Press.

Janowitz, Naomi. *Magic in the Roman World: Pagans, Jews and Christians*, 2001, Routledge.

——. *Icons of Power: Ritual Practices in Late Antiquity*, 2002, Pennsylvania State University Press.

Jacobs, Andrew S. "A Family Affair: Marriage, Class, and Ethics in the Apocryphal Acts of the Apostles," *Journal of Early Christian Studies* 7: 105-138.

Jeffers, Ann. *Magic and Divination in Ancient Palestine and Syria*, 1996, E.J. Brill.

Jennings, Theodore W. Jr. *The Man Jesus Loved: Homoerotic Narratives from the New Testament*, 2003, Pilgrim Press.

—— & Tat-Siong Benny Liew. "Mistaken Identities But Model Faith: Rereading the Centurion, the Chap, and the Christ in Matthew 8:5-13," *Journal of Biblical Literature* 123: 467-494.

Johnston, Sarah Iles. *Restless Dead: Encounters Between the Living and the Dead in Ancient Greece*, 1999, University of California Press.

——. "Songs for the ghosts: Magical solutions to deadly problems" in *The world of ancient magic*, David R. Jordan, Hugo Montgomery & Einar Thomassen, eds, 1999, Bergen.

——. *Religions of the Ancient World: A Guide*, 2004, Harvard University Press.

Jones, Prudence and Nigel Pennick. *A History of Pagan Europe*, 1995, Routledge.

Junod, Eric & Jean-Daniel Kaestli. *Acta Iohannis*, 1983, Brepols-Turnhout.

Kazhdan, Alexander. "Holy and Unholy Miracle Workers," in *Byzantine Magic*, Henry Maguire, ed, 1995, Harvard University Press.

Keck, Leander E. "Matthew and the Spirit" in *The Social World of the First Christians: Essays in Honor of Wayne A. Meeks*, L. Michael White & O. Larry Yarbrough, eds, 1995, Fortress Press.

Kee, Howard Clark. *Medicine, Miracle and Magic in New Testament Times*, 1986, Cambridge University Press.

—. "Magic and Messiah" in *Religion, Science, and Magic: In Concert and in Conflict*, Jacob Neusner, Ernst S. Frerichs & Paul Virgil McCracken Flesher, eds, 1989, Oxford University Press.

—. "The Terminology of Mark's Exorcism Stories," *New Testament Studies* 14: 232-246.

Kieckhefer, Richard. *Magic in the Middle Ages*, 1989, Cambridge University Press.

Kittel, Gerhard. "αγγελος" in *Theological Dictionary of the New Testament*, 1964, Gerhard Kittel, ed, William B. Eerdmans.

Kirby, Peter. "The Case Against the Empty Tomb," in *The Empty Tomb: Jesus Beyond the Grave*, Robert M. Price & Jeffery Jay Lowder, eds, 2005, Prometheus Books.

Klauck, Hans-Josef. *Magic and Paganism in Early Christianity: The World of the Acts of the Apostles*, 2003, Fortress Press.

—. *The Apocryphal Acts of the Apostles*, 2008, Baylor University Press.

Klijn, A.F.J. "Jewish Christianity in Egypt," in *The Roots of Egyptian Christianity*, Birger A. Pearson & James E. Goehring, eds, 1986, Fortress Press.

Koester, Helmut. *Ancient Christian Gospels: Their History and Development*, 1990, Trinity Press International.

—. "The Text of the Synoptic Gospels in the Second Century" in *Gospel Traditions in the Second Century: Origins, Recensions, Text, and Transmission*, William L. Petersen, ed, 1990, University of Notre Dame Press.

Kolenkow, Anitra B. "Relationships Between Miracle and Prophecy in the Greco-Roman World and Early Christianity," *Aufstieg und Niedergang der Römischen Welt*, II, 23.2, 1470-1506, Hildegard Temporini & Wolfgang Haase, eds, Walter de Gruyer.

Koskenniemi, Erkki. "Apollonius of Tyana: A Typical ΘΕΙΟΣ ΑΝΗΡ?" *Journal of Biblical Literature* 117: 455-467.

Kotansky, Roy. "Incantations and Prayers for Salvation on Inscribed Greek Amulets" in *Magika Hiera: Ancient Greek Magic and Religion*, Christopher Faraone & Dirk Obbink, eds, 1991, Oxford University Press.

—. *Greek Magical Amulets: The Inscribed Gold, Silver, Copper, and Bronze Lamellae, Part I, Published Texts of Known Provenance*, 1994, Westdeutscher Verlag.

—. "Greek Exorcistic Amulets" in *Ancient Magic and Ritual Power*, Marvin Meyer & Paul Mirecki, eds, 2001, Brill Academic Publishers.

Kraeling, Carl H. "Was Jesus Accused of Necromancy?" *Journal of Biblical Literature* 59: 147-157.

Kraemer, Ross S. "Implicating Herodias and Her Daughter in the Death of John the Baptizer: A (Christian) Theological Strategy?" *Journal of Biblical Literature* 125: 321-349.

Kueffler, Matthew. *The Manly Eunuch: Masculinities, Gender Ambiguity, and Christian Ideology in Late Antiquity*, 2001, University of Chicago Press.

La Fontaine, Jean. "Satanic Abuse Mythology" in *Witchcraft and Magic in Europe: The Twentieth Century*, Bengt Ankarloo & Stuart Clark, eds, 1999, University of Pennsylvania Press.

Lake, Kirsopp. *Eusebius: The Ecclesiastical History*, Books I-V, 1926, Harvard University Press.

——. *The Apostolic Fathers*, II, 1948, Harvard University Press.

Lalleman, P. J. "Polymorphy of Christ" in *The Apocryphal Acts of John*, Jan N. Bremmer, ed, 1995, Pharos.

Lane Fox, Robin. *Pagans and Christians*, 1989, Alfred A. Knopf.

Lange, Armin. "The Essene Position on Magic and Divination" in *Legal Texts and Legal Issues: Proceedings of the Second Meeting of the International Organization of Qumran Studies*, Moshe Bernstein, Florentino García Martínez, John Kampen, eds, 1997, Brill Academic Publishers.

Lapin, Hayim. "Introduction: Locating Ethnicity and Religious Community in Later Roman Palestine," in *Religious and Ethnic Communities in Later Roman Palestine*, Hayim Lapin, ed, 1998, University Press of Maryland.

Larsson, Edvin. "εχω" in *Exegetical Dictionary of the New Testament*, Horst Balz & Gerhard Schneider, eds, 1991, William B. Eerdmans.

Lenormant, François. *Chaldean Magic: Its Origin and Development*, 1875, Samuel Bagster and Sons.

Lesses, Rebecca. "Speaking with Angels: Jewish and Greco-Egyptian Revelatory Adjurations," *Harvard Theological Review* 89:41-60.

Lewis, Ioan M. *Ecstatic Religion: An Anthropological Study of Spirit Possession and Shamanism*, 1971, Penguin Books.

Lewis, Theodore J. *Cults of the Dead in Ancient Israel and Ugarit*, 1989, Scholars Press.

Licht, Hans. *Sexual Life in Ancient Greece*, 1932, George Routledge & Sons.

Liddell, Henry George, Robert Scott, Henry Stuart Jones & Roderick McKenzie. *A Greek-English Lexicon*, Revised Edition, 1996, Clarendon Press.

Lietaert Peerbolte, Bert Jan. "Paul the Miracle Worker: Development and Background of Pauline Miracle Stories" in *Wonders Never Cease: The Purpose of Narrating Miracle Stories in the New Testament and its Religious Environment*, Michael Labahn & Bert Jan Lietaert Peerbolte, eds, 2006, T & T Clark.

——. "Paul's Rapture: 2 Corinthians 12:2-4 and the Language of the Mystics," in *Experientia*, I, *Inquiry into Religious Experience in Early Judaism and Christianity*, Frances Flannery, Colleen Shantz & Rodney A. Werline, eds, 2008, Brill.

Liew, Tat-siong Benny. "Re-Markable Masculinities: Jesus, the Son of Man, and the (Sad) Sum of Manhood?" in *New Testament Masculinities*, Stephen D. Moore & Janice Capel Anderson, eds, 2003, Society of Biblical Literature.

Lipsius, Richard Adelbert & Maximillian Bonnet. *Acta Apostolorum Apocrypha*, 1959, Wissenschaftliche Buchgesellschaft Darmstadt.

Loader, William. *Sexuality and the Jesus Tradition*, 2005, William B. Eerdmans Publishing Company.

Luck, Georg. *Arcana Mundi: Magic and the Occult in the Greek and Roman Worlds,* 1985, Johns Hopkins University Press.

—. "Theurgy and Forms of Worship in Neoplatonism," in *Religion, Science, and Magic: In Concert and in Conflict,* Jacob Neusner, Ernest Frerichs & Paul Virgil McCracken Flesher, eds, 1989, Oxford University Press.

—. "Witches and Sorcerers in Classical Literature," in *Witchcraft and Magic in Europe: Ancient Greece and Rome,* Bengt Ankarloo & Stuart Clark, eds, 1999, University of Pennsylvania Press.

—. "The 'Way Out': Philological Notes on the Transfiguration of Jesus" in *Ancient Pathways and Hidden Pursuits: Religion, Morals, and Magic in the Ancient World,* 2000, University of Michigan Press.

—. "Recent Work on Ancient Magic," in *Ancient Pathways and Hidden Pursuits: Religion, Morals, and Magic in the Ancient World,* 2000, University of Michigan Press.

MacDonald, Margaret Y. "Slavery, Sexuality and House Churches: A Reassessment of Colossians 3.18-4.1 in Light of New Research on the Roman Family," *New Testament Studies* 53: 94-113.

Mack, Burton L. *The Lost Gospel: The Book of Q and Christian Origins,* 1993, Harper San Francisco.

Macleod, M. D. *Lucian: A Selection,* 1991, Aris & Phillips.

MacMullen, Ramsay. *Enemies of the Roman Order: Treason, Unrest, and Alienation in the Empire,* 1966, Harvard University Press.

—. *Christianizing the Roman Empire: A.D. 100-400,* 1984, Yale University Press.

Marcovich, Miroslav. *Iustini Martyris Dialogus cum Tryphone,* 1997, de Gruyter.

—. *Origenes: Contra Celsum Libri VIII,* 2001, Brill Academic Publishers.

Marguerat, Daniel. "Magic and Miracle in the Acts of the Apostles" in *Magic in the Biblical World: From the Rod of Aaron to the Ring of Solomon,* Todd E. Klutz, ed, 2003, T&T Clark.

Merrifield, Ralph. *The Archaeology of Ritual and Magic,* 1987, New Amsterdam.

Martin, Dale B. *Sex and the Single Savior: Gender and Sexuality in Biblical Interpretation,* 2006, Westminster John Knox Press.

Martin, Michaël. *Magie et magicians dans le monde gréco-romain,* 2005, Editions Errance.

Martinez, David. "'May She Neither Eat Nor Drink': Love Magic and Vows of Abstinence" in *Ancient Magic and Ritual Power,* Marvin Meyer & Paul Mirecki, eds, 2001, Brill Academic Publishers.

McCown, Chester Charlton. *The Testament of Solomon,* 1922, G.E. Stechert & Co.

McCullough, W.S. *Jewish and Mandaean Incantation Bowls in the Royal Ontario Museum,* 1967, University of Toronto Press.

Meier, John P. *A Marginal Jew: Rethinking the Historical Jesus,* I, 1991, Doubleday.

Metzger, Bruce M. *The New Testament: Its Background, Growth, and Content,* 2nd ed, enlarged, 1987, Abingdon Press.

Meyer, Marvin & Richard Smith. "Introduction" in *Ancient Christian Magic: Coptic Texts of Ritual Power,* 1994, Harper San Francisco.

—. "The Prayer of Mary Who Dissolves Chains in Coptic Magic and Religion," in *Magic and Ritual in the Ancient World*, Paul Mirecki & Marvin Meyer, eds, 2002, Brill.

Miller, Robert J., ed. *The Complete Gospels: Annotated Scholars Version*, Revised and Expanded Edition, 1994.

Miner, Edwin L., F. H. Sandbach & W.C. Helmbold. *Plutarch's Moralia*, 1961, William Heinemann Ltd.

Morgan, Michael A. *Sepher Ha-Razim: The Book of the Mysteries*, Harold W. Attridge, ed, 1983, Scholars Press.

Morony, Michael G. "Magic and Society in Late Sasanian Iraq," in *Prayer, Magic, and the Stars in the Ancient and Late Antique World*, Scott Noegel, Joel Walker & Brannon Wheeler, eds, 2003, Pennsylvania State University Press.

Mount, Christopher. "1 Corinthians 11:3-16: Spirit Possession and Authority in a Non-Pauline Interpolation," *Journal of Biblical Literature* 124: 313-340.

Munier, Charles. *Saint Justin: Apologie pour les Chrétiens*, 1995, Éditions Universitaires Fribourg Suisse.

Muñoz Delgado, Luis. *Léxico de magia y religión en los papiros mágicos griegos*, 2001, Consejo Superior de Investigaciones Científicas.

Myers, Ched. *Binding the Strong Man: A Political Reading of Mark's Story of Jesus*, 1988, Orbis Books.

Myllykoski, Matti. "Being There: The Function of the Supernatural in Acts 1-12" in *Wonders Never Cease: The Purpose of Narrating Miracle Stories in the New Testament and its Religious Environment*, Michael Labahn & Bert Jan Lietaert Peerbolte, eds, 2006, T&T Clark.

Naveh, Joseph and Shaul Shaked. *Magic Spells and Formulae: Aramaic Incantations of Late Antiquity*, 1993, The Magnes Press.

Neusner, Jacob. "Science and Magic, Miracle and Magic in Formative Judaism: The System and the Difference" in *Religion, Science, and Magic: In Concert and in Conflict*, Jacob Neusner, Ernest S. Frerichs & Paul Virgil McCracken Flesher, eds, 1989, Oxford University Press.

Neyrey, Jerome H. *The Resurrection Stories*, 1988, Michael Glazier.

—. "Bewitched in Galatia: Paul and Cultural Anthropology, *Catholic Biblical Quarterly* 50: 72-100.

—. "The Footwashing in John 13:6-11: Transformation Ritual or Ceremony?" in *The Social World of the First Christians: Essays in Honor of Wayne A. Meeks*, L. Michael White & O. Larry Yarbrough, eds, 1995, Fortress Press.

Nissinen, Martti. *Homoeroticism in the Biblical World*, 1998, Fortress Press.

Oesterreich, T. K. *Possession Demoniacal and Other Among Primitive Races, in Antiquity, the Middle Ages, and Modern Times*, 1966, University Books.

Ogden, Daniel. "Binding Spells: Curse Tablets and Voodoo Dolls in the Greek and Roman Worlds" in *Witchcraft and Magic in Europe: Ancient Greece and Rome*, Bengt Ankarloo & Stuart Clark, eds, 1999, University of Pennsylvania Press.

—. *Greek and Roman Necromancy*, 2001, Princeton University Press.

—. *Magic, Witchcraft and Ghosts in the Greek and Roman Worlds*, 2002, Oxford University Press.

—. *Night's Black Agents: Witches, Wizards and the Dead in the Ancient World*, 2008, Hambledon Continuum Books.

Otto, Walter F. *Dionysus: Myth and Cult*, 1965, Indiana University Press.

Oulton, J.E.L. Eusebius: *The Ecclesiastical History*, Books VI-X, 1932, Harvard University Press.

Pagels, Elaine. *The Gnostic Paul: Gnostic Exegesis of the Pauline Letters*, 1975, Trinity Press International.

—. *The Origin of Satan*, 1995, Random House.

Paige, Terence. "Who Believes in 'Spirit'? Pneuma in Pagan Usage and Implications for the Gentile Christian Mission," *Harvard Theological Review* 95: 417-436.

Paton, Lewis Bayles. *Spiritism and the Cult of the Dead in Antiquity*, 1921, The Macmillan Company.

Penny, Douglas I. and Michael O. Wise. "By the Power of Beelzebub: An Aramaic Incantation Formula from Qumran (4 Q560), *Journal of Biblical Literature* 113: 627-650.

Pesce, M. & A. Dietro. "La lavanda dei piedi di Gv 13,1-20, il Romanzo de Esopo e I Saturnalia de Macrobio," *Biblica* 80: 240-249.

Petermann, J. H. *S. Ignatii Patris Apostolici quae Feruntur Epistolae Una cum Ejusdem Martyrio*, 1849, Lipsiae.

Peters, Edward. "Superstition and Magic from Augustine to Isidore of Seville" in *Witchcraft and Magic in Europe: The Middle Ages*, Bengt Ankarloo & Stuart Clark, eds, 2002, University of Pennsylvania Press.

Pietersen, Lloyd K. "Magic/Thaumaturgy and the Pastorals" in *Magic in the Biblical World: From the Rod of Aaron to the Ring of Solomon*, Todd E. Klutz, ed, 2003, T&T Clark.

Pinch, Geraldine. *Magic in Ancient Egypt*, 1994, University of Texas Press.

Piñero, Antonio & Gonzalo del Cerro. *Hechos Apócrifos de los Apóstoles*, 2004, Biblioteca de Autores Cristianos.

Pitre, Brant James. "Blessing the Barren and Warning the Fecund: Jesus' Message for Women Concerning Pregnancy and Childbirth," *Journal for the Study of the New Testament* 81: 59-80.

Plumer, Eric. "The Absence of Exorcisms in the Fourth Gospel," *Biblica* 78: 350-368.

Podeman Sørensen, Jørgen. "The argument in ancient Egyptian magical formulae," *Acta Orientalia* 45:5-19.

Porter, Stanley E. "The Functional Distribution of Koine Greek in First-Century Palestine" in *Diglossia and Other Topics in New Testament Linguistics*, Stanley E. Porter, ed, 2000, Sheffield Academic Publishers.

Porterfield, Amanda. *Healing in the History of Christianity*, 2005, Oxford University Press.

Powell, Mark Allen. "The Magi as Wise Men: Re-examining a Basic Supposition," *New Testament Studies* 46: 1-20.

Preisendanz, Karl. *Papyri Graecae Magicae: Die Griechischen Zauberpapyri*, I & II, 2001 (reprint), K.G. Saur.

Price, Robert M. "Introduction: The Second Life of Jesus" & "Apocryphal Apparitions: 1 Corinthians 15: 3-11 as a Post-Pauline Interpolation," in *The Empty Tomb: Jesus Beyond the Grave*, Robert M. Price & Jeffery Jay Lowder, eds, 2005, Prometheus Books.

Prieur, Jean-Marc. *Acta Andreae*, 1989, Brepols—Turnhout.

Prince, Deborah Thompson. "The 'Ghost' of Jesus: Luke 24 in Light of Ancient Narratives of Post-Mortem Apparitions," *Journal for the Study of the New Testament* 29: 287-301.

Rabinowitz, Jacob. *The Rotting Goddess: The Origin of the Witch in Classical Antiquity's Demonization of Fertility Religion*, 1998, Automedia.

Rainbow, Jesse. "The Song of Songs and the Testament of Solomon: Solomon's Love Poetry and Christian Magic," *Harvard Theological Review* 100: 249-274.

Reed, Annette Yoshiko. *Fallen Angels and the History of Judaism and Christianity*, 2005, Cambridge University Press.

Reimer, Andy M. *Miracle and Magic: A Study in the Acts of the Apostles and the Life of Apollonius of Tyana*, 2002, JSNT Supplement Series 235.

Ricks, Steven D. "The Magician as Outsider in the Hebrew Bible and the New Testament" in *Ancient Magic and Ritual Power*, Marvin Meyer & Paul Mirecki, eds, 2001, Brill Academic Publishers.

Riley, Gregory J. *Resurrection Reconsidered: Thomas and John in Controversy*, 1995, Augsburg Fortress.

Ritner, Robert K. "Curses" in *Ancient Christian Magic: Coptic Texts of Ritual Power*, 1994, Harper San Francisco.

—. "Necromany in Ancient Egypt," in *Magic and Divination in the Ancient World*, Leda Ciraolo & Jonathan Seidel, eds, 2002, Brill.

Robertson, A.T. *A Grammar of the Greek New Testament in the Light of Historical Research*, 3rd ed, 1934, Broadman Press.

Robinson, James M., Paul Hoffmann and John S. Kloppenborg. *The Sayings Gospel Q in Greek and English*, 2002, Fortress Press.

Rochefort, Gabriel. *L'Empereur Julien: Oeuvres Complètes*, 1963, Société D' Édition "Les Belles-Lettres."

Rubenstein, Richard E. *When Jesus Became God: The Epic Fight over Christ's Divinity in the Last Days of Rome*, 1998, Harcourt Brace & Company.

Samain, P. "L'accusation de magie contre le Christ dans les évangiles," *Ephemerides Theologicae Lovanienses* 15: 449-490.

Sanders, Ed Parish. *The Historical Figure of Jesus*, 1993, The Penguin Press.

Schäfer, Peter. "Jewish Magic Literature in Late Antiquity and Early Middle Ages," *Journal of Jewish Studies* 41: 75-81.

—. "Magic and Religion in Ancient Judaism," in *Envisioning Magic: A Princeton Seminar and Symposium*, Peter Schäfer & Hans G. Kippenberg, eds, 1997, Brill.

—. *Jesus in the Talmud*, 2007, Princeton University Press.

Schlier, Heinrich. "δακτυλος" in *Theological Dictionary of the New Testament*, 1964, Gerhard Kittel, ed, William B. Eerdmans.

Schmidt, Brian B. *Israel's Beneficent Dead: Ancestor Cult and Necromancy in Ancient Israelite Religion and Tradition*, 1996, Eisenbrauns.

—. "The 'Witch' of Endor, 1 Samuel 28, and Ancient Near Eastern Necromancy" in *Ancient Magic and Ritual Power*, Marvin Meyer & Paul Mirecki, eds, 2001, Brill Academic Publishers.

—. "Canaanite Magic vs. Israelite Religion: Deuternomy 18 and the Taxonomy of Taboo" in *Magic and Ritual in the Ancient World*, 2002, Brill Academic Publishers.

Schnackenburg, Rudolf. *Ephesians: A Commentary*, trs by Helen Heron, 1991, T&T Clark.

Schneemelcher, Wilhelm & Rudolphe Kasser. "Acts of Paul" in *New Testament Apocrypha*, II, Wilhelm Schneemelcher, ed, 1964, The Westminster Press.

Scholem, Gershom G. *Major Trends in Jewish Mysticism*, 1941, Schocken Publishing House.

Schweitzer, Albert. *The Quest of the Historical Jesus*, 1910, Adam & Charles Black, Ltd.

Scibilia, Anna. "Supernatural Assistance in the Greek Magical Papyri," in *The Metamorphosis of Magic from Late Antiquity to the Early Modern Period*, Jan N. Bremmer & Jan R. Veenstra, eds, 2002, Peeters.

Selwyn, Edward Gordon. *The First Epistle of St. Peter. The Greek Text with Introduction, Notes and Essays*, 1952, Macmillan & Company.

Selwyn, William. *Contra Celsum*, 1876, Cambridge University Press.

Shaw, Gregory. *Theurgy and the Soul: The Neoplatonism of Iamblichus*, 1995, Pennsylvania State University Press.

Shantz, Colleen. "The Confluence of Trauma and Transcendence in the Pauline Corpus," in *Experientia*, I, *Inquiry into Religious Experience in Early Judaism and Christianity*, Frances Flannery, Colleen Shantz & Rodney A. Werline, eds, 2008, Brill.

Smith, Gregory. "The Myth of the Vaginal Soul," *Greek, Roman and Byzantine Studies* 44: 199-225.

Smith, Jay E. "The Roots of a Libertine Slogan in 1 Corinthians 6:18," *Journal of Theological Studies* 59: 61-79.

Smith, Lacey Baldwin. *Fools, Martyrs, Traitors: The Story of Martyrdom in the Western World*, 1997, Alfred A. Knopf.

Smith, Morton. *Clement of Alexandria and a Secret Gospel of Mark*, 1973, Harvard University Press.

—. *Jesus the Magician*, 1978, Harper & Row.

—. "Pauline Worship As Seen by Pagans," *Harvard Theological Review*, 73: 241-249.

—. "How Magic Was Changed by the Triumph of Christianity" in *Studies in the Cult of Yahweh*, II, Shaye J.D. Cohen, ed, 1996, E.J. Brill.

Sorensen, Eric. *Possession and Exorcism in the New Testament and Early Christianity*, 2002, Mohr Siebeck.

Stanton, Graham. *Gospel Truth? New Light on Jesus and the Gospels*, 1995, Trinity Press International.

Starr, Joshua. "The Meaning of Authority in Mark 1.22," *Harvard Theological Review* 23: 302-305.

Stone, Michael E. *Scriptures, Sects and Visions: A Profile of Judaism from Ezra to the Jewish Revolts*, 1980, Fortress Press.

Stratton, Kimberly B. *Naming the Witch: Magic, Ideology and Sterotype in the Ancient World*, 2007, Columbia University Press.

Strelen, Rick. "Who Was Bar-Jesus (Acts 13,6-12)?" *Biblica* 85: 65-87.

—. "Outside Are the Dogs and the Sorcerers…" (Revelation 22:15), *Biblical Theology Bulletin* 33: 148-157.

—. *Strange Acts: Studies in the Cultural World of the Acts of the Apostles*, 2004, Walter de Gruyter.

Stroumsa, Guy G. *Barbarian Philosophy: The Religious Revolution of Early Christianity*, 1999, Mohr Siebeck.

Taylor, Gary. *Castration: An Abbreviated History of Western Manhood*, 2000, Routledge.

Taylor, Greg. "Her Sweet Murmur: Exploring the Aural Phenomenology of Border Experiences" in *Dark Lore*, Greg Taylor, ed, 2007, Daily Grail Publishing.

Thiselton, Anthony C. "The Holy Spirit in 1 Corinthians: Exegesis and Reception History in the Patristic Era" in *The Hold Spirit and Christian Origins: Essays in Honor of James D. G. Dunn*, Graham N. Stanton, Bruce W. Longenecker & Stephen C. Barton, eds, 2004, William B. Eerdmans Publishing Company.

Thomsen, Marie-Louise. "Witchcraft and Magic in Ancient Mesopotamia" in *Witchcraft and Magic in Europe: Biblical and Pagan Societies*, Bengt Ankarloo & Stuart Clark, eds, 2001, University of Pennsylvania Press.

Tipei, John Fleter. *The Laying On of Hands in the New Testament: Its Significance, Techniques, and Effects*, 2009, University Press of America.

Trachtenberg, Joshua. *Jewish Magic and Superstition: A Study in Folk Religion*, 1970, Atheneum.

Tropper, Joseph. "Spirit of the Dead אוב" in *Dictionary of Deities and Demons in the Bible*, Karel van der Toorn, Bob Becking & Pieter W. van der Horst, eds, 1995, E.J. Brill.

Trzcionka, Silke. *Magic and the Supernatural in Fourth-Century Syria*, 2007, Routledge.

Twelftree, Graham H. "Jesus the Exorcist and Ancient Magic" in *A Kind of Magic: Understanding Magic in the New Testament and its Religious Environment*, Michael Labahm & Bert Jan Lietaert Peerbolte, eds, 2007, T&T Clark.

—. *In the Name of Jesus: Exorcism among Early Christians*, 2007, Baker Academic.

VanderKam, James C. "1 Enoch, Enochic Motifs, and Enoch in Early Christian Literature," in *The Jewish Apocalyptic Heritage in Early Christianity*, James C. VanderKam & William Adler, eds, 1996, Fortress Press.

Van Groningen, M. David & B.A. Van Groningen, *Papyrological Primer*, 4th ed, 1965, E.J. Brill.

Van Hoye, Albert. "La fuite du jeune homme nu (Mc 14,51-52)," *Biblica* 52: 401-406.

Van Voorst, Robert E. *Jesus Outside the New Testament: An Introduction to the Ancient Evidence*, 2000, William B. Eerdmans Publishing Company.

Vermes, Geza. *Jesus the Jew*, 1973, Collins.

Vermeule, Emily. *Aspects of Death in Early Greek Art and Poetry*, 1979, University of California Press.

Victor, Ulrich. *Lukian Von Samosata: Alexandros oder der Lügenprophet*, 1997, Brill.

Vitelli, G. *Papiri Greci e Latini*, 2004, Edizioni di Storia e Letteratura.

Voutiras, Emmanuel. "Euphemistic names for the powers of the nether world" in *The world of ancient magic*, David R. Jordan, Hugo Montgomery & Einar Thomassen, eds, 1999, Bergen.

Wahlen, Clinton. *Jesus and the Impurity of Spirits in the Synoptic Gospels*, 2004, Mohr Siebeck.

Wallace, Daniel B. "The Majority Text Theory: History, Methods, and Critique." In *The Text of the New Testament in Contemporary Research: Essays on the Status Quaestionis*, Bart Ehrman & Michael W. Holmes, eds, 1995, William B. Eerdmans.

—. "The Synoptic Problem." (2005) *www.bible.org*.

Wasyliw, Patricia Healy. *Martyrdom, Murder, and Magic*, 2009, Peter Lang.

Watt, Jonathan M. "Of Gutturals and Galileans: The Two Slurs of Matthew 26.73" in *Diglossia and Other Topics in New Testament Linguistics*, Stanley E. Porter, ed, 2000, Sheffield Academic Publishers.

Wenham, J.W. *The Elements of New Testament Greek*, 1991 edition, Cambridge University Press.

Werline, Rodney A. "The Experience of Prayer and Resistance to Demonic Powers in the Gospel of Mark," in *Experientia, I, Inquiry into Religious Experience in Early Judaism and Christianity*, Frances Flannery, Colleen Shantz & Rodney A. Werline, eds, 2008, Brill.

Wiens, Devon H. "Mystery Concepts in Primitive Christianity and its Environment," *Aufstieg und Niedergang der Römischen Welt*, II, 23.2, 1248-1284 Hildegard Temporini & Wolfgang Haase, eds, Walter de Gruyter.

Wikgren, Allen, Ernest Cadman Colwell and Ralph Marcus. "The Acts of Paul" in *Hellenistic Greek Texts*, 1947, University of Chicago Press.

Wilcox, Max. "Jesus in the Light of His Jewish Environment," *Aufstieg und Niedergang der Römischen Welt*, II.25.1:131-187, Hildegard Temporini & Wolfgang Haase, eds, Walter de Gruyter.

Wilken, Robert L. *The Christians as the Romans Saw Them*, 1984, Yale University Press.

Williams, Guy. "An Apocalyptic and Magical Interpretation of Paul's 'Beast Fight' in Ephesus (1 Corinthians 15:32)," *Journal of Theological Studies* 57: 42-56.

Wilson, Stephen. *Saints and their Cults: Studies in Religious Sociology, Folklore and History*, 1983, Cambridge University Press.

Winkler, John J. "The Constraints of Eros." In *Magika Hiera: Ancient Greek Magic and Religion*, Christopher Faraone & Dirk Obbink, eds, 1991, Oxford University Press.

Yarbro Collins, Adela. "The Function of 'Excommunication' in Paul," *Harvard Theological Review*, 73, 2: 251-263.

Young, Richard A. *Intermediate New Testament Greek: A Linguistic and Exegetical Approach*, 1994, Broadman.

Subject Index

A

Abrasax 321
Acts of Andrew 225
Acts of John 113, 120, 219-220, 242, 273
Acts of Paul 224
Acts of Paul and Thecla 52, 224
Acts of Thomas 31, 120
adoptionists 122
Adversus Haereses 306
Alexamenos grafitto 31
Alexander of Abonutichos 194, 320
amatorium 308
Ambrose (see *maleficus*)
Ammianus Marcellinus 222
amulet αλεξικακον 127-128, 199, 250, 255, 269, 274, 295, 301, 304-305
Ananias 218-219
androgyny 56-58, 257-259, 306
angel (see *magical assistant, spirit*) 38, 139, 156-159, 208, 232, 234, 239, 302, 318
  messengers 154
  names of 156, 220, 239
  spirit, not distinguished 157-158
Anoubis 183
antinomianism 307
Antinous 183
apocalypse 62-84, 91, 265-266, 325-327
  failure to occur 76, 81
  Qumran 70
Apollo 256, 259, 290, 318
apostolic fiction 122-123, 286
apostasy 323
Artemis 298
Asklepius 260

Asmodeus 55
Azazel 153

B

Bacchus (see *Dionysus*)
Bar-Jesus 283, 287-289
Beelzeboul 65, 129
  cast out 73
  Beelzeboul controversy 98, 187-193, 195, 224
Bethlehem 32-34, 200
bewitchment βασκανια, βασκανος 217-218
bibliomancy 36
binding δεω, δεσμος, καταδεσμος (see *oath, magic, spell*) 136-137, 162-163, 181-186, 224, 234
  curse αναθεμα 68
  erotic binding spell φιλτροκαταδεσμος, χαριτησιον 224, 226-227
  knots 136-137, 163
birds, descent of 66, 152-153
body parts, theft of 223
books, magical 138-139, 157, 213, 233, 251, 294, 298, 321
bowls (incantation) 128, 135, 147, 233
boy παιδιον 60
  Centurian, boy of 165-167
  mediums 310-311
  sexual use of 49-50, 167
brandea (see *relics*)
bull-roarer (see *magic wheel*) 271

C

Caiaphas 92-93
Carpocrates 305-309
Castration 48-51
Celibacy (see ευπαρεδρος, *magical techniques*) 75
  Jesus 46-51